Spiritual Economies

THE MIDDLE AGES SERIES

Ruth Mazo Karras, *Series Editor*
Edward Peters, *Founding Editor*

A complete list of books in the series
is available from the publisher.

Spiritual Economies

Female Monasticism in Later Medieval England

NANCY BRADLEY WARREN

PENN

UNIVERSITY OF PENNSYLVANIA PRESS   Philadelphia

Copyright © 2001 University of Pennsylvania Press
All rights reserved
Printed in the United States of America on acid-free paper

10 9 8 7 6 5 4 3 2 1

Published by
University of Pennsylvania Press
Philadelphia, Pennsylvania 19104-4011

Library of Congress Cataloging-in-Publication Data
Warren, Nancy Bradley.
 Spiritual economies : female monasticism in later medieval England / Nancy Bradley Warren.
  p. cm — (The Middle Ages series)
 Includes bibliographical references (p.   ) and index.
 ISBN 0-8122-3583-5 (cloth : alk. paper)
 1. Monasticism and religious orders for women—England—History—Middle Ages,
600–1500.   2. England—Church history—1066–1485.   I. Title.   II. Series.
BX4220.G7 W37 2001
271′.90042′0902—dc21   00-048885

Contents

Preface

In 1308, King Edward II founded a priory of Dominican friars at King's Langley to fulfill a vow.[1] The house was dependent on the Exchequer, and, after a time, Edward II became dissatisfied with this state of affairs. Because the Dominican friars could not own property, he sought to find a means of endowing the house for the support of one hundred religious.[2] To this end, Edward II determined that the Dominican friars of Guildford should surrender their house to a foundation of Dominican nuns to be created at Dartford, who would in turn hold endowments for and be subject to the Dominican friars of King's Langley.[3] Edward II sent several papal petitions regarding his desires, but he did not receive papal approval to proceed until November 1321. Before he could complete his intentions, though, he was dethroned. Edward III finally completed the plans set in motion by his father. In November 1349, he applied to the pope for confirmation of the house of nuns at Dartford,[4] and, the confirmation granted, the house at Dartford became "the complement of Langley priory."[5]

The Dominican sisters "were subject in spirituals to the Friars Preacher of King's Langley," and the prior of King's Langley appointed the friars who were to reside at Dartford with the nuns.[6] In December 1356, Edward III granted the prioress and sisters license to acquire property to the value of £300 to sustain their community and that of the friars of King's Langley.[7] In the ensuing years, Dartford received numerous endowments, always destined to support not only the sisters but also the friars at King's Langley.

In spite of its obligation to support King's Langley, Dartford became, in the course of its history, extraordinarily wealthy. At the dissolution, Dartford had a gross annual income of £488 per annum, which made it the seventh richest nunnery in England.[8] In the early sixteenth century, the prioress, Elizabeth Cressener, drew up the *Rentale* giving detailed records of the house's holdings of land and property together with the rents and services owed to the house.[9] This document testifies not only to the wealth of the house but also to the nuns' skill in business practices.

That the Dartford nuns were capable managers is not surprising, since the house was a center of female education, including Latin learning. Extracts from the records of the Masters-General of the Dominican Order include permission given in 1481 for "Sister Jane Fitzh'er" to have "a preceptor in grammar and the Latin tongue."[10] The house possessed numerous books,[11] and not only novices and nuns but also daughters (and even some sons) of the local nobility and gentry were educated at Dartford.[12]

I began with this brief account of Dartford's foundation and history because it provides a snapshot of the key issues I address in this book. First and foremost, the case of Dartford highlights the involvements of women religious in multiple, mutually informing systems of production and exchange. From the community's beginning, the Dartford nuns were enmeshed in material, symbolic, textual, political, and spiritual economies in ways which at times harmonized with and at times conflicted with each other. Exploring the relationships among these systems and considering their importance for the construction of religious identities are at the foundation of my methodology in this book. I therefore consider a wide range of sources, from monastic rules to nunneries' financial accounts, from devotional treatises to works traditionally designated as literary.

Furthermore, the case of Dartford demonstrates the permeability of the convent wall. The Dartford nuns clearly had important connections with King's Langley as well as frequent interaction with the larger community in their business and educational affairs. I thus seek to breach the cloister wall, which was not an impenetrable boundary in later medieval society but which is so often treated as such in modern scholarship, in my study of female monasticism. My analysis consequently considers the impact of "worldly" forces (for instance, economic trends and political conflicts) on "religious" life in nunneries as well as the "worldly" value of "religious" practices (for instance, politically motivated acts of monastic foundation). In doing so, I hope to breach other boundaries which have been erected in contemporary scholarship on the Middle Ages, particularly those demarcating the sacred and the secular, the material and the symbolic, the literary and the historical.[13]

Dartford's material success and the continued respect the community enjoyed from benefactors illustrate that later-medieval English nunneries for women were not, as has so often been argued, necessarily the victims of financial and spiritual decline. Nor was Dartford a community in which the women religious were uneducated and woefully incompetent at managing their affairs. These negative perceptions of later-medieval female monasticism have long been prevalent, and they have frequently led scholars either to discount the social importance of female monasticism or to treat nuns in appendix to a work on "monasticism," implicitly defined as *male* monasticism.

Eileen Power was a pioneer in women's history, and her *Medieval English Nunneries* is still valuable in many regards. Her book did much, however, to solidify the perception of later medieval nunneries as poverty stricken, ill managed, riddled with corruption, and filled with illiterate women. The work of such scholars as Jo Ann Kay McNamara, Roberta Gilchrist, Marilyn Oliva, and David Bell has done much to build on and refine Power's analysis, but far too many works on medieval religion still give short shrift to female monasticism.[14] Furthermore, the perception that female monasticism was in decline in the later Middle Ages has encouraged feminist scholars working on religion in England to pay more attention to nunneries during the Anglo-Saxon era, since monasticism is perceived to have offered women more opportunities for authority and spiritual independence during that period.

One of my aims in this book is therefore to demonstrate the complex vibrancy of material and spiritual life in later medieval nunneries. Concomitantly, I seek to emphasize the centrality of female monasticism to the flowering of later medieval female spirituality, and, indeed, its importance to later medieval culture at large. The book is thus arranged in two sections—a boundary, yes, but one across which many incursions occur in both directions. Part I explores theories and practices of monastic life; Part II examines the ways in which these theories and practices circulate in the secular world.

A return to the example of Dartford will help to make clear the logic of this organization as well as to illustrate the complex connections between the two parts. The fact that this community was founded by kings for explicitly financial reasons calls attention to the important interactions of the social, the material, and the spiritual in the most fundamental constructions of religious identity. I address such interactions in Chapter 1 on profession and visitation and in Chapter 2 on translations of monastic rules for women. These texts and ceremonies provide nuns with basic "ideological scripts" which have far-reaching implications for religious identities.[15]

Because Dartford was the only house of Dominican nuns in England, it was distinctive in more than just the circumstances of its foundation. Such distinctive aspects of religious identity in different orders are also central considerations in Chapters 1 and 2. In these chapters I direct my attention to the ways in which elements of monastic life that seem to be shared by monks and nuns of the same order, as well as by nuns of different orders, are realized in practice in profoundly different ways.

I take these differences quite seriously; thus, I consider religious traditions both individually and comparatively. In this respect, I depart from two common trends in scholarship on later medieval religion: treating female monasticism as a unified institution or studying one order in isolation. In adopting a combined approach, I hope to preserve the benefits of both macrocosmic and microcosmic analyses while avoiding some of their individual pitfalls. In order to present a nuanced portrait of female monasticism which preserves variations in monastic cultures, I focus at length on the Benedictine, Brigittine, and Franciscan traditions.

I have chosen to allow these particular religious traditions to illuminate each other for a variety of reasons. All three orders maintained a significant presence in fourteenth- and fifteenth-century England, and medieval versions of the Benedictine, Franciscan, and Brigittine rules for women are available.[16] Fairly extensive records (including financial accounts, legal and administrative documents, and letters) exist for houses of all three orders. These documents, which I investigate in Chapter 3, provide insight into nuns' everyday practices, and they give us glimpses of the ways in which nuns saw the world and their place in it. Through their involvement in the quotidian affairs of running a religious house, like the enterpreneuring activities of the Dartford nuns, women religious make visible identities which complicate and expand those shaped in foundational texts and ceremonies.

Furthermore, I have chosen to consider the Benedictine, Brigittine, and Franciscan orders because monastic texts and paradigms drawn from them circulated widely beyond the cloister, playing, as I argue in Chapter 4, important roles in identity formation for those living in the world. Interpretive schemes based on female monasticism were mobilized by clerical writers in efforts to regulate secular women's conduct and so neutralize anxieties that masculine religious and economic dominance might be waning. Images and practices drawn from female monastic traditions were also, however, embraced by secular women—and even by men—as they crafted empowered spiritual and material lives. That some of the same elements of female monasticism might be mobilized for such different, even contradictory, purposes highlights the complexities of identity formation and recalls the contradictions present in the foundations of monastic identities.

Since Dartford was created to benefit the friars and the souls of those royal founders and favorites for whom the friars were to pray, the nuns functioned as political and symbolic as well as financial resources. Similarly, as I explore in Chapters 5 and 6, female saints, nuns, and holy women served as resources of symbolic capital for those seeking to gain political legitimacy and literary success. In Chapter 5, I examine Lancastrian and Yorkist symbolic strategies to consolidate royal authority through associations with St. Birgitta, St. Anne, the Virgin Mary, and Syon Abbey. In Chapter 6, I read the Lancastrian John Lydgate's *Life of Our Lady* and the Yorkist Osbern Bokenham's *Legendys of Hooly Wummen* as texts making partisan cases for political authority as well as personal cases for literary *auctoritas*.

One final aspect of Dartford's history is instructive. The Dartford nuns did not prove to be a passive and easily controlled commodity for the friars of King's Langley, and those who mobilized female saints, nuns, and holy women also found that these women were liabilities as well as assets. In 1415, the Dartford nuns attempted to escape their subjection to King's Langley. As the result of a dispute (apparently concerning the election of the prioress), Dartford made a bid for independence, threatening the economic well-being and the spiritual authority of the friars. The friars took action, and the Provincial of the Dominican Order visited Dartford in 1415 to attempt to reimpose the nuns' obedience to the friars.[17] The matter came before the pope, and on July 16, 1418, Martin V decided entirely in favor of the Provincial and King's Langley "to whose obedience the sisters were enforced by ecclesiastical censures."[18]

In Chapters 6 and 7, I address the problematic aspects of using holy women in literary and political representational schemes. I focus first on the negotiations in which Lydgate and Bokenham must engage as they try to balance their masculinist literary, political, and clerical authority with the spiritual and social authority of the women upon whom their success depends. In Chapter 7, I then return to figures encountered in previous chapters—Richard Beauchamp, earl of Warwick; John, duke of Bedford; and Bishop William Alnwick—examining their involvements with Margery Kempe, fifteenth-century nuns, and Joan of Arc in the contexts of the Hundred Years' War, war between England and Scotland, and civil strife within England. This exploration of the relationships between political figures and holy women both heterodox and orthodox, both cloistered and uncloistered, illuminates the profound cultural anxieties that existed in fifteenth-century England about the power and value of female spirituality.

PART I

Monastic Identities in Theory and Practice

1

Vows and Visitations

Textual Transactions and the Shaping of Monastic Identity

Brides of Christ

Documents of monastic profession and visitation provide nuns with funda-mental "ideological scripts," the impacts of which exceed the textual realm, shaping nuns' participation in material, spiritual, and symbolic systems of exchange.[1] As the idea of a script suggests, these documents, and the cere-monies in which they are generated and circulated, bear witness to the inter-play of the desires of the "script writers" (those in the ecclesiastical hierarchy charged with the regulation of female monastic communities) and of the "actors" (the nuns themselves who perform religious identities). For later medieval nuns, the role of bride of Christ is central to these ideological scripts, and while this role is common to a range of women religious, what it actually means for a nun to be a bride of Christ is differently realized in different religious orders.

A nun's spousal role is, as Jacques Derrida observes of Plato's *pharmakon*, "ambivalent . . . because it constitutes the medium in which opposites are opposed, the movement and the play that links them among themselves or makes one side cross over into the other."[2] The identity of bride of Christ is at once constraining and empowering; that which necessitates supervision by the clergy also provides opportunities for spiritual and temporal autonomy. Furthermore, degrees of constraint and empowerment vary as nuptial rela-tions are constructed in different orders' foundational discourses and as the subject positions shaped for nuns by these texts are taken up in diverse socioeconomic contexts. By examining profession and visitation in the Bene-dictine, Brigittine, and Franciscan traditions, I hope to demonstrate not only

the various ways in which ideological scripts are written but also the innova-
tive ways in which they can be modified, supplemented, and rewritten as they
are put into practice.[3]

The Material and Symbolic Consequences of Profession

Because candidates formally take sacred vows and become members of preex-
isting, rule-governed communities in profession services, the future implied
by the entry discourse of a particular order conditions a postulant's expectations. For women becoming Benedictine nuns, the role of bride of Christ is the
primary one scripted in profession. For example, the fifteenth-century "furme
how A Nouice sall be made" describes the instructions the head of the house
gives the candidate before her profession. In explaining the obligations of life
under the rule, the superior says to the candidate, "þe behouis to liue chaiste,
and take god to þi spouse, and forsake all þi lust, & þi liking of þi flesche."[4]
"The Method of makeing a Nunn," also from the fifteenth century, includes the
texts of the prayers the priest uses in hallowing the nun's habit. Here, nuptial
imagery is prominent in the prayer spoken over the veil, which is "the outward
sign of inward chastity" and the "the one distinctively female part of the nun's
habit."[5] The officiating priest, referring to the story of the wise virgins who
were prepared for the bridegroom's coming (Matthew 25:1–13), prays that the
novice's body and soul be kept pure "vt quum ad perpetuam sanctorum
remuneracionem uenerit, cum prudentibus virginibus et ipsa preparata te
perducente ad perpetue felicitatis nupcias intrare meriatur. Per dominum."[6]
The "Method" also mentions the ring, which the new nun places upon the
altar with her "profession-boke" after reading her vow.[7]

The identity of bride of Christ has manifold consequences both material
and symbolic for women religious, as the focus on the body and chastity in
these excerpts from profession services suggests. Marriage, even at the imagis-
tic level, necessarily raises questions of exchange.[8] The spousal relationship
constructed in monastic profession has little in common with the ecstatic
nuptial unions found in the visionary experiences of some female mystics.
Rather, to borrow the feminist anthropologist Renée Hirschon's analysis, the
"marriage transactions" of monastic profession are means of transmitting resources "whether productive assets or personal valuables."[9] In her work on
marriage, Marilyn Strathern rightly problematizes the view that women are
exchanged as "objects," that women in marriage transactions become "things"
rather than persons.[10] The baggage accompanying the construction of the nun

as bride of Christ in later medieval England reminds us, however, that even if nuns were not simply objects of exchange, nuptial discourse limited the possibility that they could act as fully empowered agents in textual, economic, and spiritual exchanges. Roberta Gilchrist's description of nuns is particularly apt in this regard. While she does not say that nuns *were* property, she describes the brides of Christ as "metaphors for private property."[11] A striking example of such "commodification" of nuns and the alienation of their resources occurs in a promise of obedience made by the prioress and convent of St. Michael's Stamford to the abbot of Peterborough, the Benedictine abbey to which the nunnery was subject. The promise, preserved in the registers of Peterborough, "states that the nuns and all their belongings were at the disposal of the abbot and the monastery."[12]

Becoming a bride of Christ thus dramatically restricted nuns' control of both "personal valuables" and "productive assets." Nuns' "personal valuables," which many women were required to bring with them as entry gifts (often called dowries), were officially transferred to the control of the community as nuns renounced rights to private property.[13] Nuns' "productive assets"—their (licit) reproductive capabilities—were also transferred out of their control. Gilchrist observes that "in contrast to the asexuality of the celibate priest, nuns committed their virginity to the church as Brides of Christ," thus placing their bodies in the Church's possession.[14] In doing so, nuns, unlike priests, became "a private space inaccessible to others."[15]

The importance of maintaining nuns' inaccessibility, and so guarding the vital chastity of the brides of Christ, had temporal consequences exceeding in some respects those of the vow of poverty, which was in practice greatly modified for both Benedictine nuns and monks.[16] For instance, although it proved difficult to enforce, the papal bull *Periculoso* mandating strict active and passive enclosure for nuns received "sustained legal interest" throughout the fourteenth and fifteenth centuries. It was even reenacted "with the addition of stern penalties for its violation, at the Council of Trent (1545–63)."[17] The brides of Christ were not only required to be "off the market" but also out of the marketplace.[18] Nuns' chastity was a commodity whose circulation had to be closely regulated in order to protect it from devaluation and debasement, which could, as the records of episcopal visitation discussed below reveal, result even from rumors of questionable behavior, rumors often sparked by nuns' participation in the realm of commerce.

Claustration was certainly not perfectly kept in practice; later medieval episcopal communications attest to frequent breaches of the strict requirements for enclosure. For instance, in 1387, episcopal injunctions sent to

Romsey and Wherwell mention with displeasure numerous instances of nuns' leaving the cloister.[19] There are also, however, cases of apparent ecclesiastical surrender to what must have come to seem the inevitability of such breaches. The English canonist John of Ayton says of the requirement that bishops enforce *Periculoso*, "Cause to be observed! But surely there is scarce any mortal man who could do this: we must therefore here understand 'so far as lieth in the prelate's power. . . .' [W]e see in fact that these statutes are a dead letter or are ill-kept at best. Why, then, did the holy fathers thus labour to beat the air?"[20] Even the pessimistic (or perhaps merely pragmatic) John of Ayton does not give up utterly on *Periculoso*, though. He follows his grim assessment by praising prelates who do work to enforce enclosure, saying, "Yet indeed their toil is none the less to their own merit, for we look not to that which is but to that which of justice should be."[21]

Episcopal records make clear that even in the later Middle Ages some prelates did in fact attempt to enforce *Periculoso* strictly. For instance, in 1376 Bishop Brantyngham of Exeter invokes *Periculoso* in a commission sent to canons of Exeter deputed to curb "the wanderings of the nuns of Polsloe."[22] When strictly enforced by such zealous prelates, the requirement for claustration had the potential to diminish a nunnery's opportunities for economic success. As Elizabeth Makowski observes, the strict enclosure mandated by *Periculoso* "threatened to undermine the economic stability of these communities. . . . It severely limited the capacity of nuns to solicit funds from outside benefactors, to conduct schools within conventual precincts, or to engage in any kind of revenue-producing labor outside the cloister."[23]

Before comparing Brigittine and Franciscan profession services with profession for nuns in the Benedictine tradition, it is instructive to consider the distinctions that emerge in a comparison of Benedictine profession for monks and nuns. Rather than mobilizing nuptial imagery, the profession service for Benedictine monks centers on the "idea of *renovatio* of the whole person."[24] Whereas nuns become brides of Christ, monks " 'pu[t] on the new Christ'— thereby identifying themselves directly with Christ."[25] As Johnson points out, "The differences by gender emphasize the hierarchy's view of women as dependent and men as autonomous."[26] Furthermore, from the twelfth century, monks increasingly took holy orders as priests,[27] which bolstered their identification with Christ, since as priests they were Christ's earthly representatives. Benedictine monks thus share in the authority of Christ, receiving all the material and spiritual benefits such status conveys, while Benedictine nuns become Christ's spouses deeply subject to patriarchal authority.[28]

Nuns' identification as brides of Christ led to gendered interpretations of

elements of monastic life shared by monks and nuns, variations which reinforced monks' autonomy and nuns' subjection. For instance, canon lawyers
and theologians used the construction of the nun as the bride of Christ as
grounds to distinguish between monks' and nuns' vows of chastity. If a monk
broke his vow of chastity, the offense put his own soul in jeopardy. The unchastity of a nun, however, was deemed "a direct offense against her Spouse,
the King of Heaven."[29] In his gloss on the canon *Sanctimoniales* attributed to
Archbishop John Pecham, William Lyndwood, an influential fifteenth-century
English canonist, discusses the rape of Dinah, daughter of Jacob, by Shechem,
son of Hamor. Lyndwood "then explains, following a hallowed patristic tradition, that Pecham's reference to 'a more pernicious corruption' reflects the fact
that Dinah's sin was one of simple fornication, while a nun's corruption, in
view of her marriage to Christ, would be adultery."[30] This formal distinction
between monks' and nuns' vows of chastity helped encourage much stricter
enforcement of enclosure for women. Because the spouse to whom nuns were
subject was not physically present to guard their chastity and supervise their
conduct, claustration and close supervision by the clergy, the divine spouse's
earthly representatives, were necessary.

Nuptial discourse structuring profession for women thus subjects the
Benedictine nun, unlike the Benedictine monk, to a hierarchical, patriarchal
complex of familial relations. For nuns, the bishop (or the officiating priest if
the bishop did not perform the ceremony) "acted symbolically as parent and
spouse," representing both Christ the bridegroom who received her vows and
her father, who as head of the family inquired into her suitability for the
match.[31] The familial relationships such alignment evokes emphasize male
control over the nuns themselves and their material resources.

This nexus of familial relations, and the limitations that come with it, are
echoed in the textual transactions of the Benedictine profession service. In the
services for both monks and nuns, after making the vow, the candidate places
the written profession on the altar. Beyond the symmetry in this moment in
the service are implications which reinforce the different status of men and
women religious in a textual economy. For the new nun, this text, representing
her self, passes permanently out of her hands into those of the priest celebrat-
ing the mass. This priest occupies a position that the nun, unlike the monk,
can never fill. The nun is not allowed to remain in the masculine position of
scriptor, nor is she able to retain possession of the text she has written.[32] The
textual body—the writing placed on the page by female hands—and with it the
female self come irretrievably into the control of the male clergy, a group from
which women are barred.

Furthermore, the dynamics of the exchange at the altar reinforce the status of male clergy as producers of value and of women religious as vessels of a value which is alienated from their own possession. The service of profession creates new nuns, and while the nun certainly plays a role in making *herself* a bride of Christ by taking vows, she cannot perform the sacerdotal work necessary to make *more* nuns. Like the sacrament of the Eucharist, which is a key part of the profession service and which is performed at the very altar upon which the nuns have placed their written vows, the profession service represents an exclusively male, clerical form of production. It is, in a sense, a male replacement of the maternal reproduction which nuns forego upon entering religion, since profession represents not only marriage to Christ but also a "birth" into a new life of religion as spiritual daughters of clerical fathers in Christ.[33]

The identity of bride of Christ and the system of social relations it trails with it are also prominent in Franciscan and Brigittine profession services. *The Rewle of Sustres Menouresses Enclosid* highlights nuptiality in the description of the habit which the Franciscan nuns are to wear. The description reads, "it falliþ nat to hem whoche ys weddid to þe kynge perpetuel þat sche chiere none oþer but him, ne delite her in none oþer but in him."[34] According to the Middle English version of the Brigittine Rule, called *The Rewyll of Seynt Sauioure*, when a candidate has completed the year of proof before profession she is called "the newe spouse," and nuptial imagery abounds in the Brigittine consecration service.[35] As might be expected, when the bishop blesses the ring and bestows it on the candidate, such imagery is at the forefront. The bishop prays, "Almyȝty god euerlastyng. that hast spowsed to þe a newe spowse . . . blisse þoue this rynge. so þat as thi seruante beryth þe signe of a newe spowse in hir handes owtewardly. so mote she deserve to bere ynwardly thy feyth and charite"(*Rewyll* fol. 49v). Furthermore, the consecration service underlines the connection between the nun's spousal status and her status as divine "property"; the bishop says, "I blisse the in to the spouse of god. and in to his euerlastyng possession" (*Rewyll* fol. 50v).

The similarity in profession services is not surprising given the ties between the Benedictine tradition and the Brigittine and Franciscan traditions. The Brigittine Rule has close connections with the strict Cistercian interpretation of the Rule of St. Benedict,[36] and Franciscan nuns were initially professed *formaliter* under the Benedictine Rule, according to the terms of which enclosure was imposed on the women religious.[37] The Brigittine and Franciscan traditions depart from the Benedictine model of monastic life in significant ways, though, as their profession services begin to make clear.

Although nuptial discourse is quite important in Franciscan and Brigittine profession services, it is offset and partially counteracted by the imagery of maternity. Just as earthly marriage is prohibited for nuns, so too is bodily maternity. Profession services for Franciscan nuns, and, to an even greater extent, those for Brigittine nuns, though, open up the potentially empowering possibilities of the maternal in religious identity. The abbess and Mary as strong maternal figures model subject positions of authority and autonomy which the insistent nuptiality of Benedictine profession tries (although, as we shall see, not always successfully) to deny. Felice Lifshitz has rightly observed that the "maternal responsibility to nurture" does *not* contain the "maternal authority to command."[38] The abbess and Mary, however, transcend the approved function for nurturing mothers in patriarchal society, that is, the function of "maintain[ing] the social order without intervening so as to change it."[39] While the presence of the maternal in Franciscan and Brigittine profession services does not fully negate the limiting aspects of nuptial discourse as a structuring principle for female monastic identity, maternal figures do in fact intervene in the social order. They provide models of female authority and legitimate women's autonomous possession of, exchange of, and profit from their own resources.

In the Benedictine profession service for women, while the clergy symbolically stand in for spouse and father, the role of mother is largely neglected. Neither the abbess as mother nor Mary as mother figure prominently in this service in which clerics engage in the "reproductive" work of making nuns. While the abbess does play an important role in the Benedictine profession service (for instance, she "removes the novice's secular dress while the priest or prelate blesses the habit and veil"[40]), her status as mother, and the authority implied by that status, are not specifically emphasized. In the verse translation of the Benedictine rule, the chapter on receiving nuns into the community also gives Mary a mere token role. While the Latin, masculine version describes the postulant as making his vows "Coram Deo et sanctis eiis,"[41] the English briefly adds Mary to the equation. The candidate makes her vow "vnto god" and to "al halows of heuyn chere" as in the Latin but also "Vnto mary, cristes moder dere."[42] The "Method of makeing a Nunn" in MS BL Cotton Vespasian A. 25 similarly gives Mary a relatively minor role in the service—brief mentions of her as virgin mother occur in three prayers.[43]

The Franciscan vow resembles the Benedictine vow in that Mary, here not specifically named as a mother, appears in a list with others whom the candidate addresses: "I Suster . . . bihote to god & owre ladi blissid mayde marie & to seynt Fraunces, to myne ladi seint Clare & to alle seyntis" (*Rewle* 83–84).

Mary as mother nevertheless comes to the fore in the rule's description of a woman's motivation for entering this order. The rule envisions the influence of a "Marian trinity,"[44] referring to "Eche womman whiche bi þe grace & gifte of þe holi goste schal be brouht to entre in þis ordre for to nyȝe to god owre lorde Ihesu Criste & to his ful swete moder" (*Rewle* 82). While the Holy Spirit provides the desire, Mary the Mother takes her place with God the Father and Jesus the Son as those to whom the nun will draw near when she enters religion.

Moreover, the abbess as a specifically maternal authority figure is also central. The candidate does not make her profession to a clerical stand-in for husband and father but rather "in hondes of þe Abbesse bifore alle þe couent," declaring, "I Suster . . . bihote . . . in ȝoure hondes, moder, to lyue after þe rule of myne lorde þe apostle Boneface þe eytiþ correctid & approuid be alle þe time of myne life" (*Rewle* 83–84). Although as Lifshitz correctly notes, etymologically "an *abbatissa*, or abbess, is *not* a mother" but rather "a female father,"[45] the abbess here in fact *is* a mother, explicitly addressed as such. The Franciscan profession is thus an exchange between women in which women are in charge rather than a transaction in which the reproductive role is coopted by clerics and in which women are subjected to male, clerical representatives of fathers and husbands.

An extremely strong emphasis is placed on maternity in the Brigittine tradition. In St. Birgitta's revelations, when Christ describes to her the new order he wants her to found, he says, "This religion þerfore I wyll sette: ordeyne fyrst and principally by women to the worshippe of my most dere beloued modir" (*Rewyll* fol. 42r).[46] Given this emphasis, it is not surprising that the abbess as mother plays, as she does in the Franciscan service, an important role in Brigittine consecrations. While during the consecration service the candidate makes her promise of obedience to both the bishop and the abbess,[47] on the eighth day following her consecration she writes her profession in the register. The *Syon Additions for the Sisters* indicates that during this ceremony the new nun makes her promise "to the abbes of thys monastery, and to thy successours," and specifically to the abbess as mother: "I delyuer and betake to ȝour reuerent moderhode, thys wrytyng."[48] In this textual transaction, the Brigittine nun does not come into male hands and under male control as the Benedictine nun does in placing her written profession on the altar. When the new Brigittine nun writes her profession in the register, which remains in the community's possession, the textual exchange is one between women in which female, maternal authority is emphasized.

The Brigittine Rule similarly emphasizes maternal authority when it says that the abbess as mother stands in Mary's stead as head of both male and female members of the community; the abbess "for the reuerence of the most blessid virgyn marie to whomme this ordre ys halwyd. owith to be hedde and ladye. ffor þat virgyn whose stede the abbes beryth in eerth. cryst ascendynge in to heuyn. was hedde and qwene of the apostelis and disciples of cryst" (*Rewyll* fol. 56r–56v). In describing how the confessor general (the highest-ranking male official in the community) and the abbess "schal behaue them," the *Syon Additions for the Sisters* states that they "owe to be as fader and moder" (198). Then, altering the traditional hierarchy of father and mother, the text specifies that the abbess "is hede and lady of the monastery" and the confessor general is to "feythfully assiste the abbess" (*Sisters* 198).[49]

The authority constructed for the abbess in the Brigittine tradition did not go unchallenged. In the process of papal approval, the Rule encountered difficulties, since Pope Urban V disapproved of the "subordination of the men to the women." Consequently, he insisted on revisions which redefined the role of the abbess, diminishing her power over the male religious of the community.[50] The abbess at Syon was also not immune from challenges to her authority. The foundation charter initially gave her control over both spirituals and temporals, but an ecclesiastical council subsequently reduced her control to that of temporals only.

The *Syon Additions for the Sisters* itself results from a struggle between the abbess and clerical officials regarding her authority and the rights of the community. At a conference of "distinguished abbots" held in January 1416, one of a series of meetings in which the *Additions* were drawn up, "the claim of the sisters against the performance of certain kinds of manual work, such as cooking and baking, was refused: and the claim of the abbess Matilda Newton to be obeyed by the confessor and brothers was also refused."[51] The degree to which the *Syon Additions* still enables the abbess at Syon to mobilize the maternal authority originally bestowed by the Brigittine Rule is thus all the more remarkable.

In accordance with the foundation of the abbess's maternal authority in Mary's maternal authority, Mary is appropriately advanced in the Brigittine consecration service as a figure with whom the candidate is encouraged to identify. In the consecration service, the candidate asks for entry into religion in the name of Jesus Christ and in "worshipe of his holy modir mari virgyn" (*Rewyll* fol. 49r). A red banner depicting Christ's body on one side and that of the Virgin Mary on the other precedes the candidates in the procession "so that the newe spowse beholdyng þe signe of the newe spouse sufferyng on the crosse. lerne paciens and pouerte. And in beholdyng the virgyn modir: lerne chastite and mekenes" (*Rewyll* fol. 49r). The candidate is simultaneously to become Christ's "newe spowse" and "virgyn modir." Furthermore, while the bishop may stand in for Christ the spouse and for the nun's father, the candidate too can align herself with Christ, from whom she is to learn.[52] Mary and Christ, represented so frequently in Brigittine texts as co-redemptors,[53] are portrayed as two sides of the same coin, so to speak, providing equally important models for identity formation.

The instruction to Brigittine novices to learn chastity and meekness from Mary shows, on one level, the dominance of a traditional ideology of female spirituality in Brigittine texts. Brigittine texts also, however, represent Mary's meekness and chastity as empowering qualities, as sources of authority. For instance, in the *Liber celestis*, the definitive collection of Birgitta's revelations which was translated at least twice into Middle English, Christ compares Mary to "a flowr þat grew in a vale, a-bowte which vale wer v high mountaynes."[54] He identifies Mary with the vale for the "mekenes" which she had "a-fore all oþer," and he continues by saying, "This vale passed v mountaynes."[55] Thus, Mary's meekness raises her above five Old Testament leaders—Moses, Eli, Sampson, David, and Solomon. Christ also declares that Mary's chastity makes her even greater than the clergy, his earthly representatives; he says, "In thyn abstynence þu arte more than any confessore."[56]

Nuptial imagery, with all the baggage it carries, is thus not the only identity-shaping imagery available in Brigittine profession. The Brigittine consecration service contains a "complex cluster of ideas—virginity, marriage, intercourse, fertility" which lies at its heart.[57] While in the Benedictine profession service maternal reproduction is recast as the priestly production of new nuns, the language of the hymn accompanying the procession into the chapter house following the consecration highlights pointedly the combination of maternal and nuptial possibilities available to Brigittine nuns. While processing, the community sings *sponse iungendo filio*, which is also sung at compline on Thursdays; one line reads, "The wombe of mary is the chambre. her soule is the spousesse."[58] The hymn emphasizes:

that the virginal conception of Christ was, at the same time, an intimate intercourse between him and the soul of the Virgin Mary which produced a whole host of "fayre children." . . . The newly professed is thus truly what the *Extrauagantes* first called her, a daughter of the Virgin. . . . She is also . . . the spouse of the Virgin's son: at the same time, therefore, daughter, wife, and mother to be . . . , herself another Virgin Mary.[59]

Like the banner in the consecration service, the identity of the new Brigittine nun has more than one side.

It is quite appropriate that the Brigittine and Franciscan traditions work in their profession services, and, as we shall see, in their visitation practices, to shape religious identities which celebrate female spiritual power. Both orders originated with women who were profoundly committed to developing new, distinctive roles for women in religious life, and both share a common heritage of later medieval continental religious protofeminism. The Brigittine Rule, divinely revealed to St. Birgitta and ordained, in accordance with Christ's command, "first and principally by women," strives, in spite of affinities with the Cistercian tradition, to "dissociate itself from existing monastic practice."[60] Birgitta's design of a double order headed by an abbess, which was extremely unusual in the fourteenth century, also likely harkens back to an earlier attempt to carve out new religious possibilities for women—the creation of the Fontevrauldine Order by Robert of Abrissel.[61]

St. Clare of Assisi devoted her life to procuring the privilege of poverty (in her view the defining aspect of Franciscan identity) for her community at San Damiano, and she, together with Blessed Agnes of Prague, succeeded in having Pope Innocent IV remove the requirement that the nuns observe, even *formaliter*, the Rule of St. Benedict. The early versions of the Franciscan Rule for nuns were revised by Blessed Isabella, sister of Louis IX of France, into a distinctive modification known as the Isabella Rule, which, although it does not embrace the radical poverty so loved by Clare, seeks to underline the equality of Franciscan nuns and friars. That the nuns and friars are, to borrow Penelope Johnson's terms, "equal in monastic profession," is underlined by the Isabella Rule's specification that the women who follow it be called "Minoresses," so indicating their "privileged position" and "closer connection with the 'Fratres Minores' than the rest of the Order."[62] It is this rule which was followed by the English Franciscan nuns.

Through the origins of their orders in Sweden, Italy, and France, English Brigittines and Franciscans were linked with such continental developments in female spirituality as the "feminization of sanctity."[63] Ties with continental innovations in religious practices were furthered by the direct connections of English houses of Franciscan and Brigittine nuns with those in France and Scandinavia. English houses of Minoresses were settled with nuns from Isabella's foundation of Longchamp in the diocese of Paris, and nuns from the Brigittine motherhouse in Vadstena came to facilitate the beginnings of the community at Syon. Textual circulation also reinforced ties with burgeoning new forms of female spirituality across the Channel. Syon, for instance, possessed a copy of *The Orchard of Syon*, a Middle English translation of the *Dialogues* of Catherine of Siena. In these regards, the opportunities for independence both spiritual and secular offered to English Brigittine and Franciscan nuns in their profession services were part of a much larger social phenomenon.

Visitation Documents and Gendered Identity

Episcopal visitation, like profession, plays an important part in the construction of religious identity, since in visitation every element of monastic life, from performing divine service to serving meals, comes under scrutiny. Visitation also has long-term consequences, since the injunctions become part of the statutes of the house, superseding previous documents of the same kind. In visitation, documents impacting religious identity proliferate. During a typical visitation of a Benedictine religious house, upon the arrival of the diocesan, a clerk preached a sermon, and then the head of the house presented a certificate of the receipt of the summons to visitation and of its delivery to the various persons summoned. Next, the head of the house was required to exhibit certificates of election, confirmation by the diocesan, and installation in office. The superior then had to exhibit the foundation charter as well as information concerning the current financial condition of the house. Through this documentary profusion, the house accounted for its temporal circumstances and reaffirmed its material origins.

After these preliminaries of communal accountability, the business of personal accountability began. Members of the house appeared singly before the bishop or sometimes before clerks deputed to examine members simultaneously. Notaries took down the depositions, known as *detecta*, and then the *comperta* (matters discovered by the bishop) were formed from the *detecta* and the results of preliminary inquiry. At the end of the visitation proceedings, the visitor published the *detecta* and *comperta* to the assembled community and delivered brief verbal injunctions. Finally, soon after his departure, he sent written injunctions to the community which were added to the statutes of the house.[64]

The textual transactions associated with episcopal visitation have often been considered formulaic and homogenous across orders and genders;[65] just as the important imaginative work of constructing gendered identities gets done in profession services, however, so too is it performed through the seemingly bland official language of visitation documents. While it is true that episcopal visitation was a fact of monastic life for monks and nuns alike, in England nuns were more subject than monks to episcopal jurisdiction. In this respect, then, the process was not gender neutral, since not even the most powerful and important Benedictine abbeys of nuns succeeded in obtaining the kind of exemption from episcopal visitation enjoyed by some male houses of corresponding stature. In fact, even nunneries belonging to such exempt orders as the Cistercians were consistently subject to episcopal visitation.[66] In the fifteenth century, church officials, "unlike their Gregorian predecessors, aggressively sought to take the *cura mulierum* into their own hands. They wanted to direct the spiritual life of women even at the cost of carrying the burdens of responsibility."[67] Outside of the three houses of Franciscan Minoresses and the one house of Dominican nuns existing in England in the later Middle Ages, which were visited by the ministers of their orders, the only real exemptions to episcopal jurisdiction over female foundations were the communities of nuns dependent on male houses where the head of the male house sometimes acted as visitor.

As Johnson notes, prelates had a "vested interest" in maintaining strong authority over both male and female houses in their diocese or province.[68] "The obedience of a monastery increased the episcopal power base and added to the diocesan's income through court fees and procurations."[69] In addition to acquiring material resources, a diocesan could also gain symbolic capital, resources stored in nonmaterial form, by asserting his authority as visitor, as "writer" of ideological scripts, and regulator of community life.[70] Because English nuns were more subject to visitation than monks, the bishops' gain of material and symbolic capital were achieved at greater expense to the nuns— another respect in which visitation was not gender neutral.

The material burdens of visitation, while borne by nuns and monks alike, would have been comparatively greater for nuns, since nunneries were generally poorer and less well-endowed than male monasteries. Nunnery accounts indicate that these material costs could be heavy indeed. When a bishop or his deputy came to the house on the business of visitation, the nuns had to pay for the entertainment of the visitor and his retinue; they also had to pay various parties engaged in the textual transactions, such as bringing summons, returning with injunctions, and writing accounts. The treasuress's account from St. Michael's Stamford from 2–3 Richard II includes the following instances of such expenses:

Primerment pour expensus del Evesque al visitacion	xls
Item a 1 home portant la lettre del visitacion	iis
Item a 1 altre home portant 1 lettre apres le visitacion	xiid[71]

William Alnwick, bishop of Lincoln, visited St. Michael's Stamford in 1442, and a list of creditors of the house at the time of that visitation includes a debt of £8 10s to Thomas Colston.[72] Colston, a canon of Lincoln Cathedral, was Alnwick's notary and was present at the visitation, so it is quite likely that the debt is related to visitation costs. Nunneries incurred expenses even when the visitation was not performed by the bishop. A prioress's account from St. Mary de Pré (4–5 Edward IV) records "iis id in expensus" for the house's visitation by the prior and sacristan of St. Alban's together with their servants as ordered by the abbot.[73]

The gendered effects of visitation extend still further. Visitation in fact produces and reinforces very specific, differing identities for monks and nuns as men and women in religion. In visitation records and injunctions for Benedictine houses, gendered differences, which reinforce the divergent subject positions set out in profession for monks and nuns, are clearly revealed with a heightened emphasis on female weakness and vulnerability throughout. Injunctions concerning the exclusions of seculars from the cloister provide a particularly striking illustration of the way in which visitation encourages gendered religious identities. While it is the case that seculars did have access to both male and female houses on a regular basis, and indeed lived as corrodians in male and female monastic communities, ecclesiastical concern with the presence of seculars persisted. Even in cases where the theory and practice of monastic life are at odds, the continuing clerical desire to align theory and practice, and the reasons expressed for invoking the theory as the ideal, reveal gendered definitions of religious life.

In injunctions for male houses, visitors express concern with the disturbances seculars might cause to the monks. For instance, Bishop Flemyng's 1421–1422 injunctions for Huntingdon Priory prohibit seculars' passage through the cloister "in order that the devotion of the singers in quire or the peace of those who are sitting in the cloister may be in no way disturbed by those seculars."[74] In a set of late fourteenth- or early fifteenth-century injunctions for Newnham, Bishop Gray echoes these concerns, ordering that the house restrain the recourse of seculars, especially women, to cloister precincts and prevent them from sharing meals in the frater "so that the quiet of the canons in cloister at the time of contemplation or the reading in the frater at breakfast-time be in no wise hindered."[75]

The emphasis on preserving an atmosphere of quiet for the male religious' contemplation, services, and study demonstrates the Church's view of their mental and spiritual labors as valuable, productive work which seculars should not to be allowed to disrupt. These labors replaced the manual labor which had long since practically disappeared as a defining aspect of monastic life. A passage from the statutes of the 1343 chapter of the Benedictines, which was restated without change in the statutes of the 1444 chapter, indicates the importance of study and intellectual labor in monastic life: "Abbates . . . monachos suos claustrales loco operis manualis . . . certis facient exerciciis occupari, videlicet studendo, legendo, librosque scribendo, corrigendo, illuminando pariter et ligando."[76] It is clear that this passage represents a watershed change in the definition of monastic labors because, significantly, "the word *legendo* (i.e. reading with commentary to students; cf. the 'reader' at universities) is not in the corresponding decree of the chapter of 1277."[77]

The reasons visitors give for prohibiting access of seculars to female houses differ dramatically from the reasons given in injunctions for male houses. For female houses, the prohibitions tend to be expressed in terms of alarm at the spread of public slander resulting from seculars' access and corresponding concern with the damage to the nuns' reputation seculars thus caused. In his 1445 injunctions to the Benedictine nuns of Littlemore Priory, Bishop Alnwick orders that they prevent the access of outsiders because "ye and your said place are greuously noysede and sclaundrede" as a result of the "gre[te and] commune accesse" seculars have.[78] In his 1445 injunctions to the Benedictine house of Godstow, Alnwick also prohibits access of seculars with the exception of the house's officers or "other that are of your consaile and fee."[79] The reason given for this prohibition is that "youre saide monastery and diuerse singulere persones ther of are greuously noysed and sclaundred."[80] The nuns' "honesty" appears as a related concern in injunctions dealing with the access of seculars to the nuns' cloister. In 1421–1422, Bishop Gray prohibits secular boarders among the Benedictine nuns at Elstow Abbey because they damage the "purity of religion" ("religionis puritas") and the "pleasantness of honest conversation and character" ("conuersacionis honeste et morum suauitas").[81]

Contemplation, study, and divine service were as important to women as to men in monastic orders, and perhaps even more so, since women could not become priests. While English nunneries, with the exception of Syon, most likely did not have the extensive libraries available in some male houses, books appropriate for study and contemplative reading were certainly part of nuns' spiritual lives, even in houses that, unlike Syon, were not exceedingly wealthy.[82] The rhetoric of visitation records, however, appears less concerned with preserving an atmosphere conducive to contemplation, study, and divine service in female houses. The visitors' concern with the nuns' reputation rather than with their ability to engage in spiritual labor shows that the value of women religious, as far as the Church was concerned, did not lie in their work. While the Church identified monks as producers of valuable spiritual resources whose labors should be facilitated, the value of women religious did not stem so much from their contemplative and intellectual labors as from an imagined essential purity.

Indeed, clerics saw in nuns' reading and study opportunities to reinforce the kinds of proper conduct that would maintain their vital essential purity and unblemished reputation. As Anne Clark Bartlett observes in her discussion of clerical directives on how to read, "Ideally, an audience should assimilate a devotional text enthusiastically and comprehensively, attempting to reinscribe its words on their bodies by imitating the virtuous behavior that it models."[83] This clerical desire that nuns read so as to behave properly rather than so as to become learned is evident even in the translator's prologue to the Brigittine *Myroure of Oure Ladye*.[84] The translator advises the nuns, "Dresse so your entente. that your redyng & study. be not only for to be connynge or for to can speke yt fourthe to other; but pryncypally to enforme your selfe. & to set yt a warke in youre owne lyuynge."[85]

Clerical concerns with nuns' conduct and episcopal visitors' overwhelming desire that nunneries avoid slander align with canonists' assumptions that "although sexual abstinence and virginity were central values, essential to any life of religious dedication, nuns were specially blessed (or burdened) with an obligation to preserve a chastity that took on an almost mythical significance and importance."[86] For instance, Joannes Andreae "stressed that continence as well as virginity were included in the term chastity, and he equated the holiness of nuns with that single virtue."[87] According to both canonists and diocesan visitors, nuns' value lay in their chastity (so essential to their status as brides of Christ) and in the good repute which proved their intrinsic worth.

A concern not only with chastity but also with good reputation stemmed from the need to make the unknowable knowable and the invisible visible. A nun's spiritual condition was very much a public matter; *fama* or *communis fama*, defined as "the general opinion of serious and well-informed neighbors," were invoked in defining her status as holy or sinful.[88] Sherry Ortner has noted that in societies where marriage is potentially a vertical transaction for women (hypergamy), both the economic value of a woman (what she can bring as dowry to the marriage) and her mystical or spiritual value, her "inner worthiness for such an alliance," become matters of great importance.[89] Ortner observes that virginity and chastity are "particularly apt for symbolizing such value."[90] A nun's union with Christ is perhaps the ultimate instance of hypergamy, and thus those who administered and supervised the union were particularly concerned with securing the actual sexual purity of women religious as well as the reputation which provided a guarantee of value.

Episcopal injunctions concerning the proliferation of households known as *familiae* beyond the three traditionally tolerated—that is, the households of the superior, the *frater*, and the *misericord*—also reveal gendered constructions of Benedictine religious identity. *Familiae* ate together, frequently catering for themselves rather than relying on common stores. For male communities, visitors criticize numerous *familiae* as impractical, wasteful, or contrary to obedience to the monastic rule. For example, in Alnwick's 1439 visitation of Ramsey Abbey, a large male Benedictine house, numerous households eating in diverse places are said to damage religious discipline and waste temporal goods—although in the past there were only three households, "iam sunt perplurima, propter quod religio perit et bona consumuntur."[91] In the injunctions from this visitation, Alnwick orders that the almoner, sacrist, and hostilarius not keep separate households including servants because they waste the resources of the house.[92] In Thompson's three volumes of fifteenth-century visitations of religious houses in the diocese of Lincoln, *familiae* are mentioned in the visitations of five male communities. In addition to the case of Ramsey, waste figures in two other cases. At Bardney, the waste of alms through excess *familiae* is condemned,[93] while at Thornton the prior declares that, although waste has been a problem, it is not due to *familiae* but to other factors.[94] At Peterborough, the prior simply asks the bishop to affirm the steps he (the prior) has already taken in doing away with separate eating places for monks in their seynies (that is, those monks undergoing periodic bloodletting performed for health reasons) and those excused from the frater.[95] Finally, at Spalding, the bishop actually *approves* the existence of more than three households.[96]

For female houses, as in injunctions concerning the access of seculars, visitors tend to frame their concerns with excess *familiae* in terms of preventing slander. In his 1442 injunctions for Catesby Priory,[97] Bishop Alnwick commands the prioress to ensure that the nuns "aftere your rewle lyfe in commune, etyng and drynkyng in oon house, slepyng in oon house . . . levyng vtterly all pryuate hydles, chaumbers and syngulere housholdes, by the whiche hafe comen and growen grete hurte and peryle of sowles and noyesfulle sklaundere of your pryorye."[98] Concern with a house's reputation and repugnance toward public gossip about irregular activities there crop up frequently in visitation records for male and female houses. Slander is, however, only mentioned once in injunctions concerning *familiae* in a male house, and in this case (Ramsey) the slander is connected with the waste of alms rather than directly with the proliferation of *familiae*. So, since bishops use very different rhetoric to describe their concern with both enclosure and *familiae* in male and female communities, it seems fair to say that the repeated stress on reputation in the cases involving women reveals the Church's gendered ideologies of religious identity for monks and nuns.

Visitation records highlight that *familiae* allowed women religious increased autonomy and more direct control of whatever resources were available.[99] In the 1440 visitation of Gokewell, the prioress reports that "the nuns do keep divers households, to wit two by two; and yet they receive nothing of the house but bread and beer."[100] At Langley in 1440 the prioress also indicates that the nuns "keep separate households by themselves two and two." She hastens to add that they eat "in the frater every day," but she goes on to report, "the nuns receive naught from the house but their meat and drink." Finally, she indicates that "she herself keeps one household on her own account."[101]

Nunneries' financial records similarly bear witness to internal economies which allowed the women religious some personal control of resources. Each month the prioress and nuns of St. Mary de Pré (a Benedictine house dependant on St. Albans Abbey), who numbered between eight and ten, shared between 33s and 35s for their "commyns," that is, money for basic foods beyond bread and ale. St. Mary de Pré's accounts also indicate cash payments for *potages* (dishes of cooked food).[102] These developments manifest the very type of distribution of resources which injunctions limiting *familiae* sought to prevent.

The autonomy *familiae* enabled for nuns may well have prompted the clergy to focus on slander when addressing the proliferation of households. The visitors' connection of excess *familiae* and nuns' ill repute (which would potentially devalue nuns' essential purity) resonates with a common later medieval tendency to sexualize, and thus stigmatize, economic activity which allowed women any measure of independence.[103] Nuns were in fact frequently subjected to double-barreled, mutually reinforcing critiques which linked the sin of *proprietas* (that is, irregular possession of private property) with unchastity. While the link between *proprietas* and unchastity was at times made for both male and female religious, the slope leading from *proprietas* to unchastity was seen as particularly slippery and dangerous for the brides of Christ. The fifteenth-century German reformer Johann Busch declared of nuns, "First, losing the fear of God through the dissolution of their life, they fall into *proprietas* in small things; then in greater things, and then, descending farther to the personal possession of money and garments, they at last rush into the lusts of the flesh, and the incontinence of outward senses, and so to wickedness of act, not fearing to give themselves up to all filth and uncleanness."[104]

Tellingly, references to excess *familiae* appear more frequently in visitations of female houses. *Familiae* are mentioned in seventeen cases in A. Hamilton Thompson's three volumes of fifteenth-century visitations of religious houses from the diocese of Lincoln. Five references to *familiae* occur in visitations of male communities (see above), while twelve occur in visitations of female houses: the Cistercian house of Catesby,[105] the Benedictine house of Elstow (two different visitations),[106] the Benedictine house of Godstow (two different visitations),[107] the Cistercian house of Gokewell,[108] the Austin house of Gracedieu,[109] the Benedictine house of Langley,[110] the Cistercian house of Nuncoton,[111] the Benedictine house of Stainfield,[112] the Benedictine house of St. Michael's Stamford,[113] and the Cistercian house of Stixwould.[114] This difference might mean that excess *familiae* were in fact more common in female communities, a possibility given nuns' greater reliance on gifts, annuities and the like.[115] It might well mean, though, that visitors were more concerned with *familiae* and their implications in female houses.

That visitors go further in restricting *familiae* in female communities than in male communities suggests that ecclesiastical unease with the material autonomy which *familiae* enabled for nuns did lead to heightened concern about the proliferation of households. For example, rather than insisting on a return to the traditional three *familiae*, in 1440 Bishop Alnwick restricts the Benedictine nuns of St. Michael's Stamford to a single *familia*, requiring them to "stande alle holy wythe the prioresse in hire householde."[116] Alnwick similarly enjoins that the Benedictine nuns at Godstow abandon their diverse *familiae* in favor of dining all together. He additionally requires that the abbess of this house "*do* mynystre to thaym *of the commune godes of the house* mete and drynke owte [of] one selare and one kychyn."[117] This last injunction clearly reveals ecclesiastical desires to restrain the more individual administration of resources that occurred in female houses with numerous *familiae*. The point was not so much to promote the nuns' spirituality by encouraging them to live a communal life as to limit the need of the brides of Christ to engage in financial decision making in the commercial marketplace, activity which was perceived as posing such a risk to their valuable purity.

As they do in their profession services, the Franciscan and Brigittine orders demonstrate distinct similarities with the Benedictine tradition in their visitation practices, and in many respects they do not call into question male, ecclesiastical authority over women. The visitor has a great deal of authority under the Isabella Rule, which grants to the Minister Provincial "þe ordinaunce of þis ordre, þe gouernaunce, þe cure, þe visitacioun, þe correccioun, & reformacioun" (*Rewle* 95). The *Bulla Reformatoria* of Martin V, included in translation in the *Syon Additions for the Sisters*, begins by confirming episcopal jurisdiction over Brigittine houses in terms that stress a gendered, hierarchical, familial relationship between the nuns and the visitors. The bull states that English bishops in whose dioceses Brigittine foundations are located are to do all their offices as ordinary and to be "faders and iuges in al cases and causes, that toche the sustres or brethren, and also visitours and proctours of the seyd monasteryes" (*Sisters* 47).

The Brigittine and Franciscan traditions do, however, place limits on a visitor's power to impact the particular identities nuns have within them. As the preceding examples regarding *familiae* indicate, injunctions can require modifications of the community's ways of life and use of resources, aspects of monastic life fundamental to identity formation. The Isabella Rule short-circuits these potentially transformative aspects of visitation, stating, "And ouer alle þinge we defende þat none Ministre ne visitoure bi here auctorite make none constitucionis in þe Abbey ageynis þe forme & rule aforseyde" (*Rewle* 96). Any constitutions impinging on the rule could be made only "bi consentment of alle þe couent" and, strikingly, "ʒif ani soche nyew ordinaunce be made, by no maner þat þe sustres shul be boundyn þer to" (*Rewle* 96). Through these provisions, the Isabella Rule grants the nuns a significant amount of control over how visitation proceedings affect their community and their identity.

Texts associated with Brigittine visitation also place limits on visitors' powers and give the nuns significant control over the impact of visitation on the community. The *Bulla Reformatoria* limits the scope of the bishop's authority, preventing him from giving "any maner of sentence of cursynge, suspension, or interdiccion, / general or special" without "commission and special commaundmente of our see" (*Sisters* 47). Bishops visiting Syon were thus largely deprived of one of their primary tools for enjoining obedience, that is, the threat of excommunication which occurs almost universally in episcopal injunctions. Furthermore, the bull requires that the bishop commit the execution of "correccions, penaunces, and peynes, that be to be sette and enioyned to the trespasers" to "the abbes or the sadder parte of the sustres" (*Sisters* 45). Tellingly, the bull also states that the bishops are not to "aske any costes of them" (*Sisters* 47), thereby circumventing the financial burdens of visitation and mitigating the costs of hospitality which were often so heavy for houses. Since Syon's great wealth might have been a tempting prospect for a less than circumspect prelate, the papal document's assurance that material capital will remain in the nuns' hands is particularly beneficial.

Ultimately, and perhaps most significantly, Franciscan and Brigittine visitation documents blur the rigid hierarchy between observer and observed.

This distinction is an important marker of gendered, authoritative status in religion. The writing of Petrus de Ancarano, a contemporary of Joannes Andreae and, like Andreae, a commentator on *Periculoso*, is instructive on this point. In some respects Petrus is more moderate than Joannes in his interpretation of claustration; however, following Joannes's *Novella*, Petrus "agrees that even abbesses may not leave their monasteries save for expressed purposes, and that conducting visitations is *not* one of those purposes, since the abbess herself is bound by the rules such visits seek to enforce."[118] Abbots, however, could and did visit communities under their jurisdiction in lieu of the diocesan.

Franciscan and Brigittine visitation practices do not go so far as to allow abbesses to conduct visitations of houses themselves. The *Syon Additions for the Sisters*, however, specifies that the bishop is not to visit "but in hys proper persone," and he is to be accompanied by two or three companions (*Sisters* 39). Significantly, one of these companions is to be a "religious manne of the order of benett or bernarde" chosen by the abbess and confessor general in consultation with the "elder and wholer" sisters and brethren (*Sisters* 39). The members of the female community thus take an active role in organizing the visitation, and the *Syon Additions for the Sisters*, in calling for the participation of the abbess in choosing officials to carry out in the visitation, typifies the way in which Brigittine texts work to augment her position in the community of both men and women.[119]

A symbolic representation of the abbess's maternal, authoritative identity in the corporate body occurs in the Brigittine visitation ceremony itself. In bishop's registers, one of the phrases frequently used to describe the bishop's role is that he sits in the capacity of judge in a tribunal: "In primis sedente dicto domino commissario iudicialiter pro tribunali in huiusmodi visitacionis inchoande negocio."[120] The head of the house and the convent then traditionally appear before the bishop seated in this capacity. The visitation procedure to be used at Syon, however, states that when the bishop takes his seat, "he shal make the abbes to sytte on hys ryghte hande" (*Sisters* 40). The head of the house in this case does not submit to the bishop seated in judgment but rather sits in judgment with him.[121] The abbess, whom the Brigittine Rule describes as occupying the position of the Virgin Mary, is placed here on an equal level with the bishop, the representative of Christ. This placement echoes frequent description of the Virgin Mary as co-redemptrix in Brigittine service texts, and it recalls the equal focus on Mary and Christ as models for the nun in the consecration ceremony.[122] Through limiting episcopal power and foregrounding the abbess's authority, texts associated with Brigittine visitation do much to change the visitation process's "ways of making the world."[123]

The Minoresses' Isabella Rule also changes the ways in which the world of the religious community is "made" in visitation. For instance, it stipulates that the visitor's behavior is just as subject to scrutiny as the sisters' behavior. The text specifies that he is to be "soche one whoche is wel knowen of stedfastnesse of religious life & gode vertuis" (*Rewle* 92). Furthermore, if, after the visitation, "any þinge notable ageynis þe visitoure or ageynis his felawes" is found, it is to be reported to the Minister General (*Rewle* 94). He, like the sisters, may become part of a body of knowledge, a textual *corpus*. Not only those visited, but also the visitor, is subject to examination and classification. Both parties thus have the opportunity to mobilize textual practices to their own advantage.

Even more strikingly, the Isabella Rule disrupts the textual dissemination of knowledge about women religious, putting control of their textual *corpus* back into their own hands. The visitor is to "kepe priue, ne schewe hit nat bi his knowinge to none bodi" (*Rewle* 94) that which he finds in visitation. G. G. Coulton notes that in visitation records, "one of the most serious offenses contemplated is that of revealing the secrets of the chapter. . . . To reveal the details of a visitation was one of the worst and most heavily-punished monastic offenses."[124] In the case of the Minoresses, the prohibition is stated with reference to the visitor instead of the visited. Information concerning the visitation could only be reported to the Minister General of the Order "bi þe counsayle of moste wise sustris of þe couent" (*Rewle* 94).

Most dramatically, the Isabella Rule alone among rules for Franciscan nuns specifies that "assone as misdedis schal be redde & penaunce enioynid, alle þat whoche is writen schal be brent bifore þe couent" (*Rewle* 94). The visitor is not permitted to keep that which he accumulates as he writes the visitation documents. The required destruction of the texts allows the sisters following the Isabella Rule to escape being caught in the network of clerical textual exchanges. Unlike Benedictine nuns, who put themselves in textual form into clerical hands at their profession and remain in visitation documents part of a textual *corpus* permanently in the hands of ecclesiastical authorities, the Minoresses elude the defining, confining power of writing.

The wealth, aristocratic patronage, and the generally high social status of Brigittine and Franciscan nuns may have been factors enabling clerical acceptance of the less intrusive visitation practices at Syon and in houses of English Minoresses. Since important, wealthy Benedictine abbeys of nuns did not succeed in obtaining the kind of exemption from episcopal visitation enjoyed by some male houses of corresponding stature, though, money and social status did not in and of themselves ensure nuns' autonomy. In considering the more liberal visitation practices of the Brigittine and Franciscan traditions, it is also important to remember that both rules were written *for* women (not for men and then adapted for women) *by* women who were very interested in preserving distinctive religious identities. I do not wish to argue that Birgitta, Clare, and Isabella escaped or entirely rejected traditional gendered ideologies in religion. Furthermore, the rules which gained papal approval were not precisely what these women first envisioned. The Brigittine and Isabella rules do, however, bear witness to their female creators' concerns with the power dynamics in relationships between women religious and the clergy. Additionally, although Franciscan and Brigittine ceremonies of visitation, like services of profession in these traditions, have much in common with Benedictine procedures, the differences have far-reaching implications. The structures of textual, material, and symbolic exchanges in Franciscan and Brigittine visitation ceremonies are less restrictive than in the Benedictine tradition. Franciscan and Brigittine visitations reinforce nuns' legitimate access to material and spiritual resources (access grounded in profession in these orders), and they present additional opportunities for women religious to lay claim to specifically female authority.

The Benefits of a Divine Spouse, or Brides of Christ, Part 2

The preeminence of nuptial identity in Benedictine profession, which prompts clerics to stress the value of nuns' chastity, to underscore the need to protect nuns' reputation as a guarantee of that value, and, concomitantly, to emphasize claustration, clearly results in certain material detriments for Benedictine nuns. Submission to the authority of clerical stand-ins for earthly fathers and the divine spouse is not, however, the end of the story of religious identity for Benedictine brides of Christ. The identity of bride of Christ is Janus-faced; the very elements of that identity which lead to constraint also lead to empowerment. McNamara has observed that the nuptial discourse of profession metaphorically empowers the nun as "consort of the lord of the universe,"[125] an identification which suggests the symbolic capital available through profession to Benedictine women religious in conjunction with the constraining baggage of nuptiality. Additionally, while, as I have argued, the potential for the authority created for Brigittine and Franciscan nuns through mobilizations of maternity is largely absent from Benedictine profession and visitation ceremonies, the possibilities suggested by maternal imagery are not entirely un-available to Benedictine nuns in other ideological scripts. To explore these complexities of religious identity for Benedictine nuns, I turn now to the *Ordo consecrationis sanctimonialium* used at the Benedictine nunnery of St. Mary's, Winchester, and a fifteenth-century ritual for the benediction of an abbess used in Benedictine houses.

The version of the *Ordo consecrationis sanctimonialium* used at St. Mary's, Winchester, in the early sixteenth century is in MS Cambridge, University Library Mm 3.13. As Anne Bagnall Yardley, who has published an edition of the eleven primary musical portions of the *Ordo*, notes, "The manuscript is attributed to St. Mary's on the basis of the inscription on a blank leaf at the beginning of the manuscript: 'Hic liber attinet ad monasterium monialium sanctae mariae in civitate winton. Ex dono Reverendi in Christo patris, Domini Ricardi Fox, ejusdem civitatis Episcopi, et dicti monasterii benefactoris praecipi.'"[126] As Yardley points out, this manuscript provides us with a version of the service intended for use by the nuns themselves, and it therefore contains "more detailed rubrics than most of the pontificals."[127] Since it illuminates in detail the ways in which the nuns participated in the ritual, it allows us to consider the ways in which the nuns may have interpreted the ideological scripts given to them as they engaged in this highly significant performance of religious identity.

Nuptial imagery and discourse are central to the service; there is, for instance, an elaborate, complexly dramatized ceremony in which the nuns' rings are blessed and presented twice to them.[128] The chants are drawn from the liturgies for Saints Agnes and Agatha, who are certainly "appropriate female images" and saints whose "great devotion to Christ as spouse would serve as an example" for the nuns.[129] The chants which the nuns sing do not, however, merely reinforce the nuns' submission to spousal authority, since Agnes and Agatha are not simply meek and obedient brides of Christ. Indeed, the *vitae* of these saints reveal that they used their marriages to Christ as grounds to resist patriarchal authority embodied in fathers and suitors. For instance, when the prefect's son proposes to St. Agnes, offering her great treasure if she will marry him, Agnes refuses, saying she has a richer, more powerful, and more worthy lover.[130] Jocelyn Wogan-Browne has persuasively argued for the potentially empowering aspects of the stories of virgin martyrs for female audiences, aspects that supplement the regulatory elements of the hagiographical texts. She points to the "possibility of resistant readings which in particular contexts may constitute relative empowerment or recuperation."[131] She observes, for example, that the "virgin heroines can both gaze and answer back and are shown as much cleverer than their tormenters."[132] The presence of Agnes and Agatha—active and authoritative brides of Christ—via their liturgies in the ideological script of the Benedictine *Ordo* also suggests the potentially empowering dimensions of the identity of divine spouse for Benedictine nuns.

The language of the chants also reveals the symbolic capital available to the nuns through the high social status inherent in their hypergamous unions with Christ. As Johnson argues, "The rich tradition of the nun as the espoused of Christ gave to professed women a unique valued status in the Middle Ages."[133] For instance, after the ring is first placed on the nun's finger by the bishop, she sings *Anulo suo* from the liturgy of St. Agnes: "Annulo suo subarravit me Dominus meus Ihesus Christus et tanquam sponsam decoravit me corona Alleluya."[134] The instructions in the manuscript direct the nun to hold up "hir hand soo hygh that the people may see it."[135] She thus publicly proclaims that she, like Agnes whose words she sings, has the highest ranking spouse possible, and so, as the image of the crown suggests, is entitled to the social as well as the spiritual benefits of such status.

Just as the constraining baggage of nuptial discourse had material manifestations for Benedictine nuns, so too did the symbolic capital translate into concrete benefits. The Benedictine nuns of Barking, for instance, enjoyed a rich textual culture, as attested by their observation of the Benedictine requirement for the annual distribution and mandatory reading of books.[136] The nuns' status as brides of Christ may have increased their chances to read sophisticated religious texts. Their already high social rank was perhaps raised even higher by the symbolic "boost" nuns enjoyed as brides of Christ, the highest-ranking spouse of all. As Nicholas Watson has argued, in the period following Arundel's Constitutions, the aristocracy, rather than society as a whole, became the only audience permitted to read vernacular theology.[137] So, any enhancement of social status could only play a beneficial factor in enabling the Barking nuns to gain access to works of vernacular theology in the post-Arundelian era when such texts were regarded with suspicion and even criminalized. Significantly, as A. I. Doyle observes, the nuns at Barking "were in the fore-front of the public" for these works of vernacular theology, and they were "readliy supplied" with such texts as *The Clensyng of Mannes Sowle*.[138] Indeed, the nuns at Barking possessed a text which seems likely to have been regarded as especially dangerous—BL Add. MS 10596, a fifteenth-century manuscript including selections from revised translations of the Lollard Bible, which remained in the community's library at least through the late fifteenth century or early sixteenth century.[139]

Nuns, living under clerical supervision and theoretically enclosed (and so prevented from disseminating widely any threatening ideas gleaned from independent-minded reading of vernacular theology), were certainly a less troubling audience for such texts than other lay women and lay men. The vernacular translations of the Benedictine Rule examined in Chapter 2 reveal, however, that those clerics opposed to vernacular theology were not unaware of the empowerment such texts enabled for nuns, nor did they ignore what were, from their perspective, the attendant threats posed by nuns' access to these texts. These facts further highlight the significance of the sophisticated literate cultures of some Benedictine communities, attesting to the brides of Christs' ability to command respect both socially and spiritually.

The symbolic capital to which the *Ordo* suggests that Benedictine nuns had access when they became brides of Christ is accompanied in rituals for the benediction of newly elected Benedictine abbesses by opportunities to lay claim to maternal authority. In a form of the ritual used in the fifteenth century, the bishop tells the abbess, "Take here the moderly overseying and provy-dence of this the flock of God, and the cure and charge of ther bodyes and of ther sowles. And be to them a mother, a guyder, and a faythfull governer."[140] His final speech to her also grants her "plenary and full power and auctoryte of all this monastery and of all therunto belongynge, ynwardly and owtewardly, spiritually and temporally."[141]

This ritual for benediction does take pains to reinforce patriarchal hier-archy and to undercut maternal authority. The Benedictine abbess as mother is repeatedly reminded of her spousal role and of the feminine weakness which necessitate her and her nuns' subordination to paternal figures. For instance, the abbess is especially charged to keep the nuns of the monastery "pure and chaste virgyns"—that is, to preserve the essential purity vital for brides of Christ. In order to protect this crucial chastity, she is admonished to "have dylygente watche and good eye on them, that they wander not abroad."[142] She is directed to keep "the rules ordeyned of the holy fathers" as well as her "frayle nature will permytt and suffer."[143] Furthermore, the ritual opens with the abbess promising the bishop "fidelyte and true subjectyon, obedyence, and reuerence . . . to yow Reverend Father yn God."[144] In spite of these strictures, though, given an abbess's experience of the daily business of running a re-ligious community, she might easily hear the language of maternity in the benediction as a mandate for her autonomy and authority, for her "maternal right to command." Additionally, as we shall see in the second chapter, the possibilities of abbesses wielding maternal authority, and the larger implica-tions of such authority for the status of women in the spiritual realm, were disturbingly real enough to figure prominently in clerical efforts to reinforce their own authority over nuns.

The *Ordo* from St. Mary's, Winchester, and the Benedictine ritual for the benediction of an abbess underline the complexities and contradictions inherent in the construction of religious identities. These complexities and contradictions were amplified as later medieval nuns went about the daily business of living as brides of Christ in the marketplace. Ecclesiastical authorities continually reinforced material and spiritual restrictions on women religious, as the exploration of vernacular translations of monastic rules for nuns in the next chapter demonstrates. As we shall see in the third chapter, however, nuns' everyday practices continually provided "visible indices" of identities that both expanded and reinterpreted the complex identities provided for them in their foundational ideological scripts.[145]

2

The Value of the Mother Tongue

Vernacular Translations of Monastic Rules for Women

Shifting Boundaries: Translations and
Social Relations in Later Medieval England

The entry for "translaten" in the *Middle English Dictionary* includes six definitions: to relocate a person or thing (including a cleric, a saint's relics, knowledge and culture, an episcopal see, or allegiance); to take away a kingdom or duchy from its ruler or people; to take into the afterlife without death; to change the nature, condition, or appearance of someone or something; to replace, turn, or move; and—finally—to render into another language.[1] These definitions reveal that translation is an operation performed on both bodies (dead and alive) and words. The far-reaching implications of the textual exchanges of monastic profession and visitation call attention to the intimate connections between bodies and words in later medieval culture, connections that heighten the dramatic social significance of translation.[2] Corporeal and textual translation share more than a common sense of change in location or form; they are linked by their socially transformative ability to change existing boundaries.[3]

In later medieval versions of monastic rules for women the process of translation from Latin to the vernacular is, like the religious identities these rules help shape, Janus-faced; it is ambiguous in its socially transformative functions. Translation works to shift boundaries and to shore them up. The vernacular acts both as servant of orthodoxy and as agent of subversion, serving to empower as well as to constrain, and sometimes doing both at once.

The ambiguous status of the vernacular and the problematic nature of translation in Middle English monastic rules for women are intimately connected to social changes involving literacy; particularly significant are the facts that in the fifteenth century, literate culture expanded among non-noble women, and nuns were in one of the best situations available to women for gaining literacy skills.[4] The Latin literacy of later medieval nuns has been generally considered lacking; vernacular literacy, however, was another story altogether. Financial accounts and court records, for instance, manifest nuns' active participation in business affairs, involvement which would have required significant literacy skills.[5] As women religious achieved levels of pragmatic and professional literacy, "their social visibility and power" increased;[6] presumably, from a clerical point of view, their potential as a source of disruption also increased accordingly.

Further enhancing the potentially advantageous and potentially threatening position of women religious was the dearth of textual production and engagement in fifteenth-century male monasteries. In his analysis of the libraries of nuns, David Bell finds that "the interest of the nuns in fifteenth-century books and literature stands in marked contrast to the unimpressive record of their male counterparts"—interest to which the vibrant textual cultures at the Benedictine house of Barking and the Brigittine house of Syon bear witness.[7] He posits that as a result of "what most men would have seen as their limitations," nuns may have enjoyed a "richer, fuller, and, one might say, more up to date" spiritual life than male monastics, who for the most part "were still mired in the consequences of a conservative and traditional education."[8]

Burgeoning vernacular literacy among women religious was clearly not the only vernacular literacy that posed a problem in the eyes of some clerical authorities. In fact, the vernacular literacy of nuns may have been somewhat less a source of ecclesiastical anxiety than the vernacular literacy of secular women (as in the case of Lollard women) and of rebellious lay men. Women religious were, after all, at least theoretically cloistered and less able to make trouble. The Church's already conflicted attitude toward female spirituality, though, made ecclesiastical authorities ever vigilant.

Vigilance likely seemed particularly necessary since the boundary-shifting, socially transformative properties of translation, as well as the connections between bodies and words, were well understood by the clerics opposed to vernacular translation of scripture in the early fifteenth century. The antitranslation faction argued that "translation into the mother tongue will allow any old women (*vetula*) to usurp the office of teacher, which is forbidden to them (since all heresies, according to Jerome, come from women); it will bring about a world in which the laity prefers to teach than to learn, in which women (*mulierculae*) talk philosophy and dare to instruct men."[9] This is a dire vision of a "translated" world turned upside down in which the nature, condition, and appearance of society itself are dramatically altered as all "proper" boundaries are breached. The passage makes clear the negative associations of the vernacular with women, creatures of inferior bodies and minds who introduce discord and disorder.

The hysterical, even apocalyptic, tone of the antitranslation passage highlights as well the conservative clerics' anxieties about the threats posed by the vernacular to their monopoly on spiritual knowledge, which they had historically enjoyed, thanks to their virtually exclusive access to Latin learning and sacred texts.[10] By undermining the foundations of clerical authority—that is, the clergy's position as sole possessors and interpreters of these sacred texts—translation shifted boundaries demarcating hierarchies. As a result, the clergy's privileged access to cultural and material resources, which followed from their monopoly on spiritual knowledge, was threatened. The socially transformative properties of translation put the English clergy who opposed it in the position of having to, in Pierre Bourdieu's terms, "save the market."[11] Translation appeared, from a clerical perspective, as the source of diverse dangers, and so the struggle to preserve all the conditions of the social field which afforded the clergy the greatest access to symbolic and material capital likewise focused on translation.[12]

One clerical strategy to save the market emerges in Arundel's Constitutions of 1407–1409. The Constitutions sought to control the spread of the vernacular, and the social disruption perceived as accompanying it, by requiring episcopal authorization of all translations of texts containing Scripture. The requirement of episcopal authorization attempts to replace, by means of the vernacular itself, the social boundaries and hierarchies displaced by the spread of the vernacular. That is to say, the Constitutions use officially sanctioned translation to reassert clerical authority over both the vernacular language and the potentially unruly female/feminized readers of vernacular texts.[13]

The yoked threats of the feminine vernacular and the female body surface again, famously, in Hoccleve's "Remonstrance Against Oldcastle":

> Somme wommen eek, though hir wit be thynne,
> Wole argumentes make in holy writ.
> Lewed calates, sitteth down and spynne
> And kekele of sumwhat elles, for your wit
> Is al to feeble to despute of it.
> To clerkes grete apparteneth þat aart.[14]

A *callot* is, according to the *Middle English Dictionary*, a foolish woman or a harlot;[15] the connections of sexual promiscuity and lack of "wit" in Hoccleve's use of the epithet underline the association of the disruptive feminine vernacular and the disruptive female body.

While Hoccleve thus plays with the same associations evident in the argument made by the antitranslation faction, his market-saving strategy is somewhat different than Arundel's. Hoccleve styles himself in this poem as the staunch defender of orthodoxy against the rebel John Oldcastle, who, in Hoccleve's eyes has, as Ruth Nissé observes, been "feminized" through Lollardy,[16] and against Oldcastle's Lollard associates, whose vernacular translations were the target of the Constitutions. Rather than clerically authorizing the vernacular in order to replace the very boundaries it breaks down, though, Hoccleve uses a vernacular poem to position the vernacular as inferior—at least in spiritual matters—to the "aart" of "clerkes."[17] This art (learned and Latinate, and so legitimate) is definitively more worthy than the "cackling" of "lewed calates." Hoccleve at once works to reinstate a linguistic hierarchy of Latin and vernacular for spiritual subjects as well as a social hierarchy of male, clerical authorities over lay, female/feminized subjects.

In the face of the possibilities for independence both spiritual and material offered to later medieval nuns by their vernacular literacy and the increased availability of vernacular texts, clerics who made translations of monastic rules for women engaged in textual, market-saving strategies resembling those of both Arundel and Hoccleve. In other words, they used the mother tongue for their own benefit, manipulating translation, the source of instability, to replace the very boundaries it broke down or shifted. They also devalued the mother tongue and the feminized speakers of it, thus asserting their own masculine, Latinate authority.[18]

Saving the Market: The Female Body and the Feminine Vernacular in Translations of the Benedictine Rule for Women

The fifteenth-century prose and verse translations of the Benedictine Rule for women strain very hard to make translation serve traditional, hierarchical relations of masculine and feminine, Latin and vernacular, sameness and difference.[19] Just as the text of the rule is translated into the vernacular for women, so too is the version of Benedictine monasticism these rules create for women a "translation." The Benedictine Rule is adapted not only linguistically but also ideologically for women to fight social and religious transformations by enforcing a rigorously hierarchical sex/gender system.[20] Like Arundel's Constitutions, the vernacular translations of the Benedictine Rule seek to "save the market" by manipulating the vernacular to control its transgressive power and that of the women who read it, putting both firmly under the control of reaffirmed clerical authority. Like Hoccleve's "Remonstrance," the translations do their utmost to emphasize the femininity, and corresponding inferiority, of the vernacular in the spiritual realm, also attributing this combination to the audience of women religious.

Putting the vernacular "in its place" (that is, under the authority of Latin) is a step in a larger process of putting women religious firmly in their place vis-à-vis the male clergy. This process was deemed especially pressing in light of prevalent associations between the "barbarous" vernacular and "an uneducated readership with a 'carnal understanding of the truth'" who were likely to rebel.[21] The prose translation of the rule asserts the strong authority necessary to avert such danger by introducing the chapters with a phrase indicating that what follows is said by, spoken by, or commanded by St. Benedict.[22] For instance, at the beginning of chapter VII, significantly a chapter addressing meekness, the masculine authority of St. Benedict and Holy Scripture coalesce as they speak together in Latin: "Of mekenes spekis sain benet in þis sentence, & sais with hali scripture: 'Omnis qui se exaltat &c.'" (*Prose* 11). Ralph Hanna III writes, concerning translation, "Perhaps most distressing for the conservative, Englished Latin had been cut free from the Latin tradition. . . . It had become 'open.'"[23] The insertion of the figure of St. Benedict in the introductory phrases, which are not present in the Latin, links the vernacular firmly to the Latin tradition, reasserting closure. The insertion of the figure of St. Benedict, like the episcopal authorization required by Arundel's Constitutions, shores up the system of social relations in which the clergy and Latin are dominant by putting a strong authority figure in place as a prophylaxis against rebellion, as a way of ruling the potentially unruly.

Bishop Richard Fox's sixteenth-century translation of the Benedictine Rule for the nuns in his diocese of Winchester similarly contains "frequent repetitions of phrases like 'Be holde susters (sayth seint Benet)' or 'O dere susters (sayth seynt Benet).'"[24] The voice of St. Benedict in the text, to whom the "susters" are commanded to listen, merges with the voice of Fox, who also speaks to the sisters and commands obedience. The strategy works, as in the fifteenth-century prose translation, to reinforce masculine, clerical authority over the women religious, reinforcement which Fox, in spite of his open-minded humanist attitudes towards vernacular learning, was very anxious to effect.[25] Such desires are evident, for instance, in a letter Fox wrote to Cardinal Wolsey on January 18, 1527. Fox declares of the nuns in his diocese that "if I had the auctoritie and powre that your grace hathe, I wolde indever me to mure and inclose theyre monasteries accordyng to thordynance of the lawe."[26] The insertions of the figure of St. Benedict in his translation also aid Fox in advancing his aims of "legitimiz[ing] his own position as a self-conscious *auctor*,"[27] as one of the "clerkes grete" to whom the art of spiritual discourse belongs. Fox, as master of the "Latin tonge" of which the nuns "have no knowledge nor understondinge"[28] and as translator of what "sayth seint Benet," is able to claim, through Benedict and his Latin text, his proper position in the classical, clerical lineage of *auctoritas*, with all accompanying social and symbolic benefits.

The brief prayers that conclude most of the chapters in the fifteenth-century prose translation of the Benedictine Rule may not initially appear to replace boundaries by reasserting hierarchies of languages and genders as the introductory phrases do.[29] In fact, though, the prayers set up a dynamic in which the voice of masculine authority addresses and subordinates passive, feminine hearers and readers. These prayers, which are typically only one or two lines long, request help, aid, knowledge, or mercy in connection with the topic discussed in the chapter. For example, chapter XLVIII on labor and study ends with the prayer, "Lauerd for his pite giue vs sua to wirk, and sua vre lescuns at vnderstande, þat we at te ende til heuin be broght. Amen" (*Prose* 33). The prayers almost all speak in first person plural.[30] The "we" of the prayers reflects the monastic convention of praying communally and for all Christians, but the "we" is never one of full solidarity. The sameness and unity of the "we" put forth in the prayers is actually difference masked as sameness, and when this difference is unmasked, the inferiority of those who are "other" emerges.

For instance, chapter XXXVII addresses provisions for the elderly and children. The introductory phrase, "Of þe alde & of þe barnis spekis sain benet in þis sentence" (*Prose* 27), serves as a reminder of masculine, ecclesiastical authority and the right to speak. However, no prayer ends the chapter, and there is no use of the first person plural. There is no assertion by the voice of masculine authority of unity with these most feminized members of the community. Chapter LXII on the ordination of priests also lacks a prayer.[31] There can be no "we" here because the female audience cannot participate in the role of the priest treated by the chapter. Women's very bodies, "other" and, like those of the elderly and the young, less than perfect, bar them from clerical status.

Chapter VI provides perhaps the most striking illustration of the way in which the withdrawal of the first person plural in the prayers functions to replace boundaries. This chapter, which addresses silence, begins with the introductory phrase, "Sain benet spekis in þis sentence of silence, how ȝe sal it halde" (*Prose* 10). Not only is there no "we" in a prayer in this chapter, but the text also repeatedly addresses its female readers or hearers as "ȝe," saying, "he bidis þat ȝe do als þe prophete sais: 'kepe ȝour tunge, it sp[e]ke no scaþe, & ȝour lippis fra iuil, & kepe ȝow fro dedly synne.' . . . þe maistires aw at speke for to lere hyr dicipils wisdom. þe decipils sal here þar lesson & understand it" (*Prose* 10). This is a significant departure from the Latin, which speaks with a participatory first person plural in prescribing restrained speech, and, in quoting Scripture, uses the first rather than the second person: "Faciamus quod ait propheta: *Dixi: Custodiam vias meas, ut non delinquam in lingua mea.*"[32] The language and grammar of the translated passage set up a hierarchy, absent in the Latin, which goes beyond daily monastic practice of silence and which is important in considering issues of gender, power, and authority. In contrast to the female listeners, "þe maistires," a group of those (male) individuals with sufficient authority and knowledge, are to speak. Included among these "maistires" is, arguably, the translator. He has access to the original text and he, being by virtue of his knowledge and gender exempted from the requirement of silence put forth by the chapter, "leres" the hearers of the text's wisdom through the translation just as Bishop Fox does in his translation.[33] "Sain benet spekis," as does the translator, but the nuns do not. The text does its utmost to constrain the feminine vernacular and contain the female voice which would speak this language with potentially disruptive consequences.

The verse translation in MS BL Cotton Vespasian A. 25 sets up the same hierarchical relationship in which a voice of male authority subordinates a female audience. It makes the requirement of silence apply more strictly to women than to men. On the ladder of meekness, the eleventh step of humility concerns speaking few words. The Latin ends the section with the verse, "Sapiens verbis innotescit paucis" (*RB 1980* 200). The English verse translation reads:

> "Sapiens in paucis verbis expedit—
> He þat is wise in word & dede,
> His wark with fone wordes wil he spede."
> And naymly women nyght & day
> Aw to vse fune wordes alway. (*Verse* 1081–84)

While it is an indication of virtue, a sign of wisdom, for a man to use few words, women in particular (*naymly*) have an obligation to (*aw to*) use few words.[34] This emphasis reflects widespread clerical attitudes about women and speech; "aside from carnality in general, the vice most frequently assigned to women was loquacity."[35]

Differing ecclesiastical attitudes toward silence for men and women religious appear in episcopal injunctions to male and female houses, amplifying the differences evident in the verse translation of the Benedictine Rule. In his 1432 injunctions to the male Benedictine house of Ramsey Abbey, Bishop Gray enjoins that "silence be kept henceforward in the cloister, church, dorter, and frater, under pain of one penny to be paid out of the commons of every monk who shall transgress herein, towards the work of the floors aforesaid."[36] Bishop Flemyng, in his 1421–1422 injunctions for the female Benedictine house of Elstow Abbey, enjoins:

silence be kept by all without distinction at the due times and places, to wit in the house of prayer, the cloister, and the dorter, under pain of fasting on bread and water upon the Wednesday and Friday following; and, if any nun shall make default in this particular, let her be constrained to that penalty: the second time, let the same penalty be doubled; and, if she be proved to have made default in this matter a third time, let her be from that time enjoined to fast on bread and water every Wednesday and Friday for the next half year, and on Monday and Thursday, let her be content with bread and beer.[37]

Notably, the penalties for women who break silence are from the outset more severe than those for men (for whom a simple fine suffices), and the punishments mandated for women escalate with repeated offenses. The bishop, however, does not envision that the monks might engage in repeated transgressions. His description of second and third offenses by nuns manifests the general ecclesiastical perception that faults of speech were especially common for women. The bodily punishments for women, contrasted with the financial punishments for men, underline concerns about female carnality, pointing to a desire to address the source of the problem: the unruly female flesh. Significantly, the system of monetary fines in the male community does not chastise the flesh but rather ultimately contributes to the physical improvement of the house (i.e., the work of the floors), leading to better living conditions for all.

Silence and regulation of speech are clearly important parts of monastic life for both men and women.[38] The verse and prose translations, however, construct a system of social relations in which, as in Hoccleve's "Remonstrance," male authorities (significantly, in both translations those with access to Latin) have the right to speak, while female hearers are commanded to keep silent on spiritual matters, listening rather than speaking. This particular framing of monastic silence, like that constructed in the injunctions, recalls the cultural desires evident in antitranslation rhetoric—that is, the desires to keep dangerously carnal women quiet and obedient.

The verse translation does not include chapter introductions and concluding prayers as the prose version does, but it attempts to minimize the potentially disruptive power of the vernacular and of women in other ways. For example, preceding the Rule's prologue beginning "Asculta, o filia, disciplina[m] magistre tue," it contains a prologue added by the translator. This additional prologue explicitly states that the text is a translation for women who do not know Latin:

> Monkes & als all leryd men
> In latyn may it lyghtly ken,
> And wytt þarby how þay sall wyrk
> To sarue god and haly kyrk.
> Bott tyll women to mak it couth,
> Þat leris no latyn in þar ȝouth,
> In ingles is it ordand here,
> So þat þay may it lyghtly lere. (*Verse* 9–16)

This passage illustrates the translator's connection of Latin with a masculine, learned elite and the vernacular with a feminine, unlearned, inferior group. The repetition of the word *lyghtly* sets up apparent sameness that is actually difference. The prologue indicates that both men and women can easily (*lyghtly*) learn the doctrine of the Benedictine Rule; however, monks and all educated men learn it easily in Latin while women only learn it easily in English. The passage implies that the English of this version will say the same thing as the Latin, an implication proved false by a comparison of the translation with the Latin. What monks and educated men learn from the Latin is not at all the same as what women religious learn from the vernacular verse translation. The Latin and English versions of the Benedictine Rule do not shape men's and women's work, their service to Holy Church, as either the same or equal in spite of the theoretical sameness the passage implies. In the verse translation of the Benedictine Rule, language difference in fact marks gender difference, and difference is, in the course of this version, once again an indication of the lesser perfection of the feminine.

Although the verse translation lacks any references to "sain benet" that position him as an authority figure, it does retain Latin chapter headings. It also contains many more full lines of Latin in the body of the text than the prose version does. The general practice of the prose version is to include one or two words of a Latin quotation followed by a fuller version of the passage in English.[39] The verse translation, on the other hand, contains fifty-five full verse lines in Latin, and only once does it employ the technique so common in the prose translation of abbreviating with "&c."[40] The Latin lines in the verse break both meter and rhyme, standing out from the surrounding English. Thus, the Latin language of authority, the language of the original Rule as well as of the Scriptures, stands in a place of distinction from the feminine vernacular. This positioning works to assert Latin's priority, power, and authority over the vernacular. The Latin chapter headings, together with the lines of Latin included within the body of the text, attempt, like the figure of St. Benedict in the prose version, to ground the translation in a hierarchical relation with the Latin text, prioritizing the authoritative original.

The Latin chapter headings and lines suggest a correspondence between original and translation while simultaneously revealing, as does the added translator's prologue discussed above, differences. These differences further emphasize the lesser perfection and subordinate position of both the feminine vernacular and the female audience. The English translations given for the Latin lines included in the text sometimes enact this strategy by altering the meaning of the passage, and in the verse version, alterations from Latin to English tend to involve issues of authority.[41] The vernacular text reduces the scope of women's authority in religion as part of the strategy to contain potentially disruptive forces and prevent women religious from asserting newfound power.

The new opportunities for independent participation in spiritual life offered to women by the spread of vernacular literacy and the increased availability of vernacular texts proved particularly disconcerting for conservative ecclesiastical authorities, coinciding as they did with the late medieval "feminization" of sanctity.[42] This process, like that of vernacular translation, presented new spiritual possibilities to women. The paradigm of the "virile woman," in which women made themselves masculine in their pursuit of a spiritual life, gave way to one which Barbara Newman has aptly termed "womanChrist," that is, "the possibility that women, qua women, could participate in some form of the *imitatio Christi* with specifically feminine inflections and thereby attain a particularly exalted status in the realm of the spirit."[43] In the model of womanChrist, then, female particularity and difference came into their own as sources of spiritual power.

Chapter 2 of the verse version concerns the qualities and responsibilities of the superior, who in the masculine Benedictine tradition is said to hold the place of Christ in the monastery since he is addressed by a title of Christ. The Latin reads, "Christi enim agere vices in monasterio creditur, quando ipsius vocatur pronomine, dicente apostolo: *Accepistis spiritum adoptionis filiorum, in quo clamamus: abba, pater*" (*RB 1980* 172). John E. Crean, Jr., who has examined Middle High German translations of the Benedictine Rule for women, describes this passage as "pivotal in evaluating any feminine RB version. In question is the *persona* of the abbess as perceived by the editor."[44] As Crean says, the way in which a translator deals with "Christi Pronomine" is "a kind of litmus test of how intimately the abbess may be understood to 'hold the place of Christ in the monastery.' "[45]

The Middle English verse does not describe the prioress holding the place of Christ at all. Rather, it says:

> And to be honored euer hir aw;
> Bot in her-self sche sal be law,
> Pryde in hert for to haue none,
> Bot loue god euer of al his lone
> And wirchip him werld al-wais,
> Als þe apostel plainly sais
> Vn-to all folk, who so it be,
> Þat takes swilk staite of dignite:
> "Accepistis spiritum adepcionis."
> He sais: "ȝe take þe gaste of mede,
> Þat lele folk vnto lif suld lede,
> In þe whilk gaste we call & cry
> Vnto our lord god al-myghty,
> And 'fader, abbot,' þus we say." (*Verse* 327–40)

While the verse version does include the first line of the scripture passage in Latin connecting the superior with Christ, the English changes the passage's meaning. The father abbot in the English is identified with God the Father rather than with Christ as in the Latin, but the female superior herself, who is made subordinate, receives no such validation of her position.[46] The three Middle High German versions Crean examines, which range from the fourteenth century to 1505, all identify the abbess with Christ to a greater or lesser extent. The Middle English verse, however, instead instructs the abbess to be meek and to love and worship God. The translator thus constructs her "persona" to be consistent with current, sanctioned ideals of female religious life. The identification of the abbess with Christ would have made the radical possibilities inherent in the image of womanChrist all too real and would have been dangerously counterproductive to clerical strategies to save the market.

Bishop Richard Fox's early sixteenth-century translation of the Benedictine Rule for the nuns in his Winchester diocese shows less anxiety about female authority in religion than the fifteenth-century verse translation does. Fox's translation gives abbesses "the standing of diocesans, describing them as 'oure right religious diocesans.'"[47] As Barry Collett points out, "In chapter 2 . . . he ascribed to an abbess all the authority of an abbot."[48] Significantly, though, even in the humanist-influenced sociopolitical environment of the Tudor era, Fox still does not equate the abbess with Christ. He, too, modifies the Latin, and in doing so he "avoided any confusion between the full authority which pertains to an abbess, and the office of a priest. His clear belief that full authority, with its divine origin, could certainly be held by a woman did not imply that women could assume a priestly function."[49]

Other important differences between the Latin and English verse treatments of the superior arise in chapter 64, which discusses the election of a superior and outlines the qualities that make a person an ideal candidate. Strikingly, the need for learning, described as desirable for an abbot but perceived at this period as so problematic for women, is absent from the English description of the female superior. Textual knowledge and education for the abbot become simply knowledge of proper conduct for the prioress. In describing the desirable traits of an abbot, the Latin reads, "Oportet ergo sum esse doctum lege divina, ut sciat et sit unde *proferat nova et vetera*, castum, sobrium, misericordem, et semper *superexaltet misericordiam iudicio*, ut idem ipse consequatur" (*RB 1980* 282). The English verse reads:

> Al if scho be highest in degre,
> In hir-self lawest sal scho be.
> Hir aw to be gude of forthoght
> What thinges to wirk & what noght,
> Chaste & sober, meke & myld,
> Of bering bowsum os a child. (*Verse* 2263–68)

In addition to making a shift from a male superior who has textual learning to a female superior who knows how to behave properly, the different emphases in these passages exhibit a desire to neutralize the potential threat of female authority.[50] Saying that the female superior should be "lowest" echoes the stress put on meekness for the female superior in chapter 2 of the verse translation in accordance with contemporary ideals of female spirituality. While both the abbot and the prioress should be chaste and sober, the desire that the prioress be "meke & myld" is a departure from the Latin account of the abbot. The abbot is to be merciful (*misericordem*) rather than meek, and having mercy implies having power and authority.

Earlier in the Middle Ages, twelfth-century Cistercian abbots used maternal imagery in discussing the exercise of authority out of a need "to supplement their image of authority with that for which the maternal stood: emotion and nurture."[51] The description of the prioress's meekness and mildness does not, however, participate in this tradition, for indeed, she is not described here as a mother. She is not to be maternal (not even to the extent of being emotional and nurturing) but rather to be "of bering bowsum os a child." The possibilities of maternal authority available to the Benedictine abbess in the ritual for her benediction are undercut, and this diminished version of her authority would have been reiterated through required, regular readings aloud of the rule to the convent.

Unlike the translator of the fifteenth-century verse version, Bishop Fox does describe the abbess as a mother, saying, "thabbot [is] to be to his convent a fader and thabass a moder."[52] Fox's translation also exhibits a very different attitude toward female learning than the verse translation, one which resembles the attitude evident in the Brigittine *Myroure of Oure Ladye* discussed below. The treatment of women's learning in Fox's translation reveals Fox's own humanism and love of learning. Fox says that the abbess "must be well learned in the law of God, and her religion, and that she understand, and be that person that can show and teach the laws, rules and constitutions of the religion, with such histories of holy scripture and saints' lives as be most expedient for the congregation."[53] Collett notes that Fox's translation of chapter 64 "bring[s] out the point that authority rests upon clear knowledge and understanding. When he referred to learning it is clear that he assumed a fair deal of scholarship in an abbess, and that there were in his diocese educated women able to fulfil these requirements."[54]

Fox's commitment to female learning may not, however, be entirely thoroughgoing. In discussing the necessities with which the abbess is to supply the nuns, Fox mentions "bokes / and instrumentes for their crafte and occupacions,"[55] suggesting the nuns' literacy and the importance of reading in their spiritual lives. He does not, however, mention the knife, pen, and tablets listed in the Latin version. These omissions may, of course, indicate, as Greatrex suggests, that "few of them could write."[56] The omissions might also indicate, though, that Fox saw reading as a passive consumption of authoritative texts which would be entirely appropriate work for the nuns, while the production of these texts (or even the scribal reproduction of them, which would allow opportunities for making interpretations and revisions that might subsequently be accepted by future readers) was work proper to such masculine *auctors* as himself. Such an attitude would harmonize with that manifested by other Tudor era "religious authorities" who "believed in education" but whose belief in the value of learning was tempered by being situated "in a context in which the written vernacular was always liable to be seen as a dangerous instrument that needed to be corralled by any mechanism available."[57]

The fifteenth-century prose translation also contains, like the verse version, passages which change the sense of the Latin and aim to limit the dangers of the feminine. The prose translation resembles Fox's translation, though, in that it does not exhibit great anxiety about female authority in religion, since it does not emphasize the superior's meekness to the same extent as the verse translation does. Rather, the prose translator demonstrates unease with the threats posed by potentially unruly women themselves. In chapter IV the rule sets out the "Instruments of Good Works." After the instruction to deny oneself and follow Christ, the Latin instructs the monk, "*Corpus castigare*" (*RB 1980* 182). The prose translation, however, advises the nun to "halde þe in chastite, and iuil langingis do away" (*Prose* 8). The shift from a command to chastise the body to a command to keep the body chaste harmonizes with the later medieval ecclesiastical emphasis on a particularly enclosed kind of chastity in women's spirituality, an emphasis evident in the frequent reiteration of claustration requirements for nuns.[58] Rather than engaging in active physical asceticism which might lead to the excesses in corporeal spirituality so distrusted in late medieval holy women, women religious are to preserve their chastity and expel desires that might lead to its breach.[59] The change in the prose translation manifests the "static perception" of female monasticism which follows from ecclesiastical stress on the importance of chastity (and in particular, the importance of intact virginity) for women. Unlike a monk, who undertakes a "quest" to attain his spiritual ideal, a nun, in this male conception of female monasticism, ideally begins and ends in the same state.[60]

The prose translation makes another subtle change to the sense of the Latin which points to negative clerical attitudes about the ways in which female spirituality and nature differ from male spirituality and nature. Chapter XX concerns the proper way to pray. Both the Latin and the English prose version say prayer should be brief and devout; both, however, make exceptions to this rule. The Latin makes the exception "nisi forte ex affectu inspirationis divinae gratiae protendatur" (*RB 1980* 216), but the English says, "Bot yef it sua bi-tide, þat any falle in mis-trouz; þan sal scho pray gerne to god"

(*Prose* 19). According to the *Middle English Dictionary*, "mis-trouz" means doubt, disbelief, suspicion, or mistrust, quite a departure from the exception of "affectu inspirationis divinae gratiae" for which the Latin allows.[61] The Latin envisions the positive possibility of the inspiration of divine grace leading to prolonged prayer for men; the English envisions the negative possibility of a fall into doubt necessitating especially fervent prayer for women. The feminine is once again stigmatized as inferior in its difference.

The need for especially fervent prayer by nuns in the face of "mis-trouz" may also suggest, given the date of the translation, the translator's misgivings about the nuns' orthodoxy and their susceptibility (heightened, perhaps, by feminine physical and spiritual weakness) to heresy.[62] As I discuss in the first chapter, at least some Benedictine nuns had significant access to works of vernacular theology. While high social status, combined with the status the nuns commanded as brides of Christ, likely did much to enable these textual privileges, some clerics did not ignore the problematic possibility that heresy—so strongly associated with vernacular reading—might raise its head in nunneries. Indeed, William Alnwick, while bishop of Norwich, found it necessary to organize a visitation of the Benedictine priory of Redlingfield, where the prioress was accused of Lollardy.[63] As is so often the case, the vernacular simultaneously brings benefits and detriments to the nuns. Vernacular literacy and access to vernacular texts enable the nuns to expand their horizons beyond those delimited for them, but that same ability and access prompt clerical suspicion and, at least in some cases, increased supervision.

Brigittine Texts and the Power of the Feminine

The two English translations of the Benedictine Rule for women engage in diverse textual strategies to save the market for the preeminence of Latin in order to shore up clerical authority and the clergy's privileged access to material and symbolic resources. As we shall see, though, the boundary-shifting power of translation is not so easily contained, and the negative associations of the vernacular with the feminine and the female body are not perfectly stable. The later medieval translations of the Benedictine Rule for women had a competing counterpart in vernacular Brigittine texts. These English versions of Brigittine texts, unlike the fifteenth-century Benedictine translations, do not present Latin as the preeminent language of authority in an attempt to save the market. Rather, they present women religious, as well as women in the world (with whom Brigittine texts were very popular), with opportunities to mobilize the feminine vernacular and the female body in the realm of religion.[64] They thus enable women to capitalize on the power of the very differences deemed inferior in Benedictine texts.

Although the Benedictine tradition created for men has a conflicted history in shaping monastic life for women, Brigittine monasticism is founded "per mulieres primum et principaliter,"[65] or, as *The Rewyll of Seynt Sauioure* recounts Christ's declaration of the rule to St. Birgitta, "This religion þerfore I wyll sette: ordeyne fyrst and principally by women to the worshippe of my most dere beloued modir. whose ordir and statutys I shall declare most fully with myn owne mowthe."[66] In the Brigittine Rule there is no question of requiring women to "translate" themselves in order to participate in religious life. In fact, in spite of some borrowing from Benedictine and Cistercian traditions, the Brigittine Rule "takes great pains to dissociate itself from existing monastic practice."[67]

Just as the status of women is firmly established as positive and primary in the foundation of the Brigittine Rule, so is the status of the vernacular. The rule was revealed by Christ to St. Birgitta in her own mother tongue of Swedish, as was the text of the Brigittine lessons. The prologue of *The Myroure of Oure Ladye*, the English version of the Brigittine services, contains an account taken from the *Reuelaciones extravagantes* describing the way in which the Brigittine service and lessons came into existence. While St. Birgitta was in Rome, she pondered what lessons the nuns should read. She prayed, and Christ told her that he would send an angel who "shale reuele & endyte vnto the the legende"[68] (hence the name *Sermo angelicus* given to the Brigittine lessons). Christ then commanded her, "write thou yt as he saith vnto the" (*Myroure* 18). Each day after saying her hours and prayers, she collected writing materials. On the days when the angel appeared to her he "endyted the sayde legende dystynctely and in order. in the moderly tongue of saynte Brygytte, and she full deuoutly wrote yt eche day of the Aungels mouthe" (*Myroure* 19).

After the angel has revealed all the lessons to her, he tells her that he has "shapen a cote to the quiene of heuen the mother of God" and directs Birgitta "sowe ye yt togyther as ye may" (*Myroure* 19). Here the vernacular, rather than being limited and inferior, is an avenue of direct communication with the divine. The image of a vernacular text as a garment for Mary, the Queen of Heaven and Mother of God, positively associates the vernacular with the feminine and the maternal. The mother tongue is not seen as lewd, debased feminine "cackling" but rather as glorious and of high value. The angelic command that Birgitta sew together the coat also conflates women's vernacular textual work with stereotypically female textile work.[69] The association demonstrates the ability of women and the vernacular to perform the most spiritually exalted work, and it serves as an empowering counterpart to Hoccleve's dismissive command for women to leave off speaking of spiritual matters and "sitteth down and spynne."[70]

The hours and hymns of the Brigittine offices, unlike the lessons, were revealed not to St. Birgitta herself but rather to St. Birgitta's confessor "master Peter," who "taught her grammer & songe, & gouerned her & her housholde" (*Myroure* 16). As a cleric and her confessor, Peter has authority over Birgitta; through his mastery of Latin, he has greater cultural and linguistic capital. In the account of the revelations he receives, however, the dynamics of power change. The revelations to Peter are situated in relation to female authority, and it is Birgitta who receives and passes on to Peter Mary's divine authorization of the text he will bring forth. Mary stands in relation to his text as the figure of St. Benedict stands in relation to the prose translation of the Benedictine Rule. Indeed, it is Mary's effort on Peter's behalf that makes him worthy to receive the text. Mary tells Birgitta, "I haue furtheryd him so moche in to the charite of the same holy trinite, that he ys one of the pryestes that god loueth most in the worlde" (*Myroure* 16).

Even more dramatically, the assertion of clerical, paternal authority attempted by Arundel's Constitutions is reversed in the *Myroure*.[71] The text indicates that the revealed material needed to be translated into Latin for review and dissemination among "moo men of dyuerse contryes and language" (*Myroure* 20). The translation from the mother tongue to Latin is then divinely authorized through a woman when the angel tells Birgitta to take the legend to Peter "for to drawe yt in to latyn" (*Myroure* 20). Although translating the vernacular into Latin might initially threaten to recontain the mother tongue and feminine power, Latin actually serves to uphold the priority and authority of the vernacular. Rather than a vernacular translation of a Latin text receiving paternal legitimation through clerical authority, here a Latin translation of a vernacular text receives maternal authorization from Mary and Birgitta. Moreover, Mary reinforces the value of simple language and undercuts the universal values of Latin and clerical authority when, in talking about the texts revealed to Peter, she says, "For though in my songe there be no masterly makynge ne no Rhethoryke Latynne, yet thoo wordes endyted by the mouthe of this my loued frende, plese me more, then sotel wordes of eny worldely maysters" (*Myroure* 17).

In Brigittine texts, feminine authorization of the mother tongue and the vernacular's position of worthiness for the highest spiritual tasks correspond with the construction of female authority (modeled on Mary's maternal authority) as equal to, or in some cases superior to, male clerical authority. The Brigittine Rule places the abbess as the head of the entire community of men and women; whereas in Benedictine monasticism the abbot represents Christ, here the abbess represents Mary, who, after Christ ascended into heaven, was head of the apostles and disciples.[72] The alignment of the abbess and Mary gains further significance from the frequent portrayals of Mary as co-redemptrix in the Brigittine texts and from the simultaneous applications in Brigittine divine service of Scripture passages to Mary and Christ. For example, at the Sunday service of Tierce the explanation of the chapter "Et sic in Syon . . ." reads, "These wordes ar redde bothe of oure lorde Iesu cryste, and also of oure lady. for by her; we haue hym" (*Myroure* 147).[73] The Brigittine focus on Mary as co-redemptrix combats women's spiritual inferiority, their "translatedness."

Whereas Benedictine monasticism in many respects sets up a system in which the resources most readily available to women are devalued and in which women are situated as lesser because of their differences from a masculine ideal, the Brigittine tradition allows women access to the full potential inherent in the model of womanChrist. In fact, the traits that mark women as lacking, and thus inferior and subordinate, in Benedictine monasticism empower women in the Brigittine tradition. While meekness is substituted for more "masculine" traits in the description of desirable qualities for a female superior in the verse translation of the Benedictine Rule, in the Brigittine Rule meekness and humility are the foundation for female authority. "The preeminence of the Abbess is, like that of the Virgin whose deputy she is, one of humility; hence her prelacy is defined as 'onus humilitatis' (*Extrav.* 21.4)."[74] Brigittine texts wield the very terms of female spirituality that are used to subordinate women to clerical authority in the Benedictine translations to change systems of social relations in ways favorable to the status of women religious.

In spite of difficulties stemming from the generally subordinate role envisioned for men in the Brigittine order, the potentially disturbing power of the abbess,[75] and the early fifteenth-century nervousness about women assuming powerful roles in religious life, *The Rewyll of Seynt Sauioure* (unlike the fifteenth-century translations of the Benedictine Rule) does not attempt to reduce the scope of female authority. The Middle English text directly follows the Latin, which reads, concerning the abbess's authority, "Que ob reuerenciam beatissime Virginis Mariae, cui hic ordo dedicatus est, caput et domina esse debet, quia ipsa Virgo, cuius abbatissa gerit vicem in terris, ascendente

Christo in celos caput et regina extitis apostolorum et discipulorum Christi."[76] The Middle English reads, "The abbes . . . for the reuerence of the most blessid virgyn marie to whomme this ordre ys halwyd. owith to be hedde and ladye. ffor þat virgyn whose stede the abbes beryth in eerth. cryst ascendynge in to heuyn. was hedde and qwene of the apostelis and disciples of cryst" (*Rewyll* fol. 56r-56v).

This close correspondence between the description of the abbess in the Latin and the Middle English is typical of the translation practices evident in the Brigittine Rule as Englished for Syon.[77] An important aspect of the Brigittine preservation of female authority emerges in the contrast between the verse translation of the Benedictine Rule, in which textual knowledge for the abbot is changed into knowledge of proper conduct for the prioress, and the Middle English version of the Brigittine Rule, in which, as in Bishop Fox's translation of the Benedictine Rule, learning is construed as fundamental to spiritual life for all nuns and especially for the abbess. At first the Brigittine Rule allows the nuns to have only books necessary for performing divine service, but it "immediately extends this permission to cover all books needed for study."[78] Ellis notes, "Religious, indeed, are to have these books not as they need, but rather as they want, them. . . . To make desire rather than need the term of one's reading, therefore, is to set the very highest store by the getting of wisdom: to make true learning a quasi-sacramental act."[79] Mary is not only the foundation of the abbess's authority but also the model of wisdom for the order.[80] In the Brigittine order, the female wisdom embodied by Mary encompasses female learning and specifically textual knowledge.

The general absence of textual strategies to replace boundaries in the Middle English translation of the Brigittine Rule may partly be a result of the status of the Brigittine Rule itself. It was, necessarily under the terms of Lateran IV, actually accepted as constitutions to the Rule of St. Augustine rather than as an independent monastic rule. Anxieties about the status of the vernacular, and related anxieties about the status of female learning and women's place in religious life, are not, however, entirely mitigated by the officially subordinate status of the Brigittine Rule. The translation practices evident in *The Myroure of Oure Ladye* do at times reveal the translator's nervousness about the status of the feminine and the vernacular, anxieties consistent with a desire to save the market. This desire is at odds with, and perhaps even prompted by, the content of the Brigittine texts being translated.

Various candidates for authorship of the *Myroure* have been proposed. John Henry Blunt, who edited the *Myroure*, suggests Thomas Gascoigne (1403–58) of Merton College, Oxford, later vice-chancellor of Oxford, who was a lifelong devotee and scholar of St. Birgitta. A. Jeffries Collins finds Gascoigne an unlikely candidate since Gascoigne was not a professed member of the Brigittine Order and probably could not have acquired the "masterly knowledge of the Bridgettine rite and ceremonial displayed throughout the book" at Oxford.[81] Collins suggests two possibilities—Thomas Fishbourne (d. 1428), the first confessor general at Syon, and Symon Wynter, Fishbourne's contemporary in the order (d. 1448)—finding Fishbourne the more likely possibility.[82] In any case, the *Myroure* was created by a cleric in the first half, and likely some time in the second quarter, of the fifteenth century, squarely in the period in which vernacular translation was such a vexed issue.

The *Myroure*, like the verse translation and Fox's version of the Benedictine Rule, is specifically designated for women religious without knowledge of Latin in order that they "shulde haue sume maner of vnderstondynge of [their] seruyce" (*Myroure* 49). It is clear that the translator of the *Myroure* is concerned about the cultural status of the vernacular. Part II of the prologue ends with assurance that the translation of Scripture passages has been licensed by the bishop in accordance with Arundel's Constitutions. The translator writes, "And for as moche as yt is forboden vnder payne of cursynge, that no man shulde haue be drawe eny texte of holy scrypture in to englysshe wythout lycense of the bysshop dyocesan. And in dyuerse places of youre seruyce ar suche textes of holy scrypture; therfore I asked & haue lysence of oure bysshop to drawe suche thinges in to englysshe to your gostly comforte and profyt" (*Myroure* 71). The translator, who has already recounted the divine authorization of the vernacular text's translation into Latin through Mary and Birgitta, returns to episcopal authorization of translation of Latin into English. This movement works to reassert masculine control of the mother tongue and to recuperate ecclesiastical authority.

Leading up to the statement of license for translation is a complex negotiation of the relationship between Latin and English in the text of the *Myroure*, the general thrust of which is to reassert the primacy of Latin. The translator explains the physical layout of the translation, saying that the first word of each hymn, response, verse, etc. "is writen in latyn with Romeyne letter that ye may know therby where yt begynneth" (*Myroure* 70). These Latin lines do more than merely help the nuns keep their place. The Latin openings perform a function similar to that performed by the figure of St. Benedict or the Latin lines in the Benedictine translations; they remind the women of the preeminence of Latin over the vernacular, reinforcing simultaneously the inferiority inherent in the nuns' inability to access the language of divine knowledge and their necessary dependence on clerical authorities. Following the Latin opening lines is the "selfe englyshe" of the Latin "imprynted wyth a smaller letter" (*Myroure* 70). Even in the text's physical appearance, Latin is superior to and prior to the vernacular. That this reassertion of Latin's authoritative superiorty is emphasized in the layout of the printed edition, produced in 1530 by Richard Fawkes, indicates, as do elements of Fox's translation of the Benedictine Rule, the strength of clerical market-saving desires over 120 years after Arundel's Constitutions were promulgated.

That there is more at stake than convenience in the layout of the text emerges even more clearly when the translator discusses how the *Myroure* should be read aloud. He says that, depending on the nature of the passage, either the opening words of the Latin or the Latin at the beginning of each clause should be read so "that ye shulde redely knowe. when ye haue the latyn before you. what englysshe longeth to eche clause by yt selfe" (*Myroure* 71). The translator continues to specify the correct use of the translation in divine services, offering the following caveat: "This lokeynge on the englyshe whyle the latyn ys redde. ys to be vnderstonde of them that haue sayde theyre mattyns or redde theyr legende before. For else I wolde not counsell them to leue the herynge of the latyn. for the entendaunce of the englysshe" (*Myroure* 71). Hearing the Latin, even if one does not understand it, is more important in divine service than reading the English.

The extended efforts to ensure that the audience comprehend the hierarchical relationship between the vernacular and the Latin are "strategic" in Michel de Certeau's sense of the term—that is, by ensuring the place of Latin, the cleric seeks to distinguish his own place, the place of his power and will.[83] Placing controls on the vernacular works by extension to place controls on the female readers of the vernacular with whom it is so strongly associated and who might, like the women in apocalyptic antitranslation materials, gain independence and power from the access to knowledge enabled by the vernacular text.

It is significant that the efforts to reiterate the hierarchical relationship of Latin and vernacular come in a section prescribing reading methods which themselves seek to contain the potentially threatening female learning that is, according to the Rule, so fundamental to Brigittine spiritual life. The section concerning "how ye shall be gouerned in redyng of this Boke and of all other bokes" (*Myroure* 65) serves a disciplinary function, striving to limit possibilities for interpretation, for participation in the sorts of textual exchanges demonized by the antitranslation faction. In discussing Fox's translation of the Benedictine Rule, Wogan-Browne et al. observe that it envisions reading taking place in an all-female group, without clerical supervision or participation.[84]

Such a context for nuns' reading may help explain Fox's desire, as well as that of the translator of the *Myroure*, to insert a guiding clerical "presence" into the text—for Fox, the speaking figure of St. Benedict whose voice merges with his, for the Brigittine translator, a detailed methodology of correct reading.

The translator first specifies what types of books are to be read—"no worldely matters. ne worldely bokes. namely suche as ar wythout reason of gostly edyfycacyon" (*Myroure* 66). He sets out the purposes of particular kinds of books, and he describes the proper "disposition" for reading—"with meke reuerence and deuocyon" (*Myroure* 66). Finally, he puts forth a program for ensuring proper comprehension, admonishing, "ye oughte not to be hasty to rede moche at ones. but ye oughte to abyde thervpon. & som tyme rede a thynge ageyne twyes. or thryes. or oftener tyl ye understonde yt clerely" (*Myroure* 67).

The directive to read slowly in order to ensure clear understanding re-sembles directives to monks to read "ruminatively," and so is not necessarily or entirely a restriction on women's reading.[85] The translator, however, further constrains the reading process by his explanation of what texts are and his specification of the correct motivation for reading them. The translator con-ceives of books for the nuns in terms of a regulatory and corrective specularity appropriate to his title, of which he says, "And for as muche as ye may se in this boke as in a myrroure, the praysynges and worthines of oure moste excellente lady therfore I name it. Oure ladyes myroure. Not that oure lady shulde se herselfe therin, but that ye shulde se her therin as in a myroure, and so be styred the more deuoutly to prayse her, & to knowe where ye fayle in her praysinges, and to amende" (*Myroure* 4). Books provide mirrors for examining one's conduct; the nuns are exhorted, in reading the *Myroure* and other texts, to "beholde in yourselfe sadly whether ye lyue & do as ye rede or no" (*Myroure* 68). If the reader does not see her life "rewled in verteu" but feels that she lacks "suche verteows gouernaunce as [she] rede[s] of," she is directed, "kepe in mynde that lesson that so sheweth you to youre selfe & ofte to rede yt ageyne. & to loke theron. & on your selfe. with full purpose & wyll to amende you & to dresse youre lyfe therafter" (*Myroure* 68).

In conjunction with this presentation of texts as regulatory mirrors, the translator works to transform women's reading from something potentially disruptive into a means of advancing a clerically approved mode of religious life for women. Women religious are not to read in order to acquire knowledge which they can exchange for authority or resources, either material or sym-bolic. Rather, they are to read and use the knowledge gained to shape their own conduct within approved parameters. They are advised, "dresse so your entente. that your redyng & study. be not only for to be connynge. or for to can speke yt fourthe to other; but pryncypally to enforme your selfe. & to set yt a warke in youre owne lyuynge" (*Myroure* 67). This directive calls to mind the transformation of the desirable qualities of an abbot (to be learned and have textual knowledge) into those of the prioress (to be meek and have knowledge of proper conduct) in the verse translation of the Benedictine Rule. The proposed reading method denies the powers of female and vernacular particularity so prominent in Brigittine texts; it is a prophylactic against the possible escapes of the feminine, the maternal, and the mother tongue from the hierarchical relations so crucial to the designs of those who wish to save the market.

Prescribing a method of reading is not, though, the end of the story, and the prophylactic is not necessarily effective. Reading is not just a passive act, a behavior that can be contained by a method of correct training. As Certeau argues, reading is an act of productive consumption; a reader takes what she is given and "makes something of it." Reading is one of the prime opportunities for engaging in tactics, manipulations which are the "arts of the weak" enacted in the "space of the other."[86] Reading is thus, in a sense, an economic activity. What the reader produces from the text "belongs" to her, if only momentarily, and she can use that production of her own volition and to her own advantage.

The possibilities for "making something of" the text of the *Myroure* in spite of the attempts to contain interpretation are particularly rich since the text itself so resists the constraints of the feminine and the vernacular imposed upon it in the prologue. In its presentation of the Incarnation and redemption, the text of the *Myroure* sets up relationships of bodies and words, production and reproduction, language and gender, which relentlessly assert the value of female difference. The *Myroure* is thus potentially quite empowering for women religious who might wish to "play the market" by accessing the value of the female body and the mother tongue in the religious sphere. For example, the translator of the *Myroure* includes part of the *Reuelaciones extravagantes* capitulo iii to explain why the sisters say their hours after the brothers. The explanation begins with an allegory in which a poor man delivers a city besieged by a mighty man. The city is Mankind, which is saved when Mary submits her will to be the instrument of the Incarnation. On the one hand, Mary's maternity is described as submission and obedience. On the other hand, however, the explanation continues with Christ saying, "my mother & I haue saued man, as yt had be with one hart" (*Myroure* 25). Thus, Mary's maternity is not simply an instrument of, but a primary agent of, salvation.

The translator further elucidates why the brothers perform their services first by aligning Mary's poverty of spirit in submitting to the Incarnation with the poverty of spirit the sisters are to exhibit by giving precedence to the brothers. The discussion that follows, however, complicates this convenient equation. Christ says that in other churches, the custom is "to say fyrste the seruyce and houres of our lady, as lesse worthy. & afterwarde the houres of the day as more worthy" (*Myroure* 26). For the Brigittines, though, "our lorde wyl do that reuerence to his holy mother, that in thys order the houres of her shall be sayd after the houres of the day to her most worshyp" (*Myroure* 26). Mary as the genetrix of salvation receives the position of greatest prominence. Rather than subordinating themselves by allowing the brothers to say their hours first, the sisters are in fact identifying with Mary's agency in salvation and laying claim to her position of superlative worthiness. The glorification of Mary's maternal body which makes the Word flesh is mirrored by the sisters who, in saying their "most worthy" hours, themselves embody the divine word.

In an order dedicated to the Virgin Mary it is not unusual that Mary's maternity should receive significant emphasis. The importance of Mary's maternity goes beyond the miracle of the virgin birth. Luce Irigaray notes that in order to found the patriarchal lineages which undergird masculine authority, the "genealogy of women" is erased.[87] The genealogy of women, the roles of the mother and the mother tongue, are suppressed in the clerical attempt to found a universal, Latin genealogy of sacred knowledge and to preserve their concomitant privileges. Brigittine texts restore the genealogy of women, foregrounding the significance of the maternal in salvation and the mother tongue in sacred knowledge.[88]

The potentially empowering idea that salvation originates in a genealogy of women is especially clear in the service for Tuesday Matins. In this service in which language and maternity intermingle, Eve's word leads to sin and provokes God to the wrath of damnation when she "of pryde had sayd in her harte. as if she wolde be made euen to god" (*Myroure* 193). However, Mary's "worde shulde draw the charyte of god to grete comforte. to the. and to all dampned by the worde of Eue" (*Myroure* 193). Eve's word cast Adam, Eve, and all Mankind into great sorrow but "thy blessed worde o mother of wysdome. broughte the to grete ioye. and opened the gates of heuen to all that wylle enter" (*Myroure* 193). This "worde" is the Word that Mary, "mother of wysdome," brings into the world. This service clearly outlines the "genealogy of women" who, through their words and maternity, save mankind. "The frayle mother. ys Eue. the doughter ys oure lady that is mother of her father. for she is the mother of god that ys father to all that he made" (*Myroure* 194). Salvation history does not begin with Adam's *felix culpa* and proceed, through God the Father, to Christ. Rather it begins with the *felix culpa* of Eve's speech and proceeds through Mary, the mother of the Father. Women's language and women's bodies are not sources of disruption which, being inferior in their difference, must be contained. Rather, they are sources of redemptive power which are celebrated for their particular role in salvation.

In the *Myroure*, as in the nineteenth-century novels by women which Margaret Homans examines in her study of language and female experience, significantly entitled *Bearing the Word*, maternity is one of the ways in which women "reclaim their own experiences as paradigms for writing."[89] Two of the recurrent "literary situations or practices" that Homans examines in the novels are fused in the *Myroure*: "the figure of the Virgin Mary, who gives birth to and is frequently imaged carrying (thus two senses of 'bear') a child who is the Word, the embodiment of the Logos" and "the theme of women characters who perform translations from one language into another or from one medium to another."[90] The Brigittine services repeatedly focus on Christ's birth as the process of the Word being made flesh. The first lesson at Sunday Matins, for instance, declares, "Ryght so also had yt bene vnpossyble that thys worde that ys the sonne of god. shulde haue bene touched or sene. for the saluacyon of mankynde. but yf yt had bene vned to mannes body" (*Myroure* 104).[91] It is of course Mary's body that "mynystered vnto hym the mater of his holy body" (*Myroure* 141). Maternity is translation at once corporeal and textual; the *Myroure* gives female readers access to an incarnational textuality in which the "mother tongue" is salvific rather than lacking and unruly. Mary shifts cosmic boundaries by bearing the divine Logos across into the human realm; her female body translates the invisible, incomprehensible Word of God into the comprehensible and redemptory "mother tongue," the human body Christ receives from his mother. In the *Myroure*, Christ—the ultimate source of authority invoked by the very clerics opposed to vernacular translation of the Scripture—is a text in the mother tongue produced by a woman.

3

Accounting for Themselves
Nuns' Everyday Practices and
Alternative Monastic Identities

Brigittines and Minoresses: Autonomy in Practice

Profession services, visitation ceremonies, and monastic rules shape nuns' identities through their impact on nuns' participation in financial, textual, and spiritual economies. Nuns' everyday practices provide another perspective, making visible identities which at times harmonize with and at times compete with the complex interpretive schemes set out in foundational texts and ceremonies. Obedientiaries' accounts and legal documents are valuable records of such quotidian practices; they indicate what nuns possessed, what they needed, and how they obtained these things. They also provide insights on nuns' interactions with each other and with the world outside the cloister. What these documents say and the ways in which they say it illuminate women religious' views of themselves, the world, and their place in it.

The English Brigittines and Minoresses provide prime examples of nuns' temporal independence; in these communities are found degrees of financial autonomy and success in keeping with, and possibly enabled by, the enlarged spiritual and material foundations laid down in profession and visitation. I wish to stress that I am not arguing for a simple or direct correlation between modes of profession and visitation and material success or lack thereof. There were certainly Benedictine nunneries (for instance, Barking) that achieved notable economic success, and there were houses of Minoresses (for example, Bruisyard) of decidedly modest means. Furthermore, it is important to note that the much more recent origins of the Franciscan, and especially the Brigittine, Rules allowed for a closer "fit" between monastic theory and later medieval practice than that enabled by the centuries-old Rule of St. Benedict. Clare,

Isabella, and Birgitta had the advantage of observing the difficulties inherent in shaping Benedictine monasticism for women, and they were able to craft religious identities with reference to systems of social relations they themselves inhabited.

Houses of Brigittine and Franciscan nuns were fortunate to be not only generally wealthy but also largely independent of secular and ecclesiastical authorities. This status allowed them to manage their property without a great deal of outside intervention and to increase their wealth. Syon's foundation charter, for example, gives the community significant privileges. Henry V granted that during a vacancy, the nuns would have custody of all lands, rents, tenements, profits, and emoluments "without the interference of us, our heirs or successors."[1] They were not even required to present "any accounts thereof . . . to us, our heirs or successors" at the time of the vacancy.[2] When a new abbess was created, the charter ensured that the community would not have to pay any charges for the right to nominate, nor would they "be charged in future with the giving, granting, or assigning of any pension, portion or maintenance for any person or persons at the request of us, our heirs, or successors."[3] This was no small freedom, since the right of a founder to nominate women religious or corrodians was a common feature of nunneries' foundation charters. Supporting those nominated members of the community could be a financial as well as a social burden for the nuns.[4]

In 1447, Syon was granted "vast liberties . . . so that the tenants upon its estates were almost entirely exempt from royal justice."[5] Their perquisites of justice extended to "all issues and amercements, redemptions and forfeitures as well before our heirs and successors, as before the chancellor, treasurer and barons of our exchequer, the justices and commissioners of us, our heirs or successors whomsoever made, forfeited or adjudged . . . of all the people . . . in the lordships, lands, tenements, fees and possessions aforesaid."[6] In the *Valor Ecclesiasticus* Syon's income from all its perquisites of court was 133*li* 0*s* 6*d* out of a total income of 1944*li* 11*s* 5 1/4*d*,[7] so these privileges clearly did much to add to Syon's great wealth. Building on such grants and privileges, Syon became the wealthiest nunnery in England.

Syon's foundation charter also manifests the abbess's power in the Brigittine tradition, stressing her control of the house's resources. It states that Matilda Newton, whom Henry V preferred as abbess, and her successors, "shall preside over the nuns or sisters aforesaid, and take upon themselves the whole government of the aforesaid monastery, as well in spirituals as temporals, and that they shall do and execute those things which in anywise do or may belong to the abbess of the said place, (excepting only that the same confessor shall preside over the aforesaid religious men in spirituals as is aforesaid).["]8 A letter written to the abbess of Syon by a servant makes clear that the authority constructed for her in profession and visitation and reiterated in the foundation charter was recognized in materially significant ways. The servant reports to the abbess that as promised he has "delyue*r*ed to maister confessor a bill of all the some of wode in eny lordship that I haue sold & taken money for sethen I was furst offecer."9 He says that of the total sum he delivered 3*li* 11*s* 4*d* to the Lord of Surrey's officer since that officer claimed that amount of wood as his. Thus, he continues:

the hole some wi*th* that cometh to x*v*li viiis iiiid[.] [O]f this x*v*li viiis iiiid[,] xiii*li* part of xxxi*li* that my ladie alowed me in myn acount is p*ar*te ther of as the boke of acount will shewe[.] [T]his will I abide bie[.] [I]f eny p*er*sone or p*er*sones will sey the cont*r*arie[,] or that I haue done eny extorcion[,] taken eny brybes[,] or mysordered my self wetyngly & wylfully in eny cause othrwyse than a true crysten man or true offecer shuld[,] so lete hym or theym be cald be fore you & your councell & I in lyke case[.] & in eny thyng then so p*r*oued cont*r*arie to this my wrytyng take of me what ye will in satesfaccon.10

The letter attests to the abbess's active involvement in the details of the house's business, and the servant responds to her as he would to any man of business. The details show that he fully expects the abbess to comprehend accounts, and he clearly thinks that she will be up to date on the state of the house's possessions. Since Syon was a community in which female education and literacy flourished, the servant's belief that the abbess would be well equipped to manage the house's considerable resources was likely accurate.11 The servant's statement concerning the funds "that my ladie alowed me" reveals both the abbess's secular dignity in the form of address ("my ladie") and her authoritative agency in the allocation of resources. The fact that the servant reports to the abbess having delivered the bill of sale to the master confessor underscores her role as the community's chief administrator of money and property. Furthermore, the servant's concern with proving he has not taken bribes or otherwise behaved improperly highlights the abbess's status as an acknowledged judge of morality and equity with the power to punish transgressions.

The Syon servant's addressing the abbess as "my ladie" also suggests that in daily life, as in visitation practices, the high social status of the Brigittine nuns may have enhanced their independence. St. Birgitta herself was, after all, connected with the royal house of Sweden, a fact that certainly helped her further her efforts to found a new religious order (and that may well have helped to protect her from the worst sort of persecution faced by less well-connected holy women, visionaries, and religious reformers, including Margery Kempe, who identified so closely with Birgitta). Religious identity and social identity are not entirely separable, even though theoretically both men and women religious leave behind their secular identities upon entry into a monastic order. The assertion of female power at Syon is thus simultaneously an assertion of aristocratic privilege, just as the symbolic capital available to Benedictine brides of Christ works in concert with the aristocratic origins of the Barking nuns to enhance their ability to command social and spiritual respect.

English Minoresses share with the Brigittines an aristocratic heritage, tracing their lineage back to Isabella's own foundation of Longchamp. English communities of Minoresses also possessed privileges nearly as enviable as those of Syon. The London Minoresses, like the Brigittines, enjoyed significant independence from secular authority which bolstered their wealth and their ability to administer their resources. For instance, as a consequence of a 1404 grant by Henry IV, which exempted the community from all lay jurisdiction except in cases of treason or felony touching the Crown, they were entirely outside even the mayor of London's jurisdiction.[12]

The Minoresses also had important ecclesiastical freedoms which enhanced their material circumstances. Bulls from 1295 and 1296 exempted the London house "from episcopal and archiepiscopal jurisdictions, payment for chrism, sacraments, and consecration of their church and altars and excommunication by bishops and rectors." As Martha Carlin observes, "These privileges reduced the nuns' obligations to and dependence on their parish church (St. Botolph Aldgate) and its rector, the prior and convent of Holy Trinity." Additionally, in 1303, the London community's precinct was completely detached from the parish when the prior of Holy Trinity "quitclaimed to the abbess and convent all the priory's parochial rights in the precinct."[13]

The house of Minoresses at Waterbeach was covered by the thirteenth-century papal bulls which applied to the London Minoresses, and in 1343, when the Waterbeach nuns were transferred to Denney, that community received the same exemptions.[14] The founder of Denney, Mary de St. Pol, countess of Pembroke and a childless widow who was quite able in managing her own resources, worked to secure that her foundation was, like the London community, independent of external authorities.[15] In 1356, thanks to her procurement, Alan de Walshingam, prior of Ely, formally abandoned all claim that he and the convent might have on Denney Abbey and its possessions.[16] Such privileges enhanced the Franciscan nuns' ability to administer their resources and increased their wealth; the London Minoresses, for instance, were among the wealthiest nuns in England.

Throughout the Middle Ages, until about the middle of the fourteenth century, English monasteries, like other landholders, largely relied on direct exploitation of their estates. From 1350 to 1450, though, throughout England the gradual leasing of demesne was the most important change in estate administration.[17] Due to low prices of agricultural products and high costs of large-scale farming, landlords increasingly abandoned direct exploitation of lands.[18] Religious houses were as subject to these market forces as other landlords, and they likewise turned to leasing their lands rather than exploiting them directly. Setting aside London convents, which drew large portions of their income from money rents for streets of houses and shops, and setting aside a smattering of urban holdings distributed among various other houses, by the later fourteenth century the greatest proportion of nunneries' incomes was "the money derived from the possession of agricultural land, and in particular the rents paid by tenants in freehold, copyhold, customary and leasehold land."[19] Nuns thus participated in the "commercialisation" of the English economy, which R. H. Britnell argues was the key long-term trend throughout the Middle Ages.[20]

Extracts from the Court Rolls of Denney preserved in MS BL Add. 5837 provide evidence that the Minoresses' participation in "commercialisation" led to opportunities for temporal independence on a personal level.[21] These records contain detailed evidence for the distribution of resources among individual nuns in that community using the prebend system. In this system, the community as a whole approved division of the convent's property into portions for which sisters individually received rent. The prebend system thus provided occasions both for women religious to act as a corporate body independent of outside ecclesiastical authority in the distribution of portions and for them to act individually in their own names in the management of portions. For instance, in 10 Henry V, the abbess, Margaret Milly "by the Consent of the whole Convent & Chapter there, doth graunt to Johan Colcestr, & Margert Hyston, Sisters of the Abbey of Denney, one Acre & one Roode of Severall in the Marish of Waterbeche, called the Lughallough, for their Lives, without Rent."[22] This extract shows that the nuns, rather than stewards or ministers of the Franciscan order, allocated the portions, which then belonged to Joan and Margaret to manage however they saw fit.

An entry in the court records from 2 Henry V indicates that Joan Colchester already held other property as well—"one Place lying in Lugfen, abutting on the High Barke, & of another in Rushfen, late Jeffrey Burwell's." The entry shows that she claimed to hold these properties "freely of her own Purchase," and that the property was held of the abbey and convent of Denney "by the service of 4s 1d. ob. yearly."[23] That Joan purchased this property and then held it by paying a yearly fee to the house suggests that the portion may well have been property which she bought before becoming a nun and brought with her as an entry gift, and which the house subsequently returned to her for her to administer personally. It is also possible that she bought the property after becoming a nun with entry gift funds remaining in her control after her profession.

Some sisters at Denney seem to have formed lasting business relationships with members of the surrounding community through managing their portions. In 6 Henry V, Edmund Bartlett took to farm of Isabell Winter "one close, called Hetes Holt, with Oysers" for a term of ten years, paying 9s per annum.[24] Evidently, Isabell and Edmund had a satisfactory relationship, because in 5 Henry VI he takes "a Close called Letyszere nigh the Depe" for a term of ten years "by the Assent of Isabell."[25] For this he agrees to render "to the aforesaid Isabell" 12s per annum.[26]

In developing and cultivating such relationships, nuns worked to ensure their own financial security. Successful, long-term business relationships also made nuns known in the community at large as competent, independent agents in charge of resources. Such status counteracts, at least to some extent, the frequently asserted "myth of women's financial incompetence,"[27] a myth to which ecclesiastical officials frequently had recourse in seizing control of nunneries' resources and in imposing additional layers of masculine supervision. The experience of success thus opens a locus of resistance to discourses of feminine inferiority and dependence both spiritual and temporal.

The business relationships of Minoresses with others outside the convent were not always satisfactory. Legal documents recording these troubled relationships do have the advantage, however, of highlighting the ways in which the Minoresses made visible "demonstrated or desired identities."[28] Beginning in 1452, Denney had a long-running dispute with Thomas Burgoyne, whose manor of Impington adjoined their manor at Histon, regarding the convent's property and perquisites there. After Thomas Burgoyne died in 1470, the abbess Joan Ketteryche brought a case in chancery against Alys Burgoyne and John Burgoyne, Thomas's executors.[29] Ketteryche claimed that Thomas "ordeynyd by his wille and testament that his executors shulde paye and restore any Iniuries and wrongges don by hym."[30] The abbess said that the executors should therefore make satisfaction because Thomas had prevented Denney's tenants from attending Denney's courts, had stopped the convent's officers from "takyng of weyff and straye" in some of their fields, had prohibited their tenants from feeding and pasturing cattle in particular fields, and had impounded the cattle, only releasing them upon payment of a fine of 1*d* for "every fote of the bestes."[31] Furthermore, Thomas Burgoyne was "justice of peasse and keper of the bookes withynne the saide counte of Cambridge," and he "by feynyd accions" caused Denney's tenants and servants to be indicted before himself. When writs were served "for the removing of the same," Thomas would claim "ther were noo suche recordes."[32]

It is quite proper that Joan pursued this case, since female superiors had legal responsibility for their houses' holdings and possessions, and, by virtue of their office, were legal subjects. Female superiors were permitted to leave their monasteries to do homage on behalf of their communities to temporal lords, although *only* to temporal lords "since all ecclesiastical overlords would be expected to receive proctors in these cases."[33] In spite of the juridical status they had through their offices, though, the fact that female superiors were *women* religious complicated matters. In his commentary on the papal bull *Periculoso*, which required strict active and passive claustration for nuns, the fourteenth-century canonist Dominicus de Sancto Gemiano desired to limit the involvement of female superiors in legal cases, since such involvement would take them out of the cloister. He affirms the "unique right of the abbess to leave her cloister to render homage or fealty" but also "cites Roman law authority to support the case that women in general should not be compelled to appear in courts of law."[34] The abbesses of such nunneries as Shaftesbury, St. Mary's Winchester, Wilton, and Barking had baronial status as landholders; as Eileen Power drily observes, though, "the privilege of being summoned to parliament was omitted on account of their sex" even though "the duty of sending a quota of knights and soldiers to serve the King in his wars was regularly exacted."[35]

The way in which Joan Ketteryche's case plays out shows that she took her responsibilities for her house's property quite seriously and that she did not see her rights to pursue the case as being in any respect curtailed by her status as a bride of Christ. Although the result was not a total victory for Joan, it does reinforce her authority over resources. The abbess did not recover all of the money—some £883—she sought in damages,[36] but she and John Burgoyne did agree that she would have her "leets and lawdays at Impyton and they and their tenants . . . of Histon shall intercommon at Impyton with the said John and his tenants of his manor of Impyton."[37] The abbess of Denney would therefore continue to have the opportunity to act in her own name, and in the houses' name, publicly appearing as legitimate possessor and controller in temporal matters.

Another aspect of this court case demonstrates that Joan Ketteryche was in fact remarkably shrewd in taking advantage of both her distinctive gendered status as bride of Christ and her maternal authority over resources suggested in foundational Franciscan texts and ceremonies. During the dispute with Thomas Burgoyne and his executors, she wrote a letter to her kinsman John Paston asking that he aid Denney with goods left in his hands as executor of John Fastolf's estate. In this letter Joan, like the famous letter-writing Paston women with whom she is connected, mobilizes textual practices for material gain. Her rhetoric reveals not only a self-awareness of the implications of being scripted as a bride of Christ, enclosed and subject to spousal authority, but also a sophisticated ability to use this identity to achieve material goals.

Joan begins the letter with a reference to "the reverens of oure spouse ihu,"[38] and she makes the nuns' enclosure, necessitated by their status as spouses of Christ, a reason for Paston to find them deserving of help. She also takes up a gendered religious stereotype to the house's potential advantage by stressing in her request for aid that she was chosen as abbess "ful myche agens my will" and that she is "ful symple and зounge of age."[39] Her use of this terminology brings into play the ideal of nuns' detachment from material affairs and invokes the "myth of women's financial incompetence," the very myth so often reiterated by ecclesiastical officials as a reason for taking away nuns' independent control of resources, in what is in fact a calculated effort to obtain a desired economic gain.

Benedictines: Brides of Christ in the Marketplace

As the preceding examples suggest, the religious identities constructed in profession and visitation for Franciscan and Brigittine nuns and the identities to which they laid claim in practice have much in common. Disjunctions between theory and practice are somewhat more pronounced, however, when one considers what Benedictine nuns were doing in their everyday lives. A chancery case brought in 1500–1501 by Elizabeth, the prioress of Sopwell (a Benedictine nunnery dependent on St. Albans Abbey), provides a compelling illustration with which to begin probing not only gaps between theory and practice but also ways in which Benedictine nuns enlarged windows of opportunity opened for them in their foundational ideological scripts.

The case involved the terms of a lease the convent had made with Thomas Huet concerning "certeine land pasture and hegerowes within the countie of hertf." The lease reserved to the convent "all the trees wode and vnderwode growyng or standyng within the seid selwode." When the indentures were sealed, they appeared "withoute rase or enterlynyng." Thomas Huet learned, however, that the part of the indenture belonging to the prioress was in the hands of "one Dane Thomas holgrave monk keper of the place of Sopwell aforeseid and mathewe adam his clerk." The three men, evidently assuming that the nuns could not read the documents or were unaware of precisely what information they contained, then conspired to cheat the convent out of the property reserved to them in the lease, changing the "speciall poyntes" of the indentures. Elizabeth proved too sharp for their trickery though. She realized that Thomas had "rased and taken oute of the seid endenture and the same clause writtyn in a geyn to the use of the seid Thomas huet." Illustrating her grasp of the convent's rights and her command of the text, she pointed out for evidence of the men's misdeeds that "the seid rase and enterlynyng nowe playnly may appere."[40]

Elizabeth of Sopwell's court case is much like Joan Ketteryche's; both women are defending their houses' property against encroachments. Since court records are replete with such cases, Elizabeth's case is not at all unusual in some regards. It is, however, striking in that Elizabeth's performances as a textual and an economic agent serve as "visible indices" of identities which complicate the restrictions placed on Benedictine brides of Christ in foundational texts and ceremonies. As the example of Elizabeth suggests, through their typical involvements with the material world, Benedictine brides of Christ—like Brigittine and Franciscan nuns—participated in activities much like those of widows or women with "femme sole" status.[41]

I do not believe, as some scholars have implied, that nuns' independence and autonomous responsibility in material affairs were complete or that nuns of any order entirely escaped male control in their temporal business. For example, Jean Leclercq writes, "The monastic life was for many women not only a refuge from a society that had little esteem for their sex, but also at the same time a way of liberation from the restrictions and limits imposed on them by this society. . . . Nuns found themselves on equal footing with men."[42] Roberta Gilchrist and Marilyn Oliva similarly claim that women religious "managed their busy households and complicated finances without male supervision or interference."[43] Nuns were not "equal" to men, nor did they entirely escape male supervision. Bishops and other ecclesiastical officials intervened in nuns' business practices and financial affairs in ways that were much less common in male communities. For instance, the prohibition of the sale of corrodies, while occasionally invoked for male houses, occurs much more frequently in injunctions for female houses. Bishops also commonly restricted or refused to allow entirely the admittance of new members to female houses, but such constraints were very rarely placed on male communities.[44] Likewise, chances for bishops, kings, and founders to exercise the right of nominating members of the community were taken up more often for female than male communities.[45] This practice was costly to houses since nominated members did not bring entry gifts but still had to be supported for life.

In spite of such continued outside involvement, in the later Middle Ages nuns did increasingly have responsibility for administering their communities' resources and providing for their own needs. A. Hamilton Thompson shows that in the later fourteenth and fifteenth centuries, appointments of masters to nunneries became less general, and obedientiaries (primarily heads of houses, treasuresses or bursars, and cellaresses) tended to manage their own temporalities.[46] He points out that even such a house as St. Michael's Stamford, which was in theory entirely subject to Peterborough Abbey, was by this period in actuality more or less free to manage its own affairs. Power similarly observes that the practice of having a resident prior or appointing neighboring rectors as *custodes* of nunneries largely died out by the mid-fourteenth century. While she claims that the function of the *custos* was "probably performed by the steward (*senescallus*), an official often mentioned during the fourteenth and fifteenth centuries,"[47] there is a crucial difference in the relationship between the nuns and a *custos* and the nuns and a steward. The former is an administrator nominated or appointed either by the bishop or by the male community to which the nunnery is subject. The latter is a servant hired by the community, and at times the post of steward was merely honorary.[48]

In their management of material resources and direct participation in temporal affairs, Benedictine nuns engaged in what Pierre Bourdieu calls "regulated improvisations," reinterpreting the ideological scripts provided to them in profession and visitation.[49] I have chosen the nuns of St. Michael's Stamford and St. Mary de Pré to provide representative examples of these expanded religious identities made visible in everyday practices. There are several reasons that I have elected to treat these houses as representative of the "typical" (as typical as any individual houses can be) Benedictine experience for women. Both have good series of extant accounts for the period under consideration. Neither house was extremely large or extremely small, and, unlike Syon and the London Minoresses or the Benedictine house of Barking, neither house was outstandingly wealthy. In addition to being subject to secular ecclesiastical authority, both houses were dependent on male houses (St. Michael's Stamford on Peterborough and St. Mary de Pré on St. Albans), so the nuns in these houses would have been among those most subject to male control.

Monastic accounts reveal that, even in such houses as these, which were not granted the striking temporal independence of the Brigittines and Minoresses, nuns took part in hands-on administration outside the convent.[50] In spite of enclosure requirements, it is well known that nuns often traveled outside their convents. St. Michael's Stamford's obedientiaries travelled to obtain necessities for the house, as is evident from an account entry reading, "Item in expensez dame agnes & alice" (that is, the prioress Agnes Leyke and the treasuress Alice Watteryng) "in holand pur sale vid."[51] Obedientiaries also frequently travelled to tend to their house's manorial affairs in person. For example, St. Michael's Stamford held a church at Corby, and in 2–3 Richard II, the treasuress, Margaret Reding, records that she travelled with a companion to Corby: "Item mesme Dame Margarete reding & sa compaigne alant a Clopton & a Corby xviid."[52] A later treasuress's account indicates that Alice Watteryng, at that time one of the treasuresses, and Margery, likely the former treasuress, incurred expenses of 2d going "pur rent a depyngs," while the subprioress "& aultres" incurred 6d in expenses "a melton," where the house also had holdings.[53] Gilchrist and Oliva say that "it is doubtful" that heads of nunneries "ever personally appeared at their courts, gallows, sanctuaries, or markets and fairs."[54] Records of travel expenses in accounts, however, indicate otherwise. An account from St. Mary de Pré refers explicitly to the prioress attending the manorial court at Wing, stating, "in expenses for the prioresse and the steward with their servants and for hors hyre and for the wages of them that wente to kepe the courte wyth the prioresse atte Wynge atte two tymes xvjs vd, whereof the stewards fee was that of vjs viijd."[55]

Benedictine nuns' travel in order to attend personally to the house's business helped to ensure that their affairs were in order, that they paid only what they owed, and that they received all that was due to them. Their travel was, however, more than a sign of shrewd business acumen or a departure from the monastic rule for reformers to decry, which they frequently did. Their direct involvement in commercial affairs presumably reinforced to the nuns themselves the reality of their ownership and their responsibility, creating expectations of empowerment and entitlement. Additionally, Benedictine nuns' visibility through travel served to legitimate their position in the temporal economy to the secular world at large. While ecclesiastical authorities aimed for nuns' "institutional invisibility" by "inserting strict claustration into their rules,"[56] nuns' travel for business purposes counteracted this invisibility, at least to some extent. By travelling to attend directly to their property and financial affairs, women religious in effect redrew the boundaries of their community beyond the convent walls. In this way, they lay claim to and quite literally made visible identities extending far beyond that of a cloistered bride of Christ.

Obedientiaries' accounts also make clear that many people depended on nunneries for their livelihood. Nunneries, like male monasteries and, indeed, like secular landowners, relied heavily on administrative officials and servants, people outside the monastic community, to manage many aspects of their household affairs.[57] In addition to a staff of administrative officials (steward, bailiff, auditor, receiver, etc.), nunneries hired various household and agricultural servants. Treasuresses' accounts from St. Michael's Stamford include payments to a cook, gardener, carter, porter, brewster, shepherd, oxherd, swineherd, and "vadlet," as well as numerous other servants whose duties are not evident either from their surnames or from descriptions.[58] Nunneries also hired additional laborers beyond these regular servants for performing repairs, miscellaneous "odd jobs," and major agricultural tasks such as harvesting and threshing.

The existence of many dependents from the community made nuns important people who had palpable influence over the lives of members of the local economy. Although there were fluctuations over time and variations among houses, nunneries "retained fairly stable populations of household servants and guests to nuns: an average ration of two to one, a servant and lodger to each nun."[59] Nuns therefore commanded significant resources in their communities, even though these resources were generally less than those possessed by male houses. As Oliva observes in her study of nunneries in Norwich, "the presence of the great variety of people in these small houses illuminates many of the other roles these religious houses played in the broader contexts of parish and county."[60]

A positive perception of nuns as important forces in the local economy was likely increased by the fact that monastic servants were relatively well-off in comparison to laborers in the secular world. Servants often received more than a monetary stipend from a nunnery; many also received some amount of food as well as clothing or additional money in lieu of these.[61] For instance, John Leyke (probably a relative of the prioress Agnes Leyke), a servant who performed varied duties for St. Michael's Stamford, was paid 4s "pur mixture pur xii semaign." The treasuress also paid Agnes Leyke 6s 8d for "table" for John Leyke for a sixteen week period; evidently Agnes paid for John's food out of her office's funds during this time. The same account notes a payment of 6s "pur la vesture de William Bailly encountr Nowell."[62] A later account records payments for purchases of cloth "pro vestitu Johanne Brewster" (who appears in the list of servants receiving stipends) and "pro vestitu ballivo" at costs of 3s 4d and 6s 8d, respectively.[63]

Barbara Harvey observes that, in the case of Westminster Abbey's servants, when one considers board, stipends, and livery together, "To earn as much as even the lowest-paid valet in the monastic household, a journeyman craftsman would indeed have needed to work on nearly all the legitimate days for work in the year; so, too, a labourer, to equal the lowest earnings of a groom."[64] Harvey also points out that, beyond these benefits, monastic communities provided a notably secure form of employment; there was, she says, "a general attitude to servants more like that of a master to his dependents in a system of clientage than that of an employer to his employees."[65] Under this benign system, it was "probably hard to be dismissed, whatever one's behavior."[66] The fact that the same names appear in several successive accounts of both St. Michael's Stamford and St. Mary de Pré bears out Harvey's claim. So, while the servants at the nunneries considered here surely did not earn as much as those at wealthy Westminster, their situation was still better than average, because they were less subject to the common laborers' experience of "the discontinuous nature of the available employment."[67]

Rather than isolating nuns as untouchable brides of Christ, nuns' hiring servants, supervising them, and transacting business through them broke down barriers between women religious and the world outside the cloister. These activities firmly situated nuns as agents of note in local economies and as active participants in the world of production and consumption. Such economic practices complicate the limitations on Benedictine nuns' autonomy, access to resources, and control of property which profession and visitation attempt so repeatedly to put in place.

In spite of the beliefs current among ecclesiastical authorities that it was improper for women religious to participate actively in the temporal economy, in spite of the perception that nuns were by and large incapable of doing so successfully, and in spite of the lesser resources available to them, Benedictine nuns were often, like their counterparts at Denney and Syon, quite able as well as active businesswomen. Comparisons between male and female houses reveal that nuns by and large were no worse at managing their affairs than monks were.[68] In regard to almsgiving, nuns seem to have done a better job than monks, at least from the standpoint of fulfilling their mission of charity. For example, the Benedictine nuns at Blackborough Priory "spent at least seven per cent of their revenues on alms for the poor"; the Benedictine house of Redlingfield "contributed approximately thirteen per cent annually for alms."[69] In contrast, contributions made by cloistered male religious in the same diocese as these female houses averaged 3–5 percent of their yearly revenues.[70] Furthermore, small male houses were "equally, if not more, prone to poverty, mismanagement and scandal."[71] Acting publicly in their own names, being recognized as important economic agents in the larger community, having responsibility for their own affairs, and achieving reasonable degrees of success in doing so all expanded the restricted relationships with the material realm fostered in Benedictine profession and visitation. These activities additionally provided Benedictine nuns with concrete opportunities to act out the symbolic independence and authority to which some of their ideological scripts gave them at least limited recourse.

Nunnery accounts also contain evidence which indicates that women religious did not view their worth and their spiritual labor in the same passive and attenuated way that ecclesiastical officials did. Of particular interest are the sections of prioresses' accounts from St. Michael's Stamford dealing with the nuns' allowance or salary (known as the *peculium*).[72] The amounts the nuns received and the way these amounts are recorded shed light on the nuns' own conception of their status in the spiritual economy. In the account for 13 Edward IV, for instance, the relevant section is headed "salarii conue*ntus* & capellorum," and it notes, in addition to the payment of 40s to the nuns, payment of 40s to "John Alford Capello pro sallariis suo eodem anno."[73] In the account for 1–2 Richard III, the relevant section is headed "salarii monialium et capell*orum*," and the chaplains, like the nuns, receive 4li 13s 4d.[74] In the following year's account, the payments to the nuns and chaplains are grouped together with the servants' stipends. The single chaplain received 4li 14s 10d, as did the eleven nuns, and the total for the servants' stipends is 48s 4d.[75]

In each account, then, the nuns' yearly stipends are equal to those of the chaplains who served the communities, and the payments to the nuns are grouped with the payments to the chaplains in the accounts. Monastic accounts typically group payments for similar kinds of work together—servants' wages are frequently gathered under the heading *stipendia famulorum*; payments to harvest laborers, outlays for repairs to buildings, etc., are collected in individual sections. Thus, the grouping of yearly payments to the nuns and chaplains, together with the equal amounts of compensation they received, suggest that, at least within this female community, nuns' labors and priests' labors were viewed as similar kinds of work and as equally valuable work.

These Benedictine nuns did not value themselves merely as inert commodities, nor did they see their worth simply as chastity and essential purity.

Conventual seals, used to close and authenticate legal and financial transactions, provide the "image of authority chosen to represent the monastery."[76] Seals thus reveal important information about the nuns' own views of their participation in such transactions; they are visible representations of elements of nuns' identities. Significantly, many nunneries use on their seals the image of the "throne of wisdom," a scene that foregrounds the maternal authority of Mary.[77] A fifteenth-century seal from Denney bears this image, and an earlier seal from that house shows the coronation of the Virgin—another image emphasizing female authority.[78] A seal from Syon used as early as 1426 depicts "the Virgin, crowned, supporting the Child, with nimbus, seated beneath a canopy; she holds in her left hand a sceptre; at base under a four-centered arch a female figure (?St. Bridget) supports a king (?Henry V) in prayer."[79] Given the identities shaped in Franciscan and Brigittine profession and visitation, in which maternity is so important, and given the temporal independence and success of Franciscan and Brigittine houses, it is not unusual that these nuns would represent themselves with images of Mary's maternity and royalty.

Somewhat more surprising is a thirteenth-century seal from St. Mary de Pré.[80] On a seal from a Benedictine house, in light of the stress placed on nuptiality in foundational ideological scripts, one might expect an image portraying Mary as divine spouse. St Mary de Pré's seal, however, like Syon's and Denney's, depicts the throne of wisdom.[81] This seal provides further evidence that in their everyday practices later medieval Benedictine nuns could and did reinterpret ideological scripts. They extended their identities beyond that of bride of Christ, and even lay claim, publicly and visibly in the temporal realm, to the specifically maternal authority presented in the rituals for the benediction of an abbess but largely denied to them in their rule, profession service, and visitation ceremonies.

PART II

Beyond the Convent Wall

Female Monasticism in Later Medieval Culture

4

A Coin of Changing Value

Monastic Paradigms and Secular Women

The Miracle of the Pregnant Abbess: The Problem of Maternity

In the Middle English version of the miracle of the pregnant abbess, as it appears in the collection of exempla known as the *Alphabet of Tales*, "Ane abbatiss of a grete place" becomes pregnant when she "þurgh entysing of þe devull . . . lete hur carvur . . . hafe at do with hur."[1] She hides her pregnancy as long as possible, but her condition inevitably becomes obvious. The nuns, realizing that the abbess is with child, are glad of her downfall, because she has been so strict with them. Some of the sisters go to the bishop and disclose the abbess's situation, and he makes plans to visit the house. At a loss for what to do, the abbess retreats to her chapel where she "was wunt daylie als devoutlie as sho cuthe to say our ladie matyns."[2] The abbess prays to Mary for aid, and Mary appears to her, accompanied by two angels. Mary tells the abbess that she has heard her prayer, and the abbess is immediately delivered of her child, which is spirited away by the angels to be raised by a hermit.

Initially, this text appears as a straightforward portrayal of Mary's aid to a devout and repentant sinner. Like many later medieval texts about spiritual matters, however, this text has an economic valence as well. As Paul Strohm has argued, a woman's body offers "a powerful and irreducible figure for her property."[3] Similarly, pregnancy and maternity are powerful figures for women's work. While the labor of childbirth is in itself socially and spiritually important female work, it may also represent other kinds of material and spiritual work performed by women. Considered in this regard, the portrayal of maternity in the miracle might seem to provide a vision of female economic empowerment. When Mary intervenes, the abbess appears to succeed in a bid to control her own body and its productive capabilities. The disappearance from the scene of the "carvur," the child's biological father, enhances the sense that women are in charge of productive processes. As does the Brigittine *Myroure of Oure Ladye*, the miracle presents figures of maternal authority ripe for "tactical" readings which are at odds with the exemplary, regulatory force of the text.

Mary's aid to the abbess further suggests the formation of a network of women which allows them to elude the grasp of male authority and to take independent control of resources. So interpreted, the abbess's pregnancy and Mary's intervention might seem to pose a threat parallel to that posed to husbands and fathers by economically active women in the marketplace. For example, the bishop's shocked confusion when no sign of pregnancy can be found following the abbess's miraculous delivery leads to a profound disruption of hierarchical relations when he kneels before the abbess to beg forgiveness for having, he thinks, accused her falsely. But, much as the writer of the *Myroure* builds "strategic" constraints on interpretation into the text, this latent threat posed by the abbess and Mary is also quickly subjected to further narrative control. Indeed, the lengths to which the miracle goes to reign in the abbess's empowerment suggest its troubling potential. Rather than keeping the secret of her productivity and enabling women to elude male control, the abbess quickly explains what has transpired, confessing her pregnancy to the bishop and revealing Mary's aid. In doing so, she voluntarily returns herself and her productivity to the bishop's authority. With this turn of events, the miracle of the pregnant abbess colludes in and poses solutions to male anxieties about independent female initiatives.

Echoing the connections made in episcopal injunctions for nunneries between the material independence enabled by *familiae* and nuns' ill repute, the miracle reconfigures economic activities as sexual activities in order to make anxiety-producing practices easier to condemn. Such equations are evident in many late medieval texts produced in an environment in which women's entry into market production and their (at least temporary) access to greater independence, social prestige, and control of resources threatened the patriarchal household.[4] In this regard, it is significant that the miracle recounts the pregnancy of "ane abbatiss of a grete place."[5] A woman in this position is the embodiment of two particularly distressing tendencies in the later Middle Ages—female access to authority and to material resources—and the miracle resituates these threats to masculine control under a sign of sexual transgression.

The abbess's sexual activity clearly violates her monastic vow of chastity. In breaking her vow of chastity this bride of Christ has sinned against her divine spouse, and her sin may be aligned with the worldly category of transgression against the husbandly authority so crucial in maintaining masculine privilege. This aspect of her sin reinforces the miracle's economic implications; the abbess has claimed as her own to bestow according to her choice that which belongs to the spouse—her body and its reproductive capacities. This miracle's tacit linkage of economic and sexual sins is foregrounded when the bishop visits the house and deputes two clerks to examine the abbess. When they inform the bishop that they can find no sign of pregnancy, he believes that "þai had takyn som money of hur."[6] Thus, not only is the abbess's economic power figured as sexual transgression, but her sexual misconduct also begets suspicion of economic misconduct when the bishop accuses her of bribery.

The fate of the male child completes the devaluation of female labor. Upon learning the location of the abbess's child, the bishop sends his clerks to verify the story. They find the child with the hermit, and, after seven years have passed, the bishop takes the child and puts him in school, where he "encrecid gretelie in vertue & connyng, vnto so mekull þatt when þis bisshop decesid, he was made bisshop after hym nexte succedyng."[7] The transfer of the child to male hands immediately following birth, the child's adoption by the clerical establishment, and his ultimate succession as bishop illustrate a fantastic patriarchal reprocessing of motherhood, and indeed of all female labor. Even nurturing the infant, the most traditionally and stereotypically female work, becomes a man's work. In the end, it is the celibate male clergy who have reproduced, and women have become unnecessary. The miracle illustrates the "negation of the procreative mother—the consignment of this unknowable source and place to the status of unknown, to what cannot be signified."[8] Women's work is finally made insignificant, obliterated in favor of men's labors, and women acquiesce to being replaced firmly under male authority.

Much like the female body itself, the body's productivity is denied to women. The value produced is estranged from the one who produces it. The fact that the male child is placed permanently in male hands moments after birth bears out Jean-Joseph Goux's argument that the relationship between mother and child under patriarchal control is analogous to the relationship between worker and product under capitalist domination.[9] Just as it is the owner of the means of production and not the worker who benefits from the output of the worker's labor, so it is the ecclesiastical hierarchy, the stand-ins for the divine spouse to whom the abbess's body belongs, who benefit from the child produced by her body. In this respect, the miracle is a protocapitalist anticipation of subsequently visible capitalist formulations.

The miracle of the pregnant abbess resonates with contemporary fears and desires concerning the material economy. So, too, does it echo later medieval crises in the spiritual realm which are themselves connected to women's involvement in the material economy. In both realms, men in positions of power were concerned with protecting specifically masculine privileges. This miracle provides an imaginative and hypothetical space in which clerical and secular interests may be found to coincide in the devaluation of female labor and the reassertion of male control of productivity. The miracle's treatment of maternity as a complex, potentially troublesome issue is relevant to the later fourteenth and fifteenth centuries when devotional practices emphasizing the humanity of Christ (devotional practices frequently associated with women), the cult of the Virgin Mary, and, especially, the cultural power of the Eucharist and the body of Christ, were all approaching their zenith.[10] The significance of maternity and the involvement of women in the economy of salvation were ever present issues, requiring the regulation of women's material and spiritual practices and the construction of a version of maternity consistent with the interests of clerics, husbands, and fathers.

In the later Middle Ages, the body of Christ produced in the Eucharist became an almost limitless source of symbolic capital. As such, it was subject to the "economic calculation" Pierre Bourdieu sees as extending "to *all* the goods, material and symbolic without distinction, that present themselves as *rare* and worthy of being sought after in a particular social formation."[11] Such economic calculation includes attempts by those who have control over production (in this case the male clergy) to retain their advantage. The sacramental production of the body of Christ and the resultant symbolic capital are, however, rooted in the maternal, material production of the Incarnation, a relationship that complicates clerical privilege. Although women are firmly excluded from sacramental production, foundational maternity is always present, always potentially disruptive.[12] Not surprisingly, anxieties about the involvement of women in the production of the body of Christ, such as fears about the existence of Lollard women priests, surround the Eucharist in the later Middle Ages.[13]

In order to reinforce the clergy's status as privileged sacramental producers, the miracle of the pregnant abbess elevates the symbolic and represses the material. The transition of the child as a mark of the abbess's sin to the child as an exemplar of virtue worthy to be bishop, a transition effected through the education provided by the Church, marks the primacy of the symbolic. It serves "to place materiality outside of value and meaning."[14] The miracle constructs a paradigm of double reproduction like that described by Goux. The father is the "agent and the guarantor" of the superior variety of reproduction, which is "social, ideological . . . transmitted and stored in the symbolic."[15] Inferior reproduction involves "secondary, material generation" which "is the woman's function."[16] The former, though founded on the latter, supersedes and indeed negates it. When the child succeeds the bishop, the masculine and the symbolic definitively triumph over the feminine and the material. Priestly fathers able to engage in sacramental work produce, through initiation, a son who, in turn, takes his place in the lineage. The miracle, which begins with an exclusively female scene of maternal reproductive power, ends as an account of "birth done better . . . on a more exalted level than ordinary mothers do it,"[17] that is, "birth done better" symbolically and sacramentally by celibate men.

Book to a Mother: *The Contradictory Solution of Monasticism*

The miracle of the pregnant abbess was one of the most famous Marian miracles in the Middle Ages, and it is present in many Latin collections.[18] Middle English versions of this miracle did not emerge, however, until the fourteenth and fifteenth centuries, when it appeared in the Northern Homily Cycle (extant in several manuscripts), the *Alphabet of Tales* (MS BL Add. 25719), and a miscellany of vernacular religious texts (MS BL Add. 29996), a type of collection often used by women in the course of their spiritual instruction.[19] Sermons, exempla, and devotional texts are frequently directed toward regulating women's conduct, and the material in this miracle has a great deal of potential for doing precisely this in a period of rapid socioeconomic change when the group Felicity Riddy has aptly designated "male clerics and city fathers" had "a vested interest" in such regulation.[20] It also contains material that has a great deal of potential for serving just the opposite function—that is, for encouraging women's independent material and spiritual initiatives.

The miracle of the pregnant abbess thus cuts two ways at once. The abbess and the Virgin Mary as maternal authority figures provide exemplars of female self-sufficiency upon which women can model subject positions of spiritual and temporal autonomy. Female monasticism is therefore suggestive of opportunities available to women living in the world, and these opportunities in turn provoke cultural anxieties concerning women's work and women's property. The miracle simultaneously mobilizes female monasticism to provide solutions to the very anxieties it generates by proposing limits to women's material and spiritual independence.

The later fourteenth-century devotional treatise *Book to a Mother* presents a similarly multivalent treatment of female monasticism; indeed, determining the value of the coin of female monasticism in the *Book to a Mother* is even more complicated than in the miracle, since this text is explicitly directed toward male as well as female readers. The *Book to a Mother* is written by a cleric for his mother, but in his opening sentence he states, "To knowe þe bettere my purpos in þis boke, wite ȝe wel þat I desire euerych man and womman and child to be my moder, for Crist seyþ: he þat doþ his Fader wille is his broþer, suster and moder."[21]

Like the *Abbey of the Holy Ghost* and the *Charter of the Abbey of the Holy Ghost*, with which the *Book to a Mother* is found in MS Bodleian Laud Miscellaneous 210, the *Book* uses paradigms of female monasticism to suggest ways in which those in the world—men and women alike—might craft religious lives. The *Abbey of the Holy Ghost*, for instance, begins, "A dere brethir and systirs, I see þat many walde be in religyone bot þay may noghte, owthir for pouerte or for drede of thaire kyne or for band of maryage, and for-thi I make here a buke of þe religeon of þe herte, þat es, of þe abbaye of the holy goste, that all tho þat ne may noghte be bodyly in religyone, þat þay may be gostely."[22] In the *Abbey* and *Charter*, structures and procedures of female monasticism (establishing an abbey of nuns, complete with a foundation charter; staffing it with obedientiaries; and setting in motion the process of visitation when problems emerge) function as allegories for the correct regulation of the individual heart and soul by Christ and the Holy Ghost.[23] In this abbey, for example, Lady Charity is the abbess, and one is instructed to do nothing without her leave. Furthermore, in the *Abbey* and *Charter*, the "history" of the foundation represents the larger drama of salvation history in which each individual soul is involved.

The clerical writer of the *Book to a Mother* similarly turns the monastery into an allegory, transforming elements of female monastic life—for instance, claustration, which, by the later Middle Ages is almost exclusively associated with women religious—into religious directives appropriate for men and women. He advises his readers to remain within the cloister which has "foure stronge wallis, þat ben riȝtfulnes, strengþe, sleiþe and temperaunce" (*Book to a Mother* 121); alternatively, he says, the "foure wallis ben, as þe glose seiþ up Ezechiel: bileue, hope, charite and dede, þat ben eueneliche miche" (*Book to a Mother* 121).

That these texts shape a religious life for people in the world with reference to a monastic model is not particularly surprising. As Christiana Whitehead observes, allegories of the cloister are widespread in medieval literature; "fragmentary examples . . . are to be found in Latin, English, French, German, and Dutch."[24] Furthermore, in his late fourteenth-century treatise *De substan-*

tialibus regule monachialis Uthred of Boldon holds that the three substantial vows of monasticism (that is, poverty, chastity, and obedience) are "binding in some measure, not only on all monks and all Christians, but even on all men having discretion and the use of reason, by a kind of natural vow and obligation."[25] Working within this tradition, the writer of the *Book to a Mother* exhorts his readers to "make þi professioun . . . bihotinge þre þinges, as Seint Benetis rule techiþ. For alle men ben holde to kepe þulke þre upon peine of dampnacioun" (124).[26]

In spite of the prevalence of cloister allegories, the choice in the *Abbey*, *Charter*, and *Book to a Mother* of structures of female rather than male monasticism to represent an ideal religious life for lay men as well as women might seem a bit unusual. In the *Abbey* and the *Charter*, the personification of virtues as female obedientiaries harmonizes well, however, with traditional medieval presentations of virtues as female figures, and it dovetails with the very popular account of the Four Daughters of God, who figure in the *Charter*'s presentation of salvation history.[27] In fact, Mercy, Truth, Righteousness, and Peace join the abbey as nuns when it is refounded by the risen Christ: "Ane þer almihti God ordeynde þat his ffoure douhtren Merci, Truþe, Rih[t]fulnesse, and Pees, scholde be glad among þe Couent of þe abbey of the Holi-gost; and þer he bad him-self þat Merci and Truþe scholde be Charite Chapeleyns . . . and he bad also þat Rihtwysnesse scholde euermore be wiþ Wisdam, for heo was Prioresse; and he bad also þat Pees scholde beo wiþ Mekenesse, for heo was Subprioresse."[28]

Using a female religious foundation to construct an ideal religious life for women and men in the world also attests to the symbolic capital available from female monasticism and holy women in the later Middle Ages, symbolic capital exploited readily by political and literary figures alike, as I discuss in Chapters 5 and 6. Indeed, it is striking that members of royal families noted for their politically astute alliances with holy women and female monastic communities are known to have possessed manuscripts containing versions of the French treatise *Li Liure du cloistre de l'ame*, which was translated into Middle English as *The Abbey of the Holy Ghost*.[29] For instance, Marie de Bourbon, aunt of the Dauphin Charles of France, whose famous relationship with Joan of Arc is discussed in Chapter 7, owned MS BL Add. 39843. Furthermore, Oxford, Bodleian Library MS Douce 365 was written for Margaret of York, duchess of Burgundy, sister of Edward IV, whose connections with St. Birgitta and Syon are discussed in the next chapter.[30]

In addition to participating in the contemporary vogue for taking advantage of the symbolic capital available from female monasticism, the *Abbey* and

Charter also participate in the contrary contemporary trend of excoriating nuns for laxness in discipline, unchastity, and corruption. Whitehead points to the *Abbey's* "submerged text of gentle ecclesiastical criticism" and its "occasional comments" which "denigrate the motivation and commitment of some actual religious."[31] In a similar vein, the *Abbey* and *Charter* not only personify the virtues but also the vices as female, an equally common trope in medieval allegory.[32] In the *Abbey*, the Holy Ghost as visitor has to be called in because "a tyrante of þe lande" (that is, "þe fende") sent into the abbey "ffoure doghtyrs þat he hade, þat were lothely & of euyll maners"—Envy, Pride, "Gruchynge," and "False demynge of oþer."[33] These negative figures are every bit as allegorical as the virtuous ones are, but they tellingly echo the criticisms found in later medieval visitation records. This account of corruption in the (allegorical) cloister has still further resonances with later medieval ecclesiastical concerns about nuns. Because the Holy Ghost as visitor is "asked to appear as a last resort to drive out the four daughters of the devil after the abbey's inmates have proved incapable of dealing with the problem, it is apparent that the text wishes to promulgate the necessity of episcopal or other male oversight,"[34] a desire also evident, for instance, in Bishop Fox's preface to his translation of the Benedictine Rule.

Less-than-gentle criticisms of contemporary monastic life are made directly, without any mediating use of allegorical figures, in the *Book to a Mother*. For instance, the clerical writer condemns nuns' *proprietas*, rebuking those who excuse the possession of "cloþes, peces, macers and spones and oþere wordli uanites" with "a fals, feined glose excuse," saying "þat þei ben comyne" (*Book to a Mother* 124). He despises nuns' hypocrisy in presenting signs of religious life that do not correspond with true holiness, saying, "But þei haue a white, mysproude and gai, smal, ridlid, lecherous wimpel; a þicke, ryuen, lesinge abite; a ring, and a mantel treilinge aftur hem, wiþ a ueil þrefold ileid on here hed—for ellis þei helden not þer rule!—and þus be semeliche to turmentours þat comen to hem" (*Book to a Mother* 123). Female monasticism thus functions, as in the miracle of the pregnant abbess, ambiguously in the *Abbey*, *Charter*, and *Book*; it is both positive model and negative exemplum of religious life, both a source of symbolic capital and a sink of corruption.[35]

By displacing female monasticism into the "ghostly" realm, where as metaphor or figure it is applicable to men as well as women, these texts repeat the gendered movement of exegesis which passes from the literal (associated with the fleshly and the feminine) to the figurative (associated with the spiritual and the masculine).[36] Female monasticism is thus doubly disembodied. It is displaced from the bodies of actual women religious, and so removed from the carnal corruption believed to be present in contemporary nunneries; it is also removed from the feminine realm of the literal sense and so made spiritually relevant for all.

In the *Book to a Mother*, though, literal, bodily manifestations of female monasticism remain present in the text to a much greater extent than in the *Abbey* or the *Charter*. They remain precisely because the readers for whom "there can be no doubt that the instructions in the *Book* are directed . . . primarily despite the opening sentence" have female bodies (*Book to a Mother* xxvi–xxvii); in spite of his interest in educating both men and women in ways of living a religious life in the world, the clerical writer exhibits a particular concern with women's spiritual and material practices throughout the *Book to a Mother*. The *Book* would seem, as do the later medieval translations of the Benedictine Rule, to create a spiritual life which is the same for men and women. Like these translations, though, the *Book* in fact creates a gendered religious identity for women.

The multivalent significance of female monasticism, already invoked as both positive and negative template for religious life, expands still further as the clerical writer of the *Book to a Mother* responds to the anxieties generated by the female, maternal bodies of his readers by mobilizing elements drawn from female monasticism. In spite of his condemnation of corrupt nuns, such elements provide useful tools to shape subjectivities which channel women toward acceptable forms of production. Female monasticism is at once a vehicle for representing perceived contemporary problems with women— particularly their covetousness and lechery—and a solution, albeit an ambiguous one, to these same problems. The ambiguity arises because once again, in the *Book*, as in Benedictine profession services, monastic formulations that seek to control women—particularly the identity of bride of Christ—are Janus-faced, creating for women the very opportunities for access to symbolic capital and authority both temporal and spiritual which those mobilizing the formulations often seek to limit.

As in the miracle of the pregnant abbess, the spiritual instruction provided by the *Book to a Mother* has much to do with instruction in proper conduct. For example, even in the section summarizing the six excerpts from Scripture he has translated, the priest is concerned with promulgating a spiritual life lived through closely regulated material practices. He tells the mother, "be a trewe weigoere and aske alle þi conseiles henneforeward of þe weigoers . . . and principaliche of þes syxe iustices þat I spak of er, for þei weren uerrei weigoers, hauinge no propretees aʒenes here Fadur wille" (*Book to a Mother* 198).

The limitations placed on possession of property in the preceding passage sound a theme repeated frequently in the *Book*, which spends a great deal of time addressing the problems stemming from women's desire for property and the benefits of poverty. A broad-based condemnation of sinful love of property begins early in the *Book*, but proprietary sins become, as the text progresses, by and large the province of women. The priest links a condemnation of property with his criticism of women religious infected with the sin of *proprietas*, telling his mother that it is better to be of Christ's religion as described in Holy Writ than "forto haue þe mantel and þe ryng and þe wympel and þe veil, with propurte: for Crist loueþ no propurte" (*Book to a Mother* 22). He further characterizes sinful worldly possession as a particularly female problem by including a catalogue of domestic articles and household servants which the Virgin Mary did *not* possess. He admonishes, "And loke, modir, also: þou schalt not fynde aboute Marie and hure childe none gaiȝe couerelites ne testres, curtynes, docers, quischines, calabre, meniuer, ne non oþir pelure ne panter, ne boteler, ne curi[ou]se cokis" (*Book to a Mother* 49).

The priest's condemnations of property, material goods, and worldliness focus heavily on criticism of women's dress. While recounting the story of Christ's nativity the priest does critique men's frivolous fashions as well as women's, saying that in the stable in Bethlehem there were neither proud, elaborately dressed squires nor elegant ladies. His attack on women's clothing, a key sign of feminine pride, worldliness, and love of property, is, though, more biting and extended. He goes beyond decrying excess and aligns women's "maumetrie" with Eve's sin. The priest says that at Christ's birth there were no "nyce dameselis wiþ garlondis of gold ne perlis ne filettis ne bonettis, ne suche oþir maumetrie as Eue doutres disgisen hem now bi daie" (*Book to a Mother* 48–49). He further condemns all the contemporary "douȝtres" who follow "þis lessoun þe liere tauȝte Eue in Paradis," saying "þe feirer þei coueiten to seme to men, þe foulere þei semen to Godis siȝt" (*Book to a Mother* 49).

Feminine *maumetrie*, which is defined in the *Middle English Dictionary* as "misdirected worship," particularly "the worship of worldly goods," leads, in the eyes of the priestly writer, to *lecherie*.[37] As in the miracle of the pregnant abbess, sexual sins and those involving property are linked. The priest laments "hou monye men and wommen haue be lost and dampned seþ Eue bigan to teche þis lessoun, wiþ suche maumetrie sturinge hem to lecherie" (*Book to a Mother* 113).[38] The progression from *maumetrie* to *lecherie* reveals that women's desire for property is not only sinful in its own right, but, as in many monastic texts, it endangers chastity, both that of women themselves and that of men whom women tempt with their finery. The clerical writer of the *Book to a Mother* connects women's misuse of their bodies with their desire for property when he tells his mother to "þenk hou bisiliche, hou harde, hou sore þou hast traueiled wastinge awei þi bodi and þi blod wiþ alle þi / uertues niȝtes and daies, to winne wordli goodis" (*Book to a Mother* 112). The language of travailing "bisiliche," "harde," and "sore" both night and day, wasting body, blood, and virtue, has distinctly sexual resonances. The priest implies that women readily trade their body for property and that the desire for material goods makes women into whores.

The *Book's* persistent association of women's material desires with sexual transgressions echoes topics of heated discussion in the text's larger environment. Internal evidence in this treatise, which exists in four manuscripts,[39] suggests that it was composed in the later fourteenth century, a period in which concerns about women's participation in the politico-economic sphere were quite pronounced. One passage which Adrian McCarthy, the *Book's* editor, cites as evidence for the date of composition refers to the "Herods" overcome by Herodias and her daughter as well as to the "sacrifice of a 'kingdom' and to 'false reynynge of wommenliche men'" (*Book to a Mother* xxxi).[40] McCarthy argues that this passage recalls events toward the end of Edward III's reign in the 1370s, in particular his much decried relationship with Alice Perrers and the influence of John of Gaunt.[41]

In addition to being the mistress of Edward III, Alice Perrers was very shrewd in acquiring and managing property, and, not surprisingly, attacks on Perrers were directed at what were characterized as her linked sexual and economic transgressions. In his *Historia Anglicana*, Thomas Walsingham describes Perrers as a "foemina procacissima"[42] and a "meretricula."[43] Walsingham's description of Perrers as "foemina procacissima," that is, as a "most shameless" or "most bold" woman, resembles the priestly writer of the *Book's* condemnations of the "daughters of Eve" and the "wickede wommen" who "haue conquered wiþ her mametrie, bi art of þe deuel, þe moste part of þis world" (*Book to a Mother* 195). Walsingham's application of the label "little harlot" (*meretricula* is a diminutive form that intensifies the term's pejorative quality) replicates the *Book's* assessment of the sinful women who have "traueiled" both night and day with body and blood "to winne wordli goodis" (*Book to a Mother* 112).[44] Significantly, Walsingham's abbey of St. Albans had been embroiled in a property dispute with Alice Perrers over lands at Oxhey, a dispute in which Alice triumphed, shortly before he made these allegations.

In recounting the complaints made against Perrers in the Parliament of 1376, Walsingham continues to condemn Perrers's conduct as improper for a woman, writing:

Illa etenim modum mulierum nimis est supergressa; sui etenim sexus et fragilitatis immemor, nunc justa Justiciarios Regis residendo, nunc in Foro Ecclesiastico justa Doctores se collocando, pro defensione causarum suadere ac etiam contra jura postulare, minime verebatur; unde propter scandalum et grave dedecus quae exinde Regi Edwardo, non solem in hac terra sed in exteris regionibus, nimium resultabant.[45]

The Commons' complaints as characterized by Walsingham illuminate the larger sociopolitical importance of the codification and regulation of women's conduct undertaken by the *Book to a Mother*. Alice Perrers, like the pregnant abbess, like the "daughters of Eve" in the *Book*, and, as Paul Strohm argues, like Chaucer's later fourteenth-century creation the Wife of Bath, "fuses the categories of economic and sexual assertiveness into a single epitome of contemporary male dread."[46]

The priestly writer of the *Book*'s condemnation of women's sexual sins and their transgressions involving material goods culminates in a "Walsinghamesque" outburst of antifeminism. He claims that desiring, acquisitive women "wiþ here malice and here maumetrie . . . passen þe deuel, here fadur, and here dame, Dam Eue; for þei coueiteden none suche mametrie, but forte haue be like to God in konninge" (*Book to a Mother* 115). In the priest's view, neither Eve, who, according to medieval understanding of Genesis, brought sin into the world, nor the devil himself, is as evil as these contemporary women. Women's desire for property is, significantly, even more dangerous than desire for divine knowledge.

The priest's ultimate resolution to the problem of women's desires as such a socially corrosive force lies in an ideal version of female monasticism. This solution is present throughout the text, as the three substantial vows are recommended repeatedly. It emerges most strongly, though, immediately following this dire vision of women's bent for social destruction. The priest makes clear that his interest in the applicability of monasticism to people in the world is in this case gendered as well as general, since he turns to a strongly gendered element of female monasticism as a tool to regulate women's conduct. Following his antifeminist outburst, he extols the value of claustration, which was for nuns (though not for monks) in effect a fourth substantial vow, and his treatment suggests that he has in mind not only "ghostly" claustration but also the bodily variety.

In the passage in which he discusses the "foure stronge wallis," the priest returns to the theme of female finery, in this case elaborate headdresses or "hornes." He then makes a universalizing move, saying that he is not simply concerned with bodily horns but also with the "ghostliche hornes" of "grucchinge, chidinge, inpacience, inobedience, pride, wraþþe, enuie, glotenie, slouþe, lecherie and coueitise" with which "wommen and men fiȝten wiþ God" (*Book to a Mother* 119). The cleric's focus does not remain universal or ghostly, though, as he returns insistently to women and the body. Sounding once again the theme of feminine "maumetrie," he says, "Þe enchesoun whi I nempne wommen to fore men is for no worschup þat I coueite to hem for þer heiȝe hornes, but raþer desire schenschupe and schome to hem; for þei wiþ here maumetrie ben cause of alle malice and synnes þat regnen a-mong mon-kinde, and for Holi Writ seiþ: 'Þer is no malice a-boue þe malice of wommen'" (*Book to a Mother* 119). *Maumetrie* thus becomes, if not original sin, originary sin. To contain the malicious force of women, he says that "alle suche oules wiþ her heie hornus . . . schullen se þe time it hadde be bettur þat þei hadden holde Seint Benettis rule, faste iclosed in a cloister" (*Book to a Mother* 120). Like much of the *Book*, this passage implies not only a spiritual meaning— enclosure of the heart within walls of virtue—applicable to men and women alike but also a gendered, bodily valence especially for women, necessitated by their basic carnality and fundamentally disruptive, dangerous desires.

The priest reinforces the value of bodily as well as ghostly claustration for women when he says to "kepe wel þis cloister" (*Book to a Mother* 124) and to "ches þou Crist to þin Abbot" because Christ

wol ȝeue þe no leue to ride ne to go out of þi cloister for recreacioun, and so be worse whanne þou comest hom þanne whanne þou wendest out; ne se uanitees, ne telle ne here idel tales, ne to speke ueine wordes, ne to haue lustis and likinges and wordli worschupes; to be a good womman in o side of a wal, and in þat oþer side a schrewe; ne to make þi professioun o dai, and sone after haue þou asked leue to breke it in proude aparaile of cloþes, peces, macers and spones and oþere wordli uanites. (*Book to a Mother* 124)

This exhortation emphasizes the stereotypically feminine vices of vain speech and carnality, and it stresses the traditionally feminine worldly vanities of clothes and household goods; these concerns, combined with the passage's focus on defining specifically feminine virtue, highlight the cleric's particular interest in bodily enclosure as it applies to women. A good woman is, by definition, one on the right side (that is, the inside) of the wall. A woman who ventures outside enclosure must necessarily return worse than she was before she went out. Outside, for the priest, is both a physical place—in particular, the marketplace—and a moral state—the state of being beyond the law of the husband, the father, and the cleric. Bodily as well as ghostly claustration are therefore vital to keep women under male control and away from material "wordli uanites," the desire for which and the possession of which, according to the priest, lead to sin and social disorder.

As the miracle of the pregnant abbess and the *Book to a Mother* reveal, the frequent later medieval association of women's economic activities with improper sexual activities is remarkably supple. *Lecherie* in the miracle is a figure for economic assertiveness, and suspicions of bribery are an offshoot of sexual misconduct. In the *Book*, economic desires characterized as "maumetrie" lead to sexual transgression, which is in turn a figure for transgressive use of property. As in the miracle, a woman's body in the *Book* is a figure for property, and controlling sexual activity is an economic matter pertaining to the use and control of property. When a woman, going "outside," engages in sexual activity not sanctioned by those to whom her body rightly belongs (that is, her father or her spouse, be he human or divine), she is, like the pregnant abbess, using property improperly, illegitimately, and in a way harmful to the rightful owner.[47]

The priest emphasizes that women do not control their bodies according to their own will when he advises the mother, "be now sori for al þat þou hast mysused þi soule and hure uertues, þi bodi or oni oþer goodis þat God haþ suffred þe haue, oþer byinge or syllinge, oþer in ony oþer doinge aȝenus Godis wil" (*Book to a Mother* 111). In this passage, sins involving the body and sins involving property are fused; misuse of either the property of one's body or the property of one's goods is misuse of that which is given by God and is properly subject to God's will. The female body and material property also coalesce when the priest holds up the example of St. Lucy, who, like all saints, should be admired by male and female Christians alike but who also, as a virgin martyr, belongs to a category of saints whose lives are frequently presented by clerics to women as regulatory models of virtuous female conduct. In his account of her life, St. Lucy describes herself as God's possession and equates her body and material goods when she says, "Þese þre ȝer I offered none oþer offeryng bot myself to herie God: do he with his sacrifice as him likeþ" (*Book to a Mother* 22). St. Lucy's use of her body is coextensive with her use of other material resources. In her refusal to make an offering to devils, in her preserved virginity, and in her martyrdom, St. Lucy uses property correctly, in accordance with patriarchal ideology powerfully reinforced through association with "God's will." Following this account of St. Lucy's martyrdom, the priest situates his mother and the audience of female readers as possessions, objectifying them as "things" belonging to God. He admonishes, "For þan schalt þou not grucche, whatsoeuere he doþ with his owne þyng" (*Book to a Mother* 22).

That the mother the text addresses is a widow adds particular urgency to the text's admonitions about women's use of material property and the property of their bodies.[48] Widows posed an especially knotty problem for those concerned with women and their access to property in later medieval England. Their ability to dispose of their bodies and resources autonomously, since they were no longer under the control of a father or husband, resembles the privileges afforded to men, although the correspondence is by no means exact.[49] In an effort to restrict widows' potential freedoms, the priest presents the monastically influenced model of "holi Anne" from whom he directs his mother to "lerne wel . . . hou þou schalt be a good widwe" (*Book to a Mother* 52). Anna is a "good widwe" worthy of emulation because she remains "inside" both carnally and spiritually. She "wente not fro þe temple, seruinge God wiþ fastinges and preyer niʒt and dai" (*Book to a Mother* 52).

Anxieties provoked by the possibilities opened to women through widowhood also underpin the prominence of nuptial imagery in the *Book*. Nuptial imagery in the *Book* functions much like nuptial imagery in the Benedictine profession service for nuns. The possibilities for sensual pleasure inherent in becoming a bride of Christ surface briefly when the priest quotes a passage from the *Song of Songs* to describe the song of the soul possessed of the Gifts of the Holy Spirit.[50] Such potential quickly gives way, however, to a discourse of marriage which on the one hand makes women subject to male authority but which on the other hand gives the bride of Christ access to symbolic capital and opportunities to assert her independence.

As the priest refers to "þine two hosbondis—Crist and mi fadir" (*Book to a Mother* 30), nuptial discourse functions as an additional regulatory mechanism for keeping women "inside." The priest indicates that even though the mother's earthly spouse is dead, she still must comport herself as a wife who is subject to a husband's authority (i.e., that of the divine spouse and his earthly clerical representatives) in the use of her goods and her body. It is possible, however, that the mother might mobilize her marriage to Christ as a "step up." She might well be able to wield her nuptial union with Christ as many female mystics and visionaries do their unions with Christ, shaking up the power dynamics between clerical man and lay woman and circumventing clerical authority through the authority of a higher divine power.

The priest works with the idea of two husbands, one earthly and one divine, to interweave instruction to women on both earthly wedlock and the spiritual marriage between a soul and Christ, a central theme of the *Book*. As would be expected from a later medieval cleric, the priest stresses the superiority of the latter sort of marriage, which supersedes earthly unions. He says, "For eueriche hosbonde and wif ben holde upon peine of dampnacioun to forsake þe bodiliche wedlak raþer þan þe gostliche, þouȝ bestliche blinde men knowen not þis; for Crist techiþ in þe gospel hou þe bodiliche mai be departed for fornicacioun, and God mai ȝeue no leue to departe þe gostliche, for he mai ȝeue no leue to synne" (*Book to a Mother* 86). In this passage, the priest not only sets spiritual marriage and the chastity it demands over earthly marriage, which is tainted by sexual activity, but he again reminds women that even when an earthly union ends, they are still permanently subject to husbandly authority. The priest's insistence on the indissolubility of the "gostliche" marital bond between the soul and Christ creates a paradigm in which behavior contrary to the husband's will is inherently transgressive, even for a widow with no earthly husband. Such manipulation of the imagery of marriage to Christ weaves female chastity, poverty, and meek obedience together into an ideal of behavior that preserves masculine privilege.

Again, though, this nuptial discourse has a flip side. The priest's privileging of "gostliche" marriage between the soul and Christ might, for instance, be invoked by a married female reader to claim justification for taking a vow of chastity, like that taken by Margery Kempe. Vows of chastity among the married have, as Dyan Elliott has so persuasively shown, the potential to subvert patriarchal authority by undermining that authority's sexual foundations.[51] This discourse of spiritual marriage to Christ might also be used by a widow desiring to avoid remarriage by becoming a vowess. Indeed, since the clerical writer seems to want to discourage his mother from entering a monastery, becoming a vowess might be an appealing option in his view as well, since becoming a vowess would require that she take a vow of chastity before a bishop, so putting her sexuality and reproductive capacities under clerical surveillance. As we shall see in the next section of this chapter, though, a widow's vow of chastity could have strikingly liberating effects, making vowesses more, rather than less, independent and enhancing their ability to exercise control over their resources.

Although nuptial imagery works, at least potentially or partially, to counteract the freedoms available to women through widowhood, the possibilities of maternity—possibilities suggested by the miracle of the pregnant abbess—remain disturbing and must be addressed by the priestly writer. In maternity, issues of female power, female productivity, and female disposition of property merge. In a passage that turns away from a universal readership and toward an explicitly female audience, the priest draws maternity into his critique when he observes that, according to Holy Writ, " 'Þer is no malice a-boue þe malice of wommen,' for womman is þe deuelis massanger, procu[ra]toure, maister and modir" (*Book to a Mother* 119). In calling women the devil's messenger, procurator, master—and mother—the priest adds maternity to women's sexual and economic transgressions; all make women dangerous and disruptive.

Not surprisingly, bodily maternity does not appear in a positive light in the *Book*; the priest implicates it in the entwined sins of lechery and desire for property when he condemns childbearing as an expedient of those who "coueiten riches and worldly worschupes" (*Book to a Mother* 77) and those who "excusen hemself" from living chaste lives "seiynge þat it is bettur to bringe forþ children" (*Book to a Mother* 91). He argues for the superiority of spiritual maternity when he tells his mother, "þou maist conceyue þe same Crist and bere him not onlich nine monþes but wipoute ende; and þat is bettur þan to bere him bodiliche as oure Ladi dide, as Crist seiþ in þe gospel" (*Book to a Mother* 44). As in the miracle of the pregnant abbess, the best, most valuable kind of reproduction in the *Book* is nonmaterial. In addition to devaluing bodily maternity, this passage de-genders maternity. When maternity is made spiritual, its female particularity is obliterated. Maternity is removed from the sphere of the carnal and the feminine, a move that enhances its value. Maternity is no longer solely the province of women; spiritual maternity—which is "bettur þan" bearing Christ bodily—is not uniquely female work.

The chapters of the *Book* which treat the events of the Annunciation, Nativity, and Infancy further devalue the specifically female work of Mary's maternity. In the context of these events to which Mary's maternity is so central, the priest presents the Virgin Mary as a model of ideal meekness and virtue while suppressing her maternity. Referring to the etymology of Mary's name ("a bittur se or a sterre of þe see"), he says that the female reader can be Mary "gostlich" by having "a bittur sorwe" for her sins and by giving "good example to men þat þei mowen se bi þi liuinge hou þei mowen come to þe hauen toun of heuene" (*Book to a Mother* 44–45).[52] Significantly, being Mary "gostlich" has nothing at all to do with bodily, or even spiritual, maternity, but rather with repenting and setting an example of good conduct.

At the one point in these chapters when the priest encourages the female reader to participate in Mary's maternity, he follows this suggestion by quickly pointing out how wide a gulf separates the sinful reader from Mary. The priest tells the reader to "go to Marie and make couenaunt wiþ hure to kepe hure childe" (*Book to a Mother* 50), directing the reader to swaddle the Christ child, rock him, and sing lullabies to him. He continues, though, by advising the reader, "And þe while þou þus singest, be sori and þenk hou ofte þou hast receiued þi God and leid him in a foul, comyne stabele to alle þe seuene dedli synnes" (*Book to a Mother* 50).

Furthermore, Mary is by no means the sole, or even the chief, focus in these chapters in which she is certainly the central figure in the events. The priest encourages the female reader to identify with other participants in the Annunciation, Nativity, and Infancy (although, significantly, not with Christ himself), perhaps in order to discourage an identification with Mary's maternal power like that put forward in Brigittine texts. Following an affective devotional model like that of Nicholas Love in the *Mirror of the Blessed Life of Christ* (a work that has, as Nicholas Watson argues, its own agenda of shaping clerically desirable, orthodox religious practice among the laity and especially among secular women), the writer of the *Book to a Mother* offers scenes for contemplation and suggests ways in which the reader can participate in sacred history by imitating various figures.[53] He tells the female reader that she can "be angel Gabriel gostlich" by being "a good m[e]ssanger" (*Book to a Mother* 45), and that she can sing praises with the angels and seek Christ with the shepherds (*Book to a Mother* 48). She should "be wexinge in loue, and so be Ioseph, for Iosep is as muche to seien wexinge" (*Book to a Mother* 49–50); she should also rule herself "bi Godis lawe" so that her spirit overcomes the devil, the world, and the flesh "and so be a king, offringe wiþ þe þre Kinges gold and murre and sence" (*Book to a Mother* 51). Finally, she is encouraged to strive to see Christ like Simeon and to serve God as a good widow like Anna (*Book to a Mother* 52). These suggested identifications all support received ideals of female spirituality and suggest patterns of female conduct which do not threaten fathers, husbands, and clerics.

In a move that goes to striking lengths to repress the material process of childbearing and the maternal work of nurturing which are essential to Christ's Incarnation, the author replaces the fetus in the womb with a text at one of the few points where he mentions Mary's pregnancy. The *Book*'s structuring principle is that the text itself, designed to serve as a kind of spiritual manual and conduct book for women, is Christ,[54] and the priest writes, "þis Bok was closid nyne / monþe in a litel place of a maide" (*Book to a Mother* 44). In the Incarnation, specifically female work makes the divine Word flesh; the *Book*, however, makes the divine flesh into a written word. In writing the *Book*, which claims to be Christ, the priest performs a kind of textual transubstantiation. As the flesh becomes the *Book*, inscription, a process coded masculine in the later Middle Ages, replaces the Incarnation which took place in a woman's body. Just as the reproduction of Christ's body in the Eucharist excludes women and replaces the maternal process of the Incarnation, so does the production of Christ as text. Mary's role in the Incarnation disappears altogether when the priest says that in the gospel Christ "clepiþ himself Holi Writ þat his Fadur halewide and sende into þis world" (*Book to a Mother* 38). The Incarnation becomes a transaction in which the written word, enfleshed in a male body, is sent into the world by the Father alone; the paternal and the textual replace the maternal and the physical.

The transformation of fetus into text within Mary's body is analogous to the *Book*'s explicitly textual process of constructing women as nondisruptive subjects. The priest describes the text, a "bok" which "is Crist, Godis sone of heuene," as a monastic rule, calling Christ the "beste rule" (*Book to a Mother* 31). He tells the mother to "be write wiþinne and wiþoute wiþ þulke þre [poverty, chastity, and meekness] as Crist was" (*Book to a Mother* 31). The woman is not only to read the *Book* but also to be inscribed with the text of the rule. The priest elaborately sets out the creation of the female reader as a surface for inscription when he tells the mother to examine her life, and, where it is not in accordance with Christ, to "scrape it out." He further advises, "And þat þat þe lackeþ þat þou most nedis haue to holde Goddis hestis, writ in þi soule. Þy penne to write wiþ / schal be þi loue and þi wil ymad scharp wiþ drede of sharp peyne of helle" (*Book to a Mother* 38–39). In reading the writing of the *Book*, the reader is written in; the text marks the reader and makes her subject in a process which echoes the one put forth in the strategic directives for reading and conforming one's conduct to the "mirror" of the text in the *Myroure of Oure Ladye*.

Internal inscription represents the process of getting the text inside the reader and so making the reader into a desirable kind of subject. Another way the *Book* works to get the text into the reader, and thus shape the reader's identity, is through a model of reading as textual incorporation. Images of eating texts abound in the *Book*. For example, in developing the conceit that the *Book* is Christ, the priest recounts the Old Testament story in which Ezekiel is fed with a book.[55] In explaining to his mother how she should use the *Book*, the priest tells her, "lerne þis bok, as I seide, raþer; þat is, know þou þe liuinge of Crist and ofte chew hit and defie hit wiþ hot brennynge loue, so þat alle þe uertues of þi soule and of þi bodi be turned fro flescliche liuinge into Cristes liuinge, as bodiliche mete þat is chewed and defied norschiþ alle þe parties of a mannes bodi. And þanne þou etist gostliche Cristes flesch and his blod whereuere þou be" (*Book to a Mother* 32).

The image of eating texts has connections with the monastic tradition of *ruminatio*, but there is more at stake than simply contemplative, meditative reading.[56] Rather, the priest advocates a Eucharistic model of reading, a kind of reading appropriate to a work that is created through an act of textual transubstantiation. Just as eating the host differs from eating ordinary bread, incorporating this text is a special process. In medieval understanding of the Eucharist, the host is not digested and metabolized to become part of the human body.[57] Rather, by ingesting the body and blood of Christ, the recipient becomes part of the body of Christ. Here, the reader does not make something of the text by incorporating it; rather, the incorporated text makes something of the reader. The priest says that God "wol þat we ete him, as Seynt Austyn scheweþ in his Bokes of Con / fessions, þere God spekeþ to him and seiþ: 'I am mete of grete folk: be þou gret and þou schalt ete me. And þou schalt not turne me into þe, as þou dost bodily mete, bot þou schalt be turned into me' " (*Book to a Mother* 27).[58] In the process of being turned into the Christ that the *Book* itself claims to be, women are ideally turned into the kind of women the pregnant abbess turns out to be—women who do not claim the benefits of their productivity and power but instead willingly put them, and themselves, under the control of husbands, fathers, and clerics.

The Book of Margery Kempe: *Secular Women, Monastic Discourses, and Spiritual Lives in the Material World*

Such texts as the miracle of the pregnant abbess and the *Book to a Mother* circulated to serve the interests of "male clerics and city fathers," but they simultaneously provided women with "tactical" opportunities to mobilize female particularity, productivity, and authority. These opportunities were enhanced in the later Middle Ages as women increasingly controlled their own resources and entered into literate culture, book production, and manuscript ownership. The male monopolization of literature impacting female conduct was thus contested in the course of the fifteenth century. Women commissioned production of and otherwise gained access to texts that served their own "vested interests," both material and spiritual.

In this cultural environment, interpretive schemes based on female monasticism were not always imposed on secular women by ecclesiastical and civic authorities, and a Benedictine-influenced model of monastic life was not, of course, the only one on offer. Just as imagery and practices drawn from Benedictine monasticism move beyond the cloister walls in the *Book to a Mother*, so also Franciscan and Brigittine monasticism, with their portrayals of women's productivity, legitimation of women's authority, and support for women's autonomous control of resources, are textually available and at work in the secular world of later medieval England. Although the question of Margery Kempe's literacy or lack thereof is still debated by critics, we know from her *Book* that she had texts read to her, including "Bridis boke."[59] The case of Margery Kempe suggests that Franciscan and, especially, Brigittine monasticism provided powerful interpretive paradigms through which women could favorably negotiate their processes and practices of living spiritual lives in the material world.

In some ways, Margery Kempe seems a most unlikely figure to consider in exploring the importance of female monasticism in the construction of secular women's identities. As has often been observed, Margery Kempe resolutely refused to live a monastic life. She was "a *lay* woman," and, "despite the intensity of her religious aspirations, this was also part of the way she viewed herself and wanted to go on viewing herself."[60] Christ assures her that she is right to reject more conventional avenues of religious expression for women, saying, "And I haue oftyn-tymes, dowtyr, teld þe þat thynkyng, wepyng, & hy contemplacyon is þe best lyfe in erthe"—better than prayer, fasting, and penance (*Margery Kempe* 89). Margery Kempe's refusal to channel her religious devotion into a cloistered life added to the disturbances she often provoked. In fact, those hostile toward her brand of spiritual life invoked the same ideal of monastic enclosure advocated in *Book to a Mother* as a way of controlling behaviors perceived as disruptive. For instance, when Margery recounts a story from Scripture, declaring to a monk at Canterbury that she will both speak of and hear of God, he responds, "I wold þow wer closyd in an hows of ston þat þer schuld no man speke wyth þe" (*Margery Kempe* 27).

In spite of her refusal to adopt an enclosed, monastic life, and in spite of the ways in which female monasticism is wielded in attempts to circumscribe her, Margery Kempe's *Book* recounts many profitable interactions with women religious. While she is in Venice on the way to the Holy Land, she "was howselyd euery Sonday in a gret hows of nunnys & had gret cher a-mong hem" (*Margery Kempe* 65–66). During her time at this nunnery, Christ visits her with "gret deuocyon & plentyuows terys," and "þe good ladijs of þe place wer mech a-merueylyd þerof" (*Margery Kempe* 66). Nuns not only marvel at Margery's devotion, but they also find it spiritually beneficial. In describing her great weeping and crying when she contemplates the childhood of Christ, the *Book* notes that "þer wer nunnys desiryd to haue knowlach of þe creatur & þat þei xulde þe mor be steryd to deuocyon" (*Margery Kempe* 200). Margery also seeks out women religious to further her own spiritual development. When she is in Norwich, at Christ's command she visits the anchoress "Dame

Ielyan" who "good cownsel cowd ȝeuyn" (*Margery Kempe* 42). Julian of Norwich advises Margery concerning her visions and their validity, and "mych was þe holy dalyawns þat þe ankres & þis creatur haddyn be comownyng in þe lofe of owyr Lord Ihesu Crist many days þat þei were to-gedyr" (*Margery Kempe* 43).[61]

Significantly, Franciscan and Brigittine monasticism figure prominently in Margery Kempe's interactions with religious women. The *Book* reports that the abbess of Denney frequently sent for Margery to come visit the sisters, and when Margery feared to travel to the Minoresses because "it was pestylenstyme," Christ assured her that she would be safe. He commands her "to gon to Denney & comfortyn þe ladijs þat desyryd to comowynyn wyth hir" (*Margery Kempe* 202). On her last pilgrimage she visits Syon to obtain the Lammas Day pardon (*Margery Kempe* 245–46), and on her travels to the Continent she visits Brigittine houses.[62]

Margery Kempe appears early in her story as a materially acquisitive, proud, lusty woman. She boasts of her "worthy kenred" (*Margery Kempe* 9) and wears "gold pypys on hir hevyd & hir hodys with þe typettys were daggyd. Hir clokys also wer daggyd & leyd wyth dyuers colowrs be-twen þe daggys þat it schuld be þe mor staryng to mennys sygth and hir-self þe mor ben worshepd" (*Margery Kempe* 9). As a result of Christ's appearance to her while she is out of her mind following childbirth, she is transformed from being just the sort of women the *Book to a Mother* condemns to being a follower of "þe wey of hey perfeccyon" (*Margery Kempe* 2). Although the way of perfection is the way of contemplation, of pursuing poverty and chastity, and of being meek and obedient—in other words, of being the kind of woman the *Book to a Mother* praises and seeks to create—the "creatur" portrayed in the *Book of Margery Kempe* is probably not what the priestly writer of the *Book to a Mother* envisioned. The case of Margery Kempe illustrates that monastic interpretive schemes, like other interpretive systems, are not "the property of a single social segment but of society as a whole."[63] As Margery improvises on female monasticism in distinctively Franciscan and, especially, Brigittine keys, she and her *Book* demonstrate that late medieval secular women could and did capitalize on the transformability of signifiers to craft empowered spiritual lives in the material world.[64]

Distinctive elements of monastic profession make appearances in Margery Kempe's negotiation of her spiritual life and work. In addition to adopting white clothes and a mantle, a move which resembles taking the monastic habit, Margery wears a ring which calls to mind a nun's profession ring, the sign of marriage to Christ. The service of profession, especially in the Benedictine tradition, is, as I have argued, filled with language suggesting social and familial identifications marking the nuns as being possessed and exchanged by others. The description of Margery's "bone maryd ryng to Ihesu Crist" (*Margery Kempe* 78), however, is filled with language portraying Margery herself as a possessor of both material and spiritual property, recalling the ways in which Benedictine nuns might have taken advantage of the symbolic capital available through marriage to Christ: "The forseyd creatur had a ryng þe whech owyr Lord had comawndyd hir to do makyn whil she was at hom in Inglond & dede hir gravyn þerup-on, 'Ihesus est amor meus.' Sche had mech thowt how sche xulde kepe þis ryng fro theuys & stelyng as sche went be þe cuntreys, for sche thowt sche wold not a lost þe ryng for a thowsand pownde & meche mor be-cause þat sche dede it makyn be þe byddyng of God" (*Margery Kempe* 78). Since Margery had the economic wherewithal and the independent control of resources to have the ring made, she is clearly a woman with material resources. She is also a woman who possesses and uses the spiritual property of intimacy with the divine, as is demonstrated by the incident in which she loses her ring and finds it after her prayers prompt its return (*Margery Kempe* 78–79). Even the engraving on the ring, "Ihesus est amor meus," is itself a statement of possession rather than of being possessed.[65]

The mystical experience in which Margery is married to the Godhead in Rome on St. John Lateran's Day augments the access to resources she has through her nuptial relationship. Margery does not make a vow before God to become the bride of Christ as nuns do in their profession services; rather, in Margery's nuptial ceremony, God the Father makes a vow to her. In the presence of Christ, Mary, the Holy Ghost, the Twelve Apostles, St. Katherine, St. Margaret, and a multitude of saints and angels, God says to Margery, "I take þe, Margery, for my wedded wyfe, for fayrar, for fowelar, for richar, for powerar, so þat þu be buxom & bonyr to do what I byd þe do. For, dowtyr, þer was neuyr childe so buxom to þe modyr as I xal be to þe boþe in wel & in wo,—to help þe and comfort þe. And þerto I make þe suyrte" (*Margery Kempe* 87). The language of "taking" does suggest that, as in the *Book to a Mother*, Margery is God's "thing," his property to do with as he will. Nancy Partner rightly calls attention to Margery's reluctance to enter this union with God the Father, pointing out that Margery, silent after her initial refusal, never actually voices her assent.[66] It is also true that this vow entails Margery's obedience to God.

God's vow to Margery implies, however, a reciprocality in the relationship absent in the spousal relationship created by the clerical writer in the *Book to a Mother*. Margery is to "be buxom" and do as God bids her, but God will also be "buxom" to her as a child is to his mother. Even if we do not hear Margery's assent to the union, her manipulation of this reciprocal relationship of "buxom-ness" is evident throughout the text. Many times she does as she wills with the authorization of God's will. Furthermore, if Margery is figured as God's "prop-erty" in this nuptial scene, she also gains spiritual goods in recompense. God the Father declares his intention that she be wedded to the Godhead because, as he says, "I schal schewyn þe my preuyteys & my cownselys" (*Margery Kempe* 86). Through her nuptial relationship with the divine Margery be-comes, as "blyssyd Byrgytte" is described in a Brigittine prayer, "ordeyned" by Jesus "to be called thy spouse for inspyracyon of many pryuytes."[67]

Margery Kempe's vow of chastity is a striking transformation of that which is revered by the writer of the *Book to a Mother* and considered by so many clerics to be the most important of the substantial vows for nuns. Some critics have described Margery Kempe's pursuit of chastity as a practice that reaffirms patriarchal power; for instance, Sidonie Smith writes, "To the extent that she establishes her chastity within the text, to the extent that she reaffirms through the text, as well as in the text, her subordination to all fathers, she is allowed the voice of authority."[68] Many of these "fathers," however, see Marg-ery's chastity as something far more problematic; they are not at all satisfied that she is properly subordinate. Her ring and white mantle, the signs of her chaste life, repeatedly draw questions. For ecclesiastical and civic officials, her white clothes are a mark of her potential threat to their authority, and such officials frequently bring up her white clothes in the context of examinations on charges of heresy.[69] Official unease about Margery Kempe's chastity stems from the destabilizing potential of a married woman's embracing chastity.[70] Although Margery would seem to be doing just what the writer of the *Book to a Mother* recommends, in fact she, like the pregnant abbess and the women condemned in the *Book to a Mother*, is claiming her body as her own posses-sion to use according to her will.

Significantly, it is Margery's relationship with Christ, together with the combination of her divine knowledge and material resources, that enables her to impose her desire for chastity on her husband John. She wrests consent from him by making a shrewd bargain, telling him, "Grawntyth me þat ȝe schal not komyn in my bed, & I grawnt ȝow to qwyte ȝour dettys er I go to Ierusalem. & makyth my body fre to God so þat ȝe neuyr make no chalengyng in me to askyn no dett of matrimony aftyr þis day whyl ȝe leuyn" (*Margery Kempe* 25). The vow of chastity increases Margery's control of her resources, because she acquires in the negotiations the rights to her own body.[71] Rather than necessitating her enclosure, her chastity permits her to pursue her inde-pendent, highly public religious identity as visionary, prophet, and pilgrim.

Margery is not unique among later-medieval English secular women in her strategic adoption of the vow of chastity. Other women also found in it a means of maximizing their control over their material and spiritual lives. P. H. Cullum points out that the vow of chastity was the only vow taken by widows who became vowesses, many of whom were wealthy. This vow, Cullum observes, was not a "bar to continuing to manage estates or businesses."[72] Indeed, Mary Erler argues that economic freedom may well have been a key factor in widows' decisions to become vowesses.[73] Widows thus found ways to use the same life urged upon them by the writer of the *Book to a Mother* to gain precisely the economic and spiritual independence which that text works, at least on one level, to forestall.

While poverty is a less defining trait of Margery Kempe's religious practice than chastity is, it still figures importantly in her construction of a spiritual life in the material world. Margery does not accept a life of poverty easily. Even after Christ appears to her she does not immediately leave her "pride ne hir pompows aray" (*Margery Kempe* 9). Rather, "for pure coveytyse & for to maynten hir pride" (*Margery Kempe* 9) she attempts, and fails at, brewing and milling ventures. Kempe sees the failure of her enterprises as God's chastisement, and she renounces pride, covetousness, and her desire for worldly worship (*Margery Kempe* 11). This renunciation does not simply transform Kempe into a practitioner of the sort of passive poverty the priestly writer of the *Book to a Mother* advocates in his portrayal of the Virgin Mary. Instead, Margery Kempe actively and publicly seeks a more radical form of poverty.

Susan Dickman argues against Margery Kempe's interest in apostolic poverty, saying that Margery's experience of poverty only took place away from England while she was on pilgrimage.[74] This very fact does much, in my view, to align Margery's practice of poverty with the apostolic tradition. Margery Kempe wanders about, unenclosed, far from home, engaging in holy conversation and performing works of charity. While in Rome she "wyth a feruent desyr to plesyn God ʒaf a-wey swech good as sche had & sweche as sche had borwyd also" (*Margery Kempe* 92), and, when her friends did not give her food and drink, "sche beggyd hir mete fro dor to dore" (*Margery Kempe* 94). After Margery has given away all her goods, Christ encourages her to still stricter poverty, invoking the apostolic ideal of following naked the naked Christ. He says, "Dowtyr, þu art not ʒet so powr / as I was whan I heng nakyd on þe Cros for thy lofe, for þu hast clothys on thy body & I had non. And thow hast cownseld oþer men to ben powr for my sake, & þerfor þu must folwyn thyn owyn cownsel" (*Margery Kempe* 92). In these practices Margery resembles the Franciscan friars whose writings were so important in her spiritual development.[75] Margery's poverty is precisely the apostolic poverty that St. Clare desired for herself and her sisters, a desire denied to them by ecclesiastical authorities who insisted on enclosure for women religious. In her practice of poverty, Kempe identifies neither with enclosed nuns nor with Mary as she is portrayed in the *Book to a Mother*, a woman who simply does not possess or desire material goods. Rather, Margery models her version of poverty on Christ, who actively separates himself from property in acts of self-sacrifice and charity.

Franciscan friars, like many other ecclesiastical figures Margery encounters, react to her with either hearty approval or vehement disapproval; there is little middle ground. The Franciscans in the Holy Land treat Margery Kempe quite well. In Bethlehem "þe Grey Frerys whech had led hir fro place to place receyued hir in-to hem & sett hir wyth hem at þe mete þat sche xuld not etyn a-lone" (*Margery Kempe* 73). In Jerusalem, "þe Frerys of þe Tempyl mad hir gret cher and ȝouyn hir many gret relykys, desiryng þat sche schuld a dwellyd stille a-mongs hem, ȝyf sche had wold, for þe feyth þei had in hir" (*Margery Kempe* 75). It is also, however, a Franciscan friar, possibly William Melton, who throws her out of church and who subsequently preaches against her (*Margery Kempe* 148–54).

This Franciscan manifestation of ecclesiastical schizophrenia toward Margery might be connected with her enactment of Franciscan-influenced practices which, while traditional, were traditional for men instead of women. Another issue to consider in relation to Franciscan reactions to Margery is her troublingly—even radically—corporeal achievement of the pseudo-Bonaventuran *Meditationes Vitae Christi* written for a Franciscan nun and adapted by Nicholas Love in his *Mirror of the Blessed Life of Christ*,[76] a text which, as Nicholas Watson has argued, has a regulatory agenda. Margery's "rewriting" of the *Mirror*, while certainly within the affective tradition, has disturbing dimensions, including the extended weeping and crying provoked by hearing of "þe Passyon of owr Lord" (*Margery Kempe* 149). It is this behavior that leads the Franciscan preacher to throw her out of Church (*Margery Kempe* 150–51). Since the influence of Love's text is also strongly evident in the *Book to a Mother*, Margery's reinterpretive, aggressively embodied enactment may also suggest ways in which secular women might read the *Book to a Mother* "tactically," as a "map" to empowering avenues of independent spiritual development.

For Margery, adopting a life of Franciscan-like apostolic poverty ultimately works to her material advantage. After telling Margery to become one of the naked poor, Christ tells her, "But drede þe not, dowtyr, for þer is gold to-þe-ward, & I haue hyte þe befor-tyme þat I wolde neuyr fayl þe. & I xal preyn myn owyn Modir to beggyn for þe, for þu hast many tymes beggyd for me & for my Modir also" (*Margery Kempe* 92–93). In addition to receiving the spiritual benefits which accompany apostolic poverty, Margery, much like the friars, receives gifts with divine approval, since, as Christ tells her, "I haue frendys in euery cuntre & xal make my frendys to comfort þe" (*Margery Kempe* 93). For example, Dame Margarete Florentyn gives her food and drink in Rome. In Lynn, when Margery is preparing to go to St. James, "a good man" gives her forty pence and "a woman, a good frend to þis creatur" gives her seven marks "for sche xulde prey for hir whan þat sche come to Seynt Iamys" (*Margery Kempe* 106).

Margery Kempe's brand of poverty is thus both a recognizably, approvably orthodox practice and an instance of innovation. Rather than contributing to an identity that constrains women, Margery Kempe's version of poverty is a route to legitimate, autonomous use of material and spiritual resources. In this regard, Margery's negotiations of poverty resonate with the treatment of poverty and property in the Brigittine tradition. Throughout Birgitta's revelations, Christ and Mary both inform Birgitta that it is acceptable for her to possess and use property. Perhaps even more significantly, though, Birgitta's own practices of radical poverty also receive divine approval, suggesting that women have, in the end, the right to determine their own relationship to the material world.

Obedience, and the meekness which accompanies it, initially appear to be the elements of traditional female monasticism least applicable to Margery Kempe. In fact, in Margery Kempe's *Book*, disobedience to clerical authorities and spiritual advisors is a regular feature, as when she refuses to follow her confessor's order not to travel to Danzig. In ignoring this order, Margery "manages to turn this disobedience into an obedience to the higher master, who obligingly bids her to 'gon in my name, Ihesu, for I am a-bouyn thy gostly fadyr & xal excusyn þe' (227: 4–6)."[77] As Janette Dillon observes, Margery Kempe's obedience "is structured around negotiated disobedience" and "is a matter of negotiated agreement between Kempe and Christ to which confessors are mere adjuncts."[78] Just as God the Father sets up a mutual relationship of "buxomness" with Margery in their nuptial union on St. John Lateran's Day, Christ tells Margery, "ȝyf þu wilt be buxom to my wyl, I schal be buxom to thy wil" (*Margery Kempe* 158). Margery's negotiated, reciprocal obedience is clearly a departure from the monastic ideal of unquestioning, strictly hierarchical obedience. It does resemble, though, the sorts of negotiations of authority that characterize Brigittine and Franciscan visitation ceremonies, negotiations that give women religious a more active role in defining their religious identities and practices.

Margery Kempe's practice of meekness is conventionally feminine in that she bears reproof patiently and suffers slander without resistance. Even this more orthodox aspect of her meekness does not replicate the ideal of Marian meekness evident in the *Book to a Mother* or the childlike "buxomness" suggested for the female superior in the verse translation of the Benedictine Rule for women. Interpretive schemes wielded to suppress female power and devalue female productivity become, for Margery, sources of empowerment. As in Brigittine texts in which the Virgin's humility is the foundation of her authority and her meekness makes her higher than male religious leaders, Margery's meekness also raises her above ecclesiastical authorities.

Margery seeks out reproof and scorn; she "þowt it was ful mery to be reprevyd for Goddys lofe; it was to hir gret solas & cowmfort whan sche was chedyn & fletyn for þe lofe of Ihesu" (*Margery Kempe* 29). Kempe's brand of meekness in the face of slander alters the economy of salvation. Indeed, her version of meekness changes the terms of exchange to such an extent that her willingness to suffer slander guarantees her salvation, a guarantee that short-circuits clerical authority. Christ tells her that she will not experience the pains of hell and says to her, "þu xuldyst noon oþer Purgatory han þan slawndyr & speche of þe world" (*Margery Kempe* 51).

The Book of Margery Kempe further transforms the economy of salvation in a very Brigittine fashion in its treatment of maternity. As in the miracle of the pregnant abbess and the *Book to a Mother*, maternity in *The Book of Margery Kempe* is both an important manifestation of female work and a figure for other kinds of female labor. To a certain extent, in Margery Kempe's *Book*, as in the *Book to a Mother*, bodily maternity has negative associations. Clarissa Atkinson points out that although Margery Kempe is the mother of fourteen children, "she rarely mentioned her children or her experience of motherhood" in the *Book*,[79] and Margery's experience with the harsh confessor, which drives her into madness, occurs during a period of illness following childbirth. In one of her revelations, when Christ tells her that she is pregnant, her response indicates not only fear that motherhood will disrupt her communication with Christ but also a negative view of maternity tainted by sexual lust similar to that set out in *Book to a Mother*.[80] She tells Christ that she doubts her worthiness to "heryn þe spekyn & þus comown wyth myn husbond" (*Margery Kempe* 48). At this point, though, Christ himself validates bodily maternity, giving it the stamp of approval reserved for spiritual maternity in the *Book to a*

Mother. Christ tells Margery that he loves her "as wel as any mayden in þe world" (*Margery Kempe* 49) and assures her "þow xalt haue neuyr þe lesse grace, for I wyl þat þow bryng me forth mor frwte" (*Margery Kempe* 48).

The value of bodily maternity is central to Margery Kempe's experiences on the Mount of Calvary, which put maternal work back at the foundation of salvation. Margery literally enacts the medieval reading of Mary's *compassio* at Christ's crucifixion as the labor pains she did not suffer at Christ's birth.[81] When Margery visits Calvary, "sche fel down þat sche mygth not stondyn ne knelyn but walwyd & wrestyd wyth hir body, spredyng hir armys a-brode, & cryed wyth a lowde voys" (*Margery Kempe* 68). As Karma Lochrie has observed, Margery's physical posture, with her arms spread abroad, mirrors that of the crucified Jesus, while her wallowing and crying suggests a woman in labor.[82] The high value of maternal work emerges in the "language of labor"[83] used to describe Margery's participation in both Christ's passion and Mary's "maternal labor of compassion."[84] Margery is at her most Brigittine as she plays both parts in the process of co-redemption, engaging in simultaneous *imitatio Christi* and *imitatio Mariae*.[85] Like Brigittine nuns at their consecration, Margery identifies with both Mary and Christ, and she emphasizes the redemptive potential of maternal work so celebrated in Brigittine spirituality.

Similarly, Margery Kempe's experience of the Nativity, which is unlike the portrayal of the Nativity in the *Book to a Mother* but quite like that presented in Brigittine divine service and in St. Birgitta's revelations, revalues maternity. The clerical writer of the *Book to a Mother*, perhaps hoping to forestall too complete an identification between women and Mary as mother of God, suggests that the female reader should emulate the nonthreatening, exemplary behavior of various figures in the Nativity drama. In contrast, Christ tells Margery, "Dowtyr, thynke on my Modyr, for sche is cause of alle þe grace þat þow hast" (*Margery Kempe* 18). In the ensuing vision, Margery becomes intimately involved in a series of births. She is the "mayden" and "seruant" of a pregnant St. Anne, and she attends the birth of the Virgin Mary, to whom she acts as nursemaid, providing her "wyth good mete & drynke, wyth fayr whyte clothys & whyte kerchys" (*Margery Kempe* 18). Subsequently, Margery goes with Mary and Joseph to visit the pregnant St. Elizabeth, and she attends the birth of John the Baptist. Finally, after accompanying Mary and Joseph to Bethlehem and aiding them in obtaining food, shelter, and clothing for the child about to be born, Margery witnesses Christ's birth.

Much like Brigittine divine services, *The Book of Margery Kempe* presents the story of salvation as a story of pregnancies and births. In both, maternity as specifically female work reasserts its prominence. A Brigittine hymn from the

Thursday service of Matins, for instance, praises the "maydens bowels" which "bere hym. that all the worlde taketh not" and concludes with a focus on Mary as nurturing mother, declaring, "Blysse we with deuoute soulles the grete lorde. souckynge the maydenly teates of the moste meke vyrgyn. . . . Blysse we the heuenly lorde. norysshed amongest seruauntes. of the maydens breste."[86] Elizabeth's praise of Margery for her service to the Virgin Mary could be more broadly construed as praise for the work of women in this vision of salvation history shared by Margery and Birgitta; as Elizabeth tells Margery, "Dowtyr, me semyth . . . þu dost ryght wel þi deuer" (*Margery Kempe* 19).

Joseph and the angel Gabriel, suggested as appropriate models of behavior for the female reader of the *Book to a Mother*, do not play central roles in Margery's Nativity experiences. Far from appearing as a figure for identification, the angel Gabriel does not appear at all. There is no Annunciation, other than Margery's "pre-annunciation" to Mary in her youth that "ʒe schal be þe Modyr of God" (*Margery Kempe* 18); rather, after "passy[ng] awey for a certeyn tyme," the Virgin Mary simply tells Margery, "Dowtyr, now am I be-kome þe Modyr of God" (*Margery Kempe* 18). This formulation makes Mary seem to be an independent agent in the Incarnation, countering the priestly writer's version of an Incarnation without maternity (*Book to a Mother* 38). Joseph is offstage when Jesus is born, and Margery herself takes over the role of "provider" for the Virgin and Child. Margery "beggyd owyr Lady fayr whyte clothys & kerchys for to swathyn in hir Sone whan he wer born, and, whan Ihesu was born, sche ordeyned beddyng for owyr Lady to lyg in wyth hir blyssed Sone. And sythen sche beggyd mete for owyr Lady & hir blyssyd chyld" (*Margery Kempe* 19). The work of the Nativity, crucial to human redemption, is work done exclusively by women.

Margery's woman-centered experience of the Nativity closely resembles Birgitta's revelation of the birth of Jesus. In Birgitta's revelation, Joseph has a mere bit part. As the time for the birth approaches, Joseph, "a very honest olde man," brings the Virgin a candle, which he fastens to the wall and goes "owt agayne, lest he shulde be present then at the byrth."[87] The Virgin prepares clean clothes to receive the child, and gives birth painlessly as Birgitta looks on. When the child is born, even Joseph's candle loses importance: "And the candell that Joseph faystynd in the wall gave then no maner off lyght for that gloryus lyght and bryghtnes that came owt off the chylde utterly dystroiyde and putt owt the natural lyght off the candell."[88] Furthermore, Birgitta's vision of the birth focuses at length, as does Margery's, on specifically maternal details: the newborn infant miraculously clean and free from "al fylth and unclennes" who weeps and trembles "for coldnes and harndnes off the pament where apon he lay,"[89] the Virgin's womb which "was very grete afore the byrth" but afterward "swagyd and wythdrewe inwarde agayn to the state that yt was in afore she conceyvyd,"[90] and the Virgin suckling and swaddling Jesus.[91]

At Christ's birth, as at his crucifixion, Margery Kempe weeps. In her vision of the Nativity, "sche swathyd hym wyth byttyr teerys of compassyon, hauyng mend of þe scharp deth þat he schuld suffyr for þe lofe of synful men" (*Margery Kempe* 19). Tears, strongly associated with maternity in Margery's *Book*, are another kind of specifically female labor which proves quite valuable in the economy of salvation.[92] Margery Kempe's weeping is, like the labor of childbirth, redemptive work. The extraordinary salvific value of Margery's tears is evident when Christ tells her that the devil is "wroth wyth þe, for þu turmentyst hym mor wyth þi wepyng þan doth al þe fyer in helle; þu wynnyst many sowlys fro hym wyth þi wepyng" (*Margery Kempe* 51). The worth of her tears is increased still further, superseding clerical work, when Christ tells her that with the "teerys of [her] eyne" she has "ȝouyn . . . drynken ful many tymes" to "my Fadyr & to my Modyr & to alle my seyntys in Hevyn" (*Margery Kempe* 52). While priests produce the spiritual food of the Eucharist for people on earth, Margery is involved not only in the maternal labors of the Incarnation but also in the production of celestial nourishment.

The superclerical status of Margery's weeping is again evident when Christ tells her, "sumtyme whan þu receyuyst þe precyows Sacrament, I make þe to prey for thy gostly fadyr on þis wyse: þat as many men & women myth be turnyd be hys prechyng as þu woldist þat wer turnyd be þe teerys of thyn eyne" (*Margery Kempe* 212). During the sacrament of the Eucharist, which is the wellspring of clerical power and the process through which Christ's body is produced by male clerics, Christ himself positions Margery's tears as superior to priestly labors. As Dillon notes, "The direct parallel between the power of Kempe's tears and her confessor's preaching posits spiritual equality between them, while the fact that God explains this to Kempe puts her in the superior position."[93]

Margery's weeping is not the only dimension of work that achieves and even surpasses clerical status.[94] Although Margery so desires the bliss of heaven that she wishes to die, Christ tells her that she must "abyden & languren in lofe" because, he says, "I haue ordeyned þe to knele be-for þe Trynyte to prey for al þe world, for many hundryd thowsand sowlys schal be sauyd be þi prayers" (*Margery Kempe* 20). In this commission, the work of intercessory prayer, which, like weeping, is strongly associated with women, and especially with mothers, is shown to be extraordinarily productive.[95] Furthermore, that this is work to which Margery is "ordeyned" by Christ's call suggests the vocation and ordination of a priest. Margery's superclerical mission and her confidence in her ability to fulfill it are evident in the prayer which ends the *Book*. In the closing words, she casts herself as an intercessor for the world, praying, "And for alle þo þat feithyn & trustyn er xul feithyn & trustyn in my prayerys in-to þe worldys ende, sweche grace as þei desiryn, gostly er bodily, to þe profite of her sowlys, I pray þe, Lord, grawnt hem for þe multitude of þi mercy. Amen" (*Margery Kempe* 253–54).[96]

A priest is Christ's earthly representative, but Margery is more than a simple representative; she and Christ are one, and this union gives her powers beyond those of clerics. Christ says, "I am in þe, / and þow in me. And þei þat heryn þe þei heryn þe voys of God. Dowtyr, þer is no so synful man in erth leuyng, yf he wyl forsake hys synne & don aftyr þi cownsel, swech grace as þu behestyst hym I wyl confermyn for þi lofe" (*Margery Kempe* 23). Margery is able to provide direct access to God's voice, and, if her council is obeyed (a proviso that gives her striking spiritual authority), the effectiveness of her prayers is divinely guaranteed. What cleric could make such a promise? Margery's status further exceeds that of the clergy because her redemptive and intercessory abilities are like those of the saints. Faith in and devotion to her bring valuable spiritual benefits, as is clear when the Virgin Mary informs Margery that all those who believe (as well as all those until the end of time who will believe) that God loves Margery and who thank God for her will receive "þe same pardon þat was grawntyd þe . . . þat is to seyn plenowr remissyon" (*Margery Kempe* 175). Christ also tells her, "I be-hote þe þe same grace þat I be-hyte Seynt Kateryne, Seynt Margarete, Seynt Barbara, & Seynt Powle, in so mech þat what creatur in erth vn-to þe Day of Dom aske þe any bone & beleuyth þat God louyth þe he xal haue hys bone er ellys a bettyr thyng" (*Margery Kempe* 52).[97]

The combination of weeping and prayer as redemptive, maternal work in the *Book of Margery Kempe* suggests Margery's affinity with Brigittine spirituality, which focuses so sharply Mary's salvific role, and with St. Birgitta herself. In a reversal of the process by which the clergy recuperate the abbess's son in the miracle of the pregnant abbess, both Birgitta and Margery save their own sons through their maternal tears and prayers. In one of her revelations, Birgitta and Mary work together as mothers to save Birgitta's son Karl at the time of his death. Mary tells Birgitta that when her son's soul departed from his body, "I did as a womman that standith by another womman whan sche childeth."[98] His soul then appears before Jesus to be judged, where an angel and a fiend both lay claim to it. When the fiend prepares to make his case by enumerating Karl's sins, he encounters difficulties; "it semed that he [the fiend] alle-to trembled and schoke, and of grete trouble he cryed: allas and woo vn-to me, wrecche. How haue I loste my long labour? For not onely I haue loste the texte, but also all the matere is brente where-inne alle thinges werne writen."[99] The angel solves the mystery of the disappearing "texte and matere" of Karl's sins, saying, "this haue wepinges and longe labour of his modre and many prayers doo."[100]

The fiend further laments the loss of his "sak full of writinges of suche synnes as the knyght hadde purposid to haue mendid" but did not;[101] he says he has lost not only the "sak full of writinges" but even his memory of Karl's sins. Indeed, the fiend has "for-getyn his [Karl's] name."[102] These losses for the fiend and gains for Karl's soul also occur thanks to maternal labor. The angel tells the fiend, "The teres of his modre haue spoiled the and broken thy sak and distroied thy wryting, so moche hir teres plesed God."[103] The fiend has forgotten Karl's name because, according to the angel, "his name is callid in heuen 'the son of teeres'."[104] When the fiend cries out, "O cursid be þat modir of him þat had so gret a wombe þat so meche water was in,"[105] it becomes clear that the material and the maternal have triumphed over the symbolic and the paternal. Tears, associated with the womb, erase phallic inscription, and the name of the mother replaces the name of the father.[106] Materiality and maternity in this case clearly do have value and meaning.[107]

In a scene which has striking parallels although it takes place in this world rather than the next, Margery effects her son's salvation. Her son ignores her advice to "leeuyn þe worlde & folwyn Crist" (*Margery Kempe* 221); in fact, he is so stubborn that he will not even consent to her council to keep his body "klene at þe lest from womanys feleschep" until marriage (*Margery Kempe* 222). The son goes overseas, falls into "þe synne of letchery," and is afflicted with a disease that makes "hys face . . . ful of whelys & bloberys as it had ben a lepyr" (*Margery Kempe* 222). He takes his illness to be God's punishment brought on when "hys modyr had bannyd hym" (*Margery Kempe* 222). When at last, like the prodigal son, he returns to Margery, asks her blessing, and accepts her "scharp wordys of correpcyon," she agrees to pray for him (*Margery Kempe* 223). The son is subsequently healed of his sickness, marries, and lives a virtuous life in Prussia. When he returns home again to England, Margery is amazed at the change in her formerly vain and worldly son, who now wears "no daggys" and whose "dalyawns" is "ful of vertu" (*Margery Kempe* 223). Margery asks what has wrought this change, and he replies, "Modyr . . . I hope þat thorw ȝowr preyerys owr Lord hath drawyn me, and I purpose be þe grace of God to folwyn ȝowr cownsel mor þan I haue don be-forn" (*Margery Kempe* 223).

Finally, in *The Book of Margery Kempe*, textual creation becomes, as in the

Brigittine *Myroure of Oure Ladye*, not only legitimate work for a woman but also salvific work.[108] In the *Myroure*, authorization of Birgitta's confessor Peter's Latin translation of her revelations is said to come from Mary via Birgitta, and his worthiness to perform the task stems from Mary's influence in his life. Similarly, in Margery Kempe's *Book*, it is Margery's intervention that enables the second scribe to read the text written by the first scribe, and her intercession mends his faulty vision (*Margery Kempe* 4–5).[109] In Brigittine divine service, Mary's creation of the fleshly text of the divine Logos makes salvation possible; Margery's textual creation also makes salvation possible. When Margery begins the *Book*, she spends less time in prayer than previously "for sped of wrytyng" (*Margery Kempe* 216), and she worries that this may displease the Lord. The salvific dimensions of her textual labors emerge, however, when Christ reassures her that nothing pleases him more "þan ȝe don wyth ȝowr writyng, for / dowtyr, be þis boke many a man xal be turnyd to me & beleuyn þerin" (*Margery Kempe* 216).

The female reader of the *Book to a Mother* is constructed as a surface to be inscribed with a text which is Christ—that is, meekness, chastity, and poverty. Margery, in contrast, is, like Mary, the creator of a text which (in that it has Christ's authorization and will inspire belief in Christ) is Christ. In the *Book to a Mother*, textual transubstantiation transforms the Word made flesh by the female body back into the word through the priest's inscription. In Margery Kempe's *Book*, textual transubstantiation involves turning the divine word, experienced in the female flesh, into the written word.[110] Margery's rewriting of writing goes further still. She not only creates a salvific text through her labors, but she also is the text of salvation in her vision of the Book of Life, where she sees her name "at þe Trinyte foot wretyn" (*Margery Kempe* 207). Similarly, Margery becomes part of the text of Christ's body when Christ assures her of her special grace. Echoing the conceit of the Charters of Christ, in which Christ's body is inscribed in the crucifixion to become a document recording redemption, he tells Margery that nothing will harm her because he cannot forget how "þow art wretyn in myn handys & my fete" (*Margery Kempe* 30). Margery Kempe thus finally turns "vp-so down" writing itself, the very process by which women's work is devalued and masculine privilege is reinforced in the *Book to a Mother*, in translations of the Benedictine Rule for women, and, indeed, in later medieval English culture.

Margery Kempe has often been dismissed as a failed mystic or a freak—in short, as some sort of aberration. In her attraction to Brigittine spirituality and in her use of interpretive schemes drawn from Brigittine monasticism to negotiate the process of crafting a spiritual life in the material world, however,

Margery Kempe was not alone in fifteenth-century England. In fact, she had some very good company. A group of powerful, secular women exhibited some remarkably similar affinities; these women included Margaret, duchess of Clarence; Cecily, duchess of York; and Margaret, Lady Hungerford.

Margaret, duchess of Clarence, born Margaret Holand, was first married to John Beaufort, earl of Somerset. He was the eldest son of John of Gaunt and Catherine Swynford, born before their marriage and afterward legitimized in Parliament. After Beaufort's death, Margaret "was a woman of sufficient wealth and position to be a fit match for yet another Lancastrian husband Thomas, duke of Clarence (1388–1421) and brother to Henry V."[111] Margaret had great affinity for the Brigittines of Henry V's foundation of Syon. She was granted papal permission "to dwell near Syon [the only Brigittine house in England] and to be visited at her invitation by the enclosed brethren. . . . Moreover, she received permission to enter, with assent of the superiors, monasteries of enclosed nuns."[112] Furthermore, she possessed a manuscript (Yale University Beinecke MS 317) prepared for her by Symon Wynter, a brother at Syon, which included, along with other works, two of St. Birgitta's visions.[113]

Cecily, duchess of York, was the wife of Richard, duke of York, and mother of Edward IV and Richard III. While on the other side of the political fence from Margaret, duchess of Clarence, she too had strong connections with Syon and St. Birgitta. Among other bequests of books, Cecily of York left a book containing St. Birgitta's *Revelations* to her granddaughter, Anne de la Pole, who was prioress of Syon.[114] Cecily's devotion to Syon was great and led to her being included in the Syon obituary; "the vii obit is in Ester . . . for alle frendis and benefactors and specialli for the duke Richard and Cecillie his spouse parenters unto kynge Edward."[115] Cecily's household ordinances also indicate that during meals she had religious texts, including St. Birgitta's *Revelations*, read aloud.[116]

Margaret, Lady Hungerford, wife of Robert, Lord Hungerford, was not of quite the social status of Margaret of Clarence or Cecily of York. She faced more troubled personal circumstances as well; her eldest son Robert, Lord Moleyns, was attainted in 1461 and subsequently executed in 1464; his eldest son was executed in 1469. As M. A. Hicks notes, Margaret spent nearly twenty years trying to save the family inheritance in the wake of the political blunders of her relatives, and she herself was arrested three times.[117] Although tumultuous, her career exhibits the same combination of active social, political, and economic involvement with interest in Brigittine monasticism as do those of Margaret of Clarence and Cecily of York.

One of Margaret's three arrests occurred following the Lincolnshire Rebellion of March-May 1470. In the end, Edward IV showed some leniency, permitting Margaret to pay two hundred pounds and withdraw to Syon, where she was "evidently admitted as a sister, 'partner of al spiritual subsidies . . . in life and in dethe.'"[118] Margaret was able to leave Syon after Edward IV's deposition in October 1470, but while she was at the monastery she had been so impressed by the monastic life and distinctive program of Brigittine divine service that she "ordered her heart to be despatched to Syon immediately after her death, paid £100 and more for the insertion of herself and her relatives in the martyrology and adopted elements of the Syon office of compline in her own mortuary chapel."[119]

Many factors surely were involved in Margaret's, Cecily's, and Margaret's interest in Brigittine monasticism, including political factors discussed in the next chapter. A final illustration from the life of Margaret, Lady Hungerford, highlights, however, the usefulness of Brigittine interpretive schemes in women's negotiations of the spiritual and the material.[120] The seal Margaret used as a widow depicts a woman kneeling, surrounded by flowers and foliage, with a book on her lap; in the background are the arms of her father and her late husband. Carol M. Meale notes that the kneeling woman recalls "Continental representations of the Virgin of Humility" and that "the presence of the book is reminiscent of Annunciation scenes in which the Virgin is shown at her devotions."[121] In considering the seal, Meale asks, "Is the symbolism of the seal therefore more complex than it first appears, perhaps designed as a pious gloss on the public assertiveness of Margaret's political role?"[122] I believe that, in light of Margaret's intimate knowledge of Brigittine texts and services, the answer to this question is quite likely to be affirmative. The image on Margaret's seal resonates with Brigittine portrayals of the Virgin as a figure whose authority is grounded in humility and who is a model of female wisdom and learning. Margaret's seal both strengthens her secular authority through religious imagery and makes a secular woman's strong authority spiritually acceptable, goals with which Margery Kempe certainly would have sympathized, as, perhaps, would the pregnant abbess had she been able to tell her own story.

An Afterword on the Afterlife of Margery Kempe: Carthusian Monks and Conduct Books

Margery Kempe and her *Book* illustrate the continuous, complex circulation taking place between the cloister and the world. As I have argued, Margery and those noble women who show affinities with her demonstrate that paradigms drawn from female monastic traditions could be independently interpreted by—as well as clerically imposed on—women living in the world. Furthermore, the history of Margery Kempe's *Book* reveals that the interpretation of female monastic traditions by a lay woman could resonate with, and perhaps even serve as an inspiration for, not only communities of nuns but also a male monastic audience.

BL Add. MS 61823, the only surviving manuscript of Margery Kempe's book, copied by the scribe "Salthows," belonged, by the late fifteenth century, to the Carthusian Charterhouse of Mount Grace in Yorkshire. Indeed, Karma Lochrie observes, "One could . . . speculate that Mount Grace might even have commissioned the copy of Kempe's book for its library."[123] The manuscript bears four sets of annotations, the fullest from the early sixteenth century by a reader who may have been a monk at Mount Grace.[124] This reader compares Margery's practice of weeping to that of Richard Methley, a monk at Mount Grace, as well as to that of Prior Richard Norton of Mount Grace.[125] Strikingly, at the point in the text when Margery enacts her simultaneous *imitatio Christi* and *imitatio Mariae* (*Margery Kempe* 68), embodying both crucifixion and childbirth in her roaring and wresting about of her body, this reader writes in the margin, "so fa RM & f Norton" (*Margery Kempe* 68 n. 7).[126] This reader's annotations are highly significant because, as Lochrie observes, they reveal that this (presumably) monastic reader "clearly found Kempe's roaring to be a legitimate expression of religious devotion and one with which he was familiar. His notes suggest an alternative tradition to the one which is used by modern scholars to define a spiritual élite. Although he mentions Prior Norton's 'excesse,' nowhere either in this comment or elsewhere does he hint that this behavior is aberrant or inappropriate."[127] The same Margery, whom a monk at Canterbury wished to enclose in a house of stone, was a familiar, even a laudable and perhaps an exemplary, figure for these later medieval Carthusian monks enclosed in their house of stone.

Margery's story does not end with the Mount Grace manuscript, though, and it is important to remember that Mount Grace itself was not necessarily a locus of unqualified support for Margery Kempe. It is worth noting that, in spite of the fact that there were some readers from Mount Grace who show approval of Margery, during her lifetime Nicholas Love, whose *Mirror of the Blessed Life of Christ* Margery literally yet radically embodies, was prior at Mount Grace. Far from holding up Margery, or anyone resembling her, as a model, the *Mirror* elevates as an ideal of female piety St. Cecilia, a "figure for privatized and silent devotion whose mode is affective and repetitive, not progressive."[128]

The Mount Grace manuscript is as close as we can come to Margery's own version of her story since "we do not know what happened to the version of Kempe's book that she dictated to her second scribe between 1436 and 1438."[129] Until the Mount Grace manuscript came to light in 1934, Margery Kempe was known only through the excerpts drawn from her text and published by Wynkyn de Worde in 1501 (entitled *A short treatyse of contemplacyon taught by our lorde Jhesu Chryste taken out of the boke of Margerie Kempe*) and Henry Pepwell in 1521. These editions, which present a Margery much more like Love's St. Cecilia than the woman we see in her *Book*, demonstrate that even an innovator like Margery Kempe could be made to fit the mold of female virtue shaped by the miracle of the pregnant abbess and the *Book to a Mother*. Margery is thus made to serve the interests of "male clerics and city fathers," a transformation that highlights just how closely related empowerment and containment really are in later medieval culture. Lochrie tellingly labels the versions of Wynkyn de Worde and Henry Pepwell as the "disembodied text,"[130] for in them Margery receives the same treatment that female monasticism receives in the *Abbey* and the *Charter*, and that maternity receives in the miracle of the pregnant abbess and the *Book to a Mother*. In other words, female particularity is removed, and the carnal is repressed in favor of the spiritual.

Wynkyn de Worde's text largely removes Margery's own voice from the *Book*, turning public speech and visions into "private acts of prayer."[131] The *Book*, which the clerical scribe describes at the beginning as a "schort tretys and a comfortabyl for synful wrecchys" (*Margery Kempe* 1)—sinful wretches presumably both male and female—becomes in Wynkyn de Worde's version a very different kind of treatise. It is abbreviated to "a series of short sayings, mostly of Christ to Kempe" and transformed into "a new devotional text for women."[132]

Pepwell's text is an even more dramatic transformation, since it represents Margery as "a deuoute ancres."[133] As Lochrie observes, "With the experience and voice of Margery Kempe expunged from the 1501 edition, all that remains in Pepwell's edition is for the woman herself to be revised."[134] Perhaps out of anxiety that Margery Kempe's *Book* might, even in the absence of Margery herself, lead wives astray as the Mayor of Leicester fears,[135] Margery is subjected textually to the enclosure she rejected, and, in spite of the Canterbury monk's wishes, managed to escape during her lifetime. It is this retroactive enclosure of her troubling female body, combined with the textual "disembodiment" which removes her female particularity, that finally make Margery a model of female virtue, a "good woman" on the "right" side of the wall, both literally and symbolically.

5

Kings, Saints, and Nuns

Symbolic Capital and Political Authority
in Fifteenth-Century England

Emma Rawghton and Richard Beauchamp:
Holy Women and Political Men in Later Medieval England

Richard Beauchamp, earl of Warwick, son of the Appellant Thomas Beauchamp, spent much of his life in the service of Henry V. Not surprisingly,
Henry V's will specified that Richard, a powerful and trusted friend, should
play an important role in the upbringing of the infant Henry VI. On June 1,
1428, Richard Beauchamp was officially designated as Henry VI's guardian. In
Parliament, Henry VI, with the advice of his "tres chers & tres amez Oncles les
Ducs de Bedford & de Gloucestre" and the other lords of the Great Council,
granted his "tres chere & tres ame Cousin" Richard "playne poire, auctorite,
lycence, charge & commaundement especialx, primerement & devant tous
autres choses, pour prendre garde . . . la conservacion & seuretee de nre
persone."[1] The young king made particular reference to Richard's qualifications for the position, noting his "loiautee, sen, sagesse, norture, prodomie, &
discretion."[2] Richard was also given responsibility for the king's education; he
was to teach Henry "bons Meurs, Letterurer, Langages, Norture & Courtoisie,
& autres enseignementz . . . & principalment de faire son loiale devoire
& diligence pour nous enseigner, movoir & exhorter, a l'amour, honour &
creindre nre Creatour."[3] Although Richard Beauchamp was not directly involved in government, he was, by virtue of his position as Henry's "master,"
clearly quite influential in the king's household.[4]

By 1432, things looked less rosy for Richard. The situation in France was
very unsettled in spite of the dispatch of Joan of Arc (in which Richard played
a role) and Henry VI's recently held French coronation. In England squabbles

between the Duke of Bedford, the Duke of Gloucester, and Bishop Beaufort continued. Even given his influence in the royal household, Richard Beauchamp was at this time increasingly concerned about his role and about "certain pressures" exerted on the king.[5] He perceived his position as Henry VI's "master" to be somewhat precarious; as Beauchamp said when he came to the council on November 29, 1432, the young king "blessed be god . . . is grown in yeeris in stature of his persone and also in conceit and knowleche of his hiegh and Royalle auctoritee and staat þe whiche naturelly causes him and from day to day as he groweth shul causen him more and more to grucche with chastising & to lothe it."[6] Beauchamp requested and received assurance that Gloucester and the entire council would "promitte to þe said Erle and assure him þat þei shul fermely and trewely assisten him . . . in chastising of him [the king] for his defaultes and supporte þe said Erle þerinne."[7] He also received assurance of the council's support "if þe King at eny time wol conceyue for þat cause indignacion ayenis þe said Erle."[8] In spite of this at least temporary reassurance, Beauchamp's position was far from being permanently guaranteed, since, as the petition to the council itself reveals, his role as Henry VI's master "was in practice subject to the final scrutiny of the king's uncles, Bedford and Gloucester."[9]

During the difficult early years of Henry VI's reign, Richard Beauchamp needed reinforcement for his position and authority. He found one source of such reinforcement in Emma Rawghton, an anchoress at All Hallows, Northstreet, York. Emma had a revelation concerning Richard Beauchamp in which the Virgin Mary informed her, in language comfortingly echoing Richard's praise-filled appointment in Parliament, that "thorowe the Reame of Englond. was no persone lorde ne other like hym in habilite of grace and true feithfulnesse. to vertuously norisshe & governe his [Henry VI's] noble persone accordyng to his Roial astate."[10] The question with which this chapter begins is why one of the most powerful men in the realm would find a relatively obscure holy woman useful in strengthening his political position at a time of conflict and uncertainty.[11] The case of Richard Beauchamp and Emma Rawghton thus provides the starting point for an exploration of the ways in which female saints, nuns, and holy women participate in those great later medieval causes of conflict and uncertainty, the Hundred Years' War and the Wars of the Roses.

The involvement of female spirituality in political conflicts was not a new phenomenon in the fifteenth century. In the fourteenth century, "imperilled hierarchies" turned for aid and support to women's mystical discourse during the Great Schism.[12] While this ecclesiastical turn to female mysticism as a legitimating discourse helped to prepare the ground for later mobilizations like those of Richard Beauchamp, the political importance of female sanctity and spirituality has still deeper roots. André Vauchez has famously described the "feminization" of sanctity in the later Middle Ages.[13] As married women and mothers were increasingly considered eligible for sainthood, more women were canonized.[14] Additionally, devotional practices centering on affective piety and the body of Christ—practices very much associated with women—achieved prominence.[15] In later medieval culture, women were increasingly a locus of the holy and a means of access to the divine.

Eamon Duffy has noted the "striking preoccupation with women saints and female sanctity" in English rood screens dating from the period 1450–1530.[16] Duffy describes the female saints depicted on these rood screens as giving "the ordinary Christian man and woman . . . a source of power to be tapped," power grounded in the saints' "special intercessory relationship with Christ."[17] The saints provided the image-donors with "privileges and promises" as "protectresses of the marriage-bed, auxiliary midwives, fire-insurance underwriters, and guarantors against . . . 'hateful pouert.'"[18] In this religious climate, it is not surprising that magnates and kings would tap for political ends the broad-spectrum "source of power" so useful to "the ordinary Christian man and woman."

For instance, the importance Henry V placed on holy women's intercessory power in relation to his French campaign of 1415 is evident in the will he made before departing for France. He declared that he hoped to "be received into Abraham's bosom, not through any merit of his own, but 'through the prayers of Mary, the High Mother of God.'"[19] He also specified that the thirty poor men for whom the will made provision to feed and clothe for a year should say daily the Office of the Virgin Mary. The will ends with the petition, "Mother of God remember thy servant Henry who places his whole trust in thee."[20] A similar linkage of Henry's successful military undertakings with the Virgin Mary's help appears in a prayer included in MS BL Cotton Julius E IV. The prayer, which includes traditional praise for the Virgin and requests for mercy, is headed "De hympno a gente Anglorum cantando ad laudem dei genetricis Marie propter gloriossam expedicionem Regem henrici quinti et pro succursu Regni Anglie dotis sue que cunctas hereses cum heresiarcha Iohanne Oldcastel suis precibus interemit."[21]

This prayer also suggests the propagandistic potential of women as a locus of the holy and a means of access to the divine. During the Hundred Years' War and the Wars of the Roses, propaganda designed to show that "God is on our side" proliferated. The revelations of female saints and holy women contained much material that could easily be put to such service, as the

English use of St. Birgitta's revelations regarding the Hundred Years' War illustrates. Diverse permutations of her revelations outlining England's superior claim to the throne of France and directing the warring parties to procure peace through marriage were repeated in English texts. In the original version of a revelation sent to Edward III and Philip VI, St. Denis asks the Virgin Mary to intercede with Christ to procure peace for France and end the slaughter of the French people. The Virgin Mary responds by saying that Edward III has the better claim to the French throne, but that, since Philip VI was elected and did not attain the throne with violence, he should remain king throughout his life. He should, however, adopt Edward III as his son and successor.[22] Alphonse of Pecha later edited this revelation, changing it so that Christ "is seen to invite the Kings of France and England to be reconciled *per matrimonium*, in order that the Kingdom of France might have a legitimate heir at its head, born of both races."[23]

Various excerpts from St. Birgitta's revelations were mobilized according to the state of the English fortunes in France. For example, in his *Regement of Princes* Hoccleve cites the "book of reuelaciouns of Bride"[24] in urging peace through marriage so that Henry V, "That right heir is, may the reme reioyse."[25] In 1435 at the Congress of Arras and in 1439 at the conference at Calais, the English negotiators relied on St. Birgitta's revelations to stress the English king's right to the French throne. At a time when things were not going so well for the English (probably around 1436), the *Tractatus de Regimine Principum ad Regem Henricum Sextum* cites St. Birgitta in prompting the king to make peace through marriage in an arrangement that "would cost the English people neither their honour nor the conquests which they justly held."[26] In 1445, even the French, typically hostile toward St. Birgitta because of her reputation as an English partisan, quote her revelation "Volo quod fiat pax per matrimonium" in suggesting that the marriage of Henry VI and Margaret of Anjou should provide the opportunity for a permanent peace settlement.[27]

In the later Middle Ages, then, female saints and holy women had great value as sources of propaganda and intercessory power. Their cultural value, though, was not confined to these spheres. Propaganda and politically driven attempts to secure divine intercession are parts of the larger process of making visible desired identities. Roger Chartier observes that "the authority of a constituted power or the power of a group . . . depends . . . on the credit given to (or withheld from) the representations they propos[e] of themselves."[28] In later medieval England, female saints, nuns, and holy women could enhance the creditability of representations of authority, and not only for such women as Margaret, Lady Hungerford, who used an image suggesting Marian authority on her seal, or Margery Kempe, who modeled her spiritual life and writings on St. Birgitta's (among other saints). Female saints, nuns, and holy women became sources of symbolic capital fit for kings, playing crucial roles in the process of constructing royal identities.

Henry V's Constructions of Kingship: Sacred Fathers and Saintly Mothers

Henry V faced a representational task even more difficult than that facing Richard Beauchamp. Creating creditable representations of his authority was particularly complicated for Henry because his desired identity was not only as king of England but also as king of France. The contradictory bases for these claims created difficulties; while the Lancastrians wished to exclude women from the English line of succession, the English claim that Henry was the rightful heir to the throne of France depended on succession through the female line. Henry thus had to negotiate between sacred fathers and saintly mothers in his symbolic program.

Simon Walker has observed that throughout the later Middle Ages, a royal claim to priestly "special sacral status" was "advanced with increasing insistence."[29] That Henry V was particularly adept at claiming this status is evident in the pageant, described in the *Gesta Henrici Quinti*, which greeted him as he entered London on November 23, 1415, following his triumph at Agincourt.[30] The opening sequence of scenes presents images of militaristic male sanctity combined with depictions of the sacred, masculine quality of English kingship. As the king and his party entered the city, at the drawbridge they encountered "a most beautiful statue of St. George" near which were depicted the royal arms and around which stood boys representing angels singing "Benedictus qui venit in nomine Domini."[31] At the conduit in Cornhill were the arms of St. George, St. Edward, St. Edmund and England as well as escutcheons of the royal arms (*Gesta* 107). Both of these scenes, with their stress on male English national saints and royal coats of arms, emphasize a sacred, male, English lineage for Henry. Henry, who, as the boys' song indicates, comes "in the name of the Lord," is the rightful heir to a male transmission of kingship, to the name and the law of the Father.

At the entrance to Cheapside a scene appeared which most directly represents Henry V's sacral role as king of England. Here were "men of venerable old age in the garb and of the number of the apostles, having the names of the twelve apostles written in front of them, together with twelve kings of the

English succession, martyrs and confessors" (*Gesta* 107). These figures sang the psalm "Salvasti enim nos de affligentibus nos, et odientes nos confudisti," and they presented Henry with "round leaves of silver intermingled with wafers of bread, equally thin and of the same size and shape, and wine from the pipes" (*Gesta* 107–9). In this scene, Henry becomes part of Christ's lineage of apostolic succession. As he receives Eucharistic elements which manifest his priestly status, he is simultaneously incorporated into a male line of English holy kings, "martyrs and confessors." The psalm speaking of salvation further reinforces his participation in Christ's lineage as a savior of his people.[32]

That the depictions of sacral, Christological kingship are so aggressively masculine and so definitively English resonate with the Lancastrian need to deny women a place in the English line of succession. The celebration of Henry V's sacramental kingship in the pageant excludes women just as the priesthood excludes women. Similarly, the sacrament of the Eucharist is a male replacement of the female reproduction of the Incarnation. The Eucharist, Nancy Jay has observed, is, like many other sacrificial rituals, "opposed to childbirth as birth done better, under deliberate, purposeful control, and on a more exalted level than ordinary mothers do it."[33] The priestly, royal lineage depicted in this scene of the pageant, like the apostolic succession of the clergy with which it is connected, makes visible "a truly perfect 'eternal line of descent,' in which authority descends from father to father, through the one 'Son made perfect forever,' in a line no longer directly dependent on women's reproductive powers for continuity."[34]

Henry V's desired royal identity was, however, not only as king of England but also as king of France—the latter a claim that depended on acknowledging the legitimate presence of women in the line of succession. Although the apostolic depiction of Christological kingship erased women from lineages, Christological kingship proved to be a remarkably supple construction in Lancastrian hands. In addition to an apostolic identity as king of England, Henry and his supporters put forward an "incarnational" identity for him as king of France. This representation of kingship, in which women are seen to transmit the divine into the human realm as the Virgin Mary does in the Incarnation of Christ, reveals another dimension of the symbolic value of female holiness. Just as the Word becomes Flesh through Mary's female body, the divine right of kingship is transmitted through women to Henry, in whom it is made incarnate. Although apparently contradictory in many respects, these apostolic and incarnational Christological identities appear in some of the same texts; both the 1415 pageant and Syon's foundation charter manifest "incarnational politics" as well as "apostolic politics."

The political importance of the Incarnation in connection with the English claim to France did not originate with Henry V. During the early part of Edward III's reign, Pope Benedict wrote to Edward urging him not to pursue his claim to France and denying the legitimacy of succession through the female line. English oppositional documents in turn justify the claim, and "the case of the Virgin Mary and Jesus is cited as an 'excellentissimum legittime successionis exemplum' (most excellent model of legitimate succession)."[35]

Although not the originator of "incarnational politics," Henry V benefitted from the connection of the Incarnation and succession through the female line in the 1415 London pageant. The apostolic scene at Cheapside is followed by a very different scene which brings the dynamics of the Incarnation into the political realm. At Queen Eleanor's Cross, the king is greeted by "a choir of most beautiful young maidens . . . singing together with timbrel and dance . . . this song of congratulation . . . 'Welcome Henry ye fifte, Kynge of Englond and of France'" (Gesta 110–11).[36] Significantly, this is the first scene in the pageant in which women appear, and this is the first time Henry is hailed as king of England *and* France.[37]

While male figures—priestly apostles and holy English kings—celebrate Henry as king of England, virginal women hail him as king of England *and* France, bestowing the title of king upon him and so echoing the transmission of the right to that title through women.[38] The stress placed on virginity in the account of this scene is marked. The Latin description of the young women reads, "Super quem pontem exivit de castro in occursum Regis chorus pulcherimarum puellarum virginum vestitu candido et cultu virgineo limpidissime ornatarum" (Gesta 108–10). The scene is very nearly overdetermined in its suggestions of the Incarnation. The virgins' song, directed at Henry, is a sort of inverted Annunciation in which the virgins speak, rather than receive, the divine Word which is made flesh in Henry. The virginal women's speech hailing Henry as king, bestowing the title and with it the divine essence of kingship upon him, also echoes the Virgin Mary's maternal, transmissive role in the process of the Incarnation. The virgins' speech thus makes visible on multiple levels women's legitimate ability to pass along the divine right of kingship and the title of king. Significantly, the verse account of the pageant, formerly attributed to Lydgate, says:

> Virgynes out of the castell gon glyde,
> For joye of hym they were daunsyng,
> They knelyd a doun alle in that tyde,
> "Nowell," "Nowell," all thei gon syng.[39]

The virgins' song of "Nowell" makes the moment of the Incarnation, and the fundamental role of women in it, definitively present as Henry is celebrated as king of England and France.[40] Since in addition to targeting the *Gesta* toward "home consumption," the author "may have had in mind the events at the Council of Constance" where England "needed all the support against France they could obtain" (*Gesta* xxvii), this incarnational portrayal of Henry's status as rightful heir to the French throne could have done much to further the English cause.

A similarly politicized emphasis on women's participation in the Incarnation is also evident in the provisions of Henry V's 1415 will. In this will, Henry endows thousands of Masses in honor of the mysteries and joys of the Virgin, and he desires that an altar "in honor of the Annunciation of Our Lady" be erected at his tomb.[41] That he specifies an altar in honor of the Annunciation, the moment in which God's Word becomes flesh in the body of a woman, be built at the monument to his eternal remembrance reveals a particular concern with, and desire forever to be associated with, women's ability to transmit that which is divine to the human realm.[42]

Henry V and the Politics of Monastic Foundation

The 1415 London pageant confirms Henry V's well-known skill in politically savvy religious activities. Jeremy Catto notes that in Henry V's reign religion became "a matter of utmost importance to the government";[43] public worship, he observes, "is a division of propaganda . . . and Henry V was a master of the art."[44] Nowhere is this mastery clearer than in Henry V's mobilization of the symbolic capital available from female saints, nuns, and holy women. In particular, Henry's devotion to St. Birgitta and his foundation of the Brigittine house of Syon in 1415 serve his complex efforts to create creditable representations of his English and French kingship.

Even beyond her revelations which make direct reference to the Hundred Years' War, St. Birgitta and her order were quite useful for Henry V's program of constructing explicitly English and explicitly Lancastrian identities as he consolidated his royal authority. The Brigittine order was quite new in 1415 when Henry V undertook the foundation of Syon. In fact, St. Birgitta's canonization and papal approval of the order were still vexed issues. Birgitta, who died in 1373, was canonized by Boniface IX in 1391. The Brigittine Rule (officially adopted as constitutions to the Rule of St. Augustine since Lateran

IV had prohibited new orders) was confirmed by Pope Urban VI in 1379. Since the canonization and approval took place during the Great Schism, reconfirmations were sought from and granted by John XXIII in 1415. He, however, was then deposed by the Council of Constance, leading to the need for additional reconfirmations, which were finally procured from Martin V in 1418, thanks largely to the urging of Henry V and King Eric of Sweden.[45] That Henry V chose to found a monastic house likely to face ecclesiastical obstacles, and in fact persevered in the face of the obstacles which did arise, suggests the importance of the Brigittine order to Henry's symbolic program.

Henry V himself laid Syon's foundation stone on February 22, 1415, and the foundation charter is dated March 3, 1415.[46] At this precise moment, he was making preparations for a major campaign in France which would culminate in the great victory at Agincourt. In fact, on March 10, 1415, only one week after writing Syon's foundation charter, Henry made an appeal to the city of London requesting funds for his intended invasion of France (*Gesta* 15 n. 2). That Henry connected his campaign in France with St. Birgitta and the foundation of Syon is also evident in his first will, dated at Southampton on July 24, 1415. This will appeals to St. Birgitta by name,[47] and in it Henry bequeaths one thousand gold marks to the nuns of Syon for building their house.[48]

The high value of the symbolic capital available from female saints and holy women becomes clear in the impressive outlay of material resources undertaken to obtain it. Henry V's huge expenditures in founding Syon are well documented. Brigittine houses were massively expensive to found,[49] and Henry V spent correspondingly large amounts on the construction and endowment of the community. The clerk of works' accounts for Syon indicate, furthermore, that these expenses were met largely from the chamber, Henry's "highly personal fund."[50] The symbolic capital accruing from both Syon's foundation and the divine services to be performed there was so valuable to Henry at this juncture as to be worth potentially depriving himself and his successors of certain material resources. The foundation charter specifies, "henceforth nothing whatever shall be delivered or paid at the receipt of our Exchequer aforesaid, for the use and behoof of us, our heirs or successors aforesaid, or of others whomsoever, until the aforesaid abbess and convent shall by fully paid in each year the said sum of one thousand marks."[51]

One of Henry V's chief methods of endowing Syon highlights the house's place in the symbolic campaign which accompanied his military campaign to claim the French throne. In the first year of his reign, all nonconventual Alien Priories were dissolved by an act of Parliament. Henry subsequently granted properties which had belonged to St. Nicholas, Caen, Fécamp, Lodgers, Marmoutiers, St. Bertin, St. Omer, and Séez to Syon.[52] Margaret Deanesly calls it "curious" that Henry should give these possessions to "what was at first a foreign monastery itself."[53] The fact that Syon is a Brigittine house, though, gives this "foreign monastery" special status. Largely thanks to her revelations regarding the Hundred Years' War, St. Birgitta was regarded, like St. George, as "an archetypically English saint."[54] That Syon, a house of her order, should receive lands and revenues previously in French hands symbolically reinforces Henry's authority over France.

A similar transaction in which property belonging to a vanquished foe was used to advance the foundation of Syon and Henry's concomitant acquisition of symbolic capital took place in May 1415. When the Swedish nuns and brothers sent to begin the community arrived, the religious were accompanied by a Swedish bishop and Swedish knights. Upon landing in England, the bishop and knights each received a cup and a silver-gilt ewer from the property forfeited by Henry, Lord Scrope, who was executed at Southampton.[55]

Scrope and the other Southampton conspirators were reportedly drawn to treasonous plotting by "the odor of French promises or rewards."[56] Scrope's property is therefore at least purportedly tainted by this French association as well as by the obvious taint of treason. The allocation of his valuables to Syon's cause is thus symbolically shrewd in several ways. Henry V's redistribution of the property not only marks the king's triumphs over the conspirators but also over the French with whom they were linked. Tainted goods are cleansed as they are put to a holy purpose, and goods which could have purchased Henry's destruction instead buy symbolic capital and representational credit. The choice of the Swedish escorts of the Brigittine religious as the recipients further reinforces Henry's self-representation as a just, devout, divinely elected king put forth in the interpretation of the Southampton episode in the *Gesta Henrici Quinti*. The use of Scrope's property to advance Syon's foundation provides an additional illustration of Lancastrian efforts to "convert the plot into a positive opportunity for propagandist advantage."[57]

As the connection between the foundation of Syon and the Southampton plot reveals, Henry V's associations with St. Birgitta and her order were valuable not only in the representational campaign accompanying the 1415 military campaign in France but also in Henry's quest for Lancastrian legitimacy in England. Although the community moved only a few years after its foundation, the original location for Syon was near the royal manor at Sheen, the manor so closely associated with Richard II, who had it destroyed after Queen

Anne's death.[58] In choosing this location for what has been called a "gigantic chantry for the House of Lancaster,"[59] Henry V symbolically forged a connection with Richard II, eliding his father Henry IV's usurpation of the throne.[60] The foundation charter for Syon similarly works to "carefully disguis[e]" the dynastic break, presenting the foundation "as an act of royal continuity."[61]

By locating Syon near Sheen, Henry V suggests another sort of continuity as well. In describing Queen Anne's death at Sheen in 1394, Adam Usk calls her "benignissima domina,"[62] and, as both Paul Strohm and David Wallace have demonstrated, Anne was well known as a political intercessor.[63] Sheen is thus a place with which "good women" who have special intercessory talents are associated; it seems fitting that Alceste, herself a virtuous, skilled intercessor, tells Chaucer's narrator to present the *Legend of Good Women* to "the quene, / On my behalf, at Eltham or at Sheene."[64] The Virgin Mary, in whose honor Christ tells St. Birgitta the Brigittine order is to be created and to whom (with Jesus) the community at Syon was dedicated, might, even more than Queen Anne, be called "benignissima domina." She and the Brigittine nuns residing at Syon repopulate the site with "good women." The nuns and Mary also carry on a tradition of feminine, politically informed intercession, in this case interceding, at least so Henry hopes in Syon's foundation charter, with God on his behalf and on behalf of his "renowned progenitors."[65]

The charter's emphasis on Henry V's lineage of "renowned progenitors" has the additional benefit of recalling the scene at Cheapside in the 1415 pageant with its "holy English kings, martyrs and confessors." The suggestion made by this apostolic scene—that Henry V receives a divine inheritance and so takes his place in a male lineage through which he is connected with Christ—is likewise present in Syon's foundation charter. Henry describes the act of foundation as stemming from his being "earnestly desirous of imitating" the "kings and princes and our most renowned progenitors" who "have been distinguished for the said meritorious excellencies" in service to the Church militant.[66]

The parallels between the propagandist initiatives of the pageant and charter emerge even more clearly, and take on additional significance, when one considers their broader disseminations. Frank Taylor and John S. Roskell, the editors of the *Gesta*, observe that this text is not "a 'chronicle' in the accepted sense, but a piece of deliberate propaganda" which had "undoubted immediate value for home consumption" (*Gesta* xxvii). So, while the pageant was only seen by those in attendance, it was likely to have been experienced textually by a wider, politically important audience. Beckett notes that the "prologues to Sheen's and Syon's foundation charters . . . afford as forceful a written expression of Henry's programme as the *Gesta Henrici Quinti*, which was not written until a year or two afterwards."[67] He admits that the charters probably were not widely distributed, but, he adds, "we should not forget that propaganda in the Middle Ages did not have to be mass propaganda to be effective."[68]

Like the 1415 pageant with which it has so many similarities, the foundation of Syon aimed for multiple, somewhat contradictory goals. Not only does the foundation resonate with both apostolic and incarnational representational programs, but the "renowned progenitors" it celebrates are also not always the same. In addition to creating a connection with his "adopted father" Richard II as described above, the foundation charter emphasizes that Henry V is son and heir of Henry IV, who had himself shown interest in the Brigittine order.[69] In 1408 Henry IV had indicated in a letter to Brigittine authorities at Vadstena that he had given permission for Sir Henry FitzHugh to keep two monks from Vadstena at Cherry Hinton. He also stated his desire "to be the special friend and protector of the order," petitioning the pope, albeit unsuccessfully, regarding his intention to found a Brigittine house in York.[70]

A letter sent to Henry V in 1415 from Vadstena explicitly connects Henry V's foundation with one planned by Henry IV. The letter reads, "even as Solomon magnificently consummated the temple which David his father planned to build, so also may the merciful integrity of your majesty bring to due fulfillment a monastery of this kind, which the devout intention of your generous father, hindered by death, could not achieve."[71] The reference to the "merciful integrity" of Henry's "majesty" and the comparison of Henry V and Henry IV to Solomon and David are clearly calculated to please Henry V. These elements emphasize just the sort of divinely approved, legitimate royal authority Henry desired to make visible. The letter also suggests a positive father-son resemblance in generosity and religious devotion, a spiritual inheritance that would help eradicate other, more potentially unsavory inheritances. Given these connections with Henry IV in Henry V's foundation of a Brigittine house, it is fitting that the foundation charter indicates that the religious at Syon are "to celebrate divine service daily for ever, for our healthful estate whilst we live, and for the souls of our most dear lord and father Henry, late king of England, and Mary his late wife, our most dear mother; also for the souls of John late duke of Lancaster our grandfather, and Blanch our grandmother."[72] This passage specifically calls attention to Henry V's Lancastrian ancestry rather than eliding the change of dynasty and stressing connection with the previous one as the charter does elsewhere.

It is in regard to Henry V's "incarnational politics" that the distinctive program of the Brigittine nuns' divine service has particular symbolic value. Unlike the divine service performed by nuns in other orders, the Brigittine nuns' offices, which vary with the day of the week, focus on the Virgin Mary, her work in the process of the Incarnation, and her role in salvation history. The female lineage through which humankind is saved, and especially Mary's maternal transmission of salvation, appear prominently in several services. In the service for Tuesday Matins from *The Myroure of Oure Ladye*, the Middle English translation of Brigittine lessons and offices, the text declares, "oure lady . . . is mother of her father. for she is the mother of god that ys father to all that he made."[73] The service for Sunday Matins also focuses on Mary's salvific role in making the Word flesh. The first lesson states, "Ryght so also had yt bene vnpossyble. that thys worde that ys the sonne of god. shulde haue bene touched or sene. for the saluacyon of mankynde. but yf yt had bene vned to mannes body."[74] It is Mary that makes the "vnpossyble" possible; it is she who "mynystred vnto hym the mater of his holy body."[75]

The political possibilities of Brigittine divine service further emerge in the antiphon for the Wednesday service of Tierce, which calls on "Mary borne of kynges kyn."[76] Even more significant for Henry V's incarnational politics are the multiple references to Mary's place in the Tree of Jesse, an intensely politicized emblem in the later Middle Ages.[77] For instance, a chapter from the Sunday Sexte service reads, "Iesse was the father of kynge Dauyd. of whose lynage came oure lady. and therfore she is called the rodde that came oute of that rowte Iesse. And oute of her spronge a flower that is oure lorde Iesu cryste."[78] Similarly, in the explanation of the verse "Virga iesse" from the Mass used at Syon, the *Myroure* says, "The rodde of iesse hathe flowred. a virgyn hathe borne god. and man. god hathe restored peace. reconsylynge in hym lowe thynges. Iesse was the father of kynge Dauyd of whose lynage our lady came. & therfore she is called the rodde of iesse."[79]

Pamela Sheingorn observes that early versions of the Tree of Jesse, including that of Tertullian, portrayed "the rod . . . to be the Virgin Mary, descended from David (of the house of Jesse)."[80] She points out, however, that "the Tree of Jesse was soon reinterpreted in the light of the genealogy of Christ supplied in the Gospel of Matthew, and a Tree of Jesse was constructed that focused on the male line."[81] This new version of the tree "obscured the formerly central role of the Virgin" and was often used for explicitly patriarchal purposes.[82] So, the Brigittine insistence on reinserting Mary into the Tree of

Jesse is of particular significance to the project of representing women's legitimate positions in lineages.

St. Birgitta and the Brigittine order have still another useful dimension in Henry V's representation of his authority over France. While I do not want to argue that Henry V's attraction to St. Birgitta and his decision to found a Brigittine house were motivated solely by political calculation, St. Birgitta's *Revelations* and the Brigittine order do, however, emphasize women's virtue, wisdom, and authority, qualities that had long been of English concern as they pressed their claim to the French throne.[83] When Christ reveals the rule to St. Birgitta, he declares, "This religion þerfore I wyll sette: ordeyne fyrst and principally by women to the worshippe of my most dere beloued modir."[84] Additionally, the *Myroure of Oure Ladye* highlights the extraordinary value accorded to women's virtue, wisdom, and authority in this monastic tradition. One of Birgitta's revelations included in the *Myroure* to explain why the Brigittine brothers say their offices before the sisters, makes known "that not wythstondynge the vse of the chyrche ys in many londes & contres to say fyrste the seruyce and houres of our lady, as lesse worthy. & afterwarde the houres of the day as more worthy; yet our lorde wyl do that reuerence to his holy mother, that in thys order the houres of her shall be sayd after the houres of the day to her most worshyp."[85]

Furthermore, in the organization of a Brigittine community, women's role in governing takes center stage. Mary provides the ideal of wisdom in the order,[86] and the abbess's authority is modeled on that of the Virgin Mary. Indeed, the abbess stands in Mary's place in the community.[87] Interestingly, in addition to advancing the previously discussed apostolic identity for Henry V, the foundation charter for Syon also emphasizes women's authority to rule. It enlarges the already-considerable powers granted to the abbess in the Brigittine Rule. The charter gives Matilda Newton, Henry V's choice as abbess, authority in *both* temporal *and* spiritual matters, rather than only in temporal matters as the rule specifies.[88]

Henry V's symbolic program involved posing creditable representations of both his English and his French kingship; additionally, it simultaneously trumpeted not only Henry's Lancastrian ancestry but also his place in an unbroken royal lineage. These complex symbolic undertakings thus had to hold multiple contradictions in precarious balance. While at times erasing women and foregrounding sacred fathers, Henry's symbolic program as manifested in his will of 1415, Syon's foundation charter, and the London pageant also attests to the valuable versatility of female saints, nuns, and holy women in the process of consolidating royal authority.

Yorkist Reinterpretations: Edward IV, St. Anne, and St. Birgitta

The value and versatility of the symbolic capital available from female saints, nuns, and holy women emerge more fully when one considers that Henry V is not the only later medieval monarch to turn to this source in posing representations of his authority. Edward IV is not known for special personal piety or for programs of religious foundation and reform like those undertaken by Henry V. However, just as Henry V turned to St. Birgitta and the Virgin Mary as parts of a symbolic campaign accompanying his military campaign to claim the French throne, a similar symbolic program existed in conjunction with Edward IV's military campaign to reclaim the English throne in 1471.

A chronicle account by an anonymous Yorkist partisan describing Edward's march through England in the spring of 1471 tells that on April 7—Palm Sunday—Edward heard divine service in the parish church in Daventry. The chronicler recounts that during the service, an image of St. Anne, "shett, closed, and clasped, accordynge to the rulles that . . . all ymages . . . be hid from Ashe Wednesday to Estarday in the mornynge," suddenly "gave a great crak, and a little openyd."[89] The king and all those with him perceived this opening, and then, the chronicler continues, "anon, aftar, the bords drewe and closed togethars agayne, withowt any mans hand, or touchinge, and, as thowghe it had bene a thinge done with a violence, with a gretar might it openyd all abrod, and so the ymage stode, open and discovert."[90] Edward IV, who had during his exile "prayed to God, owr Lady, and Seint George, and . . . specially prayed Seint Anne to helpe hym" takes this miraculous event as "a good signe, and token of good and prosperous aventure that God wold send hym in that he had to do."[91]

This miracle, the account of which is not surprisingly absent from a Lancastrian chronicler's version of Edward's march through England,[92] is on one level, as Edward's own reported interpretation shows, a fairly straightforward, propagandistic illustration of divine approval of Edward IV as the true king. The Yorkist chronicler's account has broader symbolic resonances though. In 1471, Edward IV's claim to the throne was especially messy. Even in 1461, when he first claimed the throne, he "could not make his case on the basis of the agreement between King Henry and his father," since Henry VI was still alive.[93] The claim which Edward was trying to reassert in 1471 was won "by military victory, not in parliament."[94] In 1461, the Yorkists made their case for Edward IV by pointing up the harm that had befallen the kingdom during Henry VI's reign. This strategy led to Edward being, in effect, hoist on his own petard in 1470 when Richard Neville, earl of Warwick, accused him of causing the "realme to falle in grete pouerte of myserie."[95]

In this context, St. Anne is an ideal saint to perform a Yorkist miracle. Official recognition in England of the cult of St. Anne came in 1382 when Pope Urban ordered that, in celebration of Richard II's marriage to Anne of Bohemia, the English Church was to observe the feast of the queen's name saint. That St. Anne, so closely associated in this regard with Richard II, indicates her (and God's) approval of Edward IV creates for Edward a positive connection with Richard and his lineage much like that Henry V tried so frequently to suggest. This connection works to counterbalance the negative comparisons Richard Neville made between Edward IV and his forebears Edward II, Richard II, and Henry VI.[96]

Even more importantly, St. Anne's approval of Edward suggests his place as the rightful successor in Richard II's line, giving him a less-easily contested claim to the throne than one resting either on military victory or parliamentary agreement. The connection suggested by St. Anne's miraculous approval points to Edward as a member of a de jure lineage of kings, a lineage unlike that of the Lancastrians, who were, according to Edward IV's declaration in 1460, "kings de facto but not de jure because of Henry IV's 'intrusion and usurpation.' "[97]

The combination of St. Anne and St. George, the English national saint, as particular recipients of Edward IV's devotion further reinforces the suggestion of Edward IV's place in a sacred, unbroken line of English kings, a lineage much like those depicted at Cornhill and Cheapside in Henry V's London pageant of 1415. Even the day on which the miracle is reported to occur is symbolically beneficial for Edward's identity as the divinely approved king. That he receives this "good sign" on Palm Sunday, just before he enters London, paints Edward IV as a messianic figure who, like Christ entering Jerusalem, comes as a true king to save his people.[98] Taking a page from Henry V's book, Edward in fact explicitly lays claim to this messianic identity, "justify[ing] his tenure of the Crown in the millennial terms of a conflict with, and victory over, 'our great adversary.' "[99]

Furthermore, since the Yorkist claim to inherit the throne from Edward III through Lionel, duke of Clarence (the elder brother of John of Gaunt from whom the Lancastrian kings were descended), did depend at two points on succession through the female line, St. Anne is especially symbolically freighted.[100] Anne, mother of Mary, grandmother of Jesus, founds a lineage in which women indisputably and legitimately transmit the divine. As Kathleen Ashley and Pamela Sheingorn observe, "Anne, more than any other saint who was popular in the late Middle Ages, embodies ideas of kinship, or connection, and of relationship."[101] Sheingorn also discusses numerous instances in which Anne is specifically used to validate female lineages.[102] According to Sheila Delany, Yorkist partisans have a history of using St. Anne for this political purpose. She argues that Osbern Bokenham, in his version of the life of St. Anne, "does all he can to make his reader aware of the maternal role" in the context of furthering the claim of Edward IV's father, Richard, duke of York, to the throne.[103]

Reliance on the symbolic instrument of female sanctity by Edward IV and his supporters did not end with St. Anne and the 1471 campaign. In her recent book *Impolitic Bodies*, Sheila Delany reads Osbern Bokenham's *Legendys of Hooly Wummen* as a Yorkist retelling of lives of female saints which competes with Lancastrian antifeminist texts. Bokenham's *Legendys*, according to Delany, work to create a "positive woman-conscious atmosphere"[104] in line with the Yorkist need to validate women's ability to transmit the right of succession, a right upon which the Yorkist claim to the English throne depended. Perhaps ironically, though, Bokenham's use of female saints in this political cause in fact echoes the mobilization of St. Birgitta by that strongest of Lancastrians, Henry V, whose hereditary claim to the French throne depended on the female line.

Indeed, the Yorkist symbolic program found St. Birgitta herself to be every bit as useful as the Lancastrians had. Women in the house of York are known for attraction to St. Birgitta and involvement with Brigittine foundations. In 1495, Cecily of York, who was particularly devoted to St. Birgitta, bequeathed a book of the *Revelations* to her granddaughter Anne de la Pole, who was prioress of Syon.[105] One of Edward IV's sisters, Margaret, was named as a trustee of the Brigittine house of Gouda.[106] St. Birgitta was even finally "embodied" as a member of the house of York when Edward IV "chose the then very unusual name of Bridget for one of his daughters."[107]

F. R. Johnston posits that the interest shown in St. Birgitta by members of the house of York may be linked with the use of passages from the *Revelations* to support the Yorkist claim to the throne.[108] In fact, some of the same passages of St. Birgitta's revelations used by the Lancastrian kings to support the English claim to the French throne appear in manuscripts of Yorkist genealogical propaganda which tout Edward IV as rightful heir to the English throne. For example, the relevance of *Liber celestis* IV.iii for the English claim to the throne of France and for the Yorkist claim to the throne of England (both claims depending on succession through the female line) is evident. Christ tells St. Birgitta of a kingdom in which "þe ryghtwys ayre" is not king. Therefore, Christ continues, "þe kyngdome sall noȝt com to þe first prosperite þat it was inne, ne to þat gode astate nawþir, to þe right ayre be sett vp, þat is of succession of þe fadirs syde *or elles of þe modirs*."[109]

MS Ashmole 27, a characteristic example of Yorkist genealogical propaganda, includes an excerpt from *Liber celestis* IV.iii accompanying:

a pedigree, which shows the descent from Louis son of Philip king of France, to Edward IV on one side and to Henry VI on the other. The name of the former is written at the top of a large circle, wherein is written in red "Hec sunt nomina istius Regis qui sanctam crucem xp'i invenient secundam diversas prophecias autenticas": that of the latter in like manner over a circle containing—"Hec sunt nomina Regis istius qui injuste coronam Britannie vel Anglie occupavit secundam easdem."[110]

Even though in the English view the right king of France and the right king of England would necessarily be one and the same, it seems somewhat labored to trace Henry VI's and Edward IV's lines back to Louis IX of France in making a claim for Edward IV's legitimate occupation of the English throne. The genealogy, though, actually serves a double purpose, combining "incarnational politics" and "apostolic politics." Together with St. Birgitta's revelation, the depiction of Edward's lineage as the favored one legitimates succession through the female line. It also provides Edward IV with a holy male ancestor in Louis IX of France (St. Louis). This connection is significant because it transfers to Edward, depicted as the rightful heir, the political advantage afforded to Henry VI by genealogies such as that in MS BL Royal 15 E VI.[111] That genealogy shows Henry's dual descent from the lines of England and France, a family tree capped with a portrait of Louis IX. Much had been made during the early part of Henry VI's reign of his dual descent from English and French holy kings.[112] For instance, in the "Ballade to King Henry VI upon his Coronation," Lydgate describes Henry as the "Royal braunche descendid from twoo lynes / Of Saynt Edward and of Saynt Lowys."[113] In MS Ashmole 27, the depiction of Edward's descent from St. Louis, accompanied by the rubric which specifies that he is the king "qui sanctam crucem xp'i invenient" bolsters Edward's own position in a holy line of kings who perform sacral and messianic roles.

MS BL Cotton Vespasian E VII presents Yorkist genealogical material similar to that in MS Ashmole 27, and it also includes a copy of *Liber celestis* IV.iii in support of the genealogy.[114] This manuscript, though, contains more than genealogical propaganda supported by excerpts from St. Birgitta's *Revelations*; it also incorporates a political sermon from Edward IV's reign.[115] The sermon begins by admonishing "euery trewe cristen man of god" to "be wise and well ware hough and what oppynyons þat ye hold."[116] It advises the hearers to "applye" their "werkes" to God's will, avoiding the devil's "fals suttilte" which "disseyuyþe many a man and woman . . . with fals couetous oppinions þat nowe regnyth in moche wikkid people."[117] As quickly becomes clear, these "wikkid people" are Lancastrian supporters.

The sermon continues by explaining that God's "preuites" are unknowable, and so the Holy Spirit "hath schewyd be his inspiracion in his blyssed seruantes and holy seintes vnto us þat is most nedful & medefull for us."[118] Getting down to political brass tacks, the sermon exhorts that, for "wele bothe of body & soule," all should pay attention to the revelations given to "blyssed seruantes and holy seintes" in order to avoid the "vengeaunce þat schall fall for synful wrongus done in olde tyme be disenherityng of kynges princis and lordis of nobil progeny."[119] Making the point even clearer, the sermon declares that "now ageine wrong for syne be right is flemed oute of the lond . . . anno 1460."[120]

Following this pointed pronouncement is a detailed list of those blessed servants and holy saints who have received the Holy Spirit's revelations about past wrongs and the current corrective—that is, revelations concerning the usurpation of the Lancastrian kings and the accession of Edward IV. This list provides dramatic illustration of the Yorkist co-option of St. Birgitta for their own symbolic campaign. "Birgitt" appears as one of those who "geve credens to all þeis before rehersed hough be inspiration have stablysshed to us þe verey true and feithfull right of olde tyme in diuerse reames long tyme wrongfully kepte out."[121] St. Birgitta, so closely associated with Henry V's symbolic program, becomes an explicitly Yorkist saint, keeping company here with none other than "Ricardus Scrope."[122]

The Yorkist textual annexation of St. Birgitta and her revelations is paralleled by Edward IV's strategic involvement with Henry V's foundation of Syon.[123] Henry VI, during his reign, had undertaken his own program of foundations, most importantly Eton College and King's College, Cambridge. In his search for endowments for his new foundations, Henry VI made "stringent inquiries" into the titles of grants made to Syon by Henry V. Subsequently, in the 1440s, due to flaws in titles, Syon lost Mount St. Michael's in Cornwall; the manor of Tilshead in Wiltshire; possessions in Spalding, Lincolnshire; and the revenues of Corsham Church, Wiltshire.[124] When Edward IV came to the throne, he immediately and systematically repealed Henry VI's grants to Eton and King's College, restoring them to Syon. For instance, a charter from the first year of Edward IV's reign shows that the provost and scholars of King's College, Cambridge, "quitclaimed to the abbess [Elizabeth Gybbes] and convent of Syon and their successors all their right, title, and claim" in the priory of Mount St. Michael in Cornwall, the manor of Tilshead, the manor and rectory of Felsted, the revenues of the Church of Corsham, and "all the lands, tenements and possessions which formerly belonged to the abbey of St. Nicholas of Anjou in Spalding."[125] Like Henry V's original endowment of Syon with properties acquired from Alien Priories, Edward IV's restoration of holdings to Syon symbolically emphasizes his authority and his victory over a vanquished political foe.

Edward IV's concerted generosity to Syon continued. In addition to standard confirmations of letters patent and liberties, in 1462 Edward also granted a charter of protection for all of Syon's possessions "from all actions of distress of grievances of any kind by land or by water, through his victuallers, purveyors, and other his officers or ministers whomsoever."[126] In November of that year, he pardoned Syon from "all and all manner of fines adjudged, issues, forfeitures, amerciaments, &c. which were by them due, pertaining or belonging to him."[127]

That Edward IV would take such a kindly approach toward a foundation with such strongly Lancastrian origins might seem contradictory or even counterproductive. When one considers the symbolic stakes, however, Edward IV's program makes a great deal of sense. By his grants to Syon, Edward in effect "purchased" the symbolic capital and representational credit previously belonging to Henry V. Indeed, Edward IV became known as the "second founder" of Syon, and in 1484 an office was adopted for Edward and his consort.[128] The degree to which Edward IV's takeover of Henry V's representational credit succeeded is highlighted by the community's decision to celebrate his obit along with Henry's on August 31, the anniversary of Henry V's death.[129]

Emma Rawghton Lives On: Competing Yorkist and Tudor Representations

To return to the case with which this exploration began, the later history of Emma Rawghton reveals that the symbolic value of holy women persisted through the fifteenth century and continued to be tapped in the quest to pose politically creditable representations of authority. Emma Rawghton's revelations are preserved in two manuscript sources, both produced in the closing years of the fifteenth century, many years after Richard Beauchamp initially associated himself with the anchoress. Emma's revelations are recounted in article 6 of MS BL Cotton Julius E VI, known as the "Pageant of the Birth, Life and Death of Richard Beauchamp, Earl of Warwick."[130] This manuscript was probably commissioned by Richard Beauchamp's daughter Anne, widow of the "Kingmaker" Richard Neville, earl of Warwick, between 1485 and her death in 1493, at which time it evidently was left unfinished. The revelations also appear in the *Rous Roll*, written in the 1480s by John Rous, who was chaplain from 1444 to 1491 in the hermitage of Guy's Cliff founded by Richard Beauchamp at Emma's behest.[131]

The different ways in which Emma Rawghton and her revelations appear in the *Rous Roll* and the "Pageant" provide a final illustration of the ways in which the symbolic capital of female holiness could be manipulated for political purposes.[132] The *Rous Roll* exists in a Latin and an English version. According to Charles Ross, both were written during the reign of Richard III, probably for Richard's state visit to Warwick in the summer of 1483.[133] Ross observes, "The purpose of the whole work is to please the current lords of Warwick, King Richard III, and his wife, Queen Anne Nevill, herself daughter of Richard Nevill, Earl of Warwick."[134] Rous is known for subtle, and not-so-subtle, politically motivated textual machinations. When Henry VII prevailed at Bosworth Field and, as king, became the effective lord of Warwick, Rous "sought anxiously to destroy all record of the praise he had accorded to Richard III."[135] In addition to writing anti-Ricardian pieces, he altered the Latin version of the *Rous Roll*, expunging the portrait and description of Richard III.[136] For some reason, though, the English version remains unrevised, and it speaks of Richard III "with respect."[137] The English version thus reveals Rous's earlier desires to please Richard III by presenting the legitimacy of his claim to the throne.

The English version of the *Rous Roll* also exhibits Rous's Yorkist sympathies in its treatment of the Lancastrian monarchs. Rous virtually ignores all the Lancastrian kings; he does not mention Henry IV at all, and the only reference to Henry V is a brief note that he granted privileges to the town of Warwick. Although Richard Beauchamp, for whom Rous includes a long discussion, spent much time in the service of Henry V, Rous omits all information concerning Beauchamp's service to that king. Rous does note that Richard Beauchamp "was maister to kyng herre the syxt in hys tender age and with the helpe of the land crownyd hym twies at Westmystre as for kyng of England and at paris for kyng of fraunce."[138]

Significantly, although he does include the revelations Emma told to Richard Beauchamp concerning the founding of the chantry at Guy's Cliff (thus using Emma to enhance the prestige of his chantry and, concomitantly, his own authority), Rous does *not* include her revelations endorsing Beauchamp's position as Henry's "maister." Even more tellingly, Rous does not record the revelations recounted in the "Pageant" endorsing God's approval of Henry VI's French coronation (see below). This strategic pattern of inclusion and omission reveals Rous's desire to deny legitimacy to Lancastrian rule, saving the representational credit for Richard III. In Rous's account, Henry VI is crowned "with the help of the land,"[139] not as a legitimate successor who has the approval of God and the credit-giving authorization of a holy woman's revelation. Richard III, in contrast, is "by the grace of god kynge of ynglond and of fraunce and lord of Irelond by verrey matrimony with owt dyscontynewans or any defylynge yn the lawe by eyre male lineally dyscendyng from kynge harre the second,"[140] a description which, tellingly, stresses his legitimate, male lineage.

The "Pageant," the product of the early Tudor period, displays a profoundly different political leaning and correspondingly portrays Emma and her revelations differently. That the manuscript was created to celebrate Anne's firmly Lancastrian father itself indicates the lingering Lancastrianism which is such a well-known aspect of the Tudor era. The pro-Lancastrian tone of the "Pageant" is enhanced by the great attention given to Richard Beauchamp's service to Henry V.[141] For example, the manuscript calls attention to the Southampton Plot discussed earlier in the chapter, portraying Richard warning the king of the "prevey and sodeyn Insurreccion of traiterous heretikes which sodenly by myght purposed to haue taken & kept the kyng undre their rule & subieccion."[142] It is not surprising that in the late 1480s or early 1490s Anne would have been feeling amenable to a text with Lancastrian leanings. She had been left destitute when Richard III died, and Henry VII made provisions for her in 1486 which were augmented in 1490. In return for these provisions, she disinherited her grandson by breaking the entail and remitting her rights to the king.[143]

In addition to the revelation concerning Richard Beauchamp's qualifications as Henry VI's "master" with which this chapter begins, the "Pageant" recounts one of Emma's revelations concerning Henry VI's coronation as king of France. The caption for the picture of his coronation as king of France reads, "Here shewes howe kyng henry was after crowned Kyng of France at Seynt Denys besides parys. / Of the which coronacion in France . . . it was the will & ordenaunce of almyghty god / as or blessed lady shewed by revelacion unto Dam Emme Rawhton Recluse."[144] Henry VI's identity as king of France— the hereditary claim to which depends on the female line—is made creditable by a holy woman's revelation, and significantly this revelation is delivered to Emma by the Virgin Mary.[145]

This account of Emma's revelations concerning Henry VI's coronation as king of France does more than simply echo his father Henry V's "incarnational" strategy of legitimating his claim to the French throne. By emphasizing Henry VI's divinely approved claim to France, the "Pageant" also bolsters the legitimacy of Henry VI's kinsman Henry VII's claim to the French throne. Significantly, this text is not the only Tudor-era manuscript using holy women's revelations in conjunction with a revival of the English claim to France. In the late fifteenth century, St. Birgitta's revelations about the Hundred Years' War were included in MS BL Arundel 66, a "volume of treatises on astrology compiled for the use of Henry VII."[146] The symbolic capital which served both Lancastrians and Yorkists so well in posing creditable representations of authority and consolidating royal identities kept its value into the Tudor era, an age known for its own skillful programs of both propaganda and self-representation.

6

Liabilities and Assets

Holy Women in the Literary Economy

Unstable Commodities: Literary and Political Mobilizations of Female Holiness

The symbolic capital available from female saints, nuns, and holy women clearly benefited the most powerful men in the realm—including kings—in representing their authority. It is thus not surprising that literary figures would also turn to this source, especially literary figures with pronounced political agendas.[1] One who did so is John Lydgate. The question of whether Henry V commissioned John Lydgate to write the *Life of Our Lady* is still not definitively settled. The editors of the critical edition suggest, however, that Henry V, grateful for the success of his campaign in France and inspired by Jean Galopes's presentation of the French translation of the *Meditationes Vitae Christi*, probably asked Lydgate to write the *Life*. Lydgate likely fulfilled this request around 1421–22, not long after the Treaty of Troyes officially named Henry V as heir to the French throne.[2]

Even if Henry V did not actually commission the *Life of Our Lady*, Lydgate was a staunchly Lancastrian poet. Given Lydgate's political loyalties, it is to be expected that the *Life* would resonate with both Henry V's Marian devotion and Lancastrian symbolic interests in matters of succession and women's places in lineages.[3] Lydgate's *Life of Our Lady*, then, is not only a devotional text but also a political one; it harmonizes with the incarnational representation of Henry V as king of France at a triumphal moment when he has most fully succeeded in consolidating that royal authority through the Treaty of Troyes. Like many of Lydgate's texts, it demonstrates the ways in which, in fifteenth-century English culture, political agendas were regularly played out in the literary as well as the religious sphere.

The *Life's* legitimizing efforts are, however, not only on Henry V's behalf. The *Life* seeks to pose a creditable representation of Lydgate's own literary *auctoritas*, an attribute accessed from a lineage of literary predecessors—a male lineage much like that of apostolic succession or holy English kings.[4] To gain a place in this literary lineage, and to inherit the *auctoritas* he desires, Lydgate must prove his own right of succession.[5]

Literary and political agendas merge for writers in the Yorkist political camp as well. As I have argued, Edward IV found female saints and holy women just as useful as Henry V did, even co-opting St. Birgitta and the Brigittine house of Syon for his own symbolic program. Similarly, Osbern Bokenham found female sanctity as valuable for his political and literary purposes as the Lancastrian Lydgate did. Sheila Delany has described Osbern Bokenham's *Legendys of Hooly Wummen* as a work of Yorkist propaganda which serves to refute claims that women cannot transmit the right of succession.[6] As a text which mobilizes female saints in connection with political concerns, the *Legendys* thus has much in common with Lydgate's *Life of Our Lady*. The frequent invocations of poetic genealogies in the *Legendys of Hooly Wummen* suggest that Bokenham also shares with Lydgate a concern with literary succession and the acquisition through poetic efforts of the patrimony of *auctoritas*.[7]

The benefits of associations between female saints, nuns, and holy women with political and literary figures were not merely one-sided. While those in the world reaped the symbolic benefits provided by female spirituality, holy women reaped corresponding social and material benefits from the support of powerful lay persons. As we have seen, the nuns of Syon enjoyed dramatic wealth and far-reaching privileges from the bequests of nobles of diverse political persuasions as well as from the provisions made by both Lancastrian and Yorkist monarchs. Further down the social ladder, Margery Kempe received financial support from those who desired her prayers,[8] and Richard Beauchamp paid the expenses of an anonymous anchoress from Winchester for coming to London so he could consult with her while he was in Parliament.[9] Association with powerful lay people also provided holy women with protection and legitimation which were especially crucial in an age of extreme suspicion towards expressions of piety that deviated from an evermore narrowly defined orthodox norm. Visionary women in particular needed such support, since they were vulnerable to accusations of sorcery and heresy, accusations that could be deadly.

Furthermore, the women who commissioned female saints' lives from Bokenham evidently perceived that having such texts written for them brought social as well as spiritual benefits; they too took advantage of the symbolic capital of female sanctity. In the prolocutory to the life of Mary Magdalene, Bokenham recounts that during Twelfth Night festivities Isabel Bourchier, countess of Eu, raised the subject of the legends he had translated, including the one he had recently begun for Elizabeth Vere, countess of Oxford (*Legendys* 5035–54). Then, Bokenham reports, while he and Isabel "were besy in þis talkyng" (*Legendys* 5062), she, as though anxious not to be outdone by another countess in being part of a currently prestigious trend, said that she desired "sothely / To han made" the "lyf in englysshe" of Mary Magdalene (*Legendys* 5071–72). This passage may also hint at political competition for the symbolic capital of female sanctity, since Elizabeth and Isabel were on opposite sides of the fence, so to speak. Elizabeth Vere's husband was the Lancastrian supporter John Vere, the twelfth earl of Oxford (whose Lancastrian sympathies led to his execution for treason in 1462), while Isabel Bourchier was the sister of Richard, duke of York.

These mutually beneficial associations were, however, not without problems on both sides as well. Even though female saints and holy women were repeatedly mobilized for interwoven political and literary agendas, they were not a trouble-free, easily manageable source of symbolic capital. Symbols are always difficult to control; that rival political parties made use of some of the same texts and figures attests to the malleability of the material. Any powerful symbol or symbolically-freighted construction can, furthermore, readily take on a life of its own. As Roger Chartier observes, "Works have no stable, universal, fixed meaning. They are invested with plural and mobile meanings, constructed in the negotiation that takes place between a proposal and a reception."[10]

Female saints and holy women are not simply inert commodities. The same traits that make them valuable for posing creditable representations of political and literary authority also enable them to shake up the balance of power. Rather than bolstering the authority of the one by whom she is appropriated, a female saint or holy woman may, in the negotiation between the proposal and the reception of a representation, instead confirm her own power. Female saints and holy women may also provoke representational crises because they elude representation to some extent; aspects of their virtue remain beyond or exceed significatory attempts.

As is true of the elements of female monasticism mobilized in the miracle of the pregnant abbess and the *Book to a Mother*, female holiness proves to be a double-edged sword. It comprises a valuable symbolic resource through which political and literary aims may be accomplished and through which living holy women may benefit. Precisely because that which is valuable for male clerics, politicians, and poets also enhances the status and authority of women, though, male authorities may find themselves in troubling positions as their ultimately masculinist political and literary agendas are destabilized by the women on whom they rely. Correspondingly, female saints and holy women may find themselves subject to efforts—textual, symbolic, and material—to limit their power, efforts resembling those leveled against the pregnant abbess in the miracle who is replaced under clerical control and against the real-life abbess of Syon, whose authority is reduced by ecclesiastical officials. In short, female saints and holy women, potentially great political and literary assets, are also potentially great liabilities. Lydgate and Bokenham, as well as the political factions they support, have to perform precarious balancing acts to negotiate between their masculine, clerical, and poetic authority and the authority of the women through and by which masculine, clerical, and poetic authority are established.

The Poetics and Politics of Maternity: John Lydgate's Life of Our Lady

As I have argued, the Virgin Mary holds an important place in Henry V's "incarnational politics." Because the Virgin Mary is the pinnacle of female virtue and holiness, she is also an extraordinarily valuable resource for Lydgate in his quest for literary *auctoritas*. Her perfection, however, makes her quite possibly the most troubling of holy women, since with her perfection comes an especially strong disruptive potential. Lydgate's *Life of Our Lady* illustrates the anxieties her latent power provokes, and it illuminates the strategies Lydgate adopts to cope with these anxieties as he works to craft a supporting role for maternal productivity in his masculinist literary and political agendas.

Just as political and literary agendas overlap in the *Life of Our Lady*, the anxieties Lydgate encounters in writing a life of the Virgin Mary are perhaps magnified because they mirror the tensions inherent in the Lancastrian project of constructing a dual monarchy predicated, as I discuss in Chapter 5, on the simultaneous erasure and celebration of women. The final moments of Henry V's progress through London on November 23, 1415, illustrate the necessary, constant resonance between poles, a resonance that leads to a fundamental underlying instability. The final scene of the pageant reinforces Henry's incarnational royal identity. In each of the niches encircling the tower on the way out from Cheapside toward St. Paul's stands "a most exquisite young maiden, like a statue, decked out with emblems of chastity, richly fashioned."[11] These maidens hold golden chalices "from which, with gentlest breath scarcely perceptible, they puffed out round leaves of gold upon the king's head as he passed by."[12] The leaves made of gold, that most precious substance, carry celestial and royal connotations, and the "emblems of chastity" associate the maidens with the Virgin Mary.[13]

Although the pageant itself ends with virginal women blowing gold onto Henry V in a visible representation of women transmitting the divine right to rule, this scene is neither the end of Henry's progress through London nor indeed of the accounts of the day's events. After this final scene, the *Gesta* reports that Henry proceeds to Westminster Abbey and St. Paul's. Although the *Gesta* simply mentions that Henry went to these places, Thomas Elmham's version of the events in the *Liber Metricus* gives greater detail. Elmham notes that at St. Paul's Henry was met by prelates who led him to the high altar where he kissed the relics, made an offering, and knelt at the shrine of St. Erkenwald. At Westminster Henry then proceeded to make an offering at the Confessor's shrine.[14] Henry's apostolic identity, his masculine, priestly, and English connections, thus also get one final reinforcement.

In its own uneasy negotiation between the incarnational and the apostolic, between foregrounding and suppressing women's reproductive work, the *Life of Our Lady* manifests not only the problematic nature of Lancastrian symbolic strategy but also the problematic nature of a literary culture in which masculine *auctoritas* is transmitted via the feminine medium of texts, especially texts about women's bodies.[15] There is always the possibility that women may exceed their carefully crafted roles in representational programs; there is always tension caused by the threat of the return of the repressed. In later medieval culture, this disruptive power of holy women often manifests itself as an ability to devalue or shut down textual production, to undermine the process of constructing creditable self-representations on which both political and literary authority rely.[16]

Mary's latent, destabilizing power surfaces when Lydgate directly confronts her maternal plenitude. In addition to making the Word flesh, Mary's virginal body produces milk which has marvelous powers. This productivity overwhelms Lydgate; he describes Mary's virginal milk as a powerful, feminine agent of salvation. Mary's milk, not Christ's body, redeems the sin of Adam:

For in that licour was full remedye,
Holy refute, and pleynly medycyne

Ayayne the venyme brought in by envye,
Thorugh fals engyne and malyce serpentyne,

. . . .

But nowe the mylke of thy pappes tweyne,
Benygne lady, is to vs tryacle—
Whiche in thy brest sprenketh fro a vayne—
Ayenst dethe to be to vs obstacle.
(*Life* III 1695–98, 1702–5)

The power of Mary's milk prompts Lydgate to such high praise that the balance
of power tips in favor of the maternal body and its essential role in redemption. Her milk supervenes Christ's body, the very body reproduced by male
priests in the Eucharist. Mary recaptures the reproductive process and its
salvific possibilities for women, so undermining the eternal apostolic lineage
of fathers. The inescapable presence of the maternal at the foundation of the
paternal economies of salvation and signification is revealed. In effect, Mary's
productivity "hijacks" the text, overwhelming masculine control of both salvation and signification as she exceeds the boundaries Lydgate, and Christian
orthodoxy, erect to confine her.

To reset the balance and carve out a supporting rather than destabilizing
role for Mary's maternal plenitude in his scheme of masculine privilege, Lydgate develops a dominant male lineage in which the figure of Joseph from the
Old Testament plays an important role. On one level, the Old Testament
Joseph calls to mind that other Joseph, Mary's husband, reminding the reader
that he too has a key part in the story. At the moment when Mary's maternal
power is strongest, the figure of Joseph is introduced to counter it with paternal power, a move echoing a trend that started in the fourteenth century, when
the Church began to promote the cult of Joseph as a way of balancing the wild
popularity of the cult of the Virgin Mary.[17]

On another level, the focus on the Old Testament Joseph and on Jesus's
specifically male lineage is a way of minimizing Mary's role in the process of
salvation. Lydgate engages in the process described by Luce Irigaray as the
erasure of the genealogy of women.[18] Though Christ's human body comes
from Mary, Lydgate does not even describe Christ in his human aspect as being
like Mary. Rather, he depicts Christ as a second Joseph, emphasizing his male
kinship and lineage rather than his female kinship.[19] He says that "criste Ihesu
hym-self" is a "newe Iosephe" (*Life* III 825), and he declares, "This yonge
Ioseph, this Ioseph the secunde, / Shall by his witte helpe and Releve" (*Life* III
813–14). The formulation that the "second Joseph" will "helpe and Releve"

humankind with his "witte" is a striking one. Salvation becomes a process effected through Christ's "witte," an aspect in which he evidently resembles his earthly male forebears, rather than through his human flesh which he received from his mother. As when the abbess's child succeeds the bishop in the miracle of the pregnant abbess, the masculine and the symbolic triumph over the feminine and the material.

The figure of the Old Testament Joseph appears on the scene to shore up the male line of descent precisely when the preeminence of this lineage seems most in jeopardy. Lydgate's strategy carefully delimits the possibilities suggested by the Brigittine reinsertion of Mary into the Tree of Jesse; he makes clear that Mary is the recipient of an inheritance which passes through her but which she does not herself inherit. Invoking the image of the Jesse Tree, Lydgate describes Jesus, the child born "of the blode to be preste and kyng" (*Life* III 950), as a "burion" and "floure" (*Life* III 964) which:

> Firste gan spring to Iesse, till it raught
> And so furthe dovne, till the buddes caught
> The holy sydes of a pure virgyne,
> To bere the frute that shall mankynde save.
> (*Life* III 965–68)

Jesus, "preued pleynly to be ayre" (*Life* III 957), receives his inheritance of priesthood and royalty through Mary, whose "holy sydes" transmit these divine qualities but do not permanently contain them. The incarnational and the apostolic are reunited in a formulation that reasserts the superiority of the apostolic lineage. Unlike the earlier passage which stresses the salvific power of Mary's milk, this passage emphasizes that it is the "frute"—Jesus's male body, repository of the priestly and royal blood which pass through Mary—rather than the maternal body that saves mankind.

Lydgate moves from a strategy of dynastic containment of Mary's maternal productivity to more explicitly bodily measures in Book IV. This book addresses Christ's circumcision on the eighth day after his birth according to Jewish law. This gendered and gendering ritual focusing on the genitals is a turning point in the text. The ceremony permanently marks the male child as part of a male lineage, revealing the way in which, as Irigaray says, "the male organ" is "transformed . . . into an instrument of power with which to master maternal power (*puissance*)."[20] Mary's plenitude, power, and the salvific food of the milk produced by her body are likewise superseded by the powers of Christ's masculine body and its products, particularly his blood, which receives a great deal of emphasis in this section. For example, Lydgate recounts how the "vertu" (*Life* IV 118) of the blood and water flowing from the wound in Christ's side gave Longeus his sight again. Furthermore, Book IV focuses not only on the circumcision ceremony itself but also on Jesus's name. Just as the male organ masters maternal *puissance* and Christ's blood replaces Mary's milk, Lydgate's focus on the Holy Name and its powers represents the paternal replacement of the womb with "the matrix of language" in order "to sever this uncomfortably close link to the original matrix."[21]

When the womb is replaced by the Name, Mary the producer of excessive signification is literally silenced. Mary is largely absent from the text in Book IV; the erasure of the genealogy of women is marked by the erasure of Mary from her own story. Mary is like a prop at the circumcision ceremony, simply holding Jesus and weeping at his pain. After the infant comforts her, she disappears from the text until near the end of Book IV, where, when she reemerges in Lydgate's prayer, she is firmly placed in the nonthreatening role of meek intercessor. The disappearance of the powerful, threatening Mary suggests the "original matricide" on the basis of which "society and culture operate."[22]

The Mary who is constructed in Book IV and who appears throughout the rest of the *Life* is quite different from the Mary of the Annunciation, the pregnant virgin, and the lactating mother, who, while certainly meek, is also frightening, able to escape imposed boundaries and disturb poetic production. Although the prayer in the last stanza of Book VI, the final book of the *Life of Our Lady*, calls Mary "blissede quene" (*Life* VI 460), the account of Mary's life does not end with a discussion her Assumption. Rather, it ends with a discussion of the origins of Candlemas. This feast celebrates Mary's meek act of purification which, since she was sinless, she underwent only to "fulfille the precept of the lawe / In euery thyng and not o poynt with drawe" (*Life* VI 20–21). Not only does Lydgate exclude Mary's Assumption and her triumphant reign as queen of heaven, but he also omits any discussion of her suffering at Christ's crucifixion. Much of Mary's own life, frequently included in other Marian literature, is thus missing from Lydgate's *Life*. By omitting treatment of her salvific maternal suffering and her celestial reign, Lydgate is able to end his version of Mary's life with the focus firmly on her "mekenesse."[23]

This "properly" feminine Mary who is created in Book IV and who appears in Books V and VI serves as an example of silence, meekness, chastity, and obedience for other women to imitate. Like the clerical writer of the *Book to a Mother*, Lydgate exhorts women at length to forsake both pride and finery, calling for them to emulate instead Mary's simplicity. For example, he says:

Ye wemen all shulden take hede—
With your perle3 and your stone3 bright—
How that your quene, floure of womanhede,
Of no devyse enbroyded hath her wede,
Ne furrede with Ermyne ne with tresty graye,
Ne marten ne sable, I trowe in gode faye,
Was noon founden in her garment,
And yet she was the fayrest for to see
That euere was vndir the firmament.
(*Life* V 380–88)

Again echoing the strategy of the priestly author of the *Book to a Mother*, the monk Lydgate refuses the powerful, maternal Mary as a model for women, presenting instead a meek, subdued Mary for women to emulate. The *Life* thus endeavors to become, as do exempla, monastic rules, and devotional texts, an apparatus working to contain women's potentially disruptive urges to wield power. Lydgate's *Life*, which contains so many representations of female authority and power, seeks to limit women's direct access to both material and symbolic resources, which they should properly transmit to male recipients.

While the *Life* ends with Mary as a meek intercessor, as a portrait of nonthreatening virtue and holiness, the struggle to get her into that mold is not an easy one. Along the way, the threats posed by Mary's plenitude spawn other anxieties for Lydgate. Mary's maternity has an added anxiety-producing dimension; not only does her valuable productivity overwhelm the signifying potential of writing, but her maternal work of making the Word flesh is also a competing "textual" production which Lydgate must transform into something he can use to further his quest for literary *auctoritas*.[24]

When Lydgate begins to face Mary's productive power in Book II, the section begins with a long allegory of the daughters of God. This allegory ends, significantly, with a seamless link between the female Mercy's textual production and Mary's maternal reproduction:

And fynally, mercy shall purchace
A Chartour of pardon, lyche this mayden clene
Whiche shall for man, be so goode ameyn
That he shal nowe escape dawngerles.
(*Life* II 334–37)

Mercy's purchasing the charter of pardon is like Mary the "mayden clene"'s producing the Word made flesh which redeems mankind. The story of the

Annunciation follows immediately upon the allegory, and "with that worde" (*Life* II 365) Mary conceives. Simultaneously "with that worde" which impregnates Mary, Lydgate's fears began to multiply.

The feminine textual production of Mercy and Mary are "lyche" (*Life* II 335). For Lydgate, though, Mary's productive body assumes the status of an original which the *corpus* of his text must reproduce, and he frequently expresses doubts about his ability to accomplish such reproduction in a way that will prove his literary legitimacy. The same incarnational textuality which proves so potentially empowering for women religious in Brigittine texts is troublesome to this poet concerned with masculine literary *auctoritas*. As outbursts of poetic anxiety occurring at key moments in Lydgate's confrontations with Mary's virginal maternity indicate, encounters with maternal power repeatedly force him to confront the paternal lineage of poetic authority. For instance, when Lydgate first faces the moment when Mary conceives, he recalls St. Bernard's feelings of inadequacy in writing about the Annunciation. He cites St. Bernard's lament, and, declaring his own inferiority to St. Bernard, questions, "How dar I thanne, be so presumpcwouse / I wofull wrecche, in any manere wyse, / To take on me, this perfyte high empryse" (*Life* II 411–13).

Faced with this dilemma, the strategy Lydgate mobilizes is a striking one, essentially comprising a triumph over his predecessor and an attempt to harness Mary's maternal power for his own literary ends. He creates a sort of incarnational identity for himself, inserting himself into the place of Mary rather than Christ. He compares his anxiety about his ability "To speke or wryte, in so devoute matier" (*Life* II 443) to Mary's being distressed when Gabriel delivers the momentous news to her. Lydgate writes:

> Lytyll wondir, though I tremble and quake
> And chaunge bothe countenans and chere
> Sythen this mayde, of vertu tresorere
> Perturbed was, in loke and in visage
> Of Gabryell to hir the mesage.
> (*Life* II 444–48)

By drawing a parallel between himself and the "mayde, of vertu tresorere" (*Life* II 446), Lydgate simultaneously claims an authority superior to that of his authoritative predecessor St. Bernard and seeks to overcome the threat posed to his ability to make poetry by Mary's ability to make the Word flesh.[25] The assertion that his experience resembles Mary's reduces the unknowability and enormity of her experience, making her less disturbing. Rather than devaluing Lydgate's poetic creation, Mary's incarnational textual production comes, through this incarnational parallel, to stand for and legitimate Lydgatean aureation.

The benefits of this attempt to resolve anxiety-producing confrontations with the superiority of the authoritative past and with Mary's maternal power do not, however, last long. Lydgate returns to the scene of the Annunciation, presumably with bolstered confidence, but again coming face-to-face with the process of the Word being made flesh knocks him off-track. Just as it does in the first encounter, contemplating the Annunciation throws him back against an authoritative textual tradition. This time he turns, as the chapter rubric says, to "Howe holy men by dyvyne likenesse wrote of our lady in commendacion of hir" (*Life* II 347). The accounts of what other writers have said in praise of Mary give way first to condemnation of those who do not believe in the virgin birth and then to a long account of "proofs," which are called "ensamples . . . / Of this matier according vnto kynde" (*Life* II 650–51).

While the use of natural proofs of the virgin birth is not unusual in medieval literature, the appearance of such a list at this precise moment has particular significance. The explicit motivation Lydgate gives for including the proofs is reformist, antiheretical zeal. The heading for this section reads "Autentike conclusiouns a gayn vnbylefull men that seyne þat Criste may not be born of a Mayde," and the section opens with the address:

> O blynde man, thorough thyne Inyquyte
> Why hast thou lost, thy Reason and thy sight
> That thou of malise, list not for to see
> How criste Ihesu, thorough his gret might
> To his disciples, helde the waye Right
> Thoroughe the gates, shette by gret defence
> Withoutyn brekyng or any violence
> Why myght he not, of his magnificence
> Within a mayde, make his mansion
> And yet she stonde, in the excellence
> Of maydynhede frome all corrupcion.
> (*Life* II 652–62)

There is, however, another dimension to Lydgate's lengthy recitation of examples. The list of nearly 300 lines of proofs from nature provides a defense against being silenced by what past authorities have said and by Mary's productive power. In this prime example of what Derek Pearsall calls Lydgate's strategy of "heaping-up . . . invocation, epithet, image, and allusion . . . meant to overwhelm with excess,"[26] Lydgate expands his incarnational identity by illustrating his own textual plenitude, the seemingly endless fecundity of his rhetorical amplification.

Lydgate's multiplicatory strategy, like the others he has attempted, finally proves to be less than satisfactory, and he moves on to stronger methods. His efforts to reset the balance of power disturbed by Mary's maternity lead him, as I have discussed, to the "original matricide." Similarly, his attempts to control the silencing power of authoritative tradition at last lead him to "kill" his poetic father. In other words, the father, bearing as he does the weight of authoritative tradition, must be eliminated in order to open up a discursive space in which Lydgate can reassert rightful control over the feminine and access his own masculine, literary authority.[27]

In another encounter in which the maternal provokes a confrontation with the paternal, Lydgate begins to doubt his own ability to make poetry immediately after contemplating a scene in which Mary successfully endures an ordeal to prove her virginity and so silences the unworthy ones who did not believe her—"thorugh hir merite, she hathe the mouthes shette / And lippys closed, of men that wer in were" (*Life* II 1600–1601). Lydgate in turn fears being similarly silenced as unworthy by authoritative predecessors with superior literary power. Lydgate first speaks of Petrarch and Tullius, expressing his admiration; they, though, because of differences in language and time, do not truly threaten him:

> But oo alas, the Retorykes swete
> Of petrak Fraunces that couthe so endite
> And Tullyus, with all his wordys white
> Full longe agone, and full olde of date
> Is dede alas and passed into faate.
> (*Life* II 1623–27)

Chaucer, however, is another story. As an English poet whom Lydgate describes as the first true poet of that tongue,[28] and as a poet who, although decidedly of an earlier generation, worked during Lydgate's lifetime, Chaucer is the figure from whom Lydgate must wrest his inheritance and in reference to whom Lydgate must prove his legitimacy.

As he does with St. Bernard, Lydgate employs with Chaucer the traditional modesty topos with a twist. He writes of "my maister Chauser" who "is ygrave" (*Life* II 1628) and wishes Chaucer were available to assist his efforts at poetic creation. Another, perhaps unconscious, wish beyond a humble desire for instruction or aid operates as well.[29] The figure of Chaucer is not simply an absent teacher or mentor. Chaucer is also an overwhelming force who effectively silences all other poets, a sun so bright he outshines all other stars:

> For as the sonne, dothe in hevyn shyne
> In mydday spere, dovne to vs by lyne
> In whose presence, no ster may a pere
> Right so his dyteӡ withoutyn eny pere
> Every makyng withe his light disteyne.
> (*Life* II 1638–42)[30]

Chaucer, although physically dead, is still for Lydgate a silencing threat. Slavoj Žižek, following Lacan, writes that there are two deaths, that is, natural death of the physical body and absolute death, which is the settling of accounts, the accomplishment of symbolic destiny.[31] Chaucer still lives in the "place between two deaths,"[32] and he is still a light bright enough to prevent another star from appearing. Only the second death can "ope[n] the way for the creation of new forms of life *ex nihilo*."[33] So, in order to avoid his own literary death, Lydgate must impose this settling of accounts on his poetic father while laying claim to the masculine authority and ability possessed by that father.

In a move with striking Lancastrian resonance, Lydgate's strategy toward Chaucer resembles his patron Henry V's strategy toward Richard II. Lydgate, like Henry V, wants to end the threatening productivity of a predecessor while claiming that predecessor's inheritance—royal *dignitas* for Henry V, poetic *auctoritas* for Lydgate. As Paul Strohm argues, Henry V reburies Richard II in Westminster Abbey to impose the "second death";[34] Lydgate similarly holds a poetic "memorial service" for Chaucer.[35] Lydgate, echoing the language with which Chaucer's Clerk disposes of his own literary father Petrarch ("He is now dead and nayled in his cheste"),[36] emphasizes that Chaucer is in fact dead and buried, saying:

> I can no more, but with all my myght
> With all myne hert, and myne Inwarde sight
> Pray for hym, that liethe nowe in his cheste
> To god above, to yeve his saule goode reste.
> (*Life* II 1652–55)[37]

By definitively placing Chaucer "in his cheste" in the silent grave, he snuffs out the bright light of the "sonne" who would prevent his own poetic light from shining. At the beginning of the next stanza, Lydgate resolutely moves on, saying, "And as I can, forth I woll procede" (*Life* II 1656). Having put the haunting, silencing specter of the poetic father "maister Chaucer" firmly away, he declares, "But leve all this" (*Life* II 1662), ending once and for all any doubt that Chaucer's silencing productivity is at an end. The remaining threat to a succeeding author's discursive space is thus safely neutralized, if only—as are the challenges to the Lancastrians' securely legitimated authority—temporarily, as we shall see in the next chapter.

The Problematic Necessity of the Feminine: Osbern Bokenham's Legendys of Hooly Wummen

On the face of it, the Yorkist symbolic program does not seem to be plagued by the same contradictions that underlie Lancastrian representational strategies. After all, the Yorkists did not need simultaneously to erase and celebrate women's reproductive work. Indeed, Yorkist interests would not obviously be served by excluding women from lineages or by denying their value. For the Yorkists, even more than the Lancastrians, women were necessary both to their actual dynastic claims and to the process of creditably representing those claims.

Even the Yorkists, though, did not propose that a woman should in fact *have* the right to rule, should in fact possess political legitimacy independently. Thus, given women's high value in the Yorkist symbolic strategy, the possibility that women might harness their power for themselves was all the more troubling. Yorkists too therefore had a vested interest in making sure that women's symbolic capital remained firmly controlled, that it was kept in the "right" hands, serving masculinist aims, rather than in the hands of the women themselves.

Osbern Bokenham faced a balancing act perhaps even more difficult than that faced by Lydgate. As a writer with Yorkist proclivities at a time when the Lancastrians were in power, he had to engage in delicate political finessing as well as to negotiate constantly between his own authority and that of the holy women about whom he wrote. In addition to the political and literary importance of female saints for Bokenham's projects, women loom especially large on his horizon because they are not only the subject matter of the *Legendys of Hooly Wummen* but also the commissioners and/or dedicatees of many of the saints' lives in the collection. Bokenham's anxieties about women's necessity as it impacts his own *auctoritas* are thus further compounded by his conflicted relationships with his socially powerful female patrons, relationships made even more complex by the fact that some of his most powerful and wealthy patrons (for instance, Elizabeth Vere and Katherine Denston) had strong Lancastrian connections.[38]

Bokenham reveals his dependence on prominent female patrons when he recounts the circumstances of two commissions, that of the life of St. Mary Magdalene by Isabel Bourchier and that of St. Elizabeth by Elizabeth Vere. In both cases he indicates his inability to resist their requests. Of Isabel Bourchier he says:

> I thowt how hard it is to denye
> A-statys preyer, whych aftyr þe entent
> Of þe poete is a myhty comaundement.
> (*Legendys* 5082–84)

In the case of Elizabeth Vere's commission, he declares that he writes the life of St. Elizabeth:

> At request of hyr to whom sey nay
> I nethyr kan, ne wyl, ne may,
> So mych am I boundon to hyr goodnesse,
> I mene of Oxenforthe þe countesse,
> Dame Elyzabeth ver by hyr ryht name.
> (*Legendys* 5051–55)

Bokenham—man, cleric, textual creator—is at the mercy of a woman's command; he who, according to each of these social positions, should be in charge is instead subject to a request he cannot deny.

Bokenham depends personally and politically on women, and so he celebrates their virtues. He is also compelled, though, to play down the power and necessity of the women for whom he writes and the female saints about whom he writes as he negotiates between his and their authority. One of Bokenham's techniques to ensure that masculine power prevails is to subordinate these disturbing women to male authority. To this end, Bokenham brings the male relatives of his female patrons into the *Legendys* much as Lydgate introduces the figure of Joseph into the *Life of Our Lady*. For example, in the prologue to the life of St. Anne, Bokenham says he has made the translation for "my frende DENSTON KATERYNE" (*Legendys* 1466, capitalization in original). In addition to subordinating her given name to her married surname, Bokenham specifically situates Katherine as the wife of John Denston in a prayer which asks that St. Anne grant them a son since they already have a daughter named Anne:

> Prouide, lady, eek þat Ion denstone
> & kateryne his wyf, if it plese þe grace
> Of god aboue, thorgh þi merytes a sone
> Of her body mow haue or they hens pace,
> As they a dowghter han, yung & fayre of face,
> Wyche is anne clepyde in worship, lady, of þe
> & aftyr to blysse eterne conuey hem alle thre.
> (*Legendys* 2092–98)

The prayer for male offspring underlines the social importance of a male heir, balancing the importance women gain through their necessity.

In recounting the scene of Twelfth Night celebrations where Isabel Bourchier makes her request, Bokenham positions her in relation to her brother the Duke of York, saying:

> In presence I was of þe lady bowsere,
> Wych is also clepyd þe countesse of hu,
> Doun conueyid by þe same pedegru
> That þe duk of york is come, for she
> Hys sustyr is in egal degre.
> (*Legendys* 5004–8)

Delany argues that this genealogy reveals Bokenham's Yorkist sympathies and manifests his desire to legitimate women's ability to transmit the right of succession.[39] Beyond emphasizing that women may indeed be conduits of power, I would argue that the text shows at least equal concern with demonstrating that they may *only* be conduits—not possessors—of power. In addition to the Duke of York, Isabel's four sons also figure prominently in the account of the festivities. I believe Bokenham includes these figures, who are basically irrelevant to the commission itself, to reposition Isabel in relation to the men who are ultimately the legitimate recipients of the power and resources which she, like all women, is merely to pass on.

Delany observes that the life of Mary Magdalene which Bokenham writes for Isabel Bourchier "is the legend that most fully expresses the incarnation of Jesus."[40] She also argues that the emphasis Bokenham gives to Mary Magdalene's preaching counters the negative portrayal of women and women's language in "masculinist ecclesiastical culture."[41] The prolocutory, with its

Yorkist genealogy, together with the legend, thus creates a powerful nexus of women's maternal reproduction and feminine production of signification—the very combination Lydgate finds so troublesome in the *Life of Our Lady*. Furthermore, the life of Mary Magdalene presents, as indeed many of the lives in the collection do, a figure of a strong woman who resists patriarchal authority, asserts her will, and speaks out—a figure who, like the virgin martyrs described by Jocelyn Wogan-Browne, is very much available for "resistant readings, which in particular contexts may constitute relative empowerment or recuperation" for female readers.[42]

The scenes in which Mary Magdalene preaches are especially significant in this regard, since she engages in an activity manifestly forbidden to women in the fifteenth century. In these scenes, Bokenham's Mary Magdalene has much in common with Bokenham's contemporary Margery Kempe. Margery, although she claimed she did not preach because she "come in no pulpytt,"[43] certainly spoke publicly on the Scriptures and on spiritual topics on many occasions, and indeed defended her right to do so with recourse to the Scriptures, saying, "And also þe Gospel makyth mencyon þat, whan þe woman had herd owr Lord prechyd, sche cam be-forn hym wyth a lowde voys & seyd, 'Blyssed be þe wombe þat þe bar & þe tetys þat ʒaf þe sowkyn.' Þan owr Lord seyd a-ʒen to hir, 'Forsoþe so ar þei blissed þat heryn þe word of God and kepyn it.' And þerfor, sir, me thynkyth þat þe Gospel ʒeuyth me leue to spekyn of God."[44] When one considers that Mary Magdalene is one of the saints with whom Margery Kempe claimed special affinity, and when one remembers that, as many critics have noted, Margery patterned her life and *Book* on saints' lives, the parallels between Bokenham's Mary Magdalene and Margery Kempe illustrate the very real ways in which such texts as the *Legendys* might suggest empowering, potentially transgressive spiritual and social practices to female readers.

It is not surprising, then, that Bokenham's life of Mary Magdalene, like the account of the Twelfth Night celebrations in the prolocutory, contains a remarkably insistent subtext emphasizing masculine superiority and feminine subordination to male authority figures. The life of Mary Magdalene begins by suggesting the problems that result from female inheritance, a focus which not only resonates with Yorkist concerns about women's proper, transmissive function in lineages, but also perhaps serves as a sly warning from Bokenham to his materially well-endowed female patrons. It is after Mary Magdalene receives, with her siblings, her portion of "þe possessyoun / Of here genyturs, Syre & Euchary" (*Legendys* 5382–83) that her career as a sinner really takes off. Mary Magdalene, a woman who inherits property, uses her patrimony to fulfill her own socially-destructive desires. Bokenham points out that once she has received her inheritance, "Youthe, abundaunce, & eek beute" (*Legendys* 5397) are joined in Mary Magdalene. These elements are, in Bokenham's clerical view:

> Mynystrys . . . vn-to insolence,
> And of alle vycys þe bryngers yn,
> And so þei were in Mary Mawdelyn.
> (*Legendys* 5399–5401)

Rather than being a passive conduit of resources, she is a recipient and an active possessor who, like Eve's daughters in the *Book to a Mother*, engages in both economic and sexual transgressions. Bokenham describes her sinful exploits with a concern for female reputation worthy of his clerical status. Bokenham observes that Mary Magdalene, having inherited her portion:

> al hir youthe in dislauynesse
> Of hir body so vnshamfastely
> She dispendyd, & in synfulnesse
> So comoun she was, þat ful pytously
> Hir name she lost, for of foly
> So in þe cyte was sprungyn hir fame,
> That "Marie þe synnere" þei dede hir name.
> (*Legendys* 5402–8)

The reprivileging of masculine authority plays a key role in the transformation of Mary Magdalene into a repentant sinner and apostoless. The initial dramatization of her repentance has, naturally enough, much in common with a scene of confession and clerical absolution. Mary Magdalene anoints Jesus's feet, weeps, openly confesses her sins (*Legendys* 5444–54), and then says to Jesus, "Reforme me now, lord, for þi mercy, / And in þis greth nede be my socour" (*Legendys* 5455–56). Jesus ultimately says that "Many synnys to hyr forgeuyn now be" (*Legendys* 5499).

More subtle, and perhaps more significant, are the dynamics of the scenes in which Mary Magdalene preaches. These scenes, which on one level highlight her independence, on another level work to ensure her properly feminine subordinate status as one who submits to and even upholds masculine clerical authority. Given the prominence of mass conversions effected by the saints in many of the *Legendys of Hooly Wummen*, and given that Mary Magdalene does do quite a bit of preaching, one would expect her legend to be filled with scenes of crowds converting to Christianity. The preacher whom Delany calls "remarkably effective"[45] is strikingly ineffective in this crucial regard, though. When Mary Magdalene first preaches in Marseilles, Bokenham describes "hyr eloquency / Wych from hyr mouth cam so plesauntly" (*Legendys* 5790–91), and he says that the crowd has "delectacyoun / Stylle to stondyn & here hyr predycacyoun" (*Legendys* 5792–93). She is eloquent; her words are delightful and pleasing—but the crowd does not convert on the spot.[46]

The importance of the fact that Mary Magdalene's preaching does not lead to on-the-spot conversions emerges fully in the account of her interactions with the prince of Marseilles and his wife. The prince and his wife worship pagan gods (*Legendys* 5801–4), and in their realm "goddys seyntys dere / . . . perysshyn myscheuously" (*Legendys* 5817–18). Mary Magdalene appears twice to the prince's wife, urging the wife and her husband to repent and to aid Christians. In these first two interventions, though, Mary Magdalene has no effect. On the third attempt, she appears to the prince and his wife together, and they agree to relieve Christians. The wife fears the consequences of falling into "þe indignacyoun / Of hyr god" (*Legendys* 5880–81), but they still do not convert then and there to Christianity. Mary Magdalene sends the prince off to "oure maystyr Petyr, wych at Room is" (*Legendys* 5891), and the prince learns Christian faith and doctrine from the pope (*Legendys* 6021–43). The transmission of the faith is placed back in the hands of the clergy; the process of creating new Christians is rewritten as a paternal act of sacerdotal reproduction, and the apostolic lineage of the fathers is reprivileged.

Maternal reproduction is, like Mary Magdalene's preaching, foregrounded only to be subordinated in the life of Mary Magdalene. The prince of Marseilles and his wife are unable to conceive a child until Mary Magdalene intercedes on their behalf; the wife then gives birth to the longed-for son and heir. On the voyage to Rome, though, the wife dies, and the prince leaves the hapless infant with her body on an island, commending his son to Mary Magdalene (*Legendys* 5991–6010). On the return voyage, the prince stops at the island, where he sees a child—his son—"al nakyd rennyng" (*Legendys* 6054). The prince then sees his son go to the dead mother's body and "in hys mowth anoon hyr pappe he hent / And began to sowkyn in besy entent" (*Legendys* 6070–71). As in the miracle of the pregnant abbess, a story that seems to be about maternal reproduction turns out to be about paternal reproduction after all. The dead mother's body has miraculously nourished the son for two years, preserving the male lineage. Mary Magdalene's reproductive miracle is finally a miracle for the father and son rather than for the mother. The mother, who is not restored to life until the prince asks that she be (*Legendys* 6088–94), is important strictly as a means of keeping the heir to the throne alive.

In another scene which echoes the miracle of the pregnant abbess, Mary Magdalene, who, like the abbess, has direct contact with the divine, also voluntarily subordinates herself to a bishop. As is the case with the abbess, Mary Magdalene has the advantage over this figure of ecclesiastical authority as a result of her direct contact with celestial beings; the power dynamics between cleric and holy woman are inverted. In spite of her interaction with angels, though, Mary Magdalene positions herself as a daughter to Maximin, whom she describes as "fadyr" (*Legendys* 6273). Clerical authority is reinforced even more strongly when, as she is dying, Mary Magdalene requests and receives from Maximin "crystys body" (*Legendys* 6279), since only he as a cleric can engage in "birth done better"[47] to produce that which she desires.

Bokenham's life of St. Anne reveals further poetic maneuvering to control a female saint who is not, as I will discuss later, contained through depictions of martyrdom.[48] After the prologue, the life of St. Anne proper begins with Bokenham contemplating Mary in her mother's womb and creating a female lineage for Christ:

> for wyth-in the space
> Of hyr wombe sche dede enbrace,
> Here that is of grace the welle
> Lady of erthe & empresse of helle.
> I mene that blyssed & holy virgyne,
> Modyr of ihesu oure sauyour,
> Marye. . . . (*Legendys* 1500–1506)

As valuable as this lineage is for the Yorkist symbolic strategy, and, as Kathleen Ashley and Pamela Sheingorn demonstrate, for legitimating female lineages in general, Bokenham does not let it stand.[49] Immediately after giving Christ's female descent, he turns to a long, complex genealogical passage explaining Anne's descent from David and the male genealogies of Joachim and Joseph. He points out that male genealogy is the truly legitimate genealogy, having scriptural authority:

> The custome of scripture not vsyth, lo,
> Of wymmen to wryte the geneaolgye;
> Wherfore, as þe lyne of marye
> Is knowe be ioseph & non othyr wyse,
> So is annes be ioachym. . . . (*Legendys* 1527–31)

Descent through the female line is valid only within a system where male descent predominates.[50] Like Isabel Bourchier, like Mary in Lydgate's *Life of Our Lady*, Anne and Mary must be properly subordinate to their husbands and their husbands' lineages.[51]

In the life of a saint whose very claim to sanctity is grounded in maternity, that maternity receives strikingly little attention.[52] As in the account of the Prince of Marseilles and his son, Bokenham places more importance on the role of the father than the mother in the legend of St. Anne, focusing at length on Joachim's life rather than Anne's. Bokenham recounts in detail the bishop's reproof of Joachim for his barrenness, his life in exile in the wilderness, and the angel's appearance to him announcing that Anne will bear a child. The angel who visits Joachim has previously told Anne that the "fruht" of her body "in reuerence / & honour schal be" (*Legendys* 1788–89). Anne seems strangely uncomprehending, appearing "astoyned" and "dysconsolat" after the angel delivers his message (*Legendys* 1793–94). Joachim receives much more detailed tidings; the angel tells him that his prayers are answered, and that Anne will have a daughter "Whos name clepyd shal be marye" (*Legendys* 1888).

The angel's tidings to Joachim echo the language of the Annunciation, but with a key difference. This is an annunciation to a father, who himself has a role in the child's conception, not to a mother who conceives without the participation of a man. Delany argues that Bokenham's life of St. Anne exhibits "an implicit maculism in conflict with the recent conciliar ruling" on the doctrine of the Immaculate Conception.[53] I would argue that Bokenham's maculism does not emphasize Anne's maternity, as Delany suggests, but instead demonstrates the importance Bokenham places on fathers and paternity, since in the maculist view, Anne did not conceive alone in a purely maternal act of reproduction, but rather "naturally," with Joachim's participation.

After the angel has made several appearances to him, Joachim returns home, and a remarkably brief account of Mary's birth—which might be expected to be central to an account of Anne's life—follows, part of which is taken up with conventional Marian praise (*Legendys* 1987–2000). At this point Bokenham recommends that the reader who wishes to read more praise of Mary in English should consult "owre ladyes lyf Ihon lytgates booke" (*Legendys* 2007), a work that also exhibits a maculist stance and, as I have argued, is much preoccupied with male genealogy and the reshaping of maternal productivity to support masculinist aims.[54] The rest of Anne's life is then glossed over very quickly with no portrayal of Anne as a mother nurturing Mary. Indeed, Anne's maternal function ends with the presentation of Mary at the temple when she is three years old. While maternity is certainly important to Yorkist representational strategies, anxieties about the importance of maternity seem to overwhelm Bokenham, as they do Lydgate. Correspondingly, Bokenham dwells on maternity as little as possible, striving to make it serve masculine authorities—political, literary, and priestly—without destabilizing them.

Although Anne has two other daughters also named Mary, Bokenham declines to write about them, coyly saying he has already done so in Latin (*Legendys* 2077–82). Since this translation is made for a woman who, presumably, cannot read St. Anne's story in Latin, it is likely that Katherine Denston, to whom the life is dedicated, as well as the female readers in the nunnery to which the collection was given, cannot learn what Bokenham has to say about this aspect of Anne's maternity.[55] The offhand remark that he has already told of Anne's other daughters in Latin, the masculine language of authority, points to a much larger agenda of male co-option of maternity in particular and female power in general. That which is specifically female is made incomprehensible and unavailable to women.[56]

Making women subordinate to male relations, erasing them from their own stories, and co-opting their power do not prove to be sufficiently potent strategies for Bokenham. Like Lydgate, he turns to death, the containment strategy par excellence. Death is, of course, a necessary condition of sanctity for both male and female martyrs, and indeed, in Western Christianity, for saints generally. Bokenham's depictions of martyrdom are, however, more than just necessary parts of saints' stories. The life of St. Ursula and the eleven thousand virgins demonstrates the ways in which unambiguous death prevents a troublesome multiplication of meaning. Death provides a means of containing a disturbing avatar of female power who strongly suggests opportunities for resistant interpretations by female readers and who threatens to overwhelm masculine privilege by escaping social, literary, and religious boundaries.

St. Ursula is a strong-willed woman who, not unlike Margery Kempe and the cunning widows who take vows of chastity, manages to manipulate the terms of her marital arrangements in accordance with her own desires. Having secured a promise of conversion to Christianity from her pagan fiancé and three years to preserve her virginity (*Legendys* 3195–3207), she then collects a company of virgins with whom she travels through Europe until they are martyred in Cologne. Along the way, they attract popes, bishops, kings, and queens to join their band.

Clearly, the idea of so many women roaming around attracting followers could be perceived as a case of feminine power, particularly reproductive power, out of control. Wogan-Browne notes a connection in the lives of virgin martyrs between the voyeuristic desires of Christian clerical narrators/authors and pagan torturers.[57] In Bokenham's life of Ursula and the eleven thousand virgins, a similar affinity seems to exist between the pagan princes' fear of the virgins' powers of conversion and Christian clerical anxiety about female reproduction. The pagan princes Maxym and Affrycane have "enuye" (*Legendys* 3339) of the virgins "For-as-mych as þei seyn dayly / Euermor encresyn her company" (*Legendys* 3340–41). They decide to ask their cousin Julian to slay the virgins because

> Thys was here feer, þat more & more
> Eche day shuld growen & encrese
> Crystyn relygyoun þrogh þer lore,
> And paynymry wansyn & discrese,
> And al þer heþin rytys cese.
> (*Legendys* 3342–46)

Bokenham the poet and friar, who similarly seems to fear, consciously or unconsciously, that the virgins' power will "growen & encrese," finds martyrdom a correspondingly useful tool.

Furthermore, to add to the distress they cause, not only do these conversion-inducing virgins reproduce seemingly without limit, but they also disrupt lineages. Ursula's marital machinations break the royal line, since she will produce no heir, and, when Pope Ciriacus joins the group, the apostolic succession is broken as well. The latter disruption causes extreme resentment among the cardinals, who "blame" Ciriacus for being so "bestyal" that he is willing to forsake his "glorye pontifical" to run after "a feu fonnyd wommen" (*Legendys* 3316–20). The cardinals are so exercised that they literally eliminate the break in the apostolic succession by denying Ciriacus's papacy; "They ordeynyd hys name, wyth oon assent, / From noumbyr of popys racyd to be" (*Legendys* 3330–31).

Bokenham's method of minimizing these threats is to remind readers at frequent intervals of the women's coming death. In the brief introduction, he points immediately to their martyrdom, noting that he will tell "The lyf, þe progresse & þe passyoun, / The cause þare-of & þe occasyoun" (*Legendys* 3142–43). Once the virgins assemble and set out on their travels, Bokenham includes two announcements of their coming martyrdom within twenty-five lines (the angel's appearance to St. Ursula in 3279–85, and then the revelation to Pope Ciriacus in 3300–3302). Additional mentions of the virgins' incipient deaths occur when the bishop Jacobus of Antioch joins the company (*Legendys* 3360–69) and when Ursula's husband King Ethereus and his mother join them (*Legendys* 3384–97). After these additions to the group, the account of the actual martyrdom itself quickly follows (*Legendys* 3413–60). The frequent reminders serve as reassurance that the potentially disruptive female force is not really a threat after all.

In fact, in death these previously roaming and reproducing virgins behave precisely as idealized holy women should. A dishonest abbot takes the body of one of the martyrs from the nunnery where she was buried, but the dead virgin returns to the place from whence she was taken, as if to exhibit a desire to be permanently "cloistered" (*Legendys* 3468–502). Furthermore, in death the virgins themselves reprivilege the masculine in the spiritual realm. One of the virgins appears to a dying monk and advises him that if he says eleven thousand Pater Nosters, she and the whole company of virgins will attend his death and accompany him to God's mercy (*Legendys* 3503–44). The choice of the Pater Noster rather than, for example, a prayer for aid addressed to the virgins themselves, highlights Bokenham's strategies of privileging the paternal and the masculine.

Bokenham relies on death to control not only the destabilizing power of female saints but also that of female patrons and dedicatees. Not satisfied with simply subordinating them to masculine authority, he regularly envisions their deaths. He contemplates the death of Katherine Denston along with that of her husband in the prayer that God provide them a son (*Legendys* 2092–98); that of Isabel Bourchier along with other readers of the life of Mary Magdalene at the end of the prolocutory (*Legendys* 5255–61); that of Elizabeth Vere when he first mentions her commission (*Legendys* 5055–61), in the prologue to the life of St. Elizabeth (*Legendys* 9534–36), and in the prayer ending the life (*Legendys* 10613–16); that of Isabel Hunt along with her husband John in the prayer at the end of the life of St. Dorothy (*Legendys* 4976–78); and that of Agatha Flegge in the prologue to the life of St. Agatha (*Legendys* 8334–52). In each case the reference to the patron's or dedicatee's death is part of a pious wish evidently calculated to please. The consistency of the references suggests, however, the kind of veiled aggression evident in Lydgate's laments for Chaucer. For example, Bokenham's resentment toward being subject to female power emerges in the account of Elizabeth Vere's commission. Immediately after saying that he cannot deny her wishes (*Legendys* 5051–52), he begins to contemplate the time when she will no longer be able to impose those wishes—the time when she will die:

Dame Elyzabeth Ver by hyr rhyt name,
Whom god euere kepe from syn & shame,
And of good lyf so hyr auance
Here in þis werd syth perseueraunce,
That, whan she chaungyth hir mortal fate,
Of lyf eterne she may entryn þe gate,
Ther-ynne to dwellyn wythowtyn endyng.
(*Legendys* 5055–61)

Bokenham needs Elizabeth's patronage and prays for the eternal life of her soul; he also desires, perhaps unconsciously, the end her death will provide to the disturbing implications of the power she wields over him through her patronage.

Bokenham clearly expends a great deal of energy negotiating his position in relation to powerful female saints, patrons, and dedicatees. Negotiating the position of the "mother tongue" as he writes for his female audience and tries to lay claim to *auctoritas* demands even more strenuous textual manoeuvering, however. Like the fifteenth-century translators of the Benedictine Rule for women, Bokenham is very much aware of the link between the vernacular and the feminine. It is the feminine vernacular that, even more than the female body, prompts Bokenham's confrontation with the literary authorities of the past. His status as a translator of Latin and a vernacular poet who, living under the shadow of Arundel's Constitutions, writes about religious material makes him especially wary of his position in the culture of writing.

Theresa Kemp notes that Bokenham addresses the problem of the lack of a vernacular tradition, a problem stated in "clearly gendered terms," by " 'immasculating' the vernacular, thus displacing the threat to the authority of his project posed by the feminine."[58] He humbly compares himself to Chaucer, Gower, Lydgate, and Capgrave, stating his inferiority. Then, though, he "legitimizes his speech by placing his own writing within the lineage of these other males. The placement of Chaucer, Gower, Lydgate, and Capgrave in the company of revered Latin authors provides Bokenham with the powerful vernacular fathers he needs to overcome his 'inflectyd' and 'cankeryd' 'modur-tonge.' "[59] Just as his female patrons and saints are made less threatening to his masculine *auctoritas* when they are situated in relation to male authority figures, so too is the feminine vernacular.

In attempting to resolve the anxieties about the legitimacy of writing in the mother tongue by "immasculating" the language, Bokenham encounters another gendered poetic difficulty. He himself is now in a precarious position in relation to the "powerful vernacular fathers" he has created. Again turning to the ultimate containment strategy of death, he strives to overcome this problem through imposing the settling of accounts on his literary fathers. Bokenham's strategy resembles that of Lydgate in the *Life*; just as Lydgate focuses on his immediate predecessor Chaucer, Bokenham focuses most sharply on Lydgate, who is the vernacular father closest in proximity.[60]

In the prologue to the life of St. Agnes, Bokenham declares his intention to translate St. Ambrose's version of the life, conventionally stating, as Lydgate does, his inadequacy to perform the poetic task at hand. Pallas informs Bokenham that the freshest flowers of rhetoric have already been gathered by Gower, Chaucer, and Lydgate "Of wych tweyne han fynysshyd here fate, / But þe þrydde hath datropos yet in cherte" (*Legendys* 4056–57). Lydgate, who did not die until 1450, is in fact still alive at the time of this life's composition sometime between 1443 and 1447. Bokenham's strategy of grouping him with two poets already dead serves, however, as a reminder that Lydgate will not live forever—he is "yet" in charity with Atropos, but he will not be so permanently.

This offhand, perhaps tongue-in-cheek mention of Lydgate's future death gains significance in light of an earlier passage in which Lydgate's status is ambiguously presented.[61] Again echoing a strategy used by Lydgate, Bokenham employs the modesty topos with a twist, engaging in what becomes virtually a burlesque of Lydgate's own literary father-slaying.[62] In the prologue to the life of St. Margaret, the first life in the collection, Bokenham writes:

> But sekyr I lakke bothe eloquens
> And kunnyng swych maters to dilate,
> For I dwellyd neuere wyth the fresh rethoryens,
> Gower, Chauncers, ner wyth lytgate,
> Wych lyuyth yet, lest he deyed late.
> (*Legendys* 414–18)

It seems unlikely that Bokenham, in Stoke Clare Priory, would not have known whether his famous political and literary rival Lydgate, still quite alive in nearby Bury St. Edmunds, were living or dead. As does Bokenham's contemplation of the deaths of female saints, patrons, and dedicatees, his expression of uncertainty about Lydgate's status suggests a desire to hurry him across the threshold, to accomplish his absolute death, thus ending his authoritative predecessor's potentially silencing productivity.

Bokenham not only contemplates the deaths of his "strong vernacular fathers" but he also devalues these fathers, minimizing their *auctoritas* to magnify his own. David Lawton points out that in the prologue to the life of St. Margaret, Bokenham makes the "customary bow" to his vernacular forebears.[63] Bokenham then proceeds, however, to engage in a refusal of "thylk crafty werk" (*Legendys* 98) laying claim to "souereyn cunnynge" which "is a piety and moral uprightness superior to the merely poetic cunning Bokenham admits he lacks."[64] Bokenham thus accomplishes a "devout dethronement of Gower, Chaucer, and Lydgate," managing to make "moral virtue out of poetic deficiencies."[65]

Bokenham goes still further in his refusal of the newly masculine vernacular tradition, and the dethronement quickly becomes less devout. In addition to differentiating himself from his "vernacular fathers," Bokenham discredits the classical tradition which informed their work by associating it with the feminine as something duplicitous and false.[66] In the prologue to the life of St. Agnes, Bokenham personifies the classical tradition as the female Pallas, saying:

> For Pallas certeyn would me neuyr lede
> Of Thully Rethoryk in-to þe motleyde mede
> Flourys to gadyrn of crafty eloquens.
> (*Legendys* 4046–48)

Pallas, the fickle woman, rejects the poet, and so he rejects her and her tradition of "crafty eloquens," a phrase which itself suggests the duplicity of the feminine. In the prologue to the life of St. Anne, Bokenham further dissociates himself from a classical tradition represented through feminine images which have negative connotations, including the *raptus* of Proserpina and the figure of Orpheus, ultimately destroyed by women, seeking his wife in the underworld.[67] Bokenham, like Lydgate, rejects the feminine Muses, saying, "And þe oonly, lord, I fle on-to" (*Legendys* 5224), thus continuing to feminize and devalue the tradition of "crafty eloquens."[68]

Bokenham does not desire the ability to utter "subtyl conceytys" (*Legendys* 5227) since such writing "greth dysceyt is" (5228). Significantly, such false writing is inspired by women; practitioners of it "specyally for þere ladyis sake / . . . baladys or amalettys lyst to make" (*Legendys* 5229–30). He goes on to say these poets "feyn" (*Legendys* 5231), comparing their writing to a peacock's tail (*Legendys* 5239–40). Bokenham opts instead to found a new vernacular tradition:

Wherefore, syth Pallas me þus dede rate
And drof me a-wey so sturdyly,
I wyl neuyr-more wyth hyr debate,
Nere presume to commyn Tullius medwe ny;
And þerfore spekyn & wrytyn I wyl pleynly
Aftyr þe language of Suthfolk speche.
(*Legendys* 4059–64)

Bokenham's strategy here is the opposite of that undertaken, in Ruth Nissé's view, by Hoccleve in the "Remonstrance Against John Oldcastle" and the *Regement of Princes*. Nissé argues that Hoccleve rejects the feminized vernacular used by the Lollards to write of spiritual matters in order to refound a masculine vernacular tradition of secular, nationalistic, Chaucerian writing.[69] Bokenham, on the other hand, having created a lineage of vernacular literary fathers to legitimate the mother tongue, then rejects their secular vernacular writing as feminized, claiming instead his true literary *auctoritas* as a practitioner of *spiritual* vernacular poetry.

Like the translators of the Benedictine Rule, Bokenham seeks to connect the authority of his vernacular with Latin, although not with the classical forefathers of the feminized, secular poets. Bokenham's Latin ancestry is that of masculine divine authority, that of the clergy, which is made incarnate in his sacred vernacular poetry.[70] Significantly, the prologue to the life of St. Agnes, the prologue in which he stakes his claim to vernacular literary authority, is the only prologue (indeed, the only section of any kind) in the entire collection that begins with Latin lines. Bokenham opens by writing, "Agnes sacra sui pennam scriptoris inauret / Et det ut inceptum perficiatur opus."[71] These lines both point to the female saint as conduit of power, as one who performs the properly feminine transmissive function, and, as do the Latin lines included in the verse translation of the Benedictine Rule, reinforce the masculinity and legitimacy of Bokenham's vernacular text (and of him as rightful heir) by cementing a connection to the masculine language of authority. Bokenham's paradoxical creations of feminized literary fathers and a masculine mother tongue in order to establish himself as the legitimate heir to true *auctoritas* are thus in effect further transformations of the dynamics of incarnation in which the role of the feminine is diminished. Creating a text is an act of paternal generation, as the prologue to the life of St. Margaret suggests:

For, as the old testament beryth wytnesse,
The sone hys fadrys wykkydnesse

Shal not bere, but if he it sewe;

. . . .

Wherefore, if my werk be sure,
Lete not disdeyn it disfigure
Of the auctour, I lowly beseche;
For sekyr that were a symple wreche,
As a lytyl to-forn now here seyd is,
To slee the chyld for the fadrys mys.
(*Legendys* 61–63; 67–72)

Although Bokenham begins the digression in which he founds his new vernacular tradition in the prologue to the life of St. Agnes with a humble request that readers "not despyse" his "rude" efforts (*Legendys* 4045), he ends with a confident, "like it or lump it" exclamation. After proclaiming his intention to write "pleynly" in the "language of Suthfolk," he says, "And who-so-euere lyke not þer-by, / Whereeuyr he lyst he bettyr do seche" (*Legendys* 4065–66). Bokenham evidently now feels secure of his authoritative place in a masculine, vernacular tradition since no more expressions of anxiety occur. Bokenham has established that, in the literary lineage, as in other lineages (for instance, that of Richard, duke of York) the male heir uses a feminine transmitter to establish legitimacy. As in the story of the prince of Marseilles and his son, however, the necessity of the feminine is finally made to seem merely utilitarian rather than threatening as Bokenham firmly subordinates the feminine in his assertion of masculine power and privilege.

7

Paying the Price
Holy Women and Political Conflict

The Hidden Costs of Holiness:
Richard Beauchamp at Rouen, 1431

In 1432, as we have seen, Richard Beauchamp, earl of Warwick, the staunch Lancastrian servant and "maister" of Henry VI, found in the visionary anchoress Emma Rawghton a valuable source of symbolic capital which he used to construct creditable representations of his authority at a time when that authority was in question. A mere year earlier, though, Richard Beauchamp was deeply involved in a series of events in which he had a profoundly different experience of the power of female holiness and the impact it could have on political authority. In addition to being Henry's "maister," Richard was also governor of Rouen castle, where Joan of Arc was imprisoned and interrogated in 1430–31. Beauchamp's roles as master of the young king and governor of the castle where Joan was incarcerated converged with perhaps too much closeness for comfort during Joan's trial. On July 29, 1430, Henry VI arrived at Rouen castle, where he remained through November 1431, when he departed for his coronation in Paris. Although the boy king and "his famous enemy" were kept well apart until Joan was safely executed on May 30, 1431,[1] the implications of this convergeance did not likely escape Richard's notice, and they should not escape ours.

Emma Rawton and Joan of Arc are in some ways obvious opposites. Emma's visions reinforced Henry VI's status as divinely-sanctioned king of France; Joan's voices supported Charles VII as the rightful king. Emma, an anchoress, lived a traditional life of religion in strict enclosure. Joan, an unprofessed virgin and self-styled messenger of God, traveled about the countryside in male attire leading an army. The two are also opposites in that they represented for the Lancastrians the flip-sides of the symbolic coin of female spirituality. The convergence of Richard Beauchamp, Henry VI, and Joan of Arc at Rouen castle highlights that the same source of symbolic capital which could ensure representational success could also lead to representational disaster. In the political sphere as in the literary economy, holy women were liabilities as well as assets.[2]

Richard Beauchamp was, of course, not the only prominent Lancastrian political operative at Rouen in 1431. Indeed, in the *procès de condamnation* of Joan of Arc, one finds a veritable Lancastrian "who's who" among the Burgundian clerical officials. Of particular interest are two men who figure prominently in the lives of female saints, nuns, and holy women examined thus far. Making appearances in Rouen in those fateful early months of 1431 were John, duke of Bedford, and William Alnwick, bishop of Norwich from 1426 to 1436 and of Lincoln from 1436 to 1449. Their involvement in an enterprise as politically important as Joan's trial is to be expected, given their high-ranking positions in the Lancastrian power structure. Because they were so committed to Lancastrian royal authority, on which their individual authority depended to various degrees, it is all the more worthwhile to explore their involvement with Joan of Arc in conjunction with their previous and subsequent interactions with saints, nuns, and holy women. Such intersections bring into focus not only the significance of Joan of Arc for the Lancastrians, but also the profound cultural anxieties that existed in fifteenth-century England about the power and value of female spirituality.

A Dress Rehearsal for Rouen:
John, Duke of Bedford, at Leicester, 1417

John, duke of Bedford, is generally credited, or, perhaps more accurately, blamed, as the architect of Joan's trial and execution. Militarily, he had, of course, much on the line in France. Joan's successes in battle (notably, her raising of the siege of Orléans, which was so embarrassing for the English) were already fading into the past after a string of failures when she was captured, though. Furthermore, her influence with Charles also seemed to be declining, since he eagerly sought a peaceful reunion with the Burgundians, a policy Joan detested. Why, then, did Bedford find it so crucial that the already-captured Joan be obtained from the Burgundians, formally condemned by the Church, and physically eliminated at great expense and trouble? Other propagandists for and supporters of Charles VII, including Joan's purported associate Brother Richard and his female followers Catherine de La Rochelle and Pierronne, were, after all, dealt with less dramatically, although not necessarily more mercifully.[3]

Some light may be shed on these questions by looking to an earlier period of political turmoil during which another holy woman made an appearance on the ever-sensitive Lancastrian radar. On July 30, 1417, Henry V set off on his second great expedition to France—the expedition which the *Gesta Henrici Quinti* was in part written to justify and support.[4] Tensions already running high in England were exacerbated by the king's absence. As James Hamilton Wylie and William Templeton Waugh pithily observe, "Oldcastle was still at large and Scotland still aggressive."[5] In fact, the distress caused by the unknown whereabouts of John Oldcastle increased in the late summer of 1417 when rumors emerged that he was helping the Scots by plotting with the duke of Albany (the governor of Scotland who supposedly had Richard II in his custody).[6] In the middle of August 1417, not long after Henry's departure, and indeed, evidently taking advantage of his absence, the Scots began their "Foul Raid," besieging Berwick and Roxburgh.

John, duke of Bedford, sprang into action. By September 20, 1417, he was at Leicester, where he assembled a large body of troops to combat the Scots. While he was in the area of Leicester, in spite of the intense military preparations which were underway, he took the time to have his men arrest Margery Kempe, fresh from her trial at Leicester and her interview with the archbishop of York. Although she has just been deemed *not* to be a Lollard, as Margery is preparing to cross the Humber "ij ȝemen of þe Duke of Bedforthys . . . arestyd hir as sche wolde a takyn hir boot. . . . 'For owr Lord,' þei seyd, 'þe Duke of Bedforth hath sent for þe. And þu art holdyn þe grettest loller in al þis cuntre er a-bowte London eythyr. & we han sowt þe in many a cuntre, & we xal han an hundryd pownde for to bryng þe be-forn owr Lord.' "[7] Bedford's agents connect Margery with Oldcastle, the notorious convicted heretic and purported rebel leader, saying that she is "Combomis dowtyr & was sent to beryn lettrys abowtyn þe cuntre."[8] It is not overly surprising that Margery, whose "style," as Nancy Partner has observed, "was Lollard," would arouse official interest, especially since Leicester was a known center of Lollard activity.[9] Given the pressing situation in Scotland and the vital military preparations underway, though, even in Leicester Margery must have been more than just another garden-variety suspected Lollard to warrant the personal attention of men specially deputed by Bedford, "Lieutenant au Roi et gardein d'Engleterre."[10]

The hyperbolic language of the men's address to Margery, along with the large reward of £100 they are reportedly promised for delivering her, suggest that she is indeed, as the archbishop of York says when she is once again hauled before him, at least on some level the most-feared woman in England— "I leue þer was neuyr woman in Inglond so ferd wyth-þal as sche is & hath ben."[11] The combination of accusations leveled against Margery during her second interrogation before the archbishop reveals much about just why she was so frightening. As is Joan of Arc after her, Margery is trouble on religious, political, and symbolic fronts, the very fronts on which holy women were in difficult times such mainstays for Lancastrian politicians and propagandists.

At this crucial juncture in 1417, Henry V's efforts to gain representational credit were in full swing. The *Gesta*, with its apostolic and incarnational depictions of his kingship, was circulating at home and perhaps at the Council of Constance as well. Additionally, Henry's efforts to get his new, symbolically significant foundation of Syon up and running were well underway; although no nuns had yet been professed, the will he made before departing in 1417 "confirms all the provisions of the will made before the expedition of 1415"—a will which included the handsome bequest of one thousand marks to Syon.[12] Margery Kempe, the self-styled St. Birgitta, was not playing along with the representational program. She was not praying in a nunnery or anchorhold for divine favor to be showered on Henry and the Lancastrian dynasty, nor were her revelations politically convenient, desirable ones confirming Henry's legitimacy as king of England and France or contributing to his incarnational and apostolic representational strategies. In fact, as with Joan of Arc after her, very much the opposite was true on both counts.

In her second archiepiscopal examination, Margery is not only accused of heresy and treasonous association with the Lollard rebel Oldcastle but also of meddling in a marriage. When Bedford's men bring Margery for her return appearance before the archbishop, her relationship with Lady Westmorland and her daughter Elizabeth is a matter of particular concern. Margery protests that she had not seen Lady Westmorland for "þis too ȝer & mor,"[13] but the suffragan persists, saying, "My Lady hir owyn persone was wel plesyd wyth þe & lykyd wel thy wordys, but þu cownseledyst my Lady Greystokke to forsakyn hir husbonde, þat is a barownys wyfe & dowtyr to my Lady of Westmorlonde."[14]

Part of the trouble with Margery's marital meddling lies in the fact that her alleged interference threatened a chain of connections involving major Lancastrian players, so jeopardizing familial alliances which had important implications for English efforts to resist Scottish encroachment. The political dangers of Margery's suspected Lollardy and association with Oldcastle are thus magnified by the potentially serious consequences for the contemporary campaign in Scotland which could have resulted from a breakup of Lord and Lady Greystoke's marriage. The Lady Westmorland in question, Elizabeth's mother, is Joan Beaufort, daughter of Catherine Swynford and John of Gaunt. Ralph Griffiths notes that "the Beaufort family and its 'connection'" enjoyed great royal favor from Henry V and Henry VI, favor that brought with it "social influence and economic benefit."[15] He points out that such favor "strengthened a position among the English nobility, particularly in the north country, whereby Beaufort blood coursed through the veins of a number of lordly families."[16] Joan first married Robert de Ferrers (Elizabeth's father), and, at the time of Margery's interrogation, she was married to her second husband, Ralph Neville, earl of Westmorland. He, with the earl of Northumberland, was then leading the force against the Scots at Berwick.[17]

John's father Ralph, Lord Greystoke and Lord Fitzwilliam, was involved in the very beginning of the Lancastrian regime; he "was one of the Lords who gave his assent in Parl[iament] 23 Oct[ober] 1399, to the secret imprisonment of Richard II."[18] John's maternal grandmother is Maud, the sister of Richard Beauchamp, earl of Warwick. Any disruption to the delicate balance of familial alliances cemented in part through the marriage of John and Elizabeth had the potential to be especially troubling in Yorkshire, where "Dacre, Neville, Fitz-Hugh, Percy, Mortimer, Greystoke, and others, including the king himself, jostled each other as landowners in the county and thereby laid the foundation for personal rivalries and family disputes galore."[19] At a time when unity was needed to face the Scots in the frequently tumultuous north, any ruptures of the Greystoke-Beaufort-Westmorland connection occasioned by the trouble in John and Elizabeth's marriage could have been distracting at best, disastrous at worst.[20]

The strategic complications which could have resulted from Margery's activities call to mind, albeit indirectly, the military troubles that Joan caused for the English in France. More directly, the fissures Margery's activities have the potential to open in the system of Lancastrian political alliances in England resemble, on a smaller scale, Joan's destabilization of the connection of the thrones of England and France—a connection cemented by Treaty of Troyes—when she reasserted Charles VII as the divinely endorsed rightful heir. In both Margery's and Joan's cases, though, practical military and political matters are not the whole story, or even the most important part of it. Bedford's concern with Margery's advice to Elizabeth Greystoke in fact points to the heart of the symbolic threat Margery poses to Lancastrian representational strategies. Margery, as Joan does later, destabilizes again and again paradigms of gender and authority crucial for the success of Lancastrian representations of kingship.

Margery's encouraging Lady Greystoke to leave her husband does much to undermine these vital paradigms. In fact, the actions of which Margery is accused are doubly treasonous. Not only is she tainted by suspicions of Lollardy and association with a notorious rebel, but her nuptial meddling also falls in the category of transgression Paul Strohm calls "treason in the household." Strohm observes that "the husband in his household and the priest in his parish participate analogically and symbolically in the regality of the king."[21] Margery's encouraging a wife to leave her husband is a method of fomenting rebellion against one "to whom faith and obedience are owed."[22] Given the treasonous dimensions of Margery's purported marital aintervention, it is not surprising that the suffragan says she "hast seyd j-now to be brent for" in giving Elizabeth such advice.[23]

The suspicion that Margery Kempe is engaging in "treason in the household" as well as seditious heresy emerges when she is first questioned at Leicester on the Articles of the Faith. During this interview, the mayor of Leicester demands, "I wil wetyn why þow gost in white clothys, for I trowe þow art comyn hedyr to han a-wey owr wyuys fro us & ledyn hem wyth þe."[24] Not only is Margery suspected of rebelling against divine and royal authority by embracing Lollardy but she is also suspected of stirring up a wifely revolt which Ruth Nissé Shklar calls "essentially an all-women's version of Oldcastle's Rebellion."[25] Both the mayor of Leicester's accusations and Bedford's interest in Margery's marital advice to Elizabeth Greystoke recognize, like the extended 1352 statute of treason discussed by Strohm, "the political character of . . . ostensibly non-political institutions."[26]

The political character of seemingly nonpolitical institutions also manifests itself in Joan of Arc's trial. Unlikely as it might seem given all of the other issues they had to occupy them, Joan's interrogators are tellingly interested in her "domestic" affairs, affairs which would appear to be, as Joan so often says, "not in their case." When her judges interrogate her in prison, they bring up her involvement in a lawsuit some years previously, asking her what persuaded her to summon a man from Toul for breach of promise. She responds, "I did not have him summoned; it was he who summoned me." She also claims to have "made no promise to this man," and goes on to declare that since she first heard her voices at approximately age thirteen, she "vowed to keep her virginity as long as it should please God."[27]

Joan's responses are significant because they suggest that she has not only refused to place herself under the control of a husband, but she has also rebelled against parental authority by refusing to marry the man chosen for her.[28] Accusations of rebellion against parental authority even make it into the final Twelve Articles condensed from the original seventy. Article VII condemns Joan for leaving home at age seventeen and for obeying her voices instead of her father, describing her as "impious towards her parents" and as "contemptuous of the commandment to honor her father and mother."[29] Joan's rejections of husbandly and paternal authority serve to reinforce her spiritual and political transgressions, making her all the more "seditious" in her heresy,[30] branding her more indelibly "a traitor,"[31] and helping to condemn her as unmistakably guilty, as Henry VI says in his letter written to the prelates and noblemen of France after her execution, of "crimes de lèse-majesté divine."[32]

That Joan's judges concern themselves with these domestic, familial matters emphasizes the importance of the associations between husband, father, priest, king, and God.[33] As we have seen, Lancastrian schemes for representing royal authority make much of such parallels, and indeed, they emerge quite directly in the admonishment given to Joan on May 23, 1431, after her faults have been expounded to her. In elaborating on the crime Joan has committed by not consulting "prelates or learned ecclesiastics" to enlighten her concerning her revelations, Pierre Maurice equates ecclesiastical and royal authority. He tells her to imagine that her king has instructed her to guard a fortress, not letting anyone enter without letters or other authenticating signs. He continues, "Likewise Our Lord Jesus Christ, when He ascended into Heaven, committed the government of His Church to the apostle St. Peter and his successors, forbidding them to receive in the future those who claimed to come in His name but brought no other token than their own words."[34] Even more pointedly, he compares Joan's refusal to obey the Church and submit to its judgement to a soldier's saying, "I will not obey the king or submit to any of his officers."[35] Invoking clerical, spousal, and paternal authoritative roles in conjunction with the royal authority which initially sets up the analogy, Maurice asks Joan, "What shall you say of yourself, who, brought up in the faith of Christ by the sacrament of baptism, have become the daughter of the Church and the spouse of Christ, if you do not obey Christ's officers, that is to say, the prelates of the Church?"[36]

Both Margery's and Joan's seditious heresy and domestic treason call the crucial equivalencies among authorities into question. Margery's supposed Lollardy and Joan's rejection of the authority of the Church Militant threaten the status of the clergy as representatives of God, thus undermining not only the basis of clerical privilege but also the Lancastrian monarch's identity as priest-king.[37] Similarly, that Margery, a wife who left her husband to travel independently and who literally paid the debt of marriage to gain the freedom of chastity, may have encouraged another wife to leave her spouse deals a further blow to domestic analogues of royal and ecclesiastical power, as do Joan's refusals to obey her father and to marry. These disruptions to the very foundations of Lancastrian representational strategies surely encouraged Bedford to be "wroth" with Margery,[38] and it is for many of the same reasons that he is later "wroth" with Joan.

Bedford's wrath with Joan of Arc emerges in the earliest extant reference to her by the English, "a letter addressed by the Duke of Bedford to Charles VII from Montereau on August 7, 1429."[39] In this letter, Bedford turns his attention immediately to one of the most celebrated aspects of Joan's career—her transvestism. Bedford upbraids Charles for having accepted the aid of "plus de gens suppersticieus et reprouvés, comme d'une femme desordonée et diffammée, estant en habit d'homme et de gouvernement dissolu."[40] Much critical ink has been spilled on Joan's male attire and its meaning. Indeed, the recorders of her trial spilled plenty of their own ink on this issue, since her judges returned repeatedly to her male clothes and short hair.[41] Her resumption of male attire, together with her return to credence in her voices, are in fact the issues into which all others finally collapse in her condemnation for relapse. I want to focus here, though, on a particular aspect of Joan's transvestism which prompted intense anxiety among her judges and which cuts to the core of Lancastrian fears about Joan's threats to their symbolic enterprises.

Joan's interrogators are especially concerned that she has attended Mass and received the Sacraments in male attire, and that she has every intention of doing so again. For instance, on March 3, "Asked whether she received the said sacraments [Eucharist and Confession] in man's dress, she answered yes."[42] On Palm Sunday, when given the option of attending Mass in female clothing or not attending Mass at all, Joan responds "that as far as in her lay she would not receive the Eucharist by changing her costume for a woman's." She then "asked to be permitted to hear Mass in her male attire, adding that this attire did not burden her soul and that the wearing of it was not against the Church."[43]

Susan Schibanoff has persuasively argued that Joan in men's clothing is not a "true fiction" (as are sacred images) but rather a "false lie" (as are idols, hence the link of her male attire to idolatry when her faults are expounded to her on May 23).[44] Schibanoff further observes that the trouble with a "false lie" is not that "it is in some way true but that it has the power to become so."[45] By attending the Mass in male attire, Joan, who suggests that a woman might "become" a man, raises the problematic possibility that such a woman might— like the rumored Lollard woman priests or the legendary female pope who shares Joan's name—engage in the masculine process of sacramental production on which clerical, and, by extension, royal, authority is founded.[46] Joan's presence at the Eucharist while wearing male attire calls up the spectre of a woman's disrupting the all-male priestly succession, so putting into question the authority that lineage conveys to Lancastrian monarchs as divinely-sanctioned kings of England descended through the male line. Put bluntly, therefore, the troubling presence of Joan at the Mass in male clothing highlights that she is not just a problem for Henry VI as king of France but also as king of England.

The emphasis given by the judges to Joan's presence at the Mass in male clothing is also, significantly, closely tied to the emphasis Margery Kempe's critics place on her white clothes, which are, as in the mayor of Leicester's accusations, frequently mentioned in conjunction with charges of heresy. Margery, the "fals loller" and "fals deceyuer of þe pepyl,"[47] is, like Joan, a "false lie," since Margery's white clothes signify a virginity she manifestly does not possess.[48] Joan as a female cross-dresser "threatens to 'adulterate' man."[49] Similarly, Margery, the mother of fourteen children, in her white garments threatens to adulterate virginity, that all-important benchmark of female sanctity, virtue, and value. Joan and Margery thus both problematize a quantity which serves as a "general equivalent"—that is, "a standard measure 'which by making things commensurable, renders it possible to make them equal'"—in the Lancastrian symbolic economy.[50] As a result, all exchange relationships and valuations based on these general equivalents are disrupted.

Adulterating virginity shakes the foundation of incarnational kingship, since female purity and virtue are essential in representations of a woman's ability to transmit the divine essence of kingship to the male heir who embodies it. Without the general equivalent of virginity, the Lancastrian monarch cannot be represented as "equalling" the incarnate Christ. Adulterating masculinity similarly makes suspect the apostolic lineage, which connects the Lancastrian monarch to the source of divine authority and which draws its validity from the exclusion of women. Without pure masculinity to serve as a general equivalent, the Lancastrian monarch cannot "equal" a priest-king descended from a holy, all-male line.

The dangers of Joan's threat to pure masculinity are perhaps even more significant than Margery's threat to pure virginity and extend beyond apostolic representations of Lancastrian kingship. Masculinity is vital not only for apostolic but also for incarnational representations of kingship, since it is crucial that the heir who makes incarnate the divine essence of kingship be unquestionably male.[51] Furthermore, the adulteration of masculinity puts in jeopardy the entire system of equivalent authorities—God, king, priest, father—so fundamental to Lancastrian representational strategies, for which the "principal axis" and the "central and centralizing metaphor that anchors all other metaphors" is "none other than the *paternal metaphor.*"[52]

Not only does masculinity, or, more specifically, paternity anchor all other metaphors, but the sacramental process of symbolic production performed by priestly fathers is also, in a sense, the general equivalent of symbolic systems. The cross-dressed Joan contaminates the sacred exchange of the Mass, which, with the process of transubstantiation at its center, is the locus par excellence of equivalency and signification in their purest forms. It is the site of "ideological reproduction by fathers . . . a perfect, ideal, and supernatural transmission of image and likeness."[53] By calling into question the absolute definitions of gender, which work to set apart priests and to validate their pure, sacramental reproduction, Joan threatens the process of signification itself. It is difficult to imagine a more serious threat to a regime which was, as Strohm says in his discussion of the yoked threats of counterfeiting and Lollardy, "reliant upon signs and more signs: more efficacious, more numerous, more motile and transferrable."[54]

Joan is thus prefigured by Margery Kempe in the religious, political, and symbolic problems she creates; indeed, it is because these three realms were so interwoven in Lancastrian representational strategies that both women's threats were so potent. Through their claims that they had special knowledge sent from God for themselves alone, both women acted as possessors rather than as properly feminine transmitters of the divine. They made visible in themselves competing representations of legitimacy, so diverting symbolic capital from Lancastrian representational schemes. It is appropriate, then, that John, duke of Bedford's engineering of Margery's arrest, his offer of a monetary reward, and the re-interrogation of Margery before the Archbishop of York read like a dress rehearsal for his involvement in obtaining and trying Joan of Arc. There is, of course, one critical difference—Margery escaped alive with the ecclesiastical stamp of approval only given to Joan after her death.[55] One wonders whether Margery's escape made Bedford all the more determined to ensure that Joan did not.

William Alnwick's Episcopates: The Lessons of Heresy

Like John, duke of Bedford, William Alnwick was an important figure in the Lancastrian hierarchy. In a dispensation granted to him in May 1421, he is named as Henry V's secretary, and in December 1422, he is referred to as king's clerk.[56] He was appointed keeper of the privy seal in December 1422, and he became Henry VI's confessor about 1430.[57] As bishop of Norwich from 1426 to 1436, Alnwick was also undoubtedly, like Bedford, well aware of Margery Kempe's activities. In fact, he was involved in the drama surrounding the attempts of certain residents of Lynn (attempts strongly opposed by Margery) to obtain privileges to hold baptisms and purifications in the chapel of St. Nicholas, which was dependent on the church of St. Margaret in Lynn.[58]

Alnwick further resembles Bedford in his vigorous efforts to eradicate Lollardy; indeed, his Norwich episcopate is known for an extended series of Lollard trials. Beverly Boyd observes that William Alnwick came to Rouen for Joan of Arc's trial fresh from sending three Lollards to the stake in his diocese, and she points out that Joan's beliefs concerning ecclesiastical authority resonate with Lollard beliefs. Boyd also notes that Alnwick and such other English clerics as Robert Gilbert involved in Joan's trial had ecclesiastical authority "uppermost in [their] minds" as they "sought to stamp out the Lollard heresy which had started with Wyclif and which had found new impetus on the Continent among the followers of Hus."[59]

For lay and ecclesiastical Lancastrians alike, the connections between Joan and the Lollards likely hit closer to home than Bohemia, however, and, as we have seen, the authority both the Lollards and Joan called into question was not only ecclesiastical but also royal. Alnwick, a cleric intimately involved in the Lancastrian government, thus had multiple reasons to be interested in eradicating the Lollards and Joan of Arc. Events during the summer of 1430 likely exacerbated his hostility toward both. Just after Henry VI departed for France in late July, Lollard activity seemed to increase just as it had in 1417 at the time of Henry V's second expedition to France.[60] During this tense summer "there occurred the most serious outbreak of lollard violence since 1414,"[61] and this outbreak, which culminated with the Lollard rising of 1431, "was very much a political kind of Lollardy."[62] These Lollards were, according to Margeret Aston, particularly interested in church disendowment and social revolt—"Secular disestablishment; the disendowment of lay lords together with ecclesiastical; the accession of Lollard nominees to property as well as to government: such, apparently, was the plan."[63]

Trouble on a national scale was brewing as early as September 1429, when the chancellor opened parliament with a reminder of the continued presence of heresy in England.[64] Lollard activity intensified through 1430, as did the government's response to it. At Christmas 1430, seven women, who seem to have been suspected Lollards, were put into Fleet prison for plotting the king's death.[65] In the early months of 1431, Lollard uprisings broke out across southern England, led by William Perkins (aka William Mandeville).[66] The rising of 1431 began on March 3 in St. Giles's parish, London. During its nearly three months' duration, "it transferred its centre to Abingdon, but radiated to other towns such as Coventry, Oxford, Salisbury, Northampton, and Frome, where lollard sympathies had remained strong, and continued to rumble in the capital."[67]

Trials and executions of Lollards in England provide a sinister counterpoint to the interrogation of Joan taking place simultaneously in Rouen. The heresy trials of sixty men and women begun by Bishop Alnwick in Norwich in 1428 continued through March 1431. Thomas Bagley, a priest from Essex and a lapsed heretic, endured a public trial in London in the spring of 1431, and on March 10 of that year, in a scene eerily foreshadowing events on the horizon in Rouen, he was "solemnly burned at St. Paul's cross with the maximum publicity in the presence of Gloucester and thousands of Londoners."[68] William Perkins, along with five of his compatriots, were captured in Oxford on May 19, 1431, and Perkins was beheaded on May 22, a mere two days before Joan would recant.

We know relatively little about the role of women in the Lollard rising of 1431, although clearly they did take part. When William Perkins and his accomplices were captured, "other assorted conspirators, women among them, were rounded up elsewhere and summarily executed."[69] The account of the rising given by Nicholas Bishop, a resident of Oxford, describes the rebels' "tresun" and indicates, "A womman a mayreswyf of Coventre for this cause al so be hedyd."[70] Whatever their role in the activities of 1431, women involved in religious life, whether orthodox or heterodox, posed for such clerics as Alnwick special dangers—both actual and potential—to be taken quite seriously. In contemplating the significance of William Alnwick's participation in Joan's trial, as well as the dangers she posed to Lancastrian authority and its representations, it is useful to return to Alnwick's roles not only as a scourge of Lollards but also as a diocesan visitor of nunneries in both Norwich and Lincoln. His particular concerns in conducting visitations do much to elucidate how pervasive and politically significant was the need to keep holy women in strictly defined boundaries, valuable resources though they were to Alnwick's Lancastrian party.

The sole account of a visitation of a monastic community, male or female, preserved in Alnwick's Norwich register is that of the Benedictine nunnery of Redlingfield, which took place in September 1427. Alnwick was still acting as keeper of the privy seal at that time and was not habitually resident in the diocese until approximately August 1428 (at which point he almost immediately began the famous Lollard trials),[71] so he did not personally carry out the visitation. Rather, he deputed the responsibility to Thomas Ryngstede, dean of the college of St. Mary in the Fields in Norwich.[72] The issues which emerge in the visitation proceedings bear witness, however, to Alnwick's presence behind the scenes, and the visitation provided Alnwick with his own preparatory étude for both the upcoming Lollard trials and the trial of Joan of Arc. The visitation manifests Alnwick's abiding concern with female spirituality and its attendant dangers, concern quite possibly heightened at this moment in 1427 by his insider's awareness as keeper of the privy seal of the fragility of Lancastrian authority during the uncertain early years of Henry VI's reign.

Upon reading the account of the visitation of Redlingfield, one imagines that as soon as Alnwick got wind of rumors (to which, as we have seen in Chapter 1, he paid close attention) of events at the nunnery, the proceedings were organized posthaste. The records provide a litany of virtually every sort of troubling behavior in which women religious could engage. The prioress threatens ecclesiastical and patriarchal authority left and right. For a start, she has disobeyed previous injunctions; several items in a list detailing her faults end with such phrases as "quod est expresse contra tenorem et effectum injunctionum predictarum."[73] To make matters worse for the prioress, it is discovered that she "fuit in societate Thome Langlond ballivi sui, solus cum sola in locis suspectis, videlicet in parva aula ejusdem prioratus, ostiis undique firmiter seratis, exclusis quibuscumque et aliis personis. Et etiam compertum est quod ipsa fuit sola cum eodem in aliis locis suspectis extra dictum prioratum, sub heggerowes et sub boscis."[74] Furthermore, the prioress and this same Thomas Langland with whom she is "de incontinentia scandalizata"[75] are implicated in the economic destruction of the house. The prioress is accused as follows: "Item compertum est quod dicta priorissa alienavit bona dicti prioratus et eadem dilapidavit, videlicet Thomam Langeland, nativum dicti prioratus de sanguine alienando, ac nonnullas grossas arbores et fabricam capelle de Benyngham et etiam cuidam Willelmo Jonyour de Eye sine scientia vel consensu conventus vendendo."[76] She has compounded her financial malfeasance by failing in the keeping of accounts.[77] To make matters worse still, upon examination of the "rotulis curiarum dicti prioratus" it also comes to light that, in all such records which the prioress has had in her custody, from the time of Richard II "fuerunt rasi dumtaxat in omnibus locis quibus aliqua mentio facta fuit de nomine ejusdem Thome, et nomen ejus totaliter abrasum et deletum, maxime in suspicionem et maximam ipsius prioratus et bonorum ejusdem dilapidationem."[78]

In this combination of sexual and economic misdeeds, the prioress of Redlingfield resembles the pregnant abbess in the Marian miracle. More significantly still, this bride of Christ who has rebelled against her divine husband is yet another manifestation of that source of intense economic, sexual, and political anxiety we see in Margery Kempe—the treasonous wife. Given these similarities, it seems almost inevitable that the accusations leveled against the prioress finally tar her with the brush of that seditious heresy, Lollardy—a crime which would otherwise seem fairly unlikely for a prioress.

Heresy and sexual misconduct converge as the prioress's sin of incontinence, in which she transgresses against the authority of her divine spouse and his earthly clerical representatives, is linked with Lollardy, the great threat to the perennially-intertwined authorities of ecclesiastical orthodoxy and Lancastrian monarchy: "Item compterum est quod priorissa commisit crimen Lollardie, informando moniales sibi subditas quod minus malum est eisdem vitium incontinentie committere quam ad sui preceptum ipsam non sequi. Ac etiam ipsa priorissa dedit licentiam generalem monialibus suis ut acciperent viros vel maritos, et sic contra ipsam priorissam non amplius murmurarunt."[79] Like Margery Kempe seen through the eyes of the mayor of Leicester and the suffragan, the prioress is depicted as a corrupting threat to other wives (here, brides of Christ), leading them astray through her heresy and her self-interested encouragement of incontinence. Although the prioress objects to many other charges brought against her, and is compelled to find compurgators, when faced with the potentially capital offense of Lollardy she abjures: "Istum articulum priorissa fatetur sibi objectum, et abjuravit crimen Lollardie inantea."[80] After abjuring, the unfortunate prioress resigns her office "pure, sponte, simpliciter et absolute."[81]

It is probably a coincidence that the only surviving record of a visitation of a nunnery during Alnwick's Norwich episcopate contains an account of a prioress who abjures Lollardy, although given Alnwick's zeal in searching out Lollards, it is a fitting coincidence. The coincidence of the visitation record's survival seems all the more appropriate when one considers that William Alnwick attended Joan of Arc's trial on May 24, 1431, the day when the final sentence was read to Joan and she abjured, signing the recantation which subsequently enabled the secular authorities to execute her as a relapsed heretic. Coincidence though this situation may be, it points us to significant parallels between the visitation of Redlingfield and Joan of Arc's trial. For instance, the prioress of Redlingfield's refusal to submit to clerical authority as embodied in episcopal injunctions provides a foretaste of Joan's refusal, which Alnwick witnessed in person, to submit to "Our Holy Mother Church" and of her denial of the truth of "all that the clergy and other authorities had said and decided concerning her words and deeds."[82] Additionally, like the prioress of Redlingfield, Joan is held in suspicion for supposedly having been in the company of men "in the private offices of her room and in her secret affairs, a thing unseen and unheard of in a modest or devout woman."[83] Joan's chastity is further called into question because, the judges say, she "unashamedly walked with men, refusing to have the company or care of womenfolk, and wished to employ only men."[84] Such parallels help elucidate the dangers female spirituality could, when not properly contained, pose for politically crucial, mutually reinforcing paradigms of gender and divine authority, paradigms Alnwick and Joan's other judges sought desperately to save.

Furthermore, the trial records reveal that Joan's judges (like Alnwick's deputed visitor) were well aware that, just as Joan (like the prioress of Redlingfield) posed inextricably linked religious, political, and symbolic threats, so too did a combination of sexual, economic, and spiritual accusations have mutually reinforcing condemnatory potential. In seeking to establish Joan's heresy, her judges move easily from questioning her faith to questioning her chastity to questioning her possession and use of material resources. For instance, article LIII condemns the impropriety of Joan's acting as a military leader, saying that she "against the bidding of God and His Saints, proudly and presumptuously assumed domination over men."[85] The judges' treatment of Joan's unorthodox military pursuits also, however, hints at their concerns with her troublingly unorthodox control of money and material resources. Joan's judges interrogate her repeatedly about what money and resources she has and how she got them as she put together her military forces. They ask her, for instance, how she obtained the bishop of Senlis's hackney, how and where she got her own horse, and what riches, other than horses, she had from the king.[86] Joan's judges then bring her purported improper participation in the spiritual economy into the equation, accusing her of trading on her so-called divine revelations and prophecies by "turning them into worldly profit and advantage." They claim that "by means of them she acquired a great number of riches, great state and apparel, many officers, horses, ornaments."[87]

Joan's wearing male attire, which has clear spiritual implications in light of the oft-cited Scriptural prohibition against cross-dressing and which has, as

I have argued, important symbolic dimensions, is also treated as a transgression in which the economic and the sexual converge. The way in which Joan obtained her male clothing throws suspicion on her chastity in her judges' eyes. She is accused of having entered into "intimate relations"[88] with Robert Baudricourt, who initially provided her, albeit reluctantly, with male attire.[89] Her judges go on to describe her male attire as being "contrary to the honesty of womankind," and they say that in wearing it she has "cast aside all womanly decency . . . to the scorn of feminine modesty."[90] Worse, though, like Eve's daughters in the *Book to a Mother*, she has adopted "rich and sumptuous habits, precious stuffs and cloth of gold and furs."[91] Once again, the economic and the sexual overlap; Joan's lack of "feminine modesty" in wearing male attire, which suggests her lack of chastity, is compounded by a traditionally feminine love of worldly goods and fine clothes, faults which, as we have seen, themselves lead to lechery.

Just as Alnwick's involvement with the prioress of Redlingfield helps us to understand his and the other judges' anxieties about Joan and the strategies behind their approach to interrogating her, so too the Lancastrian prelate's participation in Joan's trial in turn sheds light on the larger social implications of his later visitations of nunneries. The records of Alnwick's visitations in Lincoln between 1436 and 1449 suggest the lessons he learned from experiences with the prioress of Redlingfield, Margery Kempe, and Joan of Arc. As I discuss in Chapter 1, in these visitations Alnwick shows an almost obsessive sensitivity to scandal, a profound concern with nuns' conduct (especially their chastity and sexual behavior), and an overriding desire to limit nuns' access to and control of material resources. Indeed, as I argue, all of these are inextricably intertwined in the construction of the ecclesiastically sanctioned identity of "bride of Christ." While there are certainly no hints of Lollardy or open rebellion among the nuns of Lincoln, the persistence of this aforementioned constellation of concerns in the visitation records, and the strictness with which Alnwick treats even the smallest lapses in these areas, highlight the nascent danger present in even the most orthodox manifestations of female spirituality. The regulation of nunneries clearly was not a matter of ecclesiastical importance alone. Because female spirituality was so valuable and so volatile a symbolic commodity, such regulation was a matter of no small political importance as well. Particularly in the 1440s, as the Lancastrians lost ground in France and faced a strengthening Yorkist challenge in England, they simply could not afford even another Redlingfield prioress or Margery Kempe, let alone another Joan of Arc.

The Price of Lancastrian Redemption

As her precursors Margery Kempe and the prioress of Redlingfield suggest, Joan did more to damage the Lancastrian cause than simply to give military support to Charles VII. Joan, like Lydgate's Virgin Mary and Bokenham's female saints, makes abundantly clear that holy women could wreak symbolic havoc as well as create symbolic order. The Lancastrians had much invested in representational schemes dependent on saints, nuns, and holy women. In Joan they were inescapably confronted by the fact that, just as those who live by the sword are apt to die by the sword, those who live symbolically through female holiness are also at risk of dying symbolically through female holiness.[92]

To avoid such symbolic disaster, the Lancastrians had to discredit Joan's version of holiness and so guarantee that proper credit was given to their self-representations which relied on carefully-delineated paradigms of gender, sanctity, and divine authority. Hence, it was not enough for Joan to remain in the hands of their ally Jean de Luxembourg after her capture at Compiègne by the Bastard of Wandomme. Rather, it was necessary to ensure her transfer first to Henry VI's hands and then to the hands of the Church, the final arbiter of sanctity and orthodox spirituality. The initial letters written to achieve these transfers set up a series of transactions calculated to extract the ultimate price from Joan and so to redeem—literally to buy back—not only Lancastrian representational credit but also the entire symbolic economy through which that credit was obtained.

Letters discussing who should properly have custody of Joan describe losses, actual and potential, for which she bears responsibility and for which reparation is vital. For instance, in writing to the duke of Burgundy to try to get him to turn Joan over to ecclesiastical authorities, the Vicar-General of the Inquisitor says that through Joan, "many and diverse errors have been sown, uttered, published, and spread abroad, and still continue to be so, whence many hurts and scandals against the divine honor and against the holy faith have resulted and do result, causing the loss of souls and of many private Christians: which cannot and must not be dissimulated nor pass without fair and appropriate reparation."[93] Both souls and honor have been diminished, and these losses must be made good. In the same vein, the faculty of the University of Paris warns the duke of Burgundy that if Joan were to escape "without fitting reparation" the damage would be "an enormous peril, obstacle, or hurt to all the estate of this realm," surpassing any "within human memory." Joan's escape would additionally "be in truth greatly to the prejudice of your honor and of the most Christian name of the house of France."[94] Similar warnings are extended to Jean de Luxembourg, who is told that "it would be an intolerable offense against the divine Majesty if it were to come to pass that this woman were set free," and "if her deliverance took place, without appropriate reparation, it would be an irreparable dishonor to your nobility and to every one concerned."[95]

The damage to Anglo-Burgundian honor, the sign of power and legitimacy, which Joan inflicts is a persistent theme in these initial letters, confirming Roger Chartier's observation that authority depends on the credit given to or withheld from self-representations. A loss of honor implies that less credit is given to Anglo-Burgundian self-representation and, concomitantly, the authority dependent on these self-representations is diminished.[96] The sums involved in acquiring and convicting Joan bear witness to the size of the symbolic liability she represented. Just as Henry V was willing to lay out significant funds to gain the symbolic payoff from founding Syon, Henry VI and the Lancastrians were willing to spend large amounts of money to obtain Joan. Pierre Cauchon, bishop of Beauvais, who presided at Joan's trial received 756 *livres* "for the pains he took to gather evidence for Joan's prosecution."[97] Richard Beauchamp personally contributed to the cause; Jules Quicherat notes, "On verra par les dépositions consignées au procès qu'il contribua de son argent aux frais du jugement."[98] Furthermore, in a letter written shortly after Joan's death, Henry VI promises that he will aid and defend "à noz propres coustz et despensz" all of the "juges, docteurs, maistres, clercs, promoteur, advocas, conseillers, notaires et autres" who were involved in condemning Joan.[99]

Joan was such a great liability, and the stakes, both material and symbolic, were so high, that Henry VI even sought to write some insurance into the deal to obtain her. The connections between Pierre Cauchon and the Lancastrians were so close that Henry's surrender of Joan to the bishop of Beauvais after he finally did obtain her from the Burgundians hardly seems a surrender at all.[100] Henry still hedges his bets, though. In the letter formally making the surrender to the Church, Henry declares that if Joan should escape ecclesiastical condemnation, he wants his expensive purchase returned to him. He writes, "Nevertheless it is our intention to retake and regain possession of this Jeanne if it comes to pass that she is not convicted or found guilty of the said crimes, or certain of them concerning or touching our faith."[101]

The stunning sums paid for gaining possession of Joan, and the lengths to which the Lancastrians, frequently strapped for funds in this period of intense and often unsuccessful military activity, had to go to obtain the necessary resources, make Henry's precautions understandable. In a summons presented to the duke of Burgundy and Jean de Luxembourg, Pierre Cauchon tenders Henry VI's offer, saying, "le Roy veult libéralment leur bailler jusques à la somme de VI mil frans, et pour ledit bastart qui l'a prinse, lui donner et assigner rente pour soustenir son estat, jusques à II or III cens livres."[102] Anticipating that this offer might not be attractive enough, the bishop sweetens the deal, stressing that, while the capture of Joan is not on par with the capture of a king, prince, or "autres gens de grant estat," even so "ledit évesque somme et requiert les dessudiz ou nom comme dessus, que ladite Pucelle lui soit délivrée en baillant seurté de ladite somme de X^m frans, pour toutes choses quelxconques."[103]

The king's ransom needed to purchase Joan was obtained by levying a special tax on the Estates of Normandy, an act which could well have had adverse political costs of its own. A letter from September 1430, written by Thomas Blount, treasurer and governor general of the king's finances in Normandy, and Pierre Surreau, the receiver general, acknowledges the receipt of the demand for the collection of the first installment of the total levy of "VI^xx mil livres tournois." Of this sum, "dix mil livres tournois" are earmarked "au paiement de l'achapt de Jehanne la Pucelle que l'en dit estre sorcière, personne de guerre, conduisant les ostz du Daulphin."[104]

The description of Joan as "sorcière" in Blount and Surreau's letter signals another sort of Lancastrian transaction—that is, their efforts to ensure the value of their own symbolic currency by devaluing Joan's. As early as August 1429 the duke of Bedford describes Joan in a letter to Henry VI as "a disciple and lyme of the Feende, called the Pucelle, that used fals enchauntements and sorcerie."[105] On May 3, 1430, an edict was issued setting forth proclamations "contra capitaneos et soldarios tergiverisantes incantationibus Puellae terrificatus,"[106] and another edict had to be issued on December 12, 1430, "De fugitivis ab exercitu quos terriculamenta Puellae exanimaverant, arestandis."[107] English efforts to make Joan into a witch, like their accusations of heresy and harlotry, are attempts permanently to secure a symbolic "debit" culminating in her payment of the ultimate price and, so the Lancastrians hoped, their own symbolic redemption—something well worth the sums spent to obtain and try Joan.

Joan, executed in May 1431, did pay the ultimate price. Lancastrian redemption, however, was not permanent. The woman executed as a heretic, traitor, and sorceress was rehabilitated within the lifetime of many of her judges and was eventually, albeit centuries later, canonized. Not only was

Lancastrian redemption remarkably short-lived, it was perhaps never securely achieved in the first place. In spite of Lancastrian expenditures both material and symbolic, Joan lived on after her death, continuing to trouble Lancastrian symbolic efforts.[108] Furthermore, even as they were working to obtain redemption by discrediting Joan, the Lancastrians found themselves subject to some of the same tactics they were mobilizing against her. At the same time they were "seeking to denigrate the 'voices' of Joan of Arc,"[109] Henry VI's delegation at the Council of Basel was compelled to defend the orthodoxy of their "champion" St. Birgitta (herself accused of sorcery during her lifetime) and her revelations "in quibus plures delusorie visiones contineri dicuntur."[110]

The potentially awkward position in which these fifteenth-century English diplomats found themselves stems from the complex cultural status of female spirituality in later medieval material, spiritual, and symbolic exchanges. Especially when women were involved, the distinctions between sanctity and sorcery, between divine inspiration and demonic possession, were notoriously difficult ones to make in the later Middle Ages, as is witnessed, for instance, by Jean Gerson's treatise *De probatione spirituum*.[111] In discussing an early sixteenth-century printed book in which Thomas à Kempis's *Imitatio Christi* is bound with the *Malleus Maleficarum*, Gerhild Scholz Williams observes the "close association . . . of spiritual progress and satanic subterfuge, of the divinity of Christ and the depravity of Satan and his most favored handmaiden, women."[112] Joan of Arc demonstrates that, like orthodoxy and heresy,[113] like sanctity and sorcery,[114] like containment and empowerment, symbolic success and symbolic disaster are two sides of the same coin, and the outcome can be as unpredictable as a coin toss.

Notes

Preface

1. William Page, ed., *The Victoria History of the County of Hertford*, vol. 4 (London: Constable, 1914), 446; hereafter *VCH Hertford*.

2. C. F. R. Palmer links Edward II's desire to endow the house of King's Langley with the presence there of the tomb of Sir Piers Gaveston. He writes that Edward II "designed to endow that house with possession sufficient for the support of one hundred religious, there to celebrate for ever the soul of his favorite" ("History of the Priory of Dartford, in Kent," *Archaeological Journal* 36 [1876]: 242).

3. William Page, ed., *The Victoria History of the County of Kent*, vol. 2 (London: St. Catherine Press, 1926), 181; hereafter *VCH Kent*.

4. Ibid.

5. *VCH Hertford*, 447.

6. Palmer, "History," 246.

7. *Calendar of Patent Rolls, 1354–1358* (London: HMSO, 1909), 486.

8. Eileen Power, *Medieval English Nunneries c. 1275 to 1535* (Cambridge: Cambridge University Press, 1922), 2.

9. MS BL Arundel 61.

10. Extract translated and printed by C. F. R. Palmer, "Notes on the Priory of Dartford, in Kent," *Archaeological Journal* 39 (1879): 178.

11. For an account of Dartford's library, see David Bell, *What Nuns Read: Books and Libraries in Medieval English Nunneries*, Cistercian Studies Series 158 (Kalamazoo, Mich.: Cistercian Publications, 1995), 130–34.

12. *VCH Kent*, 187.

13. Two contemporary scholars of women and religion who depart from narrowly defined fields of inquiry, and whose own boundary-breaching has been influential in shaping my thinking, are Jocelyn Wogan-Browne and Felicity Riddy. See in particular Wogan-Browne's work on saints' lives as well as her work on the vernacular, which has important implications for the study of female spirituality, and Riddy's analysis of conduct literature and women's reading (Jocelyn Wogan-Browne, "The Virgin's Tale," *Feminist Readings in Middle English Literature: The Wife of Bath and All Her Sect*, ed.

Ruth Evans and Lesley Johnson [London: Routledge, 1994], 165–94; Jocelyn Wogan-Browne, "Wreaths of Thyme: The Female Translator in Anglo-Norman Hagiography," *The Medieval Translator 4*, ed. Roger Ellis and Ruth Evans [Binghamton, N.Y.: Medieval and Renaissance Texts and Studies, 1994], 46–65; Jocelyn Wogan-Browne et al., eds., *The Idea of the Vernacular: An Anthology of Middle English Literary Theory, 1280–1520* [University Park: Pennsylvania State University Press, 1999]; Felicity Riddy, "Mother Knows Best: Reading Social Change in a Courtesy Text," *Speculum* 71 [1996]: 66–86; Felicity Riddy, "'Women talking about the things of God': A Late Medieval Subculture," *Women and Literature in Britain, 1150–1500*, ed. Carol M. Meale [Cambridge: Cambridge University Press, 1996], 104–27).

14. See Jo Ann Kay McNamara, *Sisters in Arms: Catholic Nuns Through Two Millennia* (Cambridge, Mass.: Harvard University Press, 1996); Roberta Gilchrist, *Contemplation and Action: The Other Monasticism*, The Archaeology of Medieval Britain 5, ed. Helen Clarke (London: Leicester University Press, 1995); Roberta Gilchrist, *Gender and Material Culture: The Archaeology of Religious Women* (London: Routledge, 1994); Roberta Gilchrist and Marilyn Oliva, *Religious Women in Medieval East Anglia: History and Archaeology c. 1000–1541*, Studies in East Anglian History 1 (Norwich: Centre of East Anglian Studies, University of East Anglia, 1993); Marilyn Oliva, *The Convent and the Community in Later Medieval England: Female Monasteries in the Diocese of Norwich, 1350–1540*, Studies in the History of Medieval Religion 12 (Woodbridge: Boydell Press, 1998); David Bell, *What Nuns Read*.

15. The concept of "ideological scripts" comes from Paul Smith, *Discerning the Subject*, Theory and History of Literature 55, ed. Wlad Godzich and Jochen Schulte-Sasse (Minneapolis: University of Minnesota Press, 1988).

16. While it is true that Syon, founded by Henry V in 1415, was the only Brigittine house in England, it was also the wealthiest nunnery in England and was quite politically important, as I discuss in Chapter 5. Furthermore, Brigittine spirituality was very popular in fifteenth-century England, as I discuss at some length in Chapter 4; Brigittine sources are even used in a fifteenth-century Assumption Day sermon preached for a community of Benedictine nuns at Carrow in Norwich (V. M. O'Mara, *A Study and Edition of Selected Middle English Sermons*, Leeds Texts and Monographs n.s. 13 [Leeds: Leeds Studies in English, 1994], 171).

17. Palmer, "History," 256.

18. Ibid., 257.

Chapter 1. Vows and Visitations

1. The concept of "ideological scripts" comes from Paul Smith, *Discerning the Subject*, Theory and History of Literature 55, ed. Wlad Godzich and Jochen Schulte-Sasse (Minneapolis: University of Minnesota Press, 1988).

2. Jacques Derrida, "Plato's Pharmacy," *Literary Theory: An Anthology*, ed. Julie Rivkin and Michael Ryan (Oxford: Blackwell, 1998), 443.

3. For useful analysis of the power of texts and writing (and the limits thereof) in later medieval society, see Steven Justice, *Writing and Rebellion: England in 1381* (Berkeley and Los Angeles: University of California Press, 1994), and Susan Crane, "The Writing Lesson of 1381," *Chaucer's England: Literature in Historical Context*, ed. Barbara Hanawalt (Minneapolis: University of Minnesota Press, 1992), 201–21. Like Justice and Crane, I am interested in the ways in which those who are subjects of texts and subject to texts rewrite, reinterpret, and even destroy those texts.

4. Ernst Kock, ed., *Three Middle-English Versions of the Rule of St. Benet and Two Contemporary Rituals for the Ordination of Nuns*, Early English Text Society o.s. 120 (Millwood, N.Y.: Kraus, 1987), 142. The "furme" follows the prose translation of the Benedictine Rule for women in MS BL Lansdowne 278.

5. Penelope D. Johnson, *Equal in Monastic Profession: Religious Women in Medieval France* (Chicago: University of Chicago Press, 1991), 236.

6. Kock, *Three Middle-English Versions*, 146. "The Method of makeing a Nunn" follows the verse translation of the Benedictine Rule for women in MS BL Cotton Vespasian A. 25.

7. Ibid., 147. René Metz points out that "la tradition de l'anneau" marks the consecration of virgins "comme un rite nuptial" (*La consécration des vierges dans l'église romaine: Etude d'histoire de la liturgie* [Paris: Presses Universitaires de France, 1954], 349 n.1), and the same holds true for the use of the ring in the general profession service for nuns.

8. Marriage played an important role in medieval culture in linking female sexuality and financial exchange. On this point, see Ruth Mazo Karras, *Common Women: Prostitution and Sexuality in Medieval England* (New York: Oxford University Press, 1996), 84–89.

9. Renée Hirschon, "Introduction: Property, Power and Gender Relations," *Women and Property—Women as Property*, ed. Renée Hirschon (London and Canberra: Croom Helm; New York: St. Martin's Press, 1984), 5.

10. See, for example, Marilyn Strathern, "Partners and Consumers: Making Relations Visible," *New Literary History* 22 (1991): 581–601 as well as her chapter in *Women and Property*.

11. Roberta Gilchrist, "The Spatial Archaeology of Gender Domains: A Case Study of Medieval English Nunneries," *Archaeological Review from Cambridge* 7 (1988): 27. Jo Ann McNamara additionally points to the "subliminal identification" of women with money stemming from "competing male needs to acquire them and protect them" (*Sisters in Arms: Catholic Nuns Through Two Millennia* [Cambridge, Mass.: Harvard University Press, 1996], 365).

12. Sally Thompson, *Women Religious: The Founding of English Nunneries After the Norman Conquest* (Oxford: Clarendon, 1991), 61.

13. The system of requiring entry gifts upon profession also reinforces the linkage of monastic profession and marriage as exchanges of both women and property. The limited endowments of nunneries, generally smaller than those of male communities, frequently led to requirements that women bring entry gifts upon reception into religion, in spite of the fact that monastic rules forbade accepting entry gifts except as alms (McNamara, *Sisters in Arms* 274; see also Thompson, *Women Religious* 188). Roberta Gilchrist and Marilyn Oliva find that the practice of requiring entry gifts was not common in East Anglia (*Religious Women in Medieval East Anglia: History and Archaeology c. 1100–1540*, Studies in East Anglian History 1 [Norwich: Centre of East Anglian Studies, University of East Anglia, 1993], 51–52), but Janet Burton points out that evidence from Yorkshire "suggest[s] that entry into a nunnery may not have been free" ("Yorkshire Nunneries in the Middle Ages: Recruitment and Resources," *Government, Religion, and Society in Northern England, 1000–1700*, ed. John C. Appleby and Paul Salton [Stroud: Sutton, 1997], 110). Using predominantly fifteenth-century records, Burton finds that the average dowry for Yorkshire nunneries was 10 marks ("Yorkshire Nunneries" 110–11). Thompson also observes, "It would appear . . . that the practice of requiring gifts on entry was widespread" (*Women Religious* 187). Because the practice was condemned as simoniacal, Thompson believes that the connection between gifts and admission was frequently obscured (*Women Religious* 187). Such obfuscation may be widespread in nunnery records since in the thirteenth century "critics of such simoniacal practices suddenly shifted the stress of their concern from entry into religion in general to the malpractices of nuns" (*Women Religious* 187–88). Nuns did not always obey the requirement that the resources they brought with them be transferred to the community. McNamara observes that women religious "rarely lost all control of their own property" and that nuns "usually retained personal items of clothing, books, and furnishings in locked chests" (*Sisters in Arms* 274). Such departures from the strict requirement of personal poverty are part of the far-reaching relaxation of this monastic vow in the later Middle Ages (on this modification of the vow of poverty, see note 16 below).

14. Roberta Gilchrist, *Gender and Material Culture: The Archaeology of Religious Women* (London: Routledge, 1994), 19.

15. Ibid. In reference to the asexuality of celibate clergy, Gilchrist cites Peter Brown's "Late Antiquity" in *A History of Private Life: From Pagan Rome to Byzantium*, ed. P. Veyne (London: Harvard University Press, 1987), 235–311. She writes, "Peter Brown . . . has commented on the loss of male sexuality upon taking monastic vows. The tonsure was a symbolic negation of personal sexuality. The celibacy which followed created a public space within the body; celibate priests became accessible to others through the creation of public space where personal sexuality had previously resided" (*Gender* 18–19).

16. While Church officials continued in the later Middle Ages to condemn the possession of private property by male and female monastics alike, they often accommodated it in practice. In fourteenth- and fifteenth-century England, the shift from direct exploitation of estates to reliance on money rents encouraged the development

of a cash economy within monasteries. As has been well-documented, the system of supplying food, clothing, and other necessities from common stores broke down in favor of a system in which monks and nuns received sums of money with which they were to provide for themselves. Furthermore, the Benedictine Chapter of 1444 declared that, because it was ancient custom, although contrary to the Rule, religious were allowed to receive and spend money, partly for necessity, partly for recreation. Such expenditures were permissible provided they were not at will, but only for certain specified things, and that faithful account was given (Robert H. Snape, *Monastic Finance in the Later Middle Ages* [Cambridge: Cambridge University Press, 1926], 64).

17. Elizabeth M. Makowski, *Canon Law and Cloistered Women: Periculoso and Its Commentators, 1298–1545* (Washington, D.C.: Catholic University of America Press, 1997), 1–2.

18. McNamara writes that as early as the end of the twelfth century, "The men who had undertaken the *cura* [of nuns] agreed that it required that women be secluded from public money-making activities. Women were neither to make money in the marketplace nor beg it on the street" (*Sisters in Arms* 275).

19. Eileen Power, *Medieval English Nunneries c. 1275 to 1535* (Cambridge: Cambridge University Press, 1922), 353.

20. Lyndwood, *Provinciale* (1679), pt. II, p. 55, qtd. in Power, *Medieval English Nunneries*, 354.

21. Ibid.

22. Power, *Medieval English Nunneries*, 313.

23. Makowski, *Canon Law*, 3.

24. Johnson, *Equal in Monastic Profession*, 63.

25. Ibid.

26. Ibid.

27. Ibid., 165.

28. The material and spiritual benefits enjoyed by monks included the sacramental ability of those who were priests to produce Christ's body, an increasingly valuable commodity in the later Middle Ages. Significantly, the sacramental ability of monks translated into increased material wealth for male religious houses in the later Middle Ages, as chantries and the endowment of masses for the souls of the dead grew in popularity. On the increasingly central role of the Eucharist in social organization in the later Middle Ages, see Miri Rubin, *Corpus Christi: The Eucharist in Late Medieval Culture* (Cambridge: Cambridge University Press, 1991).

29. G. G. Coulton, *Five Centuries of Religion*, 4 vols. (Cambridge: Cambridge University Press, 1920–1950), 2:154.

30. Makowski, *Canon Law*, 109. Makowski cites the relevant Latin: "*Provinciale* f. cxvi ad v. *longe perniciosius* 'non erat simplex fornicatio . . . sed in corruptione monialis non solum commitur fornicatio sed adulterium quod sponsa Christi . . . ' " (ibid., 109 n. 27; ellipses in original). Gratian states, "Quae Christo spiritualiter nubunt, et sacerdote velantur, si publice postea nupserint, non eas admittendas esse ad poenitentiam agen-

dam, nisi hi, quibus se junxerant, a mundo recesserint. Si enim de hominibus haec ratio custoditur, ut quaecumque vivente viro nupserit, adultera habeatur, nec ei agendae poenitentiae licentia concedatur, nisi unus de eis fuerit defunctus, quanto magis de illa tenenda est, quae ante immortali se sponso conjunxerat, et postea ad humanas nuptias transmigravit?" (Gratian, *Decretals*, vol. 1, *Patrologia Latina* 187 [Paris: Garnier, 1891], pars II, c. xxvii, q. 1, c. 10, 1377). In c. 14, gloss, he also says that whoever corrupts a nun commits both incest and adultery, incest because the nun is the bride of God our Father and adultery because she is the spouse of another.

31. Johnson, *Equal in Monastic Profession*, 64.

32. As Carolyn Dinshaw has famously argued, later medieval literary activity "has a gendered structure, a structure that associates acts of writing and related acts of signify-ing—allegorizing, interpreting, glossing, translation—with the masculine and that identifies the surfaces on which these acts are performed, or from which these acts depart, or which these acts reveal—the page, the text, the literal sense, or even the hidden meaning—with the feminine" (*Chaucer's Sexual Poetics* [Madison: University of Wisconsin Press, 1989], 9).

33. On the sacrament of the Eucharist as a male replacement of the maternal work of the Incarnation, see Chapter 4.

34. Walter W. Seton, ed., *The Rewle of Sustris Menouresses Enclosid, A Fifteenth-Century Courtesy Book and Two Franciscan Rules*, Early English Text Society o.s. 148 (London: Kegan Paul, 1914), 84 (hereafter cited parenthetically in the text as *Rewle*).

35. James Hogg, ed., *The Rewyll of Seynt Sauioure*, vol. 2 of *The Rewyll of Seynt Sauioure and Other Middle English Brigittine Legislative Texts*, Salzburger Studien zur Anglistik und Amerikanistik 6 (Salzburg: Institut für Englische Sprache und Literatur Universität Salzburg), fol. 49r (hereafter cited parenthetically in the text as *Rewyll*). Because this volume is a facsimile of MS Cambridge University Library Ff. 6. 33 (the Middle English rule) and MS St. John's College Cambridge 11 (the Latin version), I cite the *Rewyll* by folio number rather than by page number. Expansions of abbreviations in the manuscript are indicated by italics, with the exception of the various ampersands used by the scribe, which have been silently expanded. The Brigittine Rule specifies that a bishop is to conduct the service. Additionally, it uses the terms "sacre" and "consecrate" to describe the services in which a candidate makes her profession and permanently enters the order: "The consent of entre gotyn: it must be sent for the bisshop diocesan. Whiche prayed shall come and sacre hir. But ere thanne she be presentyd to the bisshop to be consecrate: she must be clipped hir here of the Abbes aftir the manere of nonnes" (*Rewyll* fol. 48r–48v). Thus, in the Brigittine tradition, "consecration" and "profession" refer to the same service, not to the consecration of virgins and the profession of other nuns.

36. Roger Ellis, *Viderunt Eam Filie Syon: The Spirituality of the English House of a Medieval Contemplative Order from its Beginnings to the Present Day*, Analecta Cartusiana 68 (Salzburg: Institut für Anglistik und Amerikanistik Universität Salzburg, 1984), 20. Ellis points out that St. Birgitta would have had a close connection to the Cistercian

tradition, since after she left Sweden, her confessor was the Cistercian Prior Peter (ibid.).

37. For a discussion of the relationships between the Benedictine Rule and the rules for Franciscan nuns, see *Rewle*, 66–68.

38. Felice Lifshitz, "Is Mother Superior? Towards a History of Feminine *Amtscharisma*," *Medieval Mothering*, ed. John Carmi Parsons and Bonnie Wheeler (New York: Garland, 1996), 119.

39. Luce Irigaray, "Women on the Market," *This Sex Which Is Not One*, trans. Catherine Porter with Carolyn Burke (Ithaca, N.Y.: Cornell University Press, 1985), 185.

40. J. B. L. Tolhurst, ed., *The Ordinale and Customary of the Benedictine Nuns of Barking Abbey (University College, Oxford, MS. 169)*, 2 vols. (London: Harrison, 1927–1928), 2:388 note for p. 350.

41. Timothy Fry et al., eds., *RB 1980: The Rule of St. Benedict in Latin and English with Notes* (Collegeville, Minn: Liturgical Press, 1981), 268.

42. Kock, *Three Middle-English Versions*, 108.

43. Ibid., 148–49.

44. On late medieval Marian trinities, see Barbara Newman, *From Virile Woman to WomanChrist: Studies in Medieval Religion and Literature* (Philadelphia: University of Pennsylvania Press, 1995), 198–209.

45. Lifshitz, "Is Mother Superior?" 122, her emphasis.

46. The importance of maternity in the account of the order's origins is discussed in detail in Chapter 2 on monastic rules.

47. See *Rewyll*, fol. 49v–50r.

48. James Hogg, ed., *The Syon Additions for the Sisters from the British Library MS Arundel 146*, vol. 4 of *The Rewyll of Seynt Sauioure and Other Middle English Brigittine Legislative Texts*, Salzburger Studien zur Anglistik und Amerikanistik 6 (Salzburg: Institut für Anglistik und Amerikanistik Universität Salzburg, 1980), 97–98 (hereafter cited parenthetically in the text as *Sisters*). Because, unlike the *Rewyll*, this volume is a printed text, I cite it by page number.

49. To answer the question Lifshitz poses in her title, then, in the Brigittine tradition the mother really *is* superior.

50. Ellis, *Viderunt Eam Filie Syon*, 32.

51. Margaret Deanesly, ed., *The Incendium Amoris of Richard Rolle of Hampole* (Manchester: University of Manchester Press; London: Longmans, 1915), 113.

52. In this respect, the Brigittine nun resembles the Benedictine monk, although not the Benedictine nun.

53. For example, Mary tells Birgitta in a revelation, "Forsothe, he was to me as mine awne hert. Þarefore methoght, when he was born of me, as halfe mi hert was born and passed oute of me, and when he suffird, me thoght þat halfe mi hert suffird. . . . Right as Adam and Eue sald þe werld for ane appill, so mi son and I boght againe þe werld as with one hert" (Roger Ellis, ed., *The Liber celestis of St. Bridget of Sweden*, vol. 1, Early English Text Society o.s. 291 [Oxford: Oxford University Press, 1987], 63).

54. William Patterson Cummings, ed., *The Revelations of Saint Birgitta Edited from the Fifteenth-Century MS in the Garrett Collection in the Library of Princeton University*, Early English Text Society o.s. 178 (1929; reprint, Millwood, N.Y.: Kraus, 1987), 56.

55. Ibid.

56. Ibid., 58.

57. Ellis, *Viderunt Eam Filie Syon*, 107.

58. John Henry Blunt, ed., *The Myroure of Oure Ladye*, Early English Text Society e.s. 19 (London: Kegan Paul, 1873), 238.

59. Ellis, *Viderunt Eam Filie Syon*, 107.

60. Ibid., 21.

61. Ibid., 20. Sally Thompson points out that "the extent of feminine supremacy" in the order of Fontevrault was "notable" (*Women Religious* 116). For instance, as in the Brigittine order, "Regulations for the brothers of Fontevrault stressed their subordinate position" (ibid.), and the abbess of Fontevrault had, as did the Brigittine abbess at Syon (at least according to the original charter), power which "extended to spiritual as well as temporal matters" (ibid., 117).

62. A. F. C. Bourdillon, *The Order of Minoresses in England*, British Society of Franciscan Studies 12 (Manchester: University of Manchester Press, 1926), 8. The majority of Franciscan nuns in medieval Europe, known as Claresses, followed the Urbanist Rule. For a concise history of the development of rules for Franciscan nuns, see McNamara, *Sisters in Arms*, 306–12.

63. The terminology "feminization of sanctity" comes from André Vauchez, *La sainteté en occident aux derniers siècles du moyen age* (Rome: Ecole française de Rome; Paris: Diffusions de Boccard, 1981).

64. This outline of visitation proceedings is based on that given by A. Hamilton Thompson in *Visitations of Religious Houses*, 3 vols., Lincoln Record Society 7, 14, 21 (Lincoln: Lincoln Record Society, 1914–1929), 1:ix–xiii. This basic procedure applied to Benedictine monks and nuns, as well as to male and female Austin communities and to Cistercian nunneries, which were typically not, like their male counterparts, exempt from visitation.

65. For instance, Penelope Johnson argues that the visitation process itself, the questions asked, and the directions given were "mostly gender neutral and appropriate to all monastics" (*Equal in Monastic Profession* 69). Johnson analyzes material from the central Middle Ages in France, so her statement may be more true for that time and place than for England in the later Middle Ages.

66. Power, *Medieval English Nunneries*, 481.

67. McNamara, *Sisters in Arms*, 418.

68. Johnson, *Equal in Monastic Profession*, 64.

69. Ibid.

70. The combination of benefits prelates received from visitations (the fees they collected and the enhancement of their authority which ensured the availability of future fees) illustrates the ready interchangeability of material and symbolic resources

or what Pierre Bourdieu terms the "undifferentiatedness of the symbolic and material aspects of the patrimony" (Pierre Bourdieu, *Outline of a Theory of Practice*, trans. Richard Nice [Cambridge: Cambridge University Press, 1977], 181).

71. PRO: SC6 1260/8. Expansions of abbreviations in this and subsequently quoted documents in the Public Record Office are indicated by italics. In expanding abbreviations, I have used the spellings found most frequently in each document.

72. PRO: SC6 1260/19.

73. PRO: SC6 867/31.

74. Thompson, *Visitations*, 1:75. "Prohibemus ingressum secularium omnini per dicta ostia, ac transitum, cursum et recursum secularium quorumcumque per loca claustralia dicti prioratus haberi, ne deuocio psallencium in choro aut quies residencium in claustro per seculares illo [sic] aliqualiter perturbentur" (ibid., 1:74–75).

75. Ibid., 1:87–88. "Item iniungimus et mandamus districcius sub pena excommunicacionis vt accessus secularium, presertim mulierum, ad loca claustralia et potissime ad claustrum, dormitorium, infirmarium et refectorium omnino cohibeatis . . . et quod nullum secularem saltem extraneum ad comedendum in refectorio tempore refeccionis canonicorum recipiatis vel recipi permittatis, sic quod quies canonicorum in claustro tempore contemplacionis aut in refectoria leccio tempore prandij nullatinus impediatur" (ibid., 1:87–88).

76. Qtd. in David Knowles and R. Neville Hadcock, *The Religious Orders in England*, vol. 2 (Cambridge: Cambridge University Press, 1957), 234 n. 1.

77. Ibid.

78. Thompson, *Visitations*, 2:218, brackets in original.

79. Ibid., 2:116.

80. Ibid., 2:115–16.

81. Ibid., 1:48.

82. For instance, David Bell cites the example of Campsey priory, which was "moderately wealthy and probably housed about twenty nuns." Pressmarks on two fifteenth-century psalters (O.E. 94 and D.D. 141) "imply that Campsey had a very large library. Just how large we do not know, but if there were at least 94 books in one *distinctio* and *gradus* and 141 in another, and if there were a plurality of *distinctiones*, the library at Campsey might have rivalled that at Christ Church, Canterbury!" (*What Nuns Read: Books and Libraries in Medieval English Nunneries*, Cistercian Studies Series 158 [Kalamazoo, Mich.: Cistercian Publications, 1995], 42–43). Furthermore, according to Bell, the Benedictine requirement of annual distribution of books was followed in at least some female communities (ibid., 42); on this practice at Barking Abbey, see note 136 below. Bell also gives an extensive inventory of manuscripts and printed books owned by nunneries.

83. Anne Clark Bartlett, *Male Authors, Female Readers: Representation and Subjectivity in Middle English Devotional Literature* (Ithaca, N.Y.: Cornell University Press, 1995), 18. Of course, directives on how and why nuns—or indeed anyone—should read were not necessarily effective. As Bartlett demonstrates, female readers could and did engage in a multiplicity of "improvisatory" readings.

84. The clerical desire to regulate nuns' reading and delimit its purposes might well have been especially strong at Syon, given the Brigittine tradition's encouragement of female learning and the authority accorded to women in the structure of the Brigittine community.

85. Blunt, *Myroure*, 67. I discuss the implications of this passage in detail in Chapter 2.

86. Makowski, *Canon Law*, 126.

87. Ibid.

88. Coulton, *Five Centuries of Religion*, 2:237.

89. Sherry Ortner, "The Virgin and the State," *Feminist Studies* 4 (1978): 32.

90. Ibid.

91. Thompson, *Visitations*, 3:303.

92. Ibid., 3:313–14.

93. Ibid., 2:14.

94. Ibid., 3:371, 380.

95. Ibid., 3:273.

96. Ibid., 3:330.

97. The visitation record designates Catesby as a Cistercian house. Cistercians followed the Benedictine Rule, and, while the Benedictine and Cistercian traditions were quite different for male monastics, in England female communities are often described as both Cistercian and Benedictine in records, indicating conflation of the traditions. In her work on Yorkshire nunneries, Janet Burton indicates that "whereas male houses could be identified by the congregation or order to which they belonged, the nature of the affiliation or self-identity of female houses was less clearly defined" ("Yorkshire Nunneries" 104). Female communities consistently designated as Cistercian are relatively rare, and even they had none of the special Cistercian privileges enjoyed by male houses of the order. Female Cistercian houses were also not bound to the parent abbey as male Cistercian houses were. See A. Hamilton Thompson, *The Archbishop of Canterbury's Committee on the Ministry of Women*, Appendix VIII (New York: Macmillan, 1919).

98. Thompson, *Visitations*, 2:52.

99. Eileen Power notes, "The control of money and goods and the division into households, catering separately for themselves, worked in together" (*Medieval English Nunneries* 331).

100. Thompson, *Visitations*, 2:117. "Domina Johanna Thorpe, priorissa, dicit quod moniales tenent diuersas familias, due videlicet adinuicem; et tamen nichil percipiunt de domo nisi panem et ceruisiam" (ibid.).

101. Ibid., 2:175. "Item dicit quod moniales bine et bine tenent diuersas familias distinctas per se, sed vt dicit comedunt omni die in refectorio. . . . Item dicit quod moniales nichil percipiunt de domo nisi esculenta et poculenta, et ipsamet tenet vnam familiam per se" (ibid.).

102. See PRO: SC6 867/30, 867/31, 867/36. These accounts also include cash

payments to the nuns for fuel. Clothing was sometimes dealt with in a similar fashion. In 1461, the ten nuns of St. Mary de Pré received 2s each to purchase their clothing individually (PRO: SC6 867/30), and a later prioress's account for the house records 16s 8d "departed amonge þe susters of the rent in cambryge for theyr clothyng" (PRO: SC6 867/35). A chambress's account for St. Michael's Stamford (a Benedictine nunnery dependent on Peterborough Abbey) for 9–10 Henry IV shows that the prioress received 5s "pour sa camise"; eleven other nuns received 4s each; and two, called "sistr" rather than "dame," received 3s each (PRO: SC6 1260/14). In 5–6 Henry VI, the treasuress's account for St. Michael's Stamford shows that the prioress received 18s for "vestitu" (PRO: SC6 1260/18). It is difficult to determine precisely how the nuns at St. Michael's Stamford obtained food. As Power points out, in this area "the account rolls of the house are not easy to interpret, because although they contain no reference to catering, other than certain pittances and feasts . . . neither do they contain any reference to commons money. No separate cellaress' accounts have survived to throw any further light upon the subject" (Medieval English Nunneries 334–35).

103. On this strategy, see Paul Strohm, Hochon's Arrow: The Social Imagination of Fourteenth-Century Texts (Princeton, N.J.: Princeton University Press, 1992), 137–39; and Karras, Common Women, 94–95, 137–38. In Chapter 4 I discuss the conflation of the sexual and the economic in texts for secular women which rely on monastic paradigms to regulate female conduct.

104. Coulton, Five Centuries of Religion, 4:131.

105. Thompson, Visitations, 2:51–52.

106. Ibid., 1:50–53, 2:89.

107. Ibid., 1:66–68, 2:113–15.

108. Ibid., 2:117.

109. Ibid., 2:119.

110. Ibid., 2:175.

111. Ibid., 3:248.

112. Ibid., 3:345.

113. Ibid., 3:350.

114. Ibid., 3:357.

115. The generally smaller endowments of nunneries meant that many nuns continued to rely on family members for support after profession, receiving money for clothing, food, fuel, and other necessities. McNamara observes that donations to nunneries "were often intended for the support of individual members of the community rather than the whole" (Sisters in Arms 263). Janet Burton also finds that "it was expected that the secular family had a financial responsibility for their nuns" ("Yorkshire Nunneries" 115). Strict enforcement of claustration may also have been a factor, since it limited the potential for nuns to augment their endowments (Makowski, Canon Law 3). Ironically, the shadow of simony cast by accepting entry gifts, along with the damaging consequences of charges of proprietas, perhaps pressed nuns into even greater reliance on entry gifts by devaluing the moral capital so important to nunneries.

Nuns had to rely on living what the Church deemed to be blameless lives in order to guarantee to benefactors the efficacy of their intercessory prayers, which were the major service they offered in exchange for donations and endowments. Thus, as McNamara observes, "accusations of simony attached to their entry gifts threatened to invalidate nuns' spiritual services" (*Sisters in Arms* 284).

116. Thompson, *Visitations*, 3:350.

117. Ibid., 2:115, emphasis in original.

118. Makowski, *Canon Law*, 81, her emphasis. Makowski cites Petrus's *Super Sexto decretalium* to VI 3.16.1, par. 3, p. 354: "Tangit circa hoc in *Novella* utrum pro visitandis monasteriis sibi subiectis abbatissa possit egredi. Iste tex. facit quod non, quia generaliter loquitur, ergo generaliter debet intelligi . . ." (ibid., 81 n. 27; ellipses in original).

119. Even though aspects of the abbess's authority, especially over the male members of the community, were reduced in changes made to the Rule in the process of papal approval, she remained a powerful figure. On the changes made during the process of papal approval, see Roger Ellis, "The Visionary and the Canon Lawyers: Papal and Other Revisions to the *Regula Salvatoris* of St. Bridget of Sweden," *Prophets Abroad: The Reception of Continental Holy Women in Late-Medieval England*, ed. Rosalyn Voaden (Cambridge: D. S. Brewer, 1996), 71–90. For a detailed discussion of the textual traditions of the rule and their relationships, see Sten Eklund, ed., *Den Heliga Birgitta Opera Minora I: Regula Salvatoris* SFSS series II, Bd. VIII:1 (Lund: Berlingska Boktryckeriet, 1975).

120. Thompson, *Visitations*, 3:355.

121. The phrasing echoes the position of Christ at the right hand of God the Father. The Brigittine abbess, unlike the Benedictine abbess, is thus aligned with Christ much as the abbot is aligned with Christ in chapter 2 of the Benedictine Rule: "Christi enim agere vices in monasterio creditur, quando ipsius vocatur pronomine" (Fry et al., *RB 1980* 172).

122. The presence of the abbess, Mary's representative, with the bishop, Christ's representative, also recalls the placement of Mary with Christ and God the Father in the late medieval Marian trinities.

123. Pierre Bourdieu, *In Other Words: Essays Towards a Reflexive Sociology*, trans. Matthew Adamson (Stanford, Calif.: Stanford University Press, 1990), 137.

124. Coulton, *Five Centuries of Religion*, 2:480.

125. McNamara, *Sisters in Arms*, 271.

126. Anne Bagnall Yardley, "The Marriage of Heaven and Earth: A Late Medieval Source of the *Consecratio virginum*," *Current Musicology* 45–47 (1990): 308. For a discussion of Bishop Fox's translation of the Benedictine Rule for the nuns in his diocese of Winchester, see Chapter 2. Although MS Cambridge, University Library, Mm 3.13, which dates to 1500–1528 (ibid., 309), is later than the period with which I am dealing in the rest of this chapter, Yardley's comparison of the chant incipits in Mm 3.13 with those in other English pontificals reveals that the chants and accompanying

actions were (with the exception of the chant *Prudentes virgines*) in use in England by the fourteenth century at the latest, and some as early as the eleventh century (ibid., table 2, 311). In the manuscript the text is designated *Ordo consecrationis sanctimonialium*, but Bagnall gives it the title *Consecratio virginum*. The profession of nuns and consecration of virgins were separate services, although there has been some scholarly confusion of the two. The text given in Mm 3.13 is indeed that of the ritual for the consecration of virgins and closely resembles the version of this service given in the *Customary* of Barking Abbey. As Dame Laurentia McLachlan observes, though, many Benedictine nuns underwent both ceremonies. The ceremony for the consecration of a virgin "took place in some instances many years after the profession. . . . The delay might be due to the candidate's being under age, for the first profession was granted to quite young girls, so young indeed even in the fifteenth century . . . that it was possible for the candidate not to have made her first Communion. . . . The solemn consecration was withheld until a ripe age had been reached" (Tolhurst, *Barking* 2:388). I therefore believe it is appropriate to consider this text in a discussion of the formation of religious identities for Benedictine nuns.

127. Yardley, "Marriage of Heaven and Earth," 309.

128. As Yardley notes, the "double delivery of the rings is presumably the only way to have a double ring ceremony with an invisible spouse" (ibid., 313).

129. Ibid., 315.

130. For late medieval versions of the lives of Saints Agnes and Agatha, versions which were in fact presented to a community of nuns, see Osbern Bokenham, *Legendys of Hooly Wummen*, ed. Mary S. Serjeantson, Early English Text Society o.s. 206 (London: Oxford University Press, 1938).

131. Jocelyn Wogan-Browne, "The Virgin's Tale," *Feminist Readings in Middle English Literature: The Wife of Bath and All Her Sect*, ed. Ruth Evans and Lesley Johnson (London: Routledge, 1994), 180.

132. Ibid., 181.

133. Penelope D. Johnson, "*Mulier et Monialis*: The Medieval Nun's Self-Image," *Thought* 64 (1989): 243.

134. Yardley, "Marriage of Heaven and Earth," 322. She translates the text, "By his ring my Lord Jesus Christ has wed me, and like a wife he has adorned me with a crown" (ibid., 313).

135. Ibid., 313.

136. The directions for the annual distribution of books at Barking are as follows: "Post terciam dum missa canitur capitalis: libraria in medio capituli extendat tapetum, libros omnes de armario superponentes. Cumque missa finita fuerit: una queque liber qui sibi anno preterito commisse fuerant: secum deferat in capitulum. Ipsa autem die solebat scolaris recipere regulam sancti benedicti, Post leccionem uero et culparume mendacionem. iubente domina abbatissa, surgat libraria et sedens in medio caplituli, legat in tabulis et nominatim indicet quem librum queque anno habuerit transacto, lectrix uero tam morose legere debet: ut inter unamquaque nominatim tam diu sileat:

quousque nominata librum reddiderit. Cumque autem unaqueque proprium nomen audierit: surgens confestim deferat librum super tapetum quod ibi est extensum, et si ipsum totum perlegerit: inclinet tantum ad crucem et redeat. Omnes qui libros/suos perlegerint eodem modo ad crucem inclinent et redeant. Onmes qui libros suos non perlegerint: prostrate coram abbatissa ueniam petant, dicentes. Mea culpa. tunc iusse surgere et accepta penetencia ab ea: redeant in stacionem suam" (Tolhurst, *Barking* 1:67–68, punctuation and capitalization as in original).

137. See Nicholas Watson, "Censorship and Cultural Change in Late-Medieval England: Vernacular Theology, the Oxford Translation Debate, and Arundel's Constitutions of 1409," *Speculum* 70 (1995): 856–57.

138. A. I. Doyle, "Books Connected with the Vere Family and Barking Abbey," *Transactions of the Essex Archaeological Society* 25 (1958): 240.

139. Doyle observes that the manuscript was made in two parts, and, while the first part may have for a time been in the possession of the Dominican house of Dartford, the second part of the manuscript (which includes the Lollard material) was always owned, and perhaps even made, at Barking. The two parts were "certainly together by the middle of the sixteenth century, the date of the present binding, and it is reasonable to suppose from the compatibility of the contents that they were put together at Barking if they were not both always there from the time of their writing" (Doyle, "Books" 242).

140. "Benedictio Abbatissae Electae," Appendix II: Fragment from the Pontifical of John [Russell] Bishop of Lincoln, *Liber pontificalis Christophori Bainbridge, Archiepiscopi Eboracensis*, Surtees Society 61 (Durham: Surtees Society, 1875), 248–49.

141. Ibid., 249. Another form of the ritual used in the fifteenth century at Barking Abbey similarly foregrounds the abbess's maternal authority. During the Mass, following the Gospel, the abbess-elect approaches the altar. She then "cum monialibus super formas ante gradus altaris uerso uultu ad episcopum monastrans episcopus primo modo in populo dicens *Ecclisie .N. mater electa. Karissimi. et cetera*" (Tolhurst, *Barking* 2:351).

142. "Benedictio Abbatissae Electae," 249.

143. Ibid., 248.

144. Ibid.

145. Roger Chartier observes that practices are the "visible indices" of demonstrated or desired identities (*Cultural History Between Practices and Representations*, trans. Lydia G. Cochrane [Ithaca, N.Y.: Cornell University Press, 1988], 10).

Chapter 2. The Value of the Mother Tongue

1. *Middle English Dictionary*, vol. 11, ed. Robert E. Lewis (Ann Arbor: University of Michigan Press, 1993), 981–84. Kathleen Ashley and Pamela Sheingorn examine the various meanings of *translatio* in rhetoric along with the specifically Christian mean-

ings relating to saints' relics in "The Translations of Foy: Bodies, Texts, and Places," *The Medieval Translator: Traduire au Moyen Age*, ed. Roger Ellis and René Tixier (Turnhout: Brepols, 1996), 26–49. They frame their argument by using the "punning potential of this word in order to explore connections among the various kinds of *translatio*" in Sainte Foy's cult ("Translations of Foy" 30). My argument exploits the multiple senses of *translatio* in a somewhat similar way, examining translations as related social phenomena.

2. On the relationship of bodies and words in medieval sign theory, especially in Augustinian ideas regarding language, see chapter 1 of Marcia Colish, *The Mirror of Language: A Study in the Medieval Theory of Language* (Lincoln: University of Nebraska Press, 1983). On the impact words have on bodies in later medieval culture, see Carolyn Dinshaw, *Chaucer's Sexual Poetics* (Madison: University of Wisconsin Press, 1989). Lori Chamberlain presents an insightful analysis of bodies and words as they participate in gendered concepts of linguistic translation in "Gender and the Metaphorics of Translation," *Rethinking Translation: Discourse, Subjectivity, Ideology*, ed. Lawrence Venuti (London: Routledge, 1992), 57–74.

3. I take the idea of translation as a process which destabilizes boundaries from Roger Ellis, who writes that translation "changes an existing boundary" (introduction to *The Medieval Translator: The Theory and Practice of Translation in the Middle Ages*, ed. Roger Ellis [Cambridge: Brewer, 1989], 3). Rita Copeland also perceptively analyzes the cultural impacts and meanings of textual translation in *Rhetoric, Hermeneutics, and Translation in the Middle Ages: Academic Traditions and Vernacular Texts* (Cambridge: Cambridge University Press, 1991).

4. Anne Clark Bartlett, *Male Authors, Female Readers: Representation and Subjectivity in Middle English Devotional Literature* (Ithaca, N.Y.: Cornell University Press, 1995), 13.

5. For instance, Anne Clark Bartlett argues that the translation of the Godstow nuns' records into English does not indicate a decline of learning but rather represents the nuns' desire to take charge of their business practices. She says that the translation ought to be seen as an indication of "the expansion of women's authority and knowledge" and as evidence for the increase, rather than the decrease, of female literacy in the later medieval period (ibid., 25). Roberta Gilchrist and Marilyn Oliva also address the "substantial administrative talents" needed by women religious to run their houses. They note, "In addition to the organizational skills necessary to provision their houses within allotted revenues, the nuns had to know how to read, write, and keep the financial records of income and expenses" (*Religious Women in Medieval East Anglia: History and Archaeology c. 1100–1540*, Studies in East Anglian History 1 [Norwich: Centre of East Anglian Studies, University of East Anglia, 1993], 55–56). I discuss nuns' involvement in business affairs in detail in Chapter 3.

6. Bartlett, *Male Authors, Female Readers*, 17.

7. David Bell, *What Nuns Read: Books and Libraries in Medieval English Nunneries* (Kalamazoo, Mich.: Cistercian Publications, 1995), 76.

8. Ibid., 77.

9. This passage comes from Richard Ullerston's protranslation *determinatio* in which he summarizes his opponents' attack on translation. The passage is paraphrased by Nicholas Watson in his article "Censorship and Cultural Change in Late-Medieval England: Vernacular Theology, the Oxford Translation Debate, and Arundel's Constitutions of 1409," *Speculum* 70 (1995): 843. My argument in this chapter owes much to the important work on religion and the rise of the vernacular done by Watson and his predecessors, in particular the work of Anne Hudson in *The Premature Reformation: Wycliffite Texts and Lollard History* (Oxford: Clarendon, 1988) and *Lollards and Their Books* (London: Hambledon, 1985) as well as that of Margaret Aston in *Lollards and Reformers: Images and Literacy in Late Medieval Religion* (London: Hambledon, 1984).

10. Susan Signe Morrison observes, "Since the learning of Latin constituted the entry into an exclusive male realm, separate from the lower-status female home, any attempt to translate and disseminate information from Latin would be seen by educated men as potentially threatening" ("Don't Ask, Don't Tell: The Wife of Bath and Vernacular Translations," *Exemplaria* 8 [1996]: 102). In "The Notion of Vernacular Theory," Ruth Evans et al. observe, "The question of who should be able to read what is pivotally important to the vernacular politics of late medieval England and is inseparable from contentious issues of gender, class, education, and community. . . . The politics of access are at least as important to English literary history as the process by which English literature invents itself through *translatio studii*" (Ruth Evans et al., "The Notion of Vernacular Theory," *The Idea of The Vernacular: An Anthology of Middle English Literary Theory, 1280–1520,* ed. Jocelyn Wogan-Browne et al. [University Park: Pennsylvania State University Press, 1999], 322–23).

11. The concept of "saving the market" comes from Pierre Bourdieu's article "The Economics of Linguistic Exchanges," *Social Science Information* 16 (1977): 645–68.

12. Given the larger difficulties facing the English clergy, it is also possible that translation may well have seemed a convenient, manageable target. In the later fourteenth and fifteenth centuries, the clergy was confronted with simultaneous, mutually reinforcing inroads on their authority, prestige, and privilege. The persistent crises of the Babylonian Captivity of 1309–1377 and the Great Schism of 1378–1417 called public attention to the increasingly political and administrative preoccupations of the Church, diminishing the clergy's stock. The conflicts weakened competing hierarchies and added to ever-growing anticlerical sentiment focusing on corruption (on this point, see André Vauchez, *The Laity in the Middle Ages: Religious Beliefs and Devotional Pratices,* trans. Margery J. Schneider [Notre Dame, Ind.: University of Notre Dame Press, 1993]). As clerical prestige declined, so did their ability to acquire and retain land, money, and other goods. Shortly before 1370, a widespread English anticlerical movement emerged, founded in the increasing discontent with the costs of the war with France and dissatisfaction with ecclesiastical freedom from taxation. Because the laity wished to ease its financial burden, demands for heavy taxation of the clergy and for the confiscation of Church property were made. The Austin friars' stand on disen-

dowment, as well as the ideas of Wyclif, provided inspiration; in the Parliament of 1371, anticlerical factions proposed that the government should be able to resume ownership of all private property, including that of the Church, for the purposes of public defenses. While no wholesale takeover of Church property resulted, the challenge to ecclesiastical possession and control of material resources persisted well into the fifteenth century (on these developments, see David Knowles and R. Neville Hadcock, *The Religious Orders in England: The End of the Middle Ages* [Cambridge: Cambridge University Press, 1957], especially chapter 7).

13. On Arundel's Constitutions, see Nicholas Watson, "Censorship," and his essay "The Politics of Middle English Writing" in *The Idea of the Vernacular*, especially 343–45. As Watson observes, in the era following Arundel's Constitutions, a "hierarchical model of the relation between clerical and lay, Latin and vernacular, remained the official line and could be applied with rigor outside the circle of privilege comprising aristocracy, gentry, and urban merchant class" ("Politics of Middle English Writing" 345).

14. Thomas Hoccleve, "Remonstrance Against Oldcastle," *Selections from Hoccleve*, ed. M. C. Seymour (Oxford: Clarendon, 1989), lines 145–150.

15. *Middle English Dictionary*, vol. 2, ed. Hans Kurath (Ann Arbor: University of Michigan Press, 1959), 24.

16. Ruth Nissé, "'Oure Fadres Olde and Modres': Gender, Heresy, and Hoccleve's Literary Politics," *Studies in the Age of Chaucer* 21 (1999): 275. Nissé points particularly to Hoccleve's assertion that "lak of faith" has "qwenchid" Oldcastle's "manhode" (Thomas Hoccleve, "The Remonstrance Against Oldcastle," line 287, qtd. in Nissé, "'Oure Fadres Olde and Modres'" 275).

17. Since Hoccleve was himself a clerk in minor orders, he may well have included himself among the entitled group. Nissé argues that in the "Remonstrance" and in the *Regement of Princes* Hoccleve goes on to promote a "remasculinized" English poetic tradition which is explicitly secular, nationalist, and Chaucerian (see "'Oure Fadres Olde and Modres,'" especially 291–99).

18. I have chosen not to analyze the Middle English version of the Isabella Rule in conjunction with the Benedictine and Brigittine translations in this chapter. Although the Isabella Rule shares with the Brigittine Rule the status of having been developed under the aegis of a women, the Isabella Rule does not have the same strongly vernacular origins that the Brigittine Rule has. While the Brigittine Rule was divinely revealed, as I discuss below, to St. Birgitta in her "mother tongue" of Swedish before it was translated into Latin and revised by clerics, the Isabella Rule was "drawn up by five of the Friars Minor who were learned masters of theology" (Walter W. Seton, ed., *The Rewle of Sustris Menouresses Enclosid, A Fifteenth-Century Courtesy Book and Two Franciscan Rules*, Early English Text Society o.s. 148 [London: Kegan Paul, 1914], 69). The English version of the Isabella Rule in MS Bodl. 585=2357 "is probably a translation from a French version of the original Latin" (ibid., 76). As a vernacular translation of a Latin original, the Isabella Rule shares something with the versions of the Benedictine

Rule analyzed in this chapter, and it is certainly true that in the early development of Franciscan monasticism for women St. Clare was involved in many conflicts about how to "translate" the life of apostolic poverty for women. The Isabella Rule, though, never attempted to construct a life of apostolic poverty for Franciscan nuns, and, unlike the Benedictine Rule, it was a "feminine" rule (that is, designed for women rather than for men) at its inception. The ideological transformations that characterize the later-medieval translations of the Benedictine Rule for women are thus not present in the Isabella Rule. Furthermore, rather than emphasizing the differences between the nuns and Franciscan friars as the translations of the Benedictine rule do with monks and nuns, the Isabella Rule actually seeks, as I argue in Chapter 1, to foreground the equality of men and women in religion.

19. The *Northern Prose Version* appears in MS BL Lansdowne 378, and it dates from the beginning of the fifteenth century (Ernst A. Kock, *Three Middle-English Versions of the Rule of St. Benet and Two Contemporary Rituals for the Ordination of Nuns*, Early English Text Society o.s. 120 [1902; reprint, Millwood, N.Y.: Kraus, 1987], x). The *Northern Verse Version* appears in MS BL Cotton Vespasian A. 25 and dates to "the former part of the 15th c" (ibid.). I cite all quotations from the prose version (hereafter *Prose*) by page number from the Kock edition and all quotations from the verse version (hereafter *Verse*) by line number from the same edition parenthetically in the text. I refer to chapters in the prose version using Roman numerals and to chapters in the verse version using Arabic numerals. Because the translators and houses with which the texts are associated are currently unknown, I focus on how the texts themselves work in later medieval English culture.

20. The argument made by Ruth Evans et al. concerning medieval understanding of the translation process is relevant here. They write, "In medieval Latin, the word *translatio* (translation) was often taken to be synonymous with *expositio* (interpretation). . . . If this equation is taken seriously, it provides a justification for understanding vernacular translations not simply as attempts to transfer meaning unchanged from one language to another but as *readings* of source texts, part of whose purpose may indeed lie in their difference from those texts" ("The Notion of Vernacular Theory" 317).

21. Watson, "Censorship," 844. The corollary to this association was that "a lack of grammatical regulation in the vernacular . . . impl[ied] the unruliness of those who speak it" (ibid.). On this point, see also Wogan-Browne et al., *The Idea of the Vernacular*, 8–10.

22. The only chapters that do not have introductory phrases are VIII–XVII, LXII, and LXV. Chapters VIII–XVII concern divine service, and in these chapters untranslated Latin appears as in the verse version discussed below. The Latin of the divine service, standing untranslated, and the institution of divine service itself, require nothing additional to secure their positions of authority. In other chapters, Latin quotations are translated, but here, since the Latin itself is present without "inferior" vernacular representation, the legitimizing aspect of the figure of St. Benedict is unnecessary.

Chapter LXII discusses priests and the Church hierarchy. Since this passage deals with the masculine ecclesiastical hierarchy, clerical authority needs no support or reinforcement from the insertion of the figure of St. Benedict. This chapter additionally appears to conceive of the abbess as male, beginning, "Yef þabbes prais for preste ouþir for dekin at be ordainde til hym-selfe, *He* sal loke, þat þai be digne þer-to at be preste" (*Prose* 40, my emphasis). Chapter LXV concerning how to choose a prioress does not contain an introductory phrase properly speaking; however, the figure of St. Benedict is introduced within the chapter.

23. Ralph Hanna III, "*Compilatio* and the Wife of Bath," *Latin and Vernacular: Studies in Late-Medieval Texts and Manuscripts*, ed. A. J. Minnis (Cambridge: Brewer, 1989), 11.

24. Joan Greatrex, "On Ministering to 'certayne devoute and religiouse women': Bishop Fox and the Benedictine Nuns of Winchester Diocese on the Eve of the Dissolution," *Women in the Church: Papers Read at the 1989 Summer Meeting and the 1990 Winter Meeting of the Ecclesiastical History Society*, ed. W. J. Sheils and Diana Wood, Studies in Church History 27 (Cambridge: Blackwell, 1990), 227–28. Greatrex does not comment on what the function of these insertions might be beyond saying that they reveal "the homely touch of a fatherly hand" (ibid., 228).

25. As Jocelyn Wogan-Browne et al. observe, Fox, in the prefatory letter to the translation, "inserts himself into a triangular structure, where the bond between male spiritual director and male auditor . . . is underwritten by the group of women in that director's charge" (*The Idea of the Vernacular* 162–63).

26. P. S. Allen and H. M. Allen, eds., *The Letters of Richard Fox, 1486–1525* (Oxford: Clarendon, 1929), 150.

27. Wogan-Browne et al., *The Idea of the Vernacular*, 162.

28. Richard Fox, "*The Rule of Seynt Benet*: Prefatory Letter," in Wogan-Browne et al., *The Idea of the Vernacular*, 164.

29. Chapters VIII–XVII on divine service lack prayers as well as introductory passages.

30. The one chapter containing a prayer which does not state directly or at least imply a "we" is chapter XXXI on the cellaress, which ends, "Lauerd, for þi merci giue hir sua hir office at do, þat so may haue þanc o god and of þe cuuent" (*Prose* 24).

31. Chapter 52 in the Latin original addresses the oratory, and chapter 60, which covers the admission of priests to the monastery, stresses that they are to observe the discipline of the order. Since in Benedict's time few monks were priests, it is not surprising that ordination of priests is not explicitly addressed in the original.

32. Timothy Fry et al., eds., *RB 1980: The Rule of St. Benedict in Latin and English with Notes* (Collegeville, Minn.: Liturgical Press, 1989), 190. Hereafter I cite this edition parenthetically in the text as *RB 1980*. In all of the quotations from this edition, the emphasis is present in the original.

33. Kock observes that the introductory phrases and concluding prayers call attention to the translator's presence in the text. "Of the originator of the version we know nothing. In an indirect manner, however, his existence is constantly brought before the

reader's mind. The chapters begin with *in this sentence spekis sain benet*, or some similar turn, and end with an added short prayer, being, as it were, an echo out of the spiritual children's hearts" (*Three Middle English Versions* xi).

34. It is possible to read "he" in line 1082 as meaning "person." Given, however, the emphasis on women in line 1083, as well as the translator's consciousness throughout that his audience is female (Kock observes that this version is, unlike the prose version, consistently "feminine" [*Three Middle English Versions* x]), the masculine valence of the pronoun "he" seems significant.

35. Barbara Newman, *From Virile Woman to WomanChrist: Studies in Medieval Religion and Literature* (Philadelphia: University of Pennsylvania Press, 1995), 24.

36. A. Hamilton Thompson, *Visitations of Religious Houses in the Diocese of Lincoln*, vol. 1, Lincoln Record Society 7 (Lincoln: Lincoln Record Society, 1914), 104. "Et quod seruetur silencium decetero in claustro, ecclesia, dormitorio et refectorio, sub pena vnius denarij soluendi de communis cuiuslibet monachi in hoc delinquentis ad opus pauimentorum predictorum" (ibid.).

37. Ibid., 52. "Item quod silencium debitis horis et locis, videlicet oratorio, claustro et dormitorio, ab omnibus indistincte obseruetur, sub pena ieiunij in pane et aqua proximis quarta et sexta feriis; et si aliqua monialis deliquerit in hac parte, compellatur ad penam illam: secundo [sic] vice duplicetur eadem pena; et si tercio conuincatur in hoc deliquisse, extunc iniungatur ei ieiunium in pane et aqua omnibus quartis et sextis feriis per proximum per proximum [sic] dimidium annum, ac secunda et quinta feria pane et ceruisia contentetur" (ibid.).

38. Newman writes, "Because the discipline of silence played such a large part in monastic life, exhortations to avoid wicked or idle speech occur frequently in the literature. These are not aimed particularly at women or at men; both sexes are instructed in the virtue of silence and the vice of an unbridled tongue. . . . But while idle words were considered a peril for all religious, the proverbial chatterbox was always female. . . . Writers who viewed all speech with a professional suspicion employed misogynistic rhetoric on this point even if they were not, in other respects, notably hostile to women" (*From Virile Woman to WomanChrist* 24–25).

39. The prose version has brief (three words or fewer) Latin headings for the prologue, primum capitulum, secundum capitulum, tercium capitulum, and capitulum IIII. Chapters I–IV are the only ones with Latin headings. Except for "Qui viuis & regnas deus per omnia secula" in chapter VII, the only full phrases of Latin occur in the chapters about divine service. In contrast, the verse translation has Latin headings, many extended, for forty-two of its chapters.

40. "Si greges meos faciam &c" (*Verse* 2300a).

41. If the presence of Latin suggests at least some ability to read the language or some knowledge of the original text, which, in spite of pessimistic views of women's Latin literacy, would not be entirely unlikely in a female monastic community, then the changes would have had an even greater impact on the female audience. M. T. Clanchy

discusses degrees of ability in Latin among those not fully literate the language in chapter 7 of *From Memory to Written Record* (London: Arnold, 1979).

42. The terminology "feminization of sanctity" comes from André Vauchez, *La sainteté en occident aux derniers siècles du moyen âge* (Rome: Ecole française de Rome; Paris: Diffusion de Boccard, 1981). Dyan Elliott discusses this process, and the nervousness it caused for some clerics, in *Spiritual Marriage: Sexual Abstinence in Medieval Wedlock* (Princeton, N.J.: Princeton University Press, 1993). As quantifiable evidence for the feminization of sanctity as the Middle Ages progressed, Donald Weinstein and Rudolph M. Bell show that the percentage of female saints rose from 11.8 percent in the twelfth century to 22.6 percent in the thirteenth century, continuing to increase to 23.4 percent in the fourteenth century and 27.7 percent in the fifteenth century (*Saints and Society: The Two Worlds of Western Christendom, 1000–1700* [Chicago: University of Chicago Press, 1982], 220–21).

43. Newman, *From Virile Woman to WomanChrist*, 3.

44. John E. Crean, Jr., "Voces Benedictinae: A Comparative Study of Three Manuscripts of the Rule of St. Benedict for Women," *Vox Benedictina* 10 (1993): 169.

45. Ibid.

46. In fact, the reference to God is perhaps more scripturally exact than the association with Christ, as Fry et al. point out, saying, "The biblical text invoked here does not actually give the title *abba* to Christ but to God the Father" (*RB 1980* 172, n. 22). Chapter II in the prose version is not really comparable to chapter 2 in the verse version, because it is definitely masculine, referring to the abbot. The connection of the abbot with God is made, although without the inclusion of the Scripture passage in either Latin or English: "For he sal be in haly kirke in godis stede for to lere his munkis wisdom and charite" (*Prose* 5).

47. Barry Collett, "The Civil Servant and Monastic Reform: Richard Fox's Translation of the Benedictine Rule for Women, 1517," *Monastic Studies: The Continuity of Tradition*, ed. Judith Loades (Bangor, Wales: Headstart History, 1990), 217.

48. Ibid.

49. Ibid., 227 n. 33. Fox does make the more scripturally exact connection between the abbess and God.

50. In chapter LXIV of the prose version, the English seems much closer to the sense of the Latin; the abbess is required to be "wise in goddis law, þat sho draȝe til witnes baþe to þe new law and til þe alde testament" (*Prose* 42).

51. Caroline Walker Bynum, *Jesus as Mother: Studies in the Spirituality of the High Middle Ages* (Berkeley and Los Angeles: University of California Press, 1982), 154.

52. Greatrex, "On Ministering," 228.

53. Collett, "Civil Servant and Monastic Reform," 218.

54. Ibid.

55. Greatrex, "On Ministering," 233.

56. Ibid.

57. Watson, "Politics of Middle English Writing," 345.

58. On the importance of enclosed chastity in female spirituality, see also Karma Lochrie, *Margery Kempe and Translations of the Flesh* (Philadelphia: University of Pennsylvania Press, 1991).

59. Caroline Walker Bynum explores the complexities of women's ascetic spirituality and clerical attempts to contain what they perceived as excesses of asceticism; see *Holy Feast and Holy Fast: The Religious Significance of Food to Medieval Women* (Berkeley and Los Angeles: University of California Press, 1987).

60. Newman writes, "The newly professed nun, unlike the monk, had the dubious advantage of beginning in the same state where she would ideally end" (*From Virile Woman to WomanChrist* 44).

61. *Middle English Dictionary*, vol. 6, ed. Hans Kurath (Ann Arbor: University of Michigan Press, 1959), 598.

62. On the ways in which women's physical makeup was thought to cause them to be especially susceptible to evil spirits and spiritual deception, see Dyan Elliott, "The Physiology of Rapture and Female Spirituality," in *Medieval Thought and the Natural Body*, ed. Peter Biller and Alistair Minnis (Woodbridge: Boydell, 1997), 141–73.

63. For a discussion of this visitation, see Chapter 7.

64. I discuss the importance of Brigittine texts to women living in the world in Chapter 4.

65. Sten Eklund, ed., *Den Heliga Birgitta Opera Minora I: Regula Salvatoris*, SFSS Ser. II, Bd. VIII: 1 (Lund: Berlingska Boktryckeriet, 1975), 105.

66. James Hogg, ed., *The Rewyll of Seynt Sauioure*, vol. 2 of *The Rewyll of Seynt Sauioure and Other Middle English Brigittine Legislative Texts*, Salzburger Studien zur Anglistik und Amerikanistik 6 (Salzburg: Institut für Englische Sprache und Literatur Universität Salzburg, 1978), fol. 42r. Hereafter I cite this edition (a facsimile MS Cambridge University Library Ff. 6. 33) as *Rewyll* parenthetically in the text by folio number. Expansions of abbreviations in the manuscript are indicated by italics, with the exception of the various ampersands used by the scribe, which have been silently expanded.

67. Roger Ellis, *Viderunt Eam Filie Syon: The Spirituality of the English House of a Medieval Contemplative Order from its Beginnings to the Present Day*, Analecta Cartusiana 68 (Salzburg: Institut für Anglistik und Amerikanistik Universität Salzburg, 1984), 21. Both the origins of the Rule in Birgitta's revelations and the status of women in the Brigittine Order caused a great deal of controversy in the creation of the order. For example, the Rule's "subordination of the men to the women . . . seems, from the very beginning, to have been a potential source of difficulty" (ibid., 32). Consequently, Urban V issued a drastically revised version of the Rule in 1370 which cut all indications that Christ dictated the Rule, and he redefined the role of the abbess. In 1378, Urban VI confirmed his predecessor's approval (ibid., 50). For an account of the changes made to the Brigittine Rule in the process of papal approval, see Roger Ellis,

"The Visionary and the Canon Lawyers: Papal and Other Revisions to the *Regula Salvatoris* of St. Bridget of Sweden," *Prophets Abroad: The Reception of Continental Holy Women in Late-Medieval England*, ed. Rosalynn Voaden (Cambridge: Brewer, 1996), 71–90. In his introduction to *Den Heliga Birgitta Opera Minora I: Regula Salvatoris*, Sten Eklund provides a comprehensive explanation of the relationships between various versions and manuscripts of the *Regula*.

68. John Henry Blunt, ed., *The Myroure of Oure Ladye*, Early English Text Society e.s. 19 (London: Kegan Paul, 1873), 18. All subsequent quotations from *The Myroure of Oure Ladye* are given parenthetically in the text by page number from the edition (hereafter *Myroure*).

69. A similar image appears in the *Reuelaciones extravagantes* 69 where the Virgin Mary appears to Birgitta and tells her to sew her daughter Catherine's tunic. Dyan Elliott comments that this revelation is a way of urging Birgitta to "maternal kindness" for this daughter whom she had initiated into a strict life of obedience and penitence (*Spiritual Marriage* 280–81). This revelation thus also reinforces a connection of the traditional female work of sewing and the labor of maternity.

70. Claire Sahlin discusses the related idea of maternity as an authorizing strategy for St. Birgitta's prophetic authority in "'A Marvelous and Great Exultation of the Heart': Mystical Pregnancy and Marian Devotion in Bridget of Sweden's *Revelations*," *Studies in St. Birgitta and the Brigittine Order*, vol. 1, Analecta Carthusiana 35, ed. James Hogg (Salzburg: Institut für Anglistik und Amerikanistik Universität Salzburg; Lewiston, N.Y.: Mellen, 1993), 108–28 and at length in "Birgitta of Sweden and the Voice of Prophecy: A Study of Gender and Religious Authority in the Later Middle Ages" (Ph.D. diss., Harvard University, 1996).

71. According to the requirements of Arundel's Constitutions, the *Myroure* does bear the episcopal stamp of approval, as discussed below.

72. See *Rewyll*, fol. 56r–56v.

73. Mary's prominence as co-redemptrix in the Brigittine tradition resonates with the two types of the "Marian trinity," that is, the Double Intercession and the Coronation of the Virgin, which were widespread in the fifteenth century. The ancient tradition of associating the Holy Spirit with the female and with a divine Mother led to the identification of the Holy Spirit with Mary. See Newman, *From Virile Woman to Woman-Christ*, especially 198–209, on the development and iconography of late medieval Marian trinities.

74. Ellis, *Viderunt Eam Filie Syon*, 27. This kind of inversion process, based on the concept of the last becoming first, undergirds the late medieval feminization of sanctity and is very much in evidence in the penitential movement in which Birgitta, a matron who did not herself become a nun, participated. See Vauchez, *Sainteté*, and Elliott, *Spiritual Marriage*, on the penitential movement.

75. In addition to causing problems in the process of papal approval of the rule, the role of the abbess caused difficulties at the foundation of Syon, leading to conflict be-

tween the appointed abbess Matilda Newton and the appointed confessor general William Alnwick (Margaret Deanesly, ed., *The Incendium Amoris* of Richard Rolle of Hampole [Manchester: Manchester University Press; London: Longmans, 1915], 110–11).

76. Eklund, *Den Heliga Birgitta Opera Minora I: Regula Salvatoris*, 161.

77. The withdrawal of descriptions of Christ speaking the rule to St. Birgitta, a move likely conceived to limit female authority as well as forestall troublesome questions concerning orthodoxy, took place during the process of papal approval, and is evident in the more widely used form of the Rule. The Middle English version of the rule (MS Cambridge University Library Ff. 6. 33) depends on the only copy of the version of the Rule connected with Syon (BL Harley 612). The Middle English, however, only restores the cut prologues to the basic text (Ellis, *Viderunt Eam Filie Syon* 51). The Middle English does not contain the chapter headings from the version indicating that Christ spoke the material in the chapter to St. Birgitta.

78. Ibid., 28. The Latin reads, "Libri quoque, quotquot necessarii fuerint ad diuinum officium peragendum, habendi sunt, plures autem nullo modo. Illos vero libros habeant, quotquot voluerint, in quibus addiscendum est vel studendum" (Eklund, *Den Heliga Birgitta Opera Minora I: Regula Salvatoris* 167). The Middle English reads, "Bookes also are to be had as many as be necessary to doo dyvyne office and moo in no wyse. Thoo bookes they shall haue as many as they wyll in whiche ys to lernne or to studye" (*Rewyll* fols. 62v–63r). On books and reading at Syon, see Mary Erler, "Syon Abbey's Care for Books: Its Sacristan's Account Rolle 1506/7–1535/6," *Scriptorium* 39 (1985): 293–307; and Ann M. Hutchison, "Devotional Reading in the Monastery and in the Late Medieval Household," *De Cella in Seculum: Religion and Secular Life and Devotion in Late Medieval England*, ed. Michael G. Sargent (Cambridge: Brewer, 1989), 215–27.

79. Ellis, *Viderunt Eam Filie Syon*, 28–29. Nicholas Watson observes that in the years following Arundel's Constitutions, only a social elite had real access to "vernacular theology" ("Censorship" 56). Syon's wealth and the generally high social status of the nuns there may have done much to mitigate clerical unease about female learning.

80. Ellis, *Viderunt Eam Filie Syon*, 28.

81. A. Jeffries Collins, *The Bridgettine Breviary of Syon*, Henry Bradshaw Society 96 (Worcester: Henry Bradshaw Society, 1969), xxxviii.

82. Ibid., xxxix–xl.

83. Michel de Certeau, *The Practice of Everyday Life*, trans. Steven Rendall (Berkeley and Los Angeles: University of California Press, 1984), 36.

84. Wogan-Browne et al., *The Idea of the Vernacular*, 163.

85. On *ruminatio*, see Jean Leclercq, *The Love of Learning and the Desire for God: A Study of Monastic Culture*, trans. Catharine Misrahi (New York: Fordham University Press, 1982), 72–73.

86. Certeau, *Practice of Everyday Life*, 37.

87. See Luce Irigaray, "Body Against Body: In Relation to the Mother," *Sexes and Genealogies*, trans. Gillian C. Gill (New York: Columbia University Press, 1993), 9–21.

88. See chapter 6 of Barbara Newman's *From Virile Woman to WomanChrist* for a discussion of other medieval attempts, such as those of the Guglielmites and Na Prous, to foreground the primacy of the maternal in salvation history.

89. Margaret Homans, *Bearing the Word: Language and Female Experience in Nineteenth-Century Women's Writing* (Chicago: University of Chicago Press, 1993), xi.

90. Ibid., 30–31.

91. Similarly, discussion of the Word made flesh occurs in the sequence of the office for the period from Christmas to Candlemas: "*Verbum ens*, The beynge worde of the hiest hathe suffered to be incorporate. takynge a body" (*Myroure* 298); in the sequence on Easter Wednesday: "*Verbum verbo*, By worde thow haste conceyued the worde. thou has broughte furthe the kynge of kynges vyrgyn unknowen of man" (ibid., 307); in the hymn at Thursday Matins: "*Maria*, Mari hathe conceyued in wombe by the trew sede of worde" (ibid., 232).

Chapter 3. Accounting for Themselves

1. George James Aungier, *The History and Antiquities of Syon Monastery, the Parish of Isleworth, and the Chapelry of Hounslow* (London: Nichols, 1840), 29.

2. Ibid.

3. Ibid.

4. For information on nominations to nunneries, see Eileen Power, *Medieval English Nunneries c. 1275 to 1535* (Cambridge: Cambridge University Press, 1922), 188–99. See also Janet Burton, "Yorkshire Nunneries in the Middle Ages: Recruitment and Resources," *Government, Religion and Society in Northern England 1000–1700*, ed. John C. Appleby and Paul Dalton (Stroud: Sutton, 1997), 106–108.

5. Power, *Medieval English Nunneries*, 103. The original charter of this grant is printed in Aungier, *History and Antiquities*, 411–18, and a translation is included, 60–67. Power quotes from this translation.

6. Power, *Medieval English Nunneries*, 104; ellipses in original.

7. Ibid.

8. Aungier, *History and Antiquities*, 28–29. In fact, the charter enlarges the powers of the abbess stated in the Brigittine Rule by giving her power over both spiritual and temporal matters. The abbess of Syon's authority was subsequently restricted to temporal affairs as the Rule specifies.

9. PRO: E135 3/12. In passages taken from this and other documents in the Public Record Office, expansions of abbreviations in the manuscripts are indicated by italics. In expanding abbreviations, I use the spellings most frequently found in each document.

10. Ibid. I have added punctuation and capitalization in square brackets for the sake of comprehensibility.

11. For information on the nuns' library at Syon, see David Bell, *What Nuns Read:*

Books and Libraries in Medieval English Nunneries, Cistercian Studies Series 158 (Kalamazoo, Mich.: Cistercian Publications, 1995), 171–210. Also see Mary C. Erler, "Syon Abbey's Care for Books: Its Sacristan's Account Rolls 1506/7–1535/6," *Scriptorium* 39 (1985): 293–307.

12. Martha Carlin, *St. Botolph Aldgate (Minories, East Side; The Abbey of St. Clare; Holy Trinity Minories)* (London: University of London Institute of Historical Research, Social and Economic Study of Medieval London, 1987), 68/1, 2–3.

13. Ibid.

14. L. F. Salzman, ed., *The Victoria History of the County of Cambridge and the Isle of Ely*, vol. 2 (London: Oxford University Press, 1948), 293, 295; hereafter *VCH Cambridge*.

15. William Keatinge Clay, *Histories of the Four Adjoining Parishes of Waterbeach, Landbeach, Horningsey, and Milton in the County of Cambridge*, Cambridge Antiquarian Society 4, 6, 7, 11 (Cambridge: Cambridge Antiquarian Society, 1861–1869), 105. In addition to overcoming early difficulties in transferring the community of Minoresses from Waterbeach to Denney, Mary de St. Pol founded the chantry-hermitage of St. Giles at Cripplegate in London as well as Pembroke College at Cambridge in 1347 (*VCH Cambridge* 295).

16. Clay, *Histories*, 105.

17. E. B. Fryde, *Peasants and Landholders in Later Medieval England* (New York: St. Martin's, 1996), 76.

18. Ibid., 3.

19. Power, *Medieval English Nunneries*, 99.

20. R. H. Britnell, *The Commercialisation of English Society 1000–1500* (Cambridge: Cambridge University Press, 1993).

21. This manuscript contains a transcription of court records of Denney made by William Cole from a manuscript in Trinity College Library Cambridge in 1746–47.

22. MS BL Add. 5837, fol. 142v.

23. Ibid., fol 141v.

24. Ibid., fol. 142v.

25. Ibid., fol. 143v. In this transaction, Edmund Bartlett's name is spelled Edmond Bertillot, but it seems unlikely that this is a different person. Cole also transcribes Isabel's last name as "Seyntour" in this transaction. It is possible that Isabel Winter and Isabel Seyntour are two different nuns. However, Clay, in what is evidently a reference to this transaction, reads the property-owner's name as Isabel Wynter: "The Lady Isabel Wynter, though resident at Denney, still possessed copyhold land, and received the rent of it. 5 Henry VI. [1426]" (*Histories* 118). He includes the following information (reading "Edward" instead of "Edmund"): "Edward Bertellet takes to farme of the Ladye Abbesse by the consent of Isabell Wynter, one of the sisters, one clause called Letysȝers, To hould during the Tearme of Tenne yeares payeinge Twelve shillinges yearely rent to the sd Isabell Wynter" (ibid.). Clay does not cite his source, but I assume he was using the original Trinity College MS transcribed by Cole, and that the discrep-

ancies result from their different readings of that manuscript. In his transcription, Cole posits that a Lady Joane Staynowre mentioned in a later transaction might be the same person as Lady Isabell Seyntour. I believe, though, given Clay's reading and the greater degrees of similarity between "Seyntour" and "Wynter" than between "Isabell" and "Joane," that Isabell Seyntour is probably Isabell Wynter. Because neither Cole nor Clay fully identifies the Trinity College manuscript, I have been unable to consult it directly.

26. MS BL Add. 5837, fol. 143v.

27. Jo Ann Kay McNamara, *Sisters in Arms: Catholic Nuns Through Two Millennia* (Cambridge, Mass.: Harvard University Press, 1996), 274.

28. Roger Chartier writes that practices are the "visible indices" of "demonstrated or desired identities" (*Cultural History Between Practices and Representations*, trans. Lydia G. Cochrane [Ithaca, N.Y.: Cornell University Press, 1988], 10).

29. *VCH Cambridge*, 299.

30. PRO: C1 40/30.

31. PRO: C1 40/32.

32. PRO: C1 40/30.

33. Elizabeth M. Makowski, *Canon Law and Cloistered Women: Periculoso and Its Commentators 1298–1545* (Washington, D.C.: Catholic University of America Press, 1997), 66.

34. Ibid., 86.

35. Power, *Medieval English Nunneries*, 185.

36. *VCH Cambridge*, 299.

37. *Calendar of Patent Rolls, 1476–1485* (London: HMSO, 1910), 304.

38. Clay, *Histories*, 112.

39. Ibid.

40. PRO: C1 245/28.

41. For a discussion of freedoms available to and restrictions on later medieval widows, see Caroline M. Barron, "Introduction: The Widow's World in Later Medieval London," *Medieval London Widows 1300–1500*, ed. Caroline M. Barron and Anne F. Sutton (London: Hambledon, 1994), xii–xxxiv.

42. Jean Leclercq, "Medieval Feminine Monasticism: Reality Versus Romantic Images," *Benedictus: Studies in Honor of St. Benedict of Nursia*, ed. E. Rozanne Elder (Kalamazoo, Mich.: Cistercian Publications, 1981), 63.

43. Roberta Gilchrist and Marilyn Oliva, *Religious Women in Medieval East Anglia: History and Archaeology c. 1100–1540*, Studies in East Anglian History 1 (Norwich: Centre of East Anglian Studies, University of East Anglia, 1991), 17–18.

44. Robert H. Snape, *Monastic Finance in the Later Middle Ages* (Cambridge: Cambridge University Press, 1926), 149.

45. David Knowles and R. Neville Hadcock, vol. 2, *The Religious Orders in England* (Cambridge: Cambridge University Press, 1957), 287.

46. A. Hamilton Thompson, "Appendix VIII: Double Monasteries and the Male

Element in Nunneries," *The Archbishop of Canterbury's Committee on the Ministry of Women* (New York: Macmillan, 1919), 162.

47. Power, *Medieval English Nunneries*, 236, 236 n. 2.

48. Power herself acknowledges, "Sometimes the office of steward was complimentary and the fee attached was nominal" (*Medieval English Nunneries* 146).

49. Pierre Bourdieu, *Outline of a Theory of Practice*, trans. Richard Nice (Cambridge: Cambridge University Press, 1977), 78.

50. For an account of typical systems of administration in nunneries, see chapter 3 in Marilyn Oliva, *The Convent and the Community in Later Medieval England: History and Archaeology c. 1000–1541*, Studies in the History of Medieval Religion 12 (Woodbridge: Boydell Press, 1998).

51. PRO: SC6 1260/18. The same account also includes a payment of 3s 1d to John Aleyn "equitat' *pour iii foitz in holand pour le dit salt*" (ibid.).

52. PRO: SC6 1260/8. In 2–3 Richard II they paid "*viis vid pour procuracione del esglise de Corby pour cest an*" (ibid.).

53. Ibid. Power notes another instance, taken from an unspecified PRO SC6 1260 series account, of such travel when the prioress was paid 1s 2 1/2d "in the expenses of . . . going to Rockingham about our woods" (*Medieval English Nunneries* 70).

54. Gilchrist and Oliva, *Religious Women in Medieval East Anglia*, 28.

55. William Dugdale, *Monasticon Anglicanum*, trans. John Caley et al., new ed., vol. 3 (London: Bohn, 1846), 359–60.

56. McNamara, *Sisters in Arms*, 290.

57. Nunneries tended to have one of two kinds of administrative staffs of servants: houses whose revenues came from scattered rents usually had a single staff of officials, while those houses which possessed various entire manors typically had a central staff as well as a bailiff and subordinate staff for each manor (Power, *Medieval English Nunneries* 99–100). As Barbara Harvey notes, servants "constituted [the house's] permanent establishment" (*Living and Dying in England 1100–1540: The Monastic Experience* [Oxford: Clarendon, 1993], 148).

58. PRO: SC6 1260/7, 1260/8, 1260/12, 1260/18.

59. Gilchrist and Oliva, *Religious Women in Medieval East Anglia*, 66.

60. Oliva, *The Convent and the Community*, 138.

61. Not all servants received food and clothing or the payments in lieu. Power indicates that some "received wages without board, others wages without livery" (*Medieval English Nunneries* 155). Harvey notes that there were two components of board, the first being bread and ale, the second being cooked food. The right to one did not guarantee the right to the other (*Living and Dying* 170).

62. PRO: SC6 1260/12.

63. PRO: SC6 1260/18.

64. Harvey, *Living and Dying*, 176.

65. Ibid., 162.

66. Ibid.

67. Christopher Dyer, *Standards of Living in the Later Middle Ages: Social Change in England c. 1200–1520* (Cambridge: Cambridge University Press, 1989), 226.

68. McNamara, *Sisters in Arms*, 273.

69. Gilchrist and Oliva, *Religious Women in Medieval East Anglia*, 64.

70. Ibid.

71. Marilyn Oliva, unpublished paper qtd. in Roberta Gilchrist, *Gender and Material Culture: The Archaeology of Religious Women* (London: Routledge, 1994), 24.

72. The *peculium* is defined as private property "applied to the yearly allowance made in certain religious houses to each brother [sic] from the common fund, and used by him [sic] for clothing, bedding and other necessaries" (A. Hamilton Thompson, *Visitations of Religious Houses*, vol. 1, Lincoln Record Society 7 [Lincoln: Lincoln Record Society, 1914], 243).

73. PRO: SC6 914/1.

74. PRO: SC6 914/13.

75. PRO: SC6 914/4. As is typical in the later accounts of this house, the distribution is not broken down into the stipend received by each individual servant.

76. Gilchrist and Oliva, *Religious Women in Medieval East Anglia*, 28.

77. Ibid.

78. *VCH Cambridge*, 302.

79. J. S. Cockburn et al., eds., *The Victoria History of the County of Middlesex*, vol. 1 (London: Oxford University Press, 1911), 190.

80. Although this seal is from a period significantly earlier than the one under consideration here, monastic seals were "a fairly conservative medium. Once established, the image chosen to represent the house was often used for hundreds of years" (Gilchrist and Oliva, *Religious Women in Medieval East Anglia* 28).

81. William Page, ed., *The Victoria History of the County of Hertford*, vol. 4 (London: Constable, 1914), 432.

Chapter 4. A Coin of Changing Value

1. Mary Macleod Banks, ed., *Alphabet of Tales*, Early English Text Society o.s. 127 (Millwood, N.Y.: Kraus, 1972), 11.

2. Ibid.

3. Paul Strohm, *Hochon's Arrow: The Social Imagination of Fourteenth-Century Texts* (Princeton, N.J.: Princeton University Press, 1992), 134–35.

4. Martha Howell, *Women, Production, and Patriarchy in Late Medieval Cities* (Chicago: University of Chicago Press, 1986), 19–21.

5. Banks, *Alphabet*, 11.

6. Ibid., 12.

7. Ibid.

8. Jean-Joseph Goux, *Symbolic Economies After Marx and Freud*, trans. Jennifer Curtiss Gage (Ithaca, N.Y.: Cornell University Press, 1990), 227.

9. Ibid., 233. In the French play *L'enfant donné au diable*, part of the collection *Miracles de Nostre Dame par personnages* in which appears a version of the miracle of the pregnant abbess, the issue of the child as property is also prominent. In *L'enfant donné au diable*, the wife makes a written contract with the devil to hand over her child, but the Virgin Mary saves the child by upholding patriarchal property rights, asserting that the mother "N'auoit riens a donner en lui" (*L'enfant donné au diable, Miracles de Nostre Dame par personnages*, vol. 1, ed. Gaston Paris and Ulysse Robert [Paris, 1876], line 1319).

10. On the rise of the Eucharist as a central symbol in later medieval culture, see Miri Rubin, *Corpus Christi: The Eucharist in Late Medieval Culture* (Cambridge: Cambridge University Press, 1991). Sarah Beckwith analyzes the importance of the body of Christ "as a *symbol* shaping and shaped by the *social vision* of the *religious culture* of the late Middle Ages in England" (*Christ's Body: Identity, Culture and Society in Late Medieval Writings* [London: Routledge, 1993], 2, her emphasis), describing the body of Christ as a symbol "subject to a very minute, material, precise and local form of economic calculation" (*Christ's Body* 108–9).

11. Pierre Bourdieu, *Outline of a Theory of Practice*, trans. Richard Nice, Cambridge Studies in Social and Cultural Anthropology 16, ed. Ernest Gellner et al. (Cambridge: Cambridge University Press, 1977), 178, his emphasis.

12. In *"Throughout Your Generations Forever": Sacrifice, Religion, and Paternity* (Chicago: University of Chicago Press, 1992), Nancy Jay writes, "Opposition between sacrifice and childbirth, or between sacrifice and childbearing women, that is, mothers or potential mothers, is present in countless different sacrificial traditions. This opposition is manifested in a number of different ways; for example, the gender roles of sacrificial practice. It is a common feature of unrelated traditions that only adult males—fathers, real and metaphorical—may perform sacrifice" (xxiii). She goes on to discuss the Eucharist as one of the practices in which the opposition between sacrifice and childbirth is present. I am grateful to Peggy McCracken for bringing Jay's work to my attention.

13. See M. E. Aston, "Lollard Women Priests?" *Journal of Ecclesiastical History* 31 (1980): 441–61. Recently, however, Shannon McSheffrey has argued that Aston and other scholars have overemphasized the opportunities Lollardy presented to women (especially in regard to literacy) and women's influence within Lollard groups. See Shannon McSheffrey, "Literacy and the Gender Gap in the Late Middle Ages: Women and Reading in Lollard Communities," *Women, the Book, and the Godly: Selected Proceedings of the St. Hilda's Conference, 1993*, vol. 1, ed. Lesley Smith and Jane H. M. Taylor (Cambridge: D. S. Brewer, 1995), 157–70; and *Gender and Heresy: Women and Men in Lollard Communities 1420–1530* (Philadelphia: University of Pennsylvania Press, 1995).

14. Goux, *Symbolic Economies*, 228.

15. Ibid., 225.

16. Ibid.

17. Jay, *"Throughout Your Generations"*, xxiv.

18. Peter Whiteford, *The Myracles of Oure Lady ed. from Wynkyn de Worde's Edition*, Middle English Texts 23, ed. M. Gorlach and O. S. Pickering (Heidelberg: Winter, 1990), 26.

19. On the Northern Homily Cycle, see Whiteford, *Myracles*, 102–4; on MS BL Add. 25719, ibid., 121–22; on MS BL Add. 29996, ibid., 117–18.

20. Felicity Riddy, "Mother Knows Best: Reading Social Change in a Courtesy Text," *Speculum* 71 (1996): 73. The convergence of the interests of "male clerics and city fathers" is evident, for instance, in the distinct parallels exhibited by conduct literature and the episcopal visitation records which express concern about nuns' chastity, reputation, and the importance of avoiding public places. In her discussion of "What the Goodwife Taught Her Daughter," Riddy remarks, "Why is the daughter warned against wandering around town and going to unsuitable entertainments? What is at stake in not being regarded as a 'strompet' or a 'gigelot'? The answer seems to be the prime bourgeois value: respectability" (ibid., 78).

21. Adrian James McCarthy, ed., *Book to a Mother: An Edition with Commentary*, Studies in the English Mystics 1, Elizabethan and Renaissance Studies 92, ed. James Hogg (Salzburg: Institut für Anglistik und Amerikanistik Universität Salzburg, 1981), 1. For a summary of textual evidence suggesting clerical authorship, see McCarthy's introduction, especially xxv–xxvi. I hereafter cite this edition parenthetically in the text as *Book to a Mother*.

22. C. Horstman, ed., *The Abbey of the Holy Ghost, Yorkshire Writers: Richard Rolle of Hampole, an English Father of the Church, and his Followers*, vol. 1 (London: Swan Sonnenschein, 1895), 321.

23. For a description of the *Abbey* and the *Charter* which summarizes the texts and places them in a tradition of architectural allegories of the cloister stretching back to Hugh of Fouilloy in the mid-twelfth century, see Christiana Whitehead, "Making a Cloister of the Soul in Medieval Religious Treatises," *Medium Aevum* 67 (1998): 1–29.

24. Ibid., 1.

25. McCarthy, *Book to a Mother*, 214 n. 22/21–3.

26. The three substantial vows are interpreted in a somewhat modified fashion, being rendered as "stabulnes in holdinge his hestis . . . chaunching of synful maners . . . uerrei obediens to þi lyues ende" (*Book to a Mother* 124–25).

27. Whitehead notes that many of the personifications of the virtues in the *Abbey* are "identical in title to the virtues personified in courtly poetry" ("Making a Cloister" 17). In particular, "Humility, Mercy, Patience, Simplicity, Courtesy, Reason, Loyalty, and Largesse are . . . all to be found in both sections of *Le Roman de la Rose*, and Courtesy, Loyalty, Generosity, Humility, Charity, and Faith all appear in Froissart's *Le Temple d'Honneur*" (ibid., 28 n. 76).

28. C. Horstman, ed., *The Charter of the Abbey of the Holy Ghost, Yorkshire Writers*, 362.

29. Whitehead, "Making a Cloister," 14.

30. On the ownership of the manuscripts, see Whitehead, "Making a Cloister," 28 n. 63. Clearly, these French texts are very close to the Middle English *Abbey*. In MS BL Add. 39843, the text begins, "La sainte abbaie et la religion doit estre fondé espirituele-ment en la conscience" (fol. 2r, qtd. in Kathleen Chesney, "Notes on Some Treatises of Devotion Intended for Margaret of York," *Medium Aevum* 20 [1951]: 14) and ends "et einsi sera l'abbaie ordenee et renformee comme devant" (fol. 5v; qtd. in Chesney, "Notes" 14). In MS Douce 365, the text, which is erroneously attributed to Jean Gerson, begins, "Cy commence ung beau traitté jadiz compilé par maistre jehan jarson, docteur en theologie. Et est intitulé L'abbaye du saint esperit. Premierement comment chascuns personne poeult icelle abbaye et religion fonder en sa conscience. Le chapitre premier. Fille regarde que moult de gens voldroient bien estre en religion maiz ilz ne peuent, ou par povreté, ou par ce qu'ilz sont par loyen de mariage retenus ou par aultre raison" (fol. Ir; qtd. in Chesney, "Notes" 13). Interestingly, in addition to owning manuscripts containing *Li Liure du cloistre de l'ame*, both Marie de Bourbon and Margaret of York were patronesses of convents of reformed Franciscan nuns founded by St. Colette of Corbie. St. Colette was intimately involved with both the Bourbon and Anglo-Burgundian factions during the Hundred Years' War, and the research I am currently pursuing on St. Colette's foundations suggests that both factions manipulated their connections with Colette and her houses to political ends, much as the opposing Lancastrians and Yorkists did with St. Birgitta and Syon, as discussed in Chapter 5.

31. Whitehead, "Making a Cloister," 17.

32. The staff of virtuous obedientiaries in the *Abbey* and *Charter* is paralleled by another staff of obedientiaries in a contemporary poem sharply critical of the life of women religious. In "Why I Can't Be a Nun," a young woman, whose father has forbidden her from entering a nunnery, sorrows until Experience shows her in a dream vision the parlous state of contemporary monastic life (Frederick J. Furnivall, ed., "Why I Can't Be a Nun," *Early English Poems and Lives of Saints, Transactions of the Philological Society* 1858, part 2, 138–48). She sees a community in which Dame Patience and Dame Charity have been ousted (lines 263–68); furthermore, "Dame Chastyte . . . / In that couent had lytelle chere" (lines 239–40). To make matters worse, Dame "devowte" has been "by vyolens" put out by "dame sclowthe and dame veyne glory" (lines 226–29). After a further litany of vices to be found in the nunnery, Experience advises the young woman that "suche bene the nunnes in euery warde" (line 312), filled with hypocrisy since their habit, wimple and veil are "a false token" (line 360) of holiness they do not possess.

33. Horstman, *Abbey*, 336.

34. Whitehead, "Making a Cloister," 18.

35. Whitehead reads the *Book to a Mother*'s treatment of female monasticism as being

more wholly negative than I do. She writes that the *Book* "appears to be on the verge of rejecting the institution of monasticism altogether, concluding it to be irrevocably corrupt" (ibid., 22).

36. This treatment of female monasticism also resembles the way in which the *Book* "consistently favors analogy, and frequently uses it to develop the 'typical sense' of Sacred Scripture" (*Book to a Mother* xxxi).

37. *Lecherie* in Middle English refers both to excessive desire for sex and material goods. The first meaning given for *lecherie* in the *Middle English Dictionary* is "A lascivious way of life; the habit or practice of adultery, fornication, etc." Subsequent definitions include the combination of sexual and economic activity in "pimping, pandering," and the more strictly materialistic "self-indulgence . . . extravagant or riotous living." There is also a specific connection with apparel as the phrase "lecherie of clothing" indicates (*Middle English Dictionary*, vol. 5, ed. Hans Kurath [Ann Arbor: University of Michigan Press, 1959], 740–41).

38. The writer of the *Charter* makes a similar connection. Eve, who is "boþe coueytous & lykerouse as comenliche wymmen ben," causes the destruction of the abbey. By eating the apple and giving it to Adam, she lets in Pride, Gluttony, Covetousness, and Folly, who bear away all the abbey's goods, drive away the "faire abbesse & þe priouresse & al here holy couent," and even make off with the charter in which God confirmed the site of the abbey, Conscience, to Adam and Eve (Horstman, *Charter* 341–43).

39. The *Book to a Mother* exists in Bodleian MSS Bodley 416 and Laud Misc. 210, in MS BL Add. 30897, and, in very fragmentary form, in MS BL Egerton 826. Bodley 416 is from about 1400; the other two manuscripts of the mostly complete text are from slightly later in the fifteenth century. Robert R. Raymo assigns the *Book* to the 1370s (*Works of Religious and Philosophical Instruction*, vol. 7 of *A Manual of the Writings in Middle English, 1050–1500*, ed. Albert E. Hartung [New Haven: Connecticut Academy of Arts and Sciences, 1986], 2267). The fact that the text, which appears primarily orthodox, indicates acceptance of the theory of the dominion of grace suggests, according to McCarthy, composition before 1380, at which point this theory began to be considered heretical and "even Oxford found it necessary to part company with Wyclif" (*Book to a Mother* xxxiii). On the orthodoxy of the *Book to a Mother*, see xlvi–xlvii.

40. For the passage in question, see *Book to a Mother*, 195.

41. Ibid., xxxii–xxxiv. This text is not the only one to associate Edward III with Herod. In *Fasciculi Zizaniorum* the Carmelite friar John Keyngham attacks Wyclif "for fawning on royal favor," and in this attack "the term used by the friar to refer to the royal family was 'the house of Herod'" (*Book to a Mother* xxxii).

42. Thomas Walsingham, *Historia Anglicana*, vol. 1, ed. Henry Thomas Riley, Rolls Series 28 pt. 1 vol. 1 (London, 1863), 320.

43. Ibid., 328.

44. Significantly, the priestly writer of the *Book to a Mother* connects the figure of Herod with prostitution as well, saying that Herod "is as muche to seie as 'ioynge in

skinnes,' or 'gloriouse skinny': Þerof is seid a comune wommon þat is ioynge in hure skyn, and gloriouse in þingus wiþoute-forth" (194).

45. Walsingham, *Historia Anglicana*, 320–21.

46. Strohm, *Hochon's Arrow*, 139.

47. This paradigm, as discussed below, is also applicable to the *Book to a Mother's* portrayal of nuptial relations between the female reader and Christ.

48. For references to her widowhood, see *Book to a Mother*, 52, 89.

49. As Caroline Barron has shown, widows had greater autonomous control than married women in their ability to buy and sell property; widows could bequeath property independently and could run businesses in their own name. See "The 'Golden Age' of Women in Medieval London," *Medieval Women in Southern England*, Reading Medieval Studies 15, ed. Keith Bate et al. (Reading: University of Reading Press, 1989), 35–58.

50. The priest writes, "And suche a soule þat haþ þese seuene ʒiftes of the Holy Gost, with þese eiʒte blessynges of Cristes mouþ, may wel synge a mornyng / song of louelikynge þat Cristes specyal syngeþ in þe Boke of Songes: 'Se, þou fayre, semely derlyng, oure litel bed is helid with floures' " (*Book to a Mother* 10–11).

51. Dyan Elliott, *Spiritual Marriage: Sexual Abstinence in Medieval Wedlock* (Princeton, N.J.: Princeton University Press, 1993), especially chapter 4.

52. The priest refers to these same Marian traits later in the text when he says, "Þerfore be þou Marie, as I seide, gostliche; and be sori for þi sinnes, and desire bisiliche to haue bittur and salte teres aʒens þe stinkinge swetnesse and lustes / in fleschliche likinges. Also desire to be a sterre, ʒeuinge liʒt to hem þat gone in dork nyʒt of synne wyþ þi good liuinge, þat þei mowe þe better se þe wei to þe blisse of heuene: and so be a sterre" (*Book to a Mother* 86).

53. On the *Mirror of the Blessed Life of Christ*, see Nicholas Watson, "Censorship and Cultural Change in Late-Medieval England: Vernacular Theology, the Oxford Translation Debate, and Arundel's Constitutions of 1409," *Speculum* 70 (1995): 852–56; the headnote to the extract from the Prologue to Love's *Mirror* in Jocelyn Wogan-Browne et al., eds., *The Idea of the Vernacular: An Anthology of Middle English Literary Theory, 1280–1520* (University Park: Pennsylvania State University Press, 1999), 252–53; Nicholas Watson, "The Politics of Middle English Writing," *The Idea of the Vernacular*, especially 343–45.

54. The priest says, "Mi leue dere modur, to speke more opunliche to þe of þe bok þat I ches bifore alle oþire, for þe moste nedful, most spedful and most medful: þis bok is Crist, Godis Sone of heuene" (*Book to a Mother* 31). The conceit of Christ as a written text is not uncommon in the later Middle Ages; for example, it appears in several of the texts known as the "Charters of Christ."

55. See *Book to a Mother*, 26.

56. On *ruminatio*, see Jean Leclercq, *The Love of Learning and the Desire for God*, trans. Catharine Misrahi (New York: Fordham University Press, 1982). The image of digest-

ing a text set out in this passage also calls to mind Michel de Certeau's model of reading as productive consumption, as a practice in which the reader makes something of the text. On this interpretation of reading, see Michel de Certeau, *The Practice of Everyday Life*, trans. Steven Rendall (Berkeley and Los Angeles: University of California Press, 1984), 165–76. The striking assertion that one eats Christ's flesh and blood "gostliche" by learning the text reveals that the priest is not simply suggesting the reading practices of *ruminatio* or productive consumption, the latter of which would do much to undermine a great deal of the regulatory work the *Book* attempts to do. The priest's intentions do not, of course, forestall the possibility that female readers engaged in just such productive consumption. In fact, as Anne Clark Bartlett points out, there are passages in the *Book to a Mother* that have a great deal of potential appeal for women. For example, the priest writes, "And þus þou maist lerne aftir þi samplerie to write a feir trewe bok and better konne Holi Writ þan ony maister of diuinite þat loueþ not God so wel as þou; for who loueþ best God, can best Holi Writ" (*Book to a Mother* 39). Bartlett observes that in this passage the *Book* "employs the discourse of familiarity, voicing the notion that women are the spiritual and intellectual equals—even potentially the superiors—of men" (*Male Authors, Female Readers: Representing Subjectivity in Middle English Devotional Literature* [Ithaca, N.Y.: Cornell University Press, 1995], 144).

57. On digestion and the host, see Rubin, *Corpus Christi*, 337–38.

58. The statement that "þou schalt not turne me into þe, as þou dost bodily mete" may also be evidence for the text's orthodoxy, as it refutes Lollard notions, as expressed, for example, by Margery Baxter, that the host is subject to digestion and excretion like ordinary food.

59. Margery Kempe, *The Book of Margery Kempe*, ed. Sanford Brown Meech and Hope Emily Allen, Early English Text Society o.s. 212 (London: Oxford University Press, 1940), 39. Hereafter I cite this edition parenthetically in the text as *Margery Kempe*. On the question of Margery's literacy, see David Lawton, "Voice, Authority, and Blasphemy in *The Book of Margery Kempe*," *Margery Kempe: A Book of Essays*," ed. Sandra J. McEntire (New York: Garland, 1992), 93–115, and Karma Lochrie, *Margery Kempe and Translations of the Flesh* (Philadelphia: University of Pennsylvania Press, 1991). In addition to telling of hearing "Bridis boke" read to her, Margery recounts a revelation in which Jesus tells her that he speaks to her just as he spoke to St. Birgitta. In the same revelation, Jesus also informs her of the Brigittine text's authenticity, saying, "I telle þe trewly it is trewe euery word þat is wretyn in Brides boke, & be þe it xal be knowyn for very trewth" (*Margery Kempe* 47). Since the publication of the Early English Text Society edition of the *Book of Margery Kempe*, the connections between Margery and Birgitta have frequently been observed. Hope Emily Allen, in her notes to the *Book of Margery Kempe*, points out, "Margery's story often suggests that she is trying to emulate St. Bridget. . . . As Danzig was the Baltic port by which the Swedes often went to Rome (where St. Bridget's relics rested, in transit to Wadstena), so Lynn was the port by which the English went to Sweden. Margery will have been aware of St. Bridget

from infancy" (280 n. 47/26). Julia Bolton Holloway believes Margery deliberately modeled her life and pilgrimages on Birgitta's life and voyages, engaging in "*imitatio Brigidae*" ("Bride, Margery, Julian, and Alice: Bridget of Sweden's Textual Community in Medieval England," *Margery Kempe: A Book of Essays*, 209); Janet Wilson similarly claims, "It is now widely accepted that Kempe consciously modeled her mystical life as a 'competitive' *imitatio* upon St. Bridget" ("Communities of Dissent: The Secular and Ecclesiastical Communities of Margery Kempe's *Book*," *Medieval Women in their Communities*, ed. Diane Watt [Toronto: University of Toronto Press, 1997], 161). Holloway also argues that *The Book of Margery Kempe* is modeled on Birgitta's *Revelations*, as are, in her view, the *Showings* of Julian of Norwich. David Lawton likewise notes the importance of Birgitta's *Liber celestis* for Margery ("Voice, Authority, and Blasphemy" 98–99). On Margery's involvement with St. Birgitta, see also Gail McMurray Gibson, *The Theater of Devotion: East Anglian Drama and Society in the Late Middle Ages* (Chicago: University of Chicago Press, 1989), especially 47–56. While much has been said about parallels between Birgitta's life and Margery's life, Birgitta's revelations and Margery's *Book*, I am particularly interested in exploring the connections between Margery's religious practices and Brigittine monasticism and spirituality.

60. Beckwith, *Christ's Body*, 102, her emphasis. Beckwith explores at length the lay influences on Kempe's religious practices, especially her participation in the life of her parish and the guild of the Trinity in Lynn, in *Christ's Body*, 102–11.

61. On Julian of Norwich's role in authorizing Margery Kempe's holy speech, see Lochrie, *Margery Kempe and Translations of the Flesh*, 106–8.

62. Holloway says that Margery's visits to Brigittine houses included the Hospice in Rome, possibly Munkaliv in Norway, and "almost certainly" the Brigittine convent of Marienbrunn at Gdansk ("Bride, Margery, Julian, and Alice" 203).

63. Strohm, *Hochon's Arrow*, 34.

64. Many critics have addressed the question of whether Margery Kempe subverts or reinforces a dominant ideology that subjects women. For example, Hope Phyllis Weissman writes that Margery Kempe shares the strategy of the Wife of Bath, "formally accepting conventional images while actually coopting them" ("Margery Kempe in Jerusalem: *Hysterica Compassio* in the Late Middle Ages," *Acts of Interpretation*, ed. Mary J. Carruthers and Elizabeth D. Kirk [Norman, Okla.: Pilgrim, 1982], 203). For nuanced arguments supporting Margery Kempe's subversive qualities, see Karma Lochrie, *Margery Kempe and Translations of the Flesh*, and Wendy Harding, "Body into Text: *The Book of Margery Kempe*," *Feminist Approaches to the Body in Medieval Literature*, ed. Linda Lomperis and Sarah Stanbury (Philadelphia: University of Pennsylvania Press, 1993): 168–97. Sarah Beckwith makes a strong case that Margery Kempe's religious practices validate female subjection in her article "A Very Material Mysticism," *Medieval Literature: Criticism, Ideology, and History*, ed. David Aers (Sussex: Harvester, 1986), 34–57. In *Christ's Body*, however, which includes Beckwith's most recent treatment of Margery Kempe, she argues that Kempe strove at once to be a part of and to criticize both clerically sanctioned religious life and bourgeois urban life, the values of

which are opposed yet inextricably tied up together (see especially 98–111). I do not see Margery Kempe's *Book* as subverting images or interpretative schemes in a process of simple inversion but rather as producing innovations within the set vocabulary of ideals and practices. The tensions inherent in her individual assertions and improvisations within a structure already in place are, I believe, the reason that her practices inspire both ecclesiastical censure and approval. With Lynn Staley and Nancy Partner, I am interested in Margery Kempe's *Book* as a text which is constructed, not as a straightforward record of a life as it "really happened" (see Lynn Staley, *Margery Kempe's Dissenting Fictions* [University Park: Pennsylvania State University Press, 1994]; Nancy Partner, "Reading the Book of Margery Kempe," *Exemplaria* 3.1 [1991]: 29–66). The Margery Kempe of the *Book* is as much a textual construction as the abbess of the miracle or the mother of the *Book to a Mother*. In all three cases historical circumstances interact with the individual desires of the texts' creators. The pregnant abbess, the mother of *Book to a Mother*, and Margery of *The Book of Margery Kempe* are the products of "facts" and, to borrow Staley's formulation, "fictions."

65. Holloway refers to the "consonance" of the engraving on Margery's ring with the motto of the Brigittine Order "Amor meus crucifixus est" ("Bride, Margery, Julian, and Alice" 209). Margery's spousal relationship with Jesus certainly exhibits sensual elements of bridal mysticism, as when Jesus tells her, "For it is conuenyent þe wyf to be homly wyth hir husbond. Be he neuyr so gret a lorde & sche so powr a woman whan he weddyth hir, ʒet þei must ly to-gedir & rest to-gedir in joy & pes. . . . Dowtyr, thow desyrest gretly to se me, & þu mayst boldly, whan þu art in þi bed, take me to þe as for þi weddyd husbond, as thy derworthy derlyng. . . . þerfor þu mayst boldly take me in þe armys of þi sowle & kyssen my mowth, myn hed, & my fete as swetly as thow wylt" (*Margery Kempe* 90). These sensual, even sexual, elements of the relationship are important, but, as much anxiety and commentary as they have produced, they are not the end of the story. Margery's spousal relationship with Jesus and the Godhead are, like the nuptial relationship of monastic profession and like the relationship created in marriage itself, constructed in profoundly social terms, as is revealed even in this sensual passage by the presence of the language of status ("Be he neuyr so gret a lorde") as she, like Benedictine nuns, receives a social "boost" through her relationship with Christ. Indeed, Margery's relationships with figures from salvation history in general are constructed in distinctly social terms.

66. Partner, "Reading the Book of Margery Kempe," 58–59.

67. John Henry Blunt, ed., *The Myroure of Oure Ladye*, Early English Text Society e.s. 19 (London: Kegan Paul, 1873), 136. This prayer is from the Sunday service of Lauds. It is tantalizingly suggestive of Brigittine influence that the descriptions of Margery's "bone maryd ryng" and her marriage to the Godhead come in a section of the *Book* describing her trip to Italy. On this trip she visits St. Birgitta's maid (*Margery Kempe* 95), acts as godmother to a child she named after St. Birgitta (*Margery Kempe* 94), kneels on the stone where Birgitta kneeled and had a revelation of her [Birgitta's] death (*Margery Kempe* 95), and visits the chamber where Birgitta died, there hearing a

"Dewche preste prechyn of hir . . . & of hir reuelacyonys & of hir maner of leuyng" (*Margery Kempe* 95).

68. Sidonie Smith, *A Poetics of Women's Autobiography: Marginality and the Fictions of Self-Representation* (Bloomington: Indiana University Press, 1987), 55.

69. Both the Mayor of Leicester (*Margery Kempe* 116) and the Archbishop of York (ibid., 124) question Margery regarding her white clothes while interrogating her on charges of being a Lollard. R. I. Moore points out that unorthodox behavior (in this case a married woman's adopting the dress of a virgin) is only identified as heretical when the conflicting claims and ideas it embodies become "a political threat to the prevailing order" (*The Formation of a Persecuting Society: Power and Deviance in Western Europe, 950–1250* (Oxford: Blackwell, 1987), 112. For a further examination of the significance of Margery's clothes and the threats they suggest, see Chapter 7.

70. On the ways in which married chastity was problematic for patriarchal authorities, including clerics as well as husbands, see Elliott, *Spiritual Marriage*, especially chapter 4.

71. Sheila Delany, the first to note the specifically economic dimensions of Margery's chastity, reads this transaction differently than I do. She views it as confirmation of Margery's status as powerless commodity. See "Sexual Economics, Chaucer's Wife of Bath, and the *Book of Margery Kempe*," *Minnesota Review* n.s. 5 (1975): 112. It is true that Margery's body is definitively marked as property in the exchange; I think it is important to remember, though, that once Margery "owns" that property, it is hers to administer. Dyan Elliott discusses in detail the relationship of the conjugal debt, vows of chastity, and patriarchal power, with particular reference to chastity as both liberatory and regulatory for women, in chapter 4 of *Spiritual Marriage*.

72. P. H. Cullum, "Vowesses and Female Lay Piety in the Province of York, 1300–1500," *Northern History* 32 (1996): 21.

73. Mary Erler, "Three Fifteenth-Century Vowesses," *Medieval London Widows 1300–1500*, ed. Caroline M. Barron and Anne F. Sutton (London: Hambledon, 1994), 180.

74. Susan Dickman, "Margery Kempe and the Continental Tradition of the Pious Woman," *The Medieval Mystical Tradition in England*, ed. Marion Glasscoe (Cambridge: Brewer, 1984): 150–68.

75. On the influence of Franciscan spirituality in Margery Kempe's development, see Lochrie, *Margery Kempe and Translations of the Flesh*; Lawton, "Voice, Authority, and Blasphemy," 99–100; Denise Despres, "Franciscan Spirituality: Margery Kempe and Visual Meditation," *FCMEN* 11 (1985): 12–18; and Gail McMurray Gibson, "St. Margery: *The Book of Margery Kempe*," *Equally in God's Image: Women in the Middle Ages*, ed. Julia Bolton Holloway et al (New York: Lang, 1990), 144–63. Alexandra Barratt posits another Franciscan connection for Margery Kempe. She argues that, while the *Revelationes Beatae Elisabeth* most likely originated with Elizabeth of Toess, O.P., "it is undeniable that the later Middle Ages universally attributed them" to St. Elizabeth of Thuringia, a Franciscan tertiary ("Margery Kempe and the King's Daughter of Hun-

gary," *Margery Kempe: A Book of Essays*, 199–200). Barratt discusses the importance of this text to Margery Kempe, and concludes, "The Friar who attacked Kempe for her noisy weeping was Franciscan, if the medieval marginal note identifying him with William Melton has any authority. But it was also an ostensibly Franciscan text (for the Latin *Revelationes Beatae Elisabeth* almost always circulated with texts of genuinely Franciscan origin) which helped give Kempe's future amanuensis the courage to defy him and help her" (ibid., 200).

76. See Gibson, "St. Margery," 145, on Margery's literal enactment of this text and Lawton, "Voice, Authority, and Blasphemy," 99, on the importance of the text to Margery Kempe's experience of the Passion. David Aers points to a way in which Margery resists the teachings of the *Mirror*. In his discussion of Margery's held-back confession in the opening chapter of the *Book of Margery Kempe*, Aers writes, "Apparently she had not heeded the conventional warnings of the contemporary prior of Mount Grace whose extremely popular translation *The Mirrour of the Blessed Lyf of Jesu Christ* has been likened to Margery's book in the meditative forms it proposes. Love, preoccupied as he often is with the threat from Lollardy, warns his readers that whatever the Church's officials teach must be accepted. . . . Unlike Lollards, Margery had not rejected the sacrament of confession, but she had sought a potentially Lollard-like autonomy of her 'souereynes' and the institution" (*Community, Gender, and Individual Identity: English Writing, 1360–1430* [London: Routledge, 1988], 84).

77. Janette Dillon, "Holy Women and Their Confessors or Confessors and Their Holy Women? Margery Kempe and the Continental Tradition," *Prophets Abroad: The Reception of Continental Holy Women in Late Medieval England*, ed. Rosalynn Voaden (Cambridge: Brewer, 1996): 134.

78. Ibid., 134–35.

79. Clarissa Atkinson, *The Oldest Profession: Christian Motherhood in the Middle Ages* (Ithaca, N.Y.: Cornell University Press, 1991), 188.

80. Concerning her fears that motherhood will disturb her religious practices, Margery says, "A, Lord, how xal I þan do for kepyng of my chylde?" (*Margery Kempe* 48). Christ responds, "Dowtyr, drede þe not, I xal ordeyn for an kepar" (ibid., 48).

81. Weissman notes that both Felix Fabri and Jacques de Vitry "associate the laments of their female subjects with the maternal agony of the Virgin; these women are thus represented as experiencing a realization of the Marian Compassion which is similar in devotional principle to the realization of Margery Kempe" ("Margery Kempe in Jerusalem" 215). On the connection of childbirth and the crucifixion, see also Caroline Walker Bynum, *Fragmentation and Redemption: Essays on Gender and the Human Body in Medieval Religion* (New York: Zone, 1991), 181–238.

82. On Kempe's physical reaction to her vision of the crucifixion, see chapter 5 of Lochrie, *Margery Kempe and Translations of the Flesh*, especially 192–93.

83. Weissman, "Margery Kempe in Jerusalem," 212. Weissman argues that what is at issue in Margery's experiences is not maternity but virginity. She says that Margery Kempe's identification with the Virgin "moves through and beyond the shameful Com-

passion to achieve a participation, both existential and metaphysical, in the act of the Virgin Birth" (ibid., 210–11). It is through this process that Margery "fulfills the deepest motivation of her vita, the recovery of a virginal purity lost in the sexual exercises of her womanhood" (ibid., 211). Weissman says that the use of the "language of labor" to describe Margery's experiences on the Mount of Calvary "suggests that her compassionate weeping is being conceived as an alternative, spiritual childbirth" (ibid., 212–13). The profound physicality of the scene, however, suggests to me not so much the creation of a redeemed spiritual alternative but rather a conflation of the spiritual and the physical in which both are equally valuable.

84. Lochrie, *Margery Kempe and Translations of the Flesh*, 192.

85. This term is from Gibson, "St. Margery." Gibson discusses the *Book's* emphasis on Mary's participation in all aspects of salvation history.

86. Blunt, *Myroure of Oure Ladye*, 232–33.

87. Bridget of Sweden, "From *The Revelations*," *Women's Writing in Middle English*, ed. Alexandra Barratt (London: Longman, 1992), 86. Barratt has edited the excerpts from the *Revelations* in this volume from the unpublished late fifteenth-century manuscript Oxford Bodley MS Rawlinson C. 41.

88. Ibid., 87.

89. Ibid., 88.

90. Ibid. Birgitta is quite struck by the Virgin's miraculous recovery, which she mentions again at the end of the revelation, saying, "In thys she nevyr chaunged her colour nor was anythyng weyke or seyke nor lakkyd anythyng off her bodyly strenght, as other women doo in tyme off byrth, but oonly that her wombe, that was so grete afore the byrth, withdrewe ytselfe to the fyrst state that yt was yn before" (ibid., 89).

91. Ibid., 88–89. In the notes for Margery's swaddling of the infant Jesus, Hope Emily Allen points to a Brigittine connection, saying, "Cp. the Bridgettine lessons, as used at Syon Abbey: 'Also the vyrgyn wrappynge and gatherynge togyther the handes and fete of her lytel sonne easely in a bande or cradel bande broughte to mynde how harde they shulde be persed thorugh on the crosse'" (*Margery Kempe* 265–66 n. 19/18).

92. On the association of tears with maternity, see Lochrie, *Margery Kempe and Translations of the Flesh*, chapter 5, and Atkinson, *Oldest Profession*, chapter 5. Partner also discusses the value of tears in "Reading the Book," 52–54.

93. Dillon, "Holy Women and Their Confessors," 132.

94. Dillon points out that Margery Kempe adopts a clerical role when, in chapter 12 of the *Book*, she tells a monk of his sins and assures him of his salvation if he confesses and reforms. Additionally, Dillon notes that Kempe "even usurps her confessor's role so far as to take responsibility for his soul, just as he does for hers" ("Holy Women and Their Confessors" 131–32). The perception that Margery Kempe was infiltrating the clerical realm of privileged access to spiritual resources and assuming clerical responsibilities through her public holy speech frequently led to trouble for her. For example, a cleric at the Archbishop's court in York, where she is accused of Lollardy, says "her

wot we wel þat sche hath a deuyl wyth-inne hir, for sche spekyth of þe Gospel" (*Margery Kempe* 126). Then "a gret clerke browt forth a boke & leyd Seynt Powyl for hys party a-geyns hir þat no woman xulde prechyn" (*Margery Kempe* 126). On the implications of Margery's response that she does not preach but rather teaches, including its relation to Lollard arguments, see Lochrie, *Margery Kempe and Translations of the Flesh*, 109–13.

95. Dhira B. Mahoney notes the "association between tears and prayers" which "constantly confirms" and "points to Kempe's power" ("Margery Kempe's Tears and the Power over Language," *Margery Kempe: A Book of Essays*, 42). Mahoney continues, "Thus, though Kempe's tears are themselves inarticulate, their explicit link with her prayers translates into an equation whereby tears equal prayers which equal power" (ibid., 43).

96. As Mahoney has observed, the prayer is not presented in the third person like the rest of the *Book* but rather "in an assured first person, speaking directly to God" (ibid., 47). In this prayer Margery also uses "the patriarchal language, the formal rhetoric of male ecclesiastics," demonstrating her "spiritual independence" and power (ibid., 48–49).

97. Many critics have commented on Margery Kempe's self-identification with various saints. The *Book* recounts several miracles Margery performs, including saving the parish church of St. Margaret's from fire, enabling the second scribe to read the poor handwriting and incomprehensible language of the first, and making a German confessor able to understand English. Gail McMurray Gibson describes Margery as a "self-styled saint," in particular as a "self-styled saint Margaret," the patron saint of childbirth ("St. Margery," 155; see also *Theater of Devotion*). Indeed, in another miraculous event Kempe does for another woman what Christ did for her in healing her of her madness following childbirth. In "Bride, Margery, Julian, and Alice," Holloway argues that Margery Kempe modeled herself and the *Book* after St. Birgitta and her book of revelations (215); she also points out that St. Birgitta and Margery shared difficult births (214). Weissman observes that Margery Kempe's *Book* is in the "approved model of the saint's vita," although it manipulates the genre for nontraditional purposes ("Margery Kempe in Jerusalem" 204).

98. William Patterson Cummings, ed., *The Revelations of Saint Birgitta Edited from the Fifteenth-Century Manuscript in the Garret Collection in the Library of Princeton University*, Early English Text Society o.s. 178 (1929; reprint Millwood, N.Y.: Kraus, 1987), 117.

99. Ibid., 121.

100. Ibid. The image of Karl's sins being written down and then burned has an interesting, although most likely coincidental, parallel in the Minoresses' visitation practices, where the list of their transgressions is burned before them at the conclusion of the visitation; for a discussion of the Minoresses' visitation practices, see Chapter 1.

101. Ibid.

102. Ibid., 123.

103. Ibid., 121.

104. Ibid., 123.

105. Ibid., 124.

106. As Sylvia Federico pointed out to me in private communication, the destruction of the "sak full of writinges" sounds a lot like castration, as does another exchange between the angel and the fiend. The angel tells the fiend to "putte oute thi tunge and schewe thy wrytyng" of Karl's sins, which the fiend has claimed are written thereon in "thousand thousandes." The fiend "ansuerde with grete yellyng, wailyng, and cryeng, and saide: allas and woo vn-to mee, for I haue not oo worde to speke; for my tunge is cutte a-way by the rootes" (ibid., 122).

107. The Middle English translation of Archbishop Gregersson's *Officium Sanctae Birgittae* recount a similar scene involving a different son. Birgitta returns home to find her son Benet desperately ill. She fears he is being punished for her sins and weeps bitterly. The devil appears to her and says, "Whi febils þou so þi sight? Wethir þat þi teres sall wende vp to heuen?" (Roger Ellis, ed., *The Liber celestis of St. Bridget of Sweden*, Early English Text Society o.s. 291 [Oxford: Oxford University Press, 1987], 3). Christ then appears and reassures her that her son's illness is not a result of her sin. He further comforts her by saying, "Before time he was called Benet, bot fro nowe furthe sall he be blissed, and he sall be called þe son of teres and of praiere" (ibid., 3–4). After five days, a sweet song is heard "betwene þe childes bed and þe wall," and "þan passed þe saule of þat child." When the child dies, "þe spirit" tells Birgitta, "Se what teres þan d[o]se nowe: þe son of teres wendes vnto riste and blisse (for teres are odious vnto þe fende)" (ibid., 4).

108. The relationship between female mystics and male clerical scribes in the process of textual creation is vexed; both visionary and scribe are perceived as bearing responsibility for the text. As Dillon observes, "The woman has the vision, but it is the scribe who is responsible for helping her to express it in a form which will not incur charges of heresy. The scribe, more than anyone else, has to be certain that the visions are within the bounds of orthodoxy, since his own safety and reputation are bound up with the woman's" ("Holy Women and Their Confessors" 137). The question of who the creator of Margery Kempe's *Book* is, and the related question of Margery Kempe's real or purported illiteracy, have attracted much attention in recent years (see, for example, Lawton, "Voice, Authority, and Blasphemy;" Lochrie, *Margery Kempe and Translations of the Flesh* 99–103; Staley, *Margery Kempe's Dissenting Fictions* 86–88; Harding, "Body into Text" 169–73, and Wilson, "Communities of Dissent" 159–62).

109. As Lochrie observes, Margery's "interdiction, that is, her insertion of her own voice between text and reader . . . becomes her authorizing practice, which not only inaugurates the book but resurfaces in the text whenever the scribe (or reader) loses faith in her authority" (*Margery Kempe and Translations of the Flesh* 100). At one point in *The Book of Margery Kempe*, the hierarchical relationship between Latin and English is called into question in a way that resembles the privileging of the vernacular and female authority in the account of the translation of Brigittine texts from Swedish to

Latin. In one of a series of linguistic and/or textual miracles, Margery is able to make a German priest who speaks no English understand her when she recounts stories from Scripture, which he then retells in Latin (*Margery Kempe* 97–98). In this "bizarre and self-conscious passage . . . English from the tongue of Kempe is the equivalent of Latin to a clerk. Divine grace bestows upon Kempe's English an honorary Latinity" (Lawton, "Voice, Authority, and Blasphemy" 98).

110. On the implications of this process as subversive to ecclesiastical authority, see chapter 3 of Lochrie's *Margery Kempe and Translations of the Flesh*.

111. George R. Keiser, "Patronage and Piety in Fifteenth-Century England: Margaret, Duchess of Clarence, Symon Wynter and Beinecke MS 317," *Yale University Library Gazette* (October 1985): 34.

112. Ibid., 37.

113. Ibid., 38–39.

114. J. G. Nichols and J. Bruce, eds., *Wills from Doctors' Commons*, Camden Society o.s. 83 (Camden Society, 1863), 1–8, quoted in Felicity Riddy, "'Women talking about the things of God': A Late Medieval Sub-Culture," *Women and Literature in Britain, 1150–1500*, ed. Carol M. Meale (Cambridge: Cambridge University Press, 1993), 122 n. 41.

115. George James Aungier, *The History and Antiquities of Syon Monastery, the Parish of Isleworth and the Chapelry of Hounslow* (London: Nichols, 1840), 527.

116. Riddy, "'Women talking,'" 110. Cecily's quasi-monastic daily routine is set out in "Orders and Rules of the House of the Princess Cecill, Mother of King Edward IV," *A Collection of Ordinances and Regulations for the Government of the Royal Household* (London: Society of Antiquaries, 1790), 37–39. C. A. J. Armstrong provides a summary of Cecily's daily services, prayers, and meditations in "The Piety of Cecily, Duchess of York: A Study in Later Mediaeval Culture," *England, France and Burgundy in the Fifteenth Century* (London: Hambledon, 1983), 140–44. He observes that the document recounting her household ordinances is "in its first half . . . wholly narrative, as if the aim of the anonymous author was to place on record a devout method of life, as a precedent for other noble ladies" (ibid., 140). Indeed, Armstrong points out that the "daily routine of Margaret Beaufort as described by St. John Fisher in his sermon on the month's mind of the Countess of Richmond conforms to the same type both outwardly and spiritually" (ibid., 141; see *English Works of John Fisher*, Early English Text Society e.s. 27 [London, 1876], 294–95). On household devotions more generally, see chapter 5 "The Household as a Religious Community" in Karen Mertes, *The English Noble Household 1250–1600: Good Governaunce and Politic Rule* (Oxford: Blackwell, 1988).

117. M. A. Hicks, "The Piety of Margaret, Lady Hungerford (d. 1478)," *Journal of Ecclesiastical History* 38 (1987): 21.

118. Ibid., 25; Hicks quotes BL MS Cotton Julius BXII, fol. 124.

119. Ibid., 26. Hicks gives detailed evidence for Brigittine influence in Margaret's mortuary chapel at Salisbury (ibid., 26–35). Ann Hutchison concurs with Hicks's views on Brigittine influence but disagrees with his "assumption that 'her book of the

use of the Brigettines of Syon' was, in fact, *The Myroure of Oure Ladye* (pp. 23–24)" ("Devotional Reading in the Monastery and in the Late Medieval Household," *De Cella in Seculum: Religious and Secular Life and Devotion in Late Medieval England*, ed. Michael G. Sargent [Cambridge: Brewer, 1989), 223 n. 26).

120. Armstrong points to the active dimension of piety among high-ranking English noblewomen. He writes, "Aristocratic ladies, who in England as on the Continent were so powerfully attracted by religious contemplation, might seek indeed to find a refuge from the strokes of fortune. But their pursuit of holiness was too positive and too vigorous to be actuated solely by a desire to escape from worldly misfortunes" ("The Piety of Cecily, Duchess of York" 136).

121. Carol M. Meale, "'. . . alle the bokes that I haue of latyn, englisch, and frensch': Laywomen and their Books in Late Medieval England," *Women and Literature in Britain, 1150–1500*, 128.

122. Ibid., 129. Meale's essay goes on to consider what the seal suggests about women's reading.

123. Lochrie, *Margery Kempe and Translations of the Flesh*, 206.

124. Ibid., 209.

125. Ibid., 209–10.

126. On this annotation, see also ibid., 210.

127. Ibid., 211.

128. Wogan-Browne et al., eds., *The Idea of the Vernacular*, 255 n. 23.

129. Lochrie, *Margery Kempe and Translations of the Flesh*, 206.

130. See Lochrie, *Margery Kempe and Translations of the Flesh*, chapter 6. On Wynkyn de Worde's version of Margery Kempe's *Book* see also Wilson, "Communities of Dissent," 156–57.

131. Lochrie, *Margery Kempe and Translations of the Flesh*, 221.

132. Ibid., 220–21.

133. Qtd. in Lochrie, *Margery Kempe and Translations of the Flesh*, 223.

134. Lochrie, *Margery Kempe and Translations of the Flesh*, 223–24.

135. After Margery has been arrested and interrogated to determine her orthodoxy, the Mayor of Leicester demands, "I wil wetyn why þow gost in white clothys, for I trowe þow art comyn hedyr to han a-wey owr wyuys fro us & ledyn hem wyth þe" (*Margery Kempe* 116).

Chapter 5. Kings, Saints, and Nuns

1. *Rotuli parliamentorum*, vol. 5 (London: 1767), 411.

2. Ibid.

3. Ibid.

4. Ralph A. Griffiths notes, "Warwick was referred to as the king's master on 8 May

1428 (*PPC*, III, 294–5)" (*The Reign of Henry VI: The Exercise of Royal Authority 1422–1461* [London: Benn, 1981], 63 n. 7). Griffiths also observes that "the care of the king was separated from the government of the realm after 1422" (ibid., 51); however, "if any single interest can be said to have dominated it [Henry VI's household] and to have influenced the king's upbringing, it is that of the Beauchamps. By Christmas 1427, and especially after the appointment of Warwick as guardian in 1428, there was recruited to the household a circle of youngish men who were engaged to wait on the royal person." Among these men were John Chetwynd, "who came from a family with deep Warwickshire roots and whose loyalties lay staunchly with the Beauchamps" and Sir Walter Beauchamp, one of Richard's kinsmen (ibid., 55).

5. Ibid., 59.

6. MS BL Add. Ch. 17228. Expansions of abbreviations in this and subsequently quoted manuscripts are indicated by italics.

7. Ibid.

8. Ibid.

9. Griffiths, *Reign of Henry VI*, 59.

10. MS BL Cotton Julius E IV fol. 24a. Although the manuscript in which this revelation is recorded was produced in the late fifteenth century, Richard Beauchamp's association with Emma Rawghton is documented as early as the first year of Henry VI's reign. In 1422–23, Richard became concerned about his lack of a male heir. He turned to Emma, who informed him that God would look favorably on the foundation of a chantry at the hermitage at Guy's Cliff. Beauchamp undertook the foundation, and two years later his wife bore a son (Ann Warren, *Anchorites and Their Patrons in Medieval Europe* [Berkeley and Los Angeles: University of California Press, 1985], 204–5). This encounter with Emma was also not the first time that Richard Beauchamp turned to a holy woman at a crucial juncture. His accounts reveal that in 1421 he paid 13s 4d for the expenses of two men sent to visit an unnamed anchoress at Winchester to obtain advice on his behalf. Later that year, when he was in London for Parliament, he paid for the Winchester anchoress to be brought to London and kept there for three days so that he could consult with her (Warren, *Anchorites* 204). So, it does not seem unreasonable to consider Emma's revelations regarding Beauchamp's position in 1432 in a contemporary context in spite of the later date of MS BL Cotton Julius E IV.

11. Emma Rawghton was not entirely an unknown figure in her own time; York wills making specific bequests indicate that there were five grants between 1430 and 1436 to "the anchoress of All Saints, North Street" (Warren, *Anchorites* 242).

12. André Vauchez, *The Laity in the Middle Ages: Religious Beliefs and Devotional Practices*, trans. Margery J. Schneider (Notre Dame: University of Notre Dame Press, 1993), 235. Vauchez observes that through this process, women, "members of the sex which was the incarnation of physical and moral weakness . . . were considered by the end of the fourteenth century to have a privileged place in the history of salvation" (ibid., 233).

13. On the "feminization" of sanctity, see André Vauchez, *La sainteté en occident aux derniers siècles du Moyen Age* (Rome: Ecole française de Rome; Paris: Diffusion de Boccard, 1981).

14. As Donald Weinstein and Rudolph Bell have noted, the percentage of female saints rose from 11.8 percent in the twelfth century to 22.6 percent in the thirteenth century, continuing to increase to 23.4 percent in the fourteenth century and 27.7 percent in the fifteenth century (*Saints and Society: The Two Worlds of Western Christendom 1000–1700* [Chicago: University of Chicago Press, 1982], 220–21).

15. On the association of these practices with women and the feminine, see Caroline Walker Bynum, *Fragmentation and Redemption: Essays on Gender and the Human Body in Medieval Religion* (New York: Zone, 1991), especially 151–238.

16. Eamon Duffy, "Holy Maydens, Holy Wyfes: The Cult of Women Saints in Fifteenth- and Sixteenth-Century England," *Women in the Church*, Papers Read at the 1989 Summer Meeting and the 1990 Winter Meeting of the Ecclesiastical History Society, ed. W. J. Sheils and Diana Wood (Cambridge: Blackwell, 1990), 176.

17. Ibid., 189–90.

18. Ibid., 190.

19. J. A. Lauritis, R. A. Klinefelter, and V. F. Gallagher, introduction to *A Critical Edition of John Lydgate's "Life of Our Lady,"* Duquesne Studies Philological Series 2 (Pittsburgh: Duquesne University Press, 1961), 7.

20. Ibid.

21. MS Bl Cotton Julius E IV, fol. 112v.

22. André Vauchez, "St. Bridget's Revelations in France at the End of the Middle Ages," *Santa Brigida Profeta Dei Tempi Nuove/Saint Bridget Prophetess of New Ages*, Proceedings of the International Study Meeting Rome October 3–7, 1991 (Rome: Casa Generalizia Suore Santa Brigida, 1991), 180–81. Vauchez notes that the first version of the revelation (which becomes *Liber celestis* Book IV chapter 104–5) is preserved in Cambridge, Corpus Christi College, MS 404 (ibid., 181 n. 16).

23. Ibid., 181.

24. Thomas Hoccleve, *Regement of Princes*, *Hoccleve's Works*, vol. 3, Early English Text Society e.s. 72 (London: Kegan Paul, 1897), line 5384.

25. Ibid., line 5396.

26. F. R. Jonathan Abergale, "The Revelations and the Hundred Years' War," *Santa Brigida Profeta Dei Tempi Nuovi*, 904.

27. Ibid., 905.

28. Roger Chartier, *On the Edge of the Cliff: History, Language, and Practices*, trans. Lydia G. Cochrane (Baltimore: Johns Hopkins University Press, 1997), 23.

29. Simon Walker, "Political Saints in Later Medieval England," *The McFarlane Legacy: Studies in Late Medieval Politics and Society*, ed. R. H. Britnell and A. J. Pollard, The Fifteenth Century Series 1, ed. Ralph A. Griffiths (Stroud: Sutton, 1995; New York: St. Martin's, 1995), 86. The construction of the priest-king and the concept of Christological kingship have a long history. See Ernst H. Kantorowicz, *The King's Two*

Bodies: A Study in Medieval Political Theology (Princeton, N.J.: Princeton University Press, 1957), especially chapter 3 "Christ-Centered Kingship."

30. For an alternative reading of this pageant, which focuses on its parallels with the liturgy of the funeral office, see Gordon Kipling, *Enter the King: Theatre, Liturgy, and Ritual in the Medieval Civic Triumph* (Oxford: Clarendon, 1998; New York: Oxford University Press, 1998), 205–9.

31. Frank Taylor and John S. Roskell, eds. and trans., *Gesta Henrici Quinti: The Deeds of Henry the Fifth* (Oxford: Clarendon, 1975; London: Oxford University Press, 1975), 105. Hereafter I cite the *Gesta Henrici Quinti* parenthetically in the text as *Gesta*. Except where the Latin is particularly important to my argument, I quote from the English translation.

32. Henry V "saw himself—and he wished his subjects to see him—as saving the kingdom, and by allying himself with Jesus the Messiah, the Saviour . . . he was casting himself in this role" (Neil Beckett, "St. Bridget, Henry V and Syon Abbey," *Studies in St. Birgitta and the Brigittine Order*, vol. 2, Analecta Carthusiana 35, ed. James Hogg [New York: Mellen, 1993], 137).

33. Nancy Jay, *"Throughout Your Generations Forever": Sacrifice, Religion, and Paternity* (Chicago: University of Chicago Press, 1992), xxiv.

34. Ibid., 37.

35. Sheila Delany, *Impolitic Bodies: Poetry, Saints, and Society in Fifteenth-Century England* (Oxford: Oxford University Press, 1998), 154.

36. Emphasis in original. This is the first song or legend in the pageant which is in the vernacular, a fact which I believe is related to its being the first speech by women.

37. A female figure, although not a living woman, does appear in the opening scene of the pageant. At the tower at the entrance to the bridge where the king's procession enters the city, there is "an image of a giant of astonishing size" holding an axe and the keys to the city. "At his right side stood a figure of a woman, not much smaller in size, wearing a scarlet mantle and adornments appropriate to her sex; and they were like a man and his wife who, in their richest attire, were bent upon seeing the eagerly awaited face of their lord and welcoming him with abundant praise" (*Gesta* 103).

38. In focusing on the legitimacy of Henry V's French as well as his English kingship, the scene at Queen Eleanor's Cross harmonizes with the larger aims of the *Gesta* itself. Antonia Grandsen says that the *Gesta*'s "main object was to stimulate support, including financial support, for the Hundred Years' War preparatory to its renewal in 1417, by persuading Henry's subjects of his own worth and the justice of his cause. . . . The *Gesta* emphasizes that Henry had a legitimate hereditary right to the territories he claimed in France" ("Propaganda in English Medieval Historiography," *Journal of Medieval History* 1 [1975]: 371).

39. Harris Nicholas, *History of the Battle of Agincourt and of the Expedition of Henry the Fifth into France in 1415*, 2nd ed. (1832; reprint, London: Müller, 1970), 327.

40. The Middle English dictionary defines "nouel" first, obviously, as "Christmas, the feast of the nativity." The second entry reads, "(a) A cry of joy at the birth of Christ,

esp. in carols of the Annunciation and the Nativity. . . . (b) a cry of general rejoicing or thanksgiving" (*Middle English Dictionary*, vol. 6, ed. Hans Kurath [Ann Arbor: University of Michigan Press, 1959], 1113). Although "nowell" may be used in this latter sense in the virgins' song, the word's associations with the Nativity are so strong that I believe the suggestion of the moment of the Incarnation is inescapable. The incarnational significance of the virgins' song of "Nowell" is further reinforced by the associations of royal entries with Advent and its liturgical imagery. Gordon Kipling observes, "The most common Latin synonym for *royal entry*, after all, was *adventus*. . . . It was perhaps only natural to view a king's first coming in terms of the Lord's First Coming" ("'Grace in This Lyf and Aftirwarde Glorie': Margaret of Anjou's Royal Entry into London," *Research Opportunities in Renaissance Drama* 29 [1986–1987]: 77). He also notes, "Cries of 'Noel! Noel!' signified general public rejoicing in the late Middle Ages and often bore no specific allusion to Christ's Nativity. However, the association of the cry with Christmas rejoicing was a strong one, and contemporaries often drew the inevitable parallel between greeting a king's royal entry with 'Noel!' and greeting Christ's Nativity with the same cry" (Kipling, *Enter the King* 59 n. 9).

41. Lauritis et al., introduction to *A Critical Edition*, 7.

42. A similar mobilization of the Annunciation in "incarnational politics" is evident in the redesigned French coin called the *salute*, which appeared in 1422 upon the accession of Henry VI. J. W. McKenna observes that the coin's depiction of the Annunciation switches the traditional placement of the angel and the Virgin; on the coin, the angel is on the viewer's right. The placement thus associates the figures of the Annunciation scene with the arms of England and France. "The angel (England) is portrayed as announcing to the Virgin (France) the coming of a saviour"—i.e., Henry V's son Henry VI (J. W. McKenna, "Henry VI of England and the Dual Monarchy: Aspects of Royal Political Propaganda, 1422–1432," *Journal of the Warburg and Courtauld Institutes* 28 [1965]: 161).

43. Jeremy Catto, "Religious Change Under Henry V," *Henry V: The Practice of Kingship*, ed. G. L. Harriss (Oxford: Oxford University Press, 1985), 97.

44. Ibid., 106.

45. Margaret Deanesly, ed., *The Incendium Amoris* of Richard Rolle of Hampole (Manchester: Manchester University Press, 1915; London: Longmans, 1915), 92–93. For a detailed account of the process of obtaining papal approval for the Brigittine Rule, see Roger Ellis, *Viderunt Eam Filie Syon: The Spirituality of the English House of a Medieval Contemplative Order from its Beginnings to the Present Day*, Analecta Carthusiana 68, ed. James Hogg (Salzburg: Institut für Anglistik und Amerikanistik Universität Salzburg, 1984).

46. As Neil Beckett has noted, Henry V did not follow the strict instructions laid out by Birgitta regarding the establishment of a Brigittine house. He rather acted with "speed" which illustrates the "urgency" with which he regarded the foundation ("St. Bridget, Henry V" 133).

47. Ibid., 127.

48. George James Aungier, *The History and Antiquities of Syon Monastery, the Parish of Isleworth and the Chapelry of Hounslow* (London: Nichols, 1849), 31.

49. Hans Cnattingius, *Studies in the Order of St. Bridget of Sweden: The Crisis in the 1420s*, Acta Universitatis Stockholmiensis Stockholm Studies in History 7 (Stockholm: Almqvist and Wiksell, 1963), 21–22, 122–23.

50. Beckett, "St. Bridget, Henry V," 131.

51. Aungier, *History and Antiquities*, 30. On the process of endowing Syon, see also Beckett, "St. Bridget, Henry V," 132.

52. J. S. Cockburn et al., eds., *The Victoria History of the County of Middlesex*, vol. 1 (London: Oxford University Press, 1911), 183; hereafter *VCH Middlesex*.

53. Deanesly, *Incendium Amoris*, 105.

54. Beckett, "St. Bridget, Henry V," 137. André Vauchez in "St. Bridget's Revelations in France at the End of the Middle Ages" and F. R. Johnston in "The English Cult of St. Bridget of Sweden," *Analecta Bollandiana* 103 (1985): 75–93 also discuss St. Birgitta's reputation as a "pro-English" saint.

55. James Hamilton Wylie, *The Reign of Henry the Fifth*, vol. 1 (Cambridge: Cambridge University Press, 1914), 222.

56. Paul Strohm, *England's Empty Throne: Usurpation and the Language of Legitimation 1399–1422* (New Haven, Conn.: Yale University Press, 1998), 94.

57. Ibid., 91. Strohm observes, "The avidly pro-Henrican *Gesta Henrici Quinti*, for example, frames the entire episode as a trial, in which God, wishing to test the constancy of his elected ruler, permits him to be assailed. . . . God's favor is revealed simply through the exposure of the plot, but it is the *just* king who is delivered" (ibid., 92, his emphasis).

58. Henry V did in fact found another monastery at Sheen itself, Sheen Charterhouse.

59. A. Jeffries Collins, *The Bridgettine Breviary of Syon Abbey*, Henry Bradshaw Society 96 (Worcester: Henry Bradshaw Society, 1969), ii n. 1.

60. The connection with Richard II and the elision of Henry IV's usurpation are moves Henry V strove to make in numerous symbolic ventures. On these ventures and on Henry's attempts to put Richard II's disturbing symbolic presence to rest while simultaneously adopting Richard as a father in place of the tainted Henry IV, see Paul Strohm, "The Trouble with Richard: The Reburial of Richard II and Lancastrian Symbolic Strategy," *Speculum* 71 (1996): 87–111 as well as the expanded version of Strohm's analysis of Richard II's reburial in chapter 4 of *England's Empty Throne*. The 1415 pageant scenes at Cornhill and the entrance tó Cheapside may also provide an additional connection with Richard II, or at least with Richard II's own program of representing his kingship. In his analysis of the Wilton Diptych, Charles Wood reads the images as providing "insights into the views of [Richard II] . . . about what he thought kingship should be" (*Joan of Arc and Richard III: Sex, Saints, and Government in the Middle Ages* [Oxford: Oxford University Press, 1988], 75). Wood, following John H. Harvey, interprets the figures of the saints Edmund Martyr, Edward the Confessor, and

John the Baptist as likenesses of Edward II, Edward III, and the Black Prince. The Diptych, in Wood's reading, also emphasizes connection with the apostles through the eleven angels (the apostles minus Judas) and "the insistence with which its gold backgrounds stress the number twelve in their patterns" (*Joan of Arc* 83). Further, the Diptych associates Richard II with Christ since John the Baptist presents Richard to the Virgin and Child, "directly touching him and . . . seeming to say: 'This is my beloved son, in whom I am well pleased' " (*Joan of Arc* 81). Henry V's London pageant similarly highlights both his legitimate earthly descent from holy English kings and his status as recipient of divine favor.

61. Beckett, "St. Bridget, Henry V," 137.

62. Adam Usk, *Chronicon Adae de Usk*, ed. and trans. Edward Maunde Thompson, 2nd ed. (London: Frowde, 1904), 8.

63. See Paul Strohm, *Hochon's Arrow: The Social Imagination of Fourteenth-Century Texts* (Princeton, N.J.: Princeton University Press, 1992), 105–19, and David Wallace, *Chaucerian Polity: Absolutist Lineages and Associational Forms in England and Italy* (Stanford, Calif.: Stanford University Press, 1997), 366ff.

64. Geoffrey Chaucer, *Legend of Good Women*, *The Riverside Chaucer*, 3rd ed., ed. Larry D. Benson (Boston: Houghton, 1987), F Prologue 496–97.

65. Aungier, *History and Antiquities*, 26.

66. Ibid.

67. Beckett, "St. Bridget, Henry V," 136.

68. Ibid.

69. The most famous tradition connected with the origin of Syon is that the foundation was part of Henry V's fulfillment of Henry IV's vow to found three religious houses to expiate his participation in the deaths of Richard II and Archbishop Scrope. Whether or not Henry IV ever undertook these expiatory foundations is uncertain, but, as Neil Beckett observes, even if Henry IV never undertook the project, "it is still quite possible that Henry V fulfilled it" ("St. Bridget, Henry V" 139). Beckett continues, "What may really have mattered was not whether Henry IV did or did not make his alleged undertaking, but the fact that he was thought to have made it" (ibid.). The construction of Henry V's identity, the public representation of his dynastically solid and divinely sanctioned kingship, benefitted either way.

70. Ibid., 127.

71. *Diplomatorium* iii no. 2082, qtd. in Deanesly, *Incendium Amoris*, 104.

72. Aungier, *History and Antiquities*, 27.

73. John Henry Blunt, ed., *The Myroure of Oure Ladye*, Early English Text Society e.s. 19 (London: Kegan Paul, 1873), 194.

74. Ibid., 104.

75. Ibid., 141.

76. Ibid., 216.

77. On the political significance of the Jesse Tree see J. W. McKenna, "Henry VI of England," and Richard Osberg, "The Jesse Tree in the 1432 London Entry of Henry VI:

Messianic Kingship and the Rule of Justice," *Journal of Medieval and Renaissance Studies* 16 (1986): 213–32.

78. Blunt, *Myroure*, 147.

79. Ibid., 295.

80. Pamela Sheingorn, "Appropriating the Holy Kinship: Gender and Family History," *Interpreting Cultural Symbols: Saint Anne in Late Medieval Society* (Athens: University of Georgia Press, 1990), 170.

81. Ibid.

82. Ibid., 170–71.

83. For examples of the recurrence of these issues in English texts and documents dealing with the claim to the French throne, see Delany, *Impolitic Bodies*, 144ff.

84. *Rewyll of Seynt Sauioure*, vol. 2 of *The Rewyll of Seynt Sauioure and Other Middle English Brigittine Legislative Texts*, ed. James Hogg, Salzburger Studien zur Anglistik und Amerikanistik 6 (Salzburg: Institut für Englische Sprache und Literatur Universität Salzburg, 1978), fol. 42r. Expansions of abbreviations in the manuscript of which this edition is a facsimile are indicated by italics, with the exception of the various ampersands used by the scribe, which have been silently expanded.

85. Blunt, *Myroure*, 26. For a further discussion of the implications of this passage, see Chapter 2.

86. Ellis, *Viderunt Eam Filie Syon*, 28.

87. See *Rewyll of Seynt Sauioure*, fol. 56r–56v.

88. Aungier, *History and Antiquities*, 28–29. These enlarged powers were, however, taken away from the abbess by a conference of theologians in January 1416 (Deanesly, *Incendium Amoris* 113).

89. John Bruce, ed., *Historie of the Arrivall of Edward IV in England and the Finall Recouerye of his Kingdomes from Henry VI*, *Three Chronicles of the Reign of Edward IV* (Gloucester: Sutton, 1988), 160.

90. Ibid.

91. Ibid., 159–60.

92. John Warkworth, *A Chronicle of the First Thirteen Years of the Reign of King Edward the Fourth*, ed. James Orchard Halliwell, *Three Chronicles of the Reign of Edward IV*, does not include the miracle of St. Anne in the account of Edward's activities of the week before Easter 1471 (37–38). Keith Dockray observes, "Unusually for a narrative composed during the reign of Edward IV, *Warkworth's Chronicle* not only displays considerable sympathy for Henry VI and his plight but also has a distinctly pro-Lancastrian tinge throughout" (introduction to *Three Chronicles of the Reign of Edward IV* ix).

93. William Huse Dunham, Jr. and Charles T. Wood, "The Right to Rule in England: Depositions and the Kingdom's Authority, 1327–1485," *American Historical Review* 81 (1976): 752.

94. Ibid.

95. Neville's accusation is quoted in Charles Ross, "Rumour, Propaganda, and Popular Opinion During the Wars of the Roses," *Patronage, the Crown, and the Provinces in*

Later Medieval England, ed. Ralph A. Griffiths (Gloucester: Sutton, 1981; Atlantic Heights, N.J.: Humanities Press, 1981), 26.

96. In 1469, Warwick had publicized "the occasions and verray causes of the grete inconveniencies and mischeves that fall in this lond in the dayes of [Edward II, Richard II, and Henry VI] . . . to the destruccion of them, And to the gret hurt and empourysshing of this lond" (Ross, "Rumour" 26, brackets in original).

97. Dunham and Wood, "Right to Rule," 752.

98. Richard Osberg observes that the N-Town play of the entry into Jerusalem makes the "connection between the entry of Christ into Jerusalem and the royal entry of secular authority" ("Jesse Tree" 218). He also notes, "Iconographically, the connection between Christ entering Jerusalem and the king entering his city is perhaps most clearly illustrated in the illumination from Harley MS 4380, fol 174b of Henry of Derby being welcomed into the City of London (Froissart, Book IV)" (ibid., 219).

99. Walker, "Political Saints," 90.

100. Edward IV's connection to Edward III through Lionel, duke of Clarence, comes through his paternal grandmother Anne Mortimer, who was the granddaughter of Philippa (Lionel's daughter) and Edmund Mortimer. The line thus runs: Edward III-Lionel-Philippa-Roger Mortimer-Anne Mortimer-Richard, duke of York-Edward IV. Edward IV could also claim descent from Edward III through his paternal grandfather Richard, earl of Cambridge, whose father was Edmund, duke of York. Edmund was, however, the younger brother of John of Gaunt.

101. Kathleen Ashley and Pamela Sheingorn, introduction to *Interpreting Cultural Symbols*, 53.

102. On using St. Anne to validate female lineages, see Sheingorn, "Appropriating the Holy Kinship."

103. Delany, *Impolitic Bodies*, 161.

104. Ibid., 181.

105. Felicity Riddy, "'Women talking about the things of God': A Late Medieval Subculture," *Women and Literature in Britain, 1150–1500*, ed. Carol M. Meale, (Cambridge: Cambridge University Press, 1996), 122 n. 41.

106. Johnston, "English Cult," 87.

107. Ibid., 86.

108. Ibid., 87.

109. Roger Ellis, ed., *The Liber celestis of St. Bridget of Sweden*, vol. 1, Early English Text Society o.s. 291 (Oxford: Oxford University Press, 1987), 253, my emphasis. As Roger Ellis observes, the discussion of "rights of heredity and elective kingship" and the "question of enforced resignation of the Crown" in *Liber celestis* IV.iii provided support not only for the English claim to France but also for those opposing Henry IV's usurpation in 1399. Excerpts from *Liber celestis* IV.iii were then also used to "urge the rights of Edward IV" ("'Flores ad fabricandam . . . coronam': An Investigation into the Uses of the Revelations of St. Bridget of Sweden in Fifteenth-Century England," *Medium Aevum* 51 [1982]: 173). Material in MS Cotton Vespasian E VII (discussed below)

appears to have been used successively against Henry IV and for Edward IV. In addition to the texts written during Edward IV's reign, the manuscript contains tracts which are "probably an Oxford product of the northern opposition to Henry IV in the years 1403–1405" (J. W. McKenna, "Popular Canonization as Political Propaganda: The Cult of Archbishop Scrope," *Speculum* 45 [1970]: 620).

110. William Henry Black, *Catalogue of the Ashmolean Manuscripts* (Oxford: Oxford University Press, 1845), 12.

111. MS BL Royal 15 E VI is a lavishly decorated book of romances and treatises presented to Queen Margaret by John Talbot, earl of Shrewsbury, upon her marriage to Henry VI. The genealogy is reproduced in McKenna, "Henry VI of England," plate 27. Linne R. Mooney observes that John Talbot "had been a commander in the war in France in the 1430s and early 1440s, and had been raised to his earldom in 1442 for his military achievements there" ("Lydgate's 'Kings of England' and Another Verse Chronicle of the Kings," *Viator* 20 [1989]: 269). Mooney concurs with B. J. H. Rowe that in presenting Margaret of Anjou with this pedigree, the earl wanted to remind Margaret that Henry descended from the royal house of France and to suggest that Henry's claim to the French throne was legitimate (269; see also B. J. H. Rowe, "King Henry VI's Claim to France in Picture and Poem," *The Library* 4th ser. 13 [1933]: 80 n. 1).

112. Through associations of Henry VI's genealogy with the Jesse Tree, his propagandists used his dual descent to get a great deal of mileage from the kind of "incarnational politics" so skillfully mobilized by Henry V. Discussing the 1432 pageant for Henry VI's entry into London, in which the Jesse Tree appears, McKenna says that the "striking combination of the royal family tree with the Tree of Jesse shows . . . the lengths to which the English royal administrators were prepared to go to advertise the dynastic claims of Henry VI" ("Henry VI of England" 161). Richard Osberg also analyzes the importance of the Jesse Tree in constructing a representation of messianic kingship in this pageant; see "The Jesse Tree in the 1432 London Entry of Henry VI: Messianic Kingship and the Rule of Justice." Similarly, in a pageant presented for Queen Margaret in 1456 at the feast of the Holy Cross, Margaret appears as "a kind of 'secular parallel' of the Divine Queen; she is the French rod of Jesse from which an English flower will grow. Her son Edward, the 'fragrante floure,' becomes the Christ-like Prince who will bring unity and peace to a divided land" (Osberg, "Jesse Tree" 218).

113. John Lydgate, "Ballade to King Henry VI upon his Coronation," *The Minor Poems of John Lydgate*, part 2, ed. Henry Noble MacCracken, Early English Text Society e.s. 107 (London: Oxford University Press, 1933), lines 9–10.

114. MS BL Cotton Vespasian E VII, fol. 117r. The manuscript contains a Latin version of the passage from the *Liber celestis* quoted above in Middle English, ending "istud non venient ad priorem gloriam & feliciorem statum verus heres consurgat aut ex patria successione aut materna" (ibid.).

115. According to C. A. J. Armstrong, J. O. Haliwell identifies this sermon as that

preached by George Neville, bishop of Exeter, at St. Paul's Cross (C. A. J. Armstrong, "The Inauguration Ceremonies of the Yorkist Kings and their Title to the Throne," *Transactions of the Royal Historical Society* 4th ser., 30 [1948]: 57). Armstrong, however, says that this identification, although widely accepted, "must be pronounced spurious" (ibid.). Armstrong argues, "On internal evidence it is impossible to accept the identification . . . with Neville's sermon at St. Paul's. The author of the 'pseudo-Neville', and of much else in the miscellany, was an ardent Welsh patriot who saw in the accession of Edward IV, descended from a daughter of Llewelyn ap Joworth (fol. 68v), the restoration of the British race and princes. . . . It is unlikely that George Neville was interested in Welsh patriotism, and it is unreasonable to suppose that he would have introduced the theme preaching to Londoners on behalf of Edward IV's title. The 'pseudo-Neville', which in the manuscript is without note of authorship, is rather a survey of the prophecies relating the fortunes of the Welsh with the Yorkist dynasty" (ibid., 57–58 n. 7).

116. MS BL Cotton Vespasian E VII, fol. 21v.

117. Ibid.

118. Ibid.

119. Ibid.

120. Ibid., fol. 22r.

121. Ibid., 22v.

122. The list reads, "þus it is knowen & proued of oure lord by reuelacion in oure lady aungell Sibill Quene of þe Souþe a doughter of seint Germaine Seint Edwarde [erasure] Birgitt Bede Gildas Ric*ar*dus Scrope & many moo &c" (ibid., fol. 22v). The erasure, made, according to J. W. McKenna, during the Reformation, reads "seint Thomas of Caunterbury" ("Popular Canonization" 620). This manuscript also bears witness to another Yorkist co-option of a Lancastrian symbolic strategy. It contains an illustrated genealogy that depicts Edward IV with a triple crown. McKenna observes, "From the dual crowns of Henry VI evolved the triple crown of Edward IV, an interesting though abortive symbol of the Yorkist tripartite claim to the thrones of England, France and Spain" ("Henry VI of England" 162).

123. That his niece Anne de la Pole is ultimately prioress at the house may well be connected with Edward's generosity to the community.

124. *VCH Middlesex*, 185.

125. Aungier, *History and Antiquities*, 68.

126. Ibid., 69.

127. Ibid.

128. Collins, *Bridgettine Breviary*, iv n. 5.

129. Ibid.

130. Article 6 of this manuscript was bound separately in 1858. Although it was once bound with the article containing the *Gesta Henrici Quinti* discussed above, as Taylor and Roskell point out, "It is important to note that the conjunction of the six

articles in this manuscript is entirely fortuitous; they were brought together at a date between 160[–] and 1621" (*Gesta* xvi–xvii).

131. Emma's presence in the *Rous Roll* may be partially explained by the fact that Rous in a sense owed his position at Guy's Cliff to Emma's revelations. When Richard Beauchamp approached her with his concern about his lack of a male heir, she advised him, as discussed above, to found a chantry in the chapel of the hermitage of Guy's Cliff. The *Rous Roll* reports that according to the revelation of "a holy anchoras namyd dam Em Rawghtone" the chantry of two priests "in tyme to cum . . . shuld be . . . a gracious place to seke to for eny dises or gref and on of Seynt Gyes Eyris shuld bryng hys Reliks a geyn to the same place" (John Rous, *Rous Roll, The Rous Roll with an Historical Introduction on John Rous and the Warwick Roll by Charles Ross* [Gloucester: Sutton, 1980], sect. 50). Hereafter I cite this volume as *Rous Roll*.

132. It has been suggested that John Rous was responsible for the "Pageant" as well as the *Rous Roll*. The table of contents inscribed inside MS BL Cotton Julius E IV attributes the "Pageant" to John Rous: "Vita et gesta Richardi Beauchamp Comitis Warwicensis illustre picturis per Iohannem Rossum Warwicensem." The spine of the binding for article 6 also reads, "John Rous Life and Acts of Richard Beauchamp Earl of Warwick Illustrated by Drawings." The 1802 catalogue to the Cottonian manuscripts similarly makes this attribution, describing article 6 as "The history of the life and acts of Richard Beauchamp Earl of Warwick; illustrated with drawings by John Ross of Warwick" (*A Catalogue of the Manuscripts in the Cottonian Library, Deposited in the British Museum* [London: 1802], 18 col. 1). In their introduction to the 1914 facsimile of the "Warwick Pageant," Viscount Dillon and W. H. St. John Hope posit that John Rous contributed the captions (Viscount Dillon and William Henry St. John Hope, eds., *Pageant of the Birth, Life and Death of Richard Beauchamp, Earl of Warwick, K.G., 1389–1439* [London: Longmans, 1914]), and P. Tudor-Craig argues that "Rous was the author, but not the illuminator of the Beauchamp Pageant itself" (*Richard III, Catalogue of National Portrait Gallery Exhibition* [1973], 48–9, 57–8, qtd. in Ross, introduction to *Rous Roll* vii n. 5). Archibald Russell claims that the attribution of the drawings in the "Pageant" to John Rous is "untenable" ("The *Rous Roll*," *Burlington Magazine* 30 [1917]: 23), but in the introduction to the 1980 reedition of the *Rous Roll*, Charles Ross indicates a possible connection between the *Rous Roll* and the "Pageant." Ross says that John Rous likely wrote and illustrated the Latin version of the *Rous Roll*, while the artwork in the English version, which is "much superior, more sophisticated and delicately refined," is perhaps the product of "an English artist influenced by Flemish artists, perhaps himself a Fleming, who probably knew the drawings in the Beauchamp Pageant" (introduction to *Rous Roll* vi). Russell says that it is "probable" that "Rous was personally acquainted with the accomplished Fleming who was the draughtsman of the Warwick MS in the British Museum" ("The *Rous Roll*" 24). More recently, Antonia Gransden has argued that, while the "Pageant" was formerly attributed to Rous, "nowadays scholars agree that he was not the artist; nor is it at all certain that he was the

author of the text" (*Historical Writing in England*, vol. 2 [London: Routledge and Kegan Paul, 1982], 313). She points, however, to the presence of Emma's revelations in the "Pageant" and the *Rous Roll*, as well as to another shared passage concerning Thomas, earl of Warwick's visit to eastern Europe, as evidence for her assertion that it is "likely . . . that the *Pageant* was either executed under Rous's supervision or that the text was composed by someone with similar interests and who had access to the 'Yorkist' roll" (*Historical Writing* 313). If John Rous is partially or entirely responsible for the "Pageant" as well as the *Rous Roll*, his political machinations and the differences in the accounts of Emma's revelations are all the more dramatic.

133. Ross, introduction to *Rous Roll*, vi.

134. Ibid., xiv–xv.

135. Ibid., xvii.

136. For a detailed description of the alterations, see the introduction to William Pickering's 1859 edition of the *Rous Roll* included in the 1980 reedition. The changes are so far reaching that the Latin version is dubbed the "Lancastrian" roll and the English the "Yorkist" roll.

137. Martin Lowry, "John Rous and the Survival of the Neville Circle," *Viator* 19 (1988): 337.

138. *Rous Roll*, sect. 50.

139. Ibid.

140. Ibid., sect. 63.

141. Lowry observes that the "overriding purpose of the whole work is to emphasize the loyalty of Earl Richard Beauchamp to the Lancastrian dynasty, and in the circumstances of 1485–1486, that was an obvious hint" ("Survival of the Neville Circle" 338). The document does, however, also show a move toward Tudor unification. For example, the depiction of Richard Beauchamp's baptism shows him flanked by figures identified as his two godfathers "Kyng Richard the secund and Seynt Richard Scrope" (MS BL Cotton Julius E VI fol. 1b). The description of Scrope as a saint in this Lancastrian text manifests the quality of "political saints" so astutely described by Simon Walker, who notes, "The power of the saints, and their value in political life, was not in preventing disorder or rebellion, for this they manifestly could not do. It was in helping to restore a measure of harmony after the strife was over" ("Political Saints" 90–91).

142. MS BL Cotton Julius E VI, fol. 12a.

143. M. A. Hicks, "Descent, Partition and Extinction: The 'Warwick Inheritance'," *Bulletin of the Institute of Historical Research* 52 (1979): 126. Lowry, who dates the text to the mid-1480s, says that it "can hardly be accidental" that the "Pageant" was produced "just as the issue of Anne Neville and her inheritance came into the public eye" ("Survival of the Neville Circle" 337).

144. MS BL Cotton Julius E VI, fol. 24a.

145. In contrast, the caption for the picture showing Henry VI's coronation as king

of England simply states, "Here shewes how kyng henry the vjth beyng in his tendre age was crowned kyng of England as Westm*inster* wt gret solempnyte" (ibid., fol. 23b).

146. Abergale, "The Revelations and the Hundred Years' War," 905–6.

Chapter 6. Liabilities and Assets

1. The proliferation of stories of "good" or "holy" women in the later Middle Ages attests to the widespread perception of this value. In addition to Lydgate's *Life of Our Lady* and Osbern Bokenham's *Legendys of Hooly Wummen* with which this chapter is primarily concerned, the list includes Chaucer's *Legend of Good Women*, Boccaccio's *De claris mulieribus*, Christine de Pisan's *Livre de la cité des dames*, and such collections of Marian miracles as the plays in the *Miracles de nostre dame par personnages*. Ian Johnson, discussing Bokenham's *Legendys*, points to the particular value of the spiritual authority of female saints in creating (masculine) literary authority. Bokenham's work, he says, "incorporates key features of gendered authority, such as the efficient causality of the saints in the making of the hagiographic texts, the self-interested and affective relationship between saint and writer, the personal experience of the writer of the saint's gracious powers, and the spiritual puissance imminent in hagiographic textuality itself" ("*Auctricitas*? Holy Women and Their Middle English Texts," *Prophets Abroad: The Reception of Continental Holy Women in Late-Medieval England*, ed. Rosalynn Voaden [Cambridge: Brewer, 1996], 189).

2. J. A. Lauritis, R. A. Klinefelter, and V. F. Gallagher, introduction to *A Critical Edition of John Lydgate's "Life of Our Lady,"* Duquesne Studies Philological Series 2 (Pittsburgh: Duquesne University Press, 1961), 4–10. All quotations from the *Life of Our Lady* are cited from this edition (hereafter *Life*) parenthetically in the text by book and line number. On the issue of Henry V's patronage, see also George R. Keiser, "*Ordinatio* in the Manuscripts of John Lydgate's *Lyf of Our Lady*: Its Value for the Reader, Its Challenge for the Modern Editor," *Medieval Literature: Texts and Interpretations*, ed. Tim William Machan, Medieval and Renaissance Texts and Studies 79 (Binghamton, N.Y.: Medieval and Renaissance Texts and Studies, 1991), 139–57. Keiser claims that Henry's commission "fits very well with what we know of Henry's intense devotionalism and with his commission of the French translation of the *Meditationes*" ("*Ordinatio*" 146). For evidence of the culture of Marian devotion at Lydgate's monastery of Bury St. Edmunds, which would harmonize well with Henry's devotion to the Virgin Mary, see Gail Gibson's article, "Bury St. Edmunds, Lydgate, and the *N-Town Cycle*," *Speculum* 56 (1981): 56–90, especially 70–74. Derek Pearsall argues that he does not find the rubrics indicating Henry V's patronage to be reliable because the poem contains no internal reference to the patronage "such as Lydgate invariably makes in a major poem" (*John Lydgate* [Charlottesville: University of Virginia Press, 1970], 286). While he believes it is possible that Henry V suggested the work to Lydgate but did not live to see

his suggestion carried out, Pearsall thinks that the *Life* was written for a monastic community (ibid.). Keiser, however, points out that there is also no internal evidence for Pearsall's suggestion that the *Life* was written for a monastic community ("*Ordinatio*" 146 n. 16), and Lee Patterson, like Keiser and the editors of the *Life*, comes down in favor of Henry V's patronage, saying that "in all likelihood" Henry commissioned the work (Lee Patterson, "Making Identities: Henry V and Lydgate," *New Historical Literary Study: Essays on Reproducing Texts, Representing History*, ed. Jeffrey N. Cox and Larry J. Reynolds [Princeton, N.J.: Princeton University Press, 1993], 74).

3. As Alan S. Ambrisco and Paul Strohm observe in relation to the prologue to Lydgate's *Troy Book*, "An aspect of John Lydgate's poetry fully commensurate with its Lancastrian environment is his recurring concern with matters of succession" ("Succession and Sovereignty in Lydgate's Prologue to *The Troy Book*," *The Chaucer Review* 30 [1995]: 40). Karen Winstead analyzes two other texts about female sanctity in which Lancastrian political concerns merge with literary issues: the anonymous prose *Lyf of Seynt Katerine*, composed c. 1420, and John Capgrave's legend of St. Katherine, written c. 1445. The *Lyf* "resonates with the nationalism that was vigorously promoted during Henry V's reign" (*Virgin Martyrs: Legends of Sainthood in Late Medieval England* [Ithaca, N.Y.: Cornell University Press, 1997], 158) and "uses Katherine to provide a straightforward model for pious lay readers" (Winstead, *Virgin Martyrs* 156). In contrast, Capgrave "explores the social and political ramifications of Katherine's scholarship, at once encouraging lay learning and warning of its dangers" (Winstead, *Virgin Martyrs* 156). For a detailed comparison of political and literary concerns in these texts, see "The Politics of Reading" in *Virgin Martyrs*.

4. As Ambrisco and Strohm argue, Lydgate's negotiation of literary succession "possesses an urgent and particular Lancastrian resonance" ("Succession and Sovereignty" 47). *Auctoritas*, the power to engage credibly in writing, is undeniably a masculine trait in later medieval culture. On the masculinity of *auctoritas*, Ian Johnson writes, "For the Middle Ages the term *auctor* and *auctoritas* are the masculine/general terms for originating and governing cultural and textual power" ("*Auctricitas*?" 177). David Lawton treats issue of influence and literary authority from a very useful perspective in "Dullness and the Fifteenth Century," *ELH* 54 (1987): 761–99, and Seth Lerer analyzes literary lineages and paternity in detail in *Chaucer and His Readers: Imagining the Author in Late-Medieval England* (Princeton, N.J.: Princeton University Press, 1993). Lerer argues that Lydgate and Chaucer's other fifteenth-century followers are "infantilized." He says these writers are "subjugate[d] . . . into childhood and incompetence" (*Chaucer and His Readers* 5). I believe that the anxieties about gender I discuss in this chapter are very much present in the kind of father-son relationship Lerer posits. Sons not only have to prove their adulthood, they also have to prove their manhood, their masculinity. In the culture of writing, this means proving their ability and legitimacy in the process of signification. Just as in the Oedipal drama the son fears castration, the literary son fears the castrating experience of being silenced. Significantly, in the anxieties about silence which paternal predecessors provoke for literary sons there is a

connection with Lerer's concept of "infantilization," since an infant is *in-fans*, not speaking.

5. To realize the extent to which Lydgate's self-legitimating efforts succeeded, one has only to look at *The Title and Pedigree of Henry VI*, commissioned by Richard Beauchamp, earl of Warwick. As Robert J. Meyer-Lee observes, this text contains an "elaborate poetic signature," an important feature because "Lydgate's name had become a political and cultural commodity." Meyer-Lee further argues, "The fact that *The Title and Pedigree of Henry VI* represents itself as the voice of specifically John Lydgate lent it more, not less, authority. Having poetry on your side—or on your mantle—was one thing, but having Lydgate's poetry was better" (Robert J. Meyer-Lee, "Lydgate's Lyric Ego," unpublished paper read at the Thirty-Fourth International Congress on Medieval Studies, Kalamazoo, Mich., May 9, 1999). My thanks to Robert for kindly providing me with a copy of his paper.

6. See Sheila Delany's introduction to her translation of the *Legendys* (Sheila Delany, trans., *A Legend of Holy Women: Osbern Bokenham, Legends of Holy Women* [Notre Dame: University of Notre Dame Press, 1992], xii, xxvii–xxxiii) and the expansion of this argument in her book *Impolitic Bodies: Poetry, Saints, and Society in Fifteenth Century England* (Oxford: Oxford University Press, 1998), especially chapters 4, 7, and 8. She gives particular emphasis to Bokenham's inclusion of Isabel Bourchier's genealogy, which includes Richard, duke of York, as evidence of Bokenham's political sympathies. Although my reading of the *Legendys* differs in some key regards from Delany's, her work on Bokenham has been an invaluable resource to me. In contrast to Delany, A. S. G. Edwards observes that Bokenham's fondness for the house of York may not have been motivated solely by political sympathy. Edwards says that it is at least as likely, if not more so, that "Bokenham's regard for Richard stemmed from his role as 'patronus' of Clare" ("The Transmission and Audience of Osbern Bokenham's *Legendys of Hooly Wummen*," *Late-Medieval Religious Texts and Their Transmission: Essays in Honour of A. I. Doyle*, ed. A. J. Minnis [Cambridge: Brewer, 1994], 166 n. 44).

7. See, for instance, Osbern Bokenham, *Legendys of Hooly Wummen*, ed. Mary S. Serjeantson, Early English Text Society o.s. 206 (London: Oxford University Press, 1938), lines 414–18, 4054–58. All quotations from the *Legendys of Hooly Wummen* (hereafter *Legendys*) are cited parenthetically in the text by line number from this edition.

8. For instance, when she is preparing to go to on pilgrimage to Santiago de Compostela and needs money, "a woman, a good frend to þis creatur" gives her "vij marke for sche xulde prey for hir whan þat sche come to Seynt Iamys" (Margery Kempe, *The Book of Margery Kempe*, ed. Sanford Brown Meech and Hope Emily Allen, Early English Text Society o.s. 212 [London: Oxford University Press, 1940], 106).

9. Ann Warren, *Anchorites and Their Patrons in Medieval Europe* (Berkeley and Los Angeles: University of California Press, 1982), 204.

10. Roger Chartier, *On the Edge of the Cliff: History, Language and Practices*, trans. Lydia G. Cochrane (Baltimore: Johns Hopkins University Press, 1997), 21.

11. Frank Taylor and John S. Roskell, eds. and trans., *Gesta Henrici Quinti: The Deeds of Henry the Fifth* (Oxford: Clarendon, 1975; London: Oxford University Press, 1975), 111.

12. Ibid.

13. The scene itself also strategically recalls another visual depiction of transmission of the right to rule. Walsingham reports that in the pageant for Richard II's coronation, the citizens constructed a castle at Cheapside. From each tower of the castle, maidens showered Richard II with gold leaves, and a gold angel offered him a crown (Thomas Walsingham, *Historia Anglicana*, vol. 1, ed. Henry Thomas Riley, Rolls Series 28, pt.1, vol. 1 [London, 1863], 331–32). Walsingham writes, "Factum etiam fuerat quoddam castrum habens turres quatuor, in superiori parte Fori venalium, qoud 'Chepe' nuncupatur. . . . In turribus autem ejus quatuor virgines speciosissimae collocatae fuerant, staturae et aetatis regiae, vestibus albis indutae, in qualibet turri una; quae adventanti Regi procul aurea folia in ejus faciem efflaverunt, et propius accedenti, florenos aureos, sed sophisticos, super eum et ejus dextrarium projecerunt. . . . In summitate castelli, quae ad modum tali inter quatuor turres elevata fuerat, positus erat angelus aureus, tenens auream coronam in manibus, qui tali ingenio factus fuerat, ut adventanti Regi coronam porrigeret inclinando" (ibid.). Such visual depictions continued to be politically useful throughout the fifteenth century; J. W. McKenna notes the parallel between the angelic coronation of Henry VI portrayed in the genealogy of MS BL Royal 15 E VI and the angelic coronation described by Walsingham ("Henry VI of England and the Dual Monarchy: Aspects of Royal Political Propaganda 1422–1432," *Journal of the Warburg and Courtauld Institutes* 28 [1965]: 152 n. 23).

14. Taylor and Roskell, *Gesta*, 112–13 n. 3. Taylor and Roskell indicate that the accounts of Walsingham and Adam of Usk also contain many of the details given in the *Liber Metricus* (ibid.).

15. On texts as a feminine medium, see Carolyn Dinshaw, *Chaucer's Sexual Poetics* (Madison: University of Wisconsin Press, 1989), 9.

16. In both political and literary mobilizations, female saints and holy women are meant to "be" rather than "have" the Phallus. They serve, in Judith Butler's analysis of Lacan's terminology, to "reflect the power of the Phallus, to signify that power . . . to signify the Phallus through 'being' . . . the dialectical confirmation of its identity" (*Gender Trouble: Feminism and the Subversion of Identity* [New York: Routledge, 1990], 44). As Butler further observes, though, even in this apparently safe capacity of "being," women have a dangerous, latent power; "Lacan clearly suggests that power is wielded by this feminine position of not-having, that the masculine subject who 'has' the Phallus requires this Other to confirm and, hence, be the Phallus" (ibid.).

17. David Herlihy points out that in the fourteenth century, "several prominent churchmen undertake a vigorous campaign to promote devotion to Joseph" (*Medieval Households* [Cambridge: Cambridge University Press, 1985], 127). Jean Gerson was particularly energetic in his efforts, and in his sermons, tracts, and poetry he proposed that the Church establish a major feastday for St. Joseph. Gerson did much to trans-

form the saint's image from feeble old man to vigorous husband and provider and to "downplay the image of Mary" (ibid., 128). Herlihy posits that the zealous promotion of the cult of Joseph by late medieval Church leaders may have been a reaction to the "feminization of sainthood and sanctity" and a response to the belief that "in their tumultuous times, fathers needed stronger spiritual patrons and models than the ranks of recent saints were supplying" (ibid., 129). Rosemary Drage Hale discusses the transformation of St. Joseph in the later Middle Ages from a feeble old man to a "mature, productive layman" ("Joseph as Mother: Adaptation and Appropriation in the Construction of Male Virtue," *Medieval Mothering*, ed. John Carmi Parsons and Bonnie Wheeler [New York: Garland, 1996], 102). Additionally, she observes, "Devotion to the Holy Family and veneration of Joseph as an intercessor and protector did not replace or displace Mary as an intercessor, but most likely diminished the near-goddess cult of the later Middle Ages" ("Joseph as Mother" 111). Hale also notes the appropriation into St. Joseph's cult of elements from the Marian cult, such as the "Madonna pose" and the lily as an emblem of purity. Such appropriation further serves to undercut the preeminence of Mary as mother.

18. Luce Irigaray, "Body Against Body: In Relation to the Mother," *Sexes and Genealogies*, trans. Gillian C. Gill (New York: Columbia University Press, 1993), 19.

19. Similarly, the painting by the "Master of the Holy Kinship" of "a young Joseph and older Peter taking the Child for a walk" displaces a female lineage with a male one (Hale, "Joseph as Mother" 112). As Hale observes, "In profoundly significant ways this image echoes the popular late medieval iconography of Anne, Mary, and the Child, in which Anne often carried a book and held or sat near her daughter and grandchild. Here, Peter, placed symbolically in Anne's position, carries a book, and Joseph takes the Child's hand" (ibid.). Lydgate's focus on Christ's male lineage also recalls the male lineages presented in Henry V's London pageant of 1415.

20. Irigaray, "Body Against Body," 17.

21. Ibid., 14. It is possible to read the focus on the circumcision in Book IV as a focus on Christ's suffering, bleeding, feeding flesh, a type of reading for which Caroline Walker Bynum persuasively argues in her discussion of Christ's wounded body as it appears in diverse medieval textual and visual representations (she does not discuss the *Life of Our Lady*, however). See *Fragmentation and Redemption: Essays on Gender and the Human Body in Medieval Religion* (New York: Zone, 1992), 79–117. In the *Life of Our Lady*, though, the relationship between Christ's blood and Mary's milk does not seem to be one of equality, suggesting "double intercession" and co-redemption as in many of the cases discussed by Bynum. Rather, given the stress on Jesus' name which accompanies the circumcision, together with the subsequent "disappearance" of Mary from her life discussed below, the dynamic seems to be one of replacement, of establishing proper hierarchy between male heir and mother.

22. Irigaray, "Body Against Body," 11.

23. Pearsall observes that "Lydgate . . . despite the 5,932 lines of his poem, only gets as far as the Purification, and an explanation of Candlemas. It may have been that the

apocryphal material from here to the Passion was too thin to sustain any sort of biographical treatment, or that he did not relish the prospect of the Passion. Whatever the reason, he seems to have left it a fragment" (*John Lydgate* 285). Lauritis et al. note, though, that "the first part of the *Meditationes* [that is, the *Meditationes Vitae Christi*, a major source for the *Life of Our Lady*], those meditations devoted to Monday, related the life of the Virgin Mary from her birth to the Purification, the exact extent of Lydgate's *Life of Our Lady*. Margaret Deanesly points out that this was a popular tradition in medieval lives of Mary" (introduction to *A Critical Edition*, 6; for Deanesly's views, see "The Gospel Harmony of John de Caulibus," *Collectanea Franciscana* X [1922], 17). So, it is quite possible that the *Life of Our Lady* is not a fragment, and that Lydgate may have meant the section on the Purification to be the end of the work.

24. There is also another respect in which Mary is a competing textual authority. As Ian Johnson observes, "The figure of Mary is not only an exemplary role model for meditation and devotion, she is also acknowledged as an *auctrix* behind the evangelical *auctores* for it was she who told them the details of the Nativity and Infancy of Christ" ("*Auctricitas?*" 179). Thus, even scriptural authority, one of the masculine textual authorities par excellence, has a necessary feminine foundation.

25. Lydgate's logic of "self-feminization" which works ultimately to assert his masculine superiority is similar to that described by Caroline Walker Bynum in her analysis of St. Bernard's description of monks as women. Bynum notes, "To call monks women, as St. Bernard does, is to use the feminine as something positive (humility) but also to imply that such is *not* the opinion of society" (*Jesus as Mother: Studies in the Spirituality of the High Middle Ages* [Berkeley and Los Angeles: University of California Press, 1982], 144).

26. Pearsall, *John Lydgate*, 268.

27. As A. C. Spearing observes, with reference to numerous classical examples including Lucretius, Epicurus, and Horace, "There is ample precedent for seeing the authority of the literary precursor over his successors as analogous to the authority of the father over his sons. . . . Descent and inheritance from father to son provide a basic explanatory model for literary history, and the model retains its power, for example in Harold Bloom's conception of the tensely Oedipal relation of son to father as characterizing the whole of English poetic history from Milton to the present" (*From Medieval to Renaissance in English Poetry* [Cambridge: Cambridge University Press, 1985], 92). In his recent astute analysis of the dynamics of the paternal relationship between Chaucer and Hoccleve, Ethan Knapp argues that Hoccleve's praise and eulogies for Chaucer "present a strategy for poetic usurpation" ("Eulogies and Usurpations: Hoccleve and Chaucer Revisited," *Studies in the Age of Chaucer* 21 [1999]: 249). Lydgate's strategy seems not unlike Hoccleve's, and it also bears witness to the Oedipal drama described by Harold Bloom in *The Anxiety of Influence: A Theory of Poetry* (New York: Oxford University Press, 1973).

28. He says Chaucer "made firste, to distille and rayne / The golde dewe, dropes, of speche and eloquence / Into our tunge" (*Life* II 1632–34).

29. As Knapp points out, "The paradox of aggressivity hidden within the elegy is as old as the elegy itself, and is a paradox of which Chaucer had been well aware" ("Eulogies and Usurpations" 262). Indeed, Lydgate's position vis-á-vis Chaucer resembles that of Chaucer's Clerk in relation to his own *auctor* Petrarch as Carolyn Dinshaw describes it: feminized, Griselda-like, and aggressive toward the one in authority. See "Griselda Translated" in *Chaucer's Sexual Poetics*, especially 132–37.

30. A certain amount of resentment is evident in the continuation of the poet's lament: "Right so his dyteʒ withoutyn eny pere / Euery makyng with his light disteyne / In sothefastness, who so takethe hede / Wherefore no wondre, thof my hert pleyne / Vpon his dethe" (*Life* II 1641–45). The break between the verb "pleyne" at the end of line 1644 and its completion in the phrase "Vpon his dethe" at the beginning of line 1645 allows a moment in which it is ambiguous precisely *what* the poet laments. It is briefly possible to imagine that the poet "pleynes" that Chaucer "Euery makyng withe his light disteyne, / In sothefastness," a possibility perhaps subtly emphasized by the rhyming of "disteyne" and "pleyne."

31. Slavoj Žižek, *The Sublime Object of Ideology* (London: Verso, 1989), 135.

32. Ibid.

33. Ibid., 134.

34. Paul Strohm, "The Trouble with Richard: The Reburial of Richard II and Lancastrian Symbolic Strategy," *Speculum* 71 (1996): 87–111. See also the expanded version of this argument in chapter 4 of *England's Empty Throne: Usurpation and the Language of Legitimation 1399–1422* (New Haven, Conn.: Yale University Press, 1998).

35. Knapp argues that Hoccleve's strategy of poetic usurpation directed against the father Chaucer in the *Regement of Princes* similarly resonates with events happening at the time of its composition within the house of Lancaster—the conflict between Prince Henry, for whom the *Regement* was written, and Henry IV ("Eulogies and Usurpations" 268–73).

36. Geoffrey Chaucer, *The Canterbury Tales*, *The Riverside Chaucer*, 3rd ed., ed. Larry D. Benson (Boston: Houghton, 1987), IV 29.

37. Chaucer's Clerk continues his lament for Petrarch by similarly remarking, "But Deeth, that wol nat suffre us dwellen heer, / But as it were a twynklyng of an ye, / Hem bothe hath slayn, and alle shul we dye" (*Canterbury Tales* IV 36–38). Dinshaw points out that this remark is illustrative of the Clerk's aggression toward Petrarch and that he "dwells a moment too long to be innocent on the power and inevitability of death" (*Chaucer's Sexual Poetics* 136). Spearing similarly observes that the Clerk finds "those nails . . . that keep Petrarch in his coffin" to be "reassuring" (*From Medieval to Renaissance* 103).

38. In addition to Elizabeth Vere and Katherine Denston, Bokenham's female patrons include Katherine Howard, Isabel Bourchier, Agatha Flegge, and Isabel Hunt. For accounts of the familial and social connections of these patrons, see Delany, *Impolitic Bodies*, 15–22, and Eileen S. Jankowski, "Reception of Chaucer's Second Nun's Tale: Osbern Bokenham's Lyf of S. Cycyle," *The Chaucer Review* 30 (1996): 307–8, 317

n. 12. The description of Lydgate's relationships with patrons and literary traditions given by Ruth Evans et al. seems quite applicable to Bokenham as well, since he too is a "vernacular writer, situated between authoritative sources and authoritative patrons whose demands pull him in such different directions that he has to assume a double attitude of simultaneous deference and assertiveness" ("The Notion of Vernacular Theory," *The Idea of the Vernacular: An Anthology of Middle English Literary Theory, 1280–1520*, ed. Jocelyn Wogan-Browne et al. [University Park: Pennsylvania State University Press, 1999], 321).

39. See Delany, *Impolitic Bodies*, 21–22 and chapter 7, especially 130–33 and 144ff.

40. Ibid., 94.

41. Ibid., 91.

42. Jocelyn Wogan-Browne, "The Virgin's Tale," *Feminist Readings in Middle English Literature: The Wife of Bath and All Her Sect*, ed. Ruth Evans and Lesley Johnson (London: Routledge, 1994), 180.

43. *Margery Kempe*, 126.

44. Ibid. On Margery's strategy in this encounter, see Karma Lochrie, *Margery Kempe and Translations of the Flesh* (Philadelphia: University of Pennsylvania Press, 1991), chapter 3, especially 110–13.

45. Delany, *Impolitic Bodies*, 91.

46. The only "on the spot" conversion involving Mary Magdalene takes place in Aguens, and it is not effected by her preaching but rather by unspecified miracles: "Whan þis was don þei went þens / Blyssyd Mawdelyn & hir company, / And come to a cyte clepyd Aguens, / Wych, wyth myracles shewyde plenteuously, / To cryst was conuertyd ryht redyly" (*Legendys* 6144–48).

47. Nancy Jay, *"Throughout Your Generations Forever": Sacrifice, Religion, and Paternity* (Chicago: University of Chicago Press, 1992), xxiv.

48. Of the thirteen saints whose lives are recounted in the *Legendys*, ten of them are virgin martyrs. Besides St. Anne and St. Mary Magdalene, the other saint who is neither a virgin nor a martyr is St. Elizabeth, to whom Bokenham applies similar strategies. St. Elizabeth is situated, for instance, as subordinate to her father, her husband, and her confessor.

49. Kathleen Ashley and Pamela Sheingorn, introduction to *Interpreting Cultural Symbols: Saint Anne in Late-Medieval Society* (Athens: University of Georgia Press, 1990), 1–68.

50. While some mention of a saint's parents and the nobility of her family is common at the beginning of Bokenham's saints' lives, as it is in many medieval saints' lives, it is telling that the long and complex genealogy given for St. Anne has no precise parallel in the *Legendys* except the rather complicated family tree of Isabel Bourchier discussed above.

51. There is no life of St. Anne in the *Legenda Aurea*, which is one of Bokenham's main sources. Mary Serjeantson reports that for the life of St. Anne "the immediate source (or sources) cannot be traced, but seems to have been a Latin legend based on

(or on the same originals as) the *Evangelium de Nativitate S. Mariae* and the *Historia de Nativitate Mariae et de Infantia Salvatoris*" (introduction to *Legendys* xxii). Delany argues, "Given the gospel origins of the savior's pedigree and the lack of other information, Bokenham can do little to augment the matrilineal dimension"; however, even within these constraints Bokenham "does all he can to make his reader aware of the matrilineal role" (*Impolitic Bodies* 161). It is true, as Delany points out, that Bokenham names David's wife as well as both of Anne's parents. I do not agree, though, that it would have been impossible for Bokenham to emphasize an exclusively female lineage, especially in light of the examples of such lineages described by Ashley and Sheingorn. It seems that Bokenham foregrounds female lineage for his political purposes but is careful to contain the potentially disturbing implications this strategy entails by keeping male lineage clearly in the picture.

52. Delany, on the other hand, views maternity as central to the life of St. Anne, arguing that it is "centrally about childbirth" (*Impolitic Bodies* 82) and associating it with the womb in her "corporeal" reading of the *Legendys*.

53. Ibid., 85. In the debate concerning the conception of Mary, the "maculists" held that Mary was conceived naturally, through sexual intercourse; the "immaculists" held that Mary was conceived miraculously, without sexual intercourse, and hence without the stain (the *macula*) of original sin.

54. Lydgate writes, "And she conceyved, this faythfull trwe wyf / By Ioachym, the holy frute of lyfe" (*Life* I 125–26). On Lydgate's maculism, see Delany, *Impolitic Bodies*, 83–84.

55. The sole extant manuscript of the text belonged to an unnamed nunnery as the epilogue explains: "Translatyd in-to englys be a doctor of dyuyni / te clepyd Osbern Bokenham frere Austyn of the / conuent of Stok-clare and was doon wrytyn in Cane / bryge by hys soun Frere Thomas Burgh. The yere of our lord / a thousand foure hundryth seuyn & fourty Whose expence dreu / thretty schyligys & yafe yt onto this holy place of nunnys / that þei shulde haue mynd on hym & of hys systyr Dame / Betrice Burgh Of þe wych soulys ihesu haue mercy. Amen" (*Legendys* page 289).

56. Dinshaw makes a similar point in discussing Petrarch's translation of the story of Griselda into Latin, saying that the translation of this woman's story "excludes all but those who can negotiate Latin 'heigh stile'" (*Chaucer's Sexual Poetics* 149); women in particular are thus by and large denied access.

57. Wogan-Browne, "The Virgin's Tale," 174.

58. Theresa Kemp, "Incriminating Women: Identity, Resistance and Early English Literary Women" (Ph.D. diss., Indiana University, 1994), 39–40.

59. Ibid., 40.

60. Delany notes, "Several factors affect Bokenham's attitude toward Lydgate. Institutional rivalry was one, for regional jurisdictional disputes were common among religious houses in the same area, and competition for land and money bequests was ongoing. Politically, the firm Lancastrian commitment of Lydgate and his establishment must have been viewed with hostility by a Yorkist convent and its inmates. Also,

the old competition between monks and friars is not irrelevant to Lydgate and Boken-ham. Besides the social reasons for a negative approach to Lydgate, there is also the matter of what and how he wrote" (*Impolitic Bodies* 46). In particular, Delany believes Bokenham, objecting to Lydgate's hagiographical fundraising efforts such as "St. Austin at Compton," may have "perceived a need to cleanse hagiography of its courtly ironic and its bureaucratic accretions to return to the fundamentals of faith" (ibid., 65).

61. I am grateful to Steven G. Weiskopf who in private communication called my attention to the possibility of something sinister in Bokenham's attitude toward Lydgate at this point in the text.

62. As Jocelyn Wogan-Browne et al. observe regarding the prologue to the life of St. Margaret, "The tone . . . is partly comic, as though Bokenham is aware of writing not for a national audience but for provincial coteries, and as though vernacular writing may not be taken too seriously by his Cambridge contemporaries" (*The Idea of the Vernacular* 65).

63. Lawton, "Dullness and the Fifteenth Century," 766.

64. Ibid.

65. Ibid., 766–67. In discussing the development of the relationship of Bokenham with Chaucer, Delany develops an extended comparison of the *Legendys of Hooly Wummen* and Chaucer's *Legend of Good Women*, saying that Bokenham's text replaces a pseudohagiography with a real one in an act of both homage and critique (see chapters 2 and 3 of *Impolitic Bodies*).

66. In using this strategy, Bokenham engages in a sort of gendered variation on the strategy that Rita Copeland sees Chaucer using in the *Legend of Good Women* and Gower using in the *Confessio Amantis*. According to Copeland, Chaucer and Gower claim equality with classical sources while simultaneously insisting upon their inde-pendence as vernacular poets. See chapter 7 of *Rhetoric, Hermeneutics, and Translation in the Middle Ages: Academic Translations and Vernacular Texts* (Cambridge: Cambridge University Press, 1991); see also the discussion of Copeland's work in Ruth Evans et al., "The Notion of Vernacular Theory," especially 315–19.

67. Bokenham writes, "I neuer slepte, ne neuer dede seche / In ethna flowrs, wher, as claudian doþe telle, / Proserpina was rapt; nor of þe sugird welle / In elicona, my rudnesse to leche, / I neuer dede taste, to me so felle / Wher euer the muses, & þe cruel wreche / Of orpheus, whiche hys wyf dede seche / In helle, of me wolde neuer take hede, / Nor of his armonye oo poynt me teche / In musical proporcyon rymes to lede" (*Legendys* 1455–64).

68. Lydgate writes, "And though my penne, be quakyng ay for drede / Neythir to Cleo, ne to Caliope / Me luste not calle, forto helpe me / Ne to no muse, my poyntell forto gye" (*Life* II 1658–61).

69. Ruth Nissé, " 'Oure Fadres Olde and Modres': Gender, Heresy, and Hoccleve's Literary Politics," *Studies in the Age of Chaucer* 21 (1999), especially 291–99.

70. Delany discusses Bokenham's rejection of classicism, especially his rejection of the Muses, as a manifestation of his concern with the proper Christian use of classical

material. Bokenham the friar gives, she says, "a polemic against, first, the abuse of classicism and then abuse of courtly rhetoric" (*Impolitic Bodies* 58). Bokenham's *Legendys* might also be seen as a prime example of what Ruth Evans et al. call the "double sense of dependence on and difference from Latin thought and literature" evident in many Middle English texts ("The Notion of Vernacular Theory" 318).

71. *Legendys of Hooly Wummen*, page 110. On the authority female saints can bring to hagiographical texts as well as to the authors who pen such texts, see Johnson, "*Auctricitas?*" especially 189.

Chapter 7. Paying the Price

1. Marina Warner, *Joan of Arc: The Image of Female Heroism* (New York: Knopf, 1981), 113.

2. Paul Strohm makes a related argument about the difficulties inherent in a different sort of political manipulation of women by the Lancastrians—in this case foreign brides—in "Joanne of Navarre: That Obscure Object of Desire" (*England's Empty Throne: Usurpation and the Language of Legitimation, 1399–1422* [New Haven, Conn.: Yale University Press, 1998], 153–72). Discussing Joanne's betrothal by proxy to Henry IV, Strohm writes, "And so are women generally brought forward in Lancastrian texts in a range of capacities, each of which might be though a less than adequate representation of the historical woman, a more than adequate way of shaping her representation to the requirements of the task at hand. This range of capacities includes such superficially different incarnations as mother, mediatrix, sorceress, and whore. Yet for all their apparent variety such roles must be seen as alternative forms of effacement in their complete subservience to processes of male fantasy" (ibid., 161). Strohm goes on to examine Joanne's case as an example of the complications that ensue from her "disruptive potentialities," her existence as "something more than the sum of the roles" assigned to her (ibid., 172).

3. Brother Richard was an itinerant preacher and initially a supporter of the Anglo-Burgundian cause. He was, however, "converted by the progress of Joan through enemy territory to Rheims" and "went over to the other side at Troyes" (Warner, *Joan of Arc* 83). Bedford despised Brother Richard and believed him to be Joan's "mentor in the black arts—'that mendicant friar, a seditious apostate'" (ibid.). Joan said to her interrogators that she had never seen Brother Richard when she came before Troyes and that she thought that "the people of Troyes . . . sent him to her, saying that they were afraid she was not from God; and when he drew near her, he made the sign of the Cross and sprinkled holy water, and she said to him: 'Come boldly, I shall not fly away'" (W. P. Barrett, *The Trial of Jeanne D'Arc Translated into English from the Original Latin and French Documents* [London: Gotham House, 1932], 81). Catherine de La Rochelle also, like Brother Richard, switched sides, in her case more than once. After Joan cast doubt upon Catherine's reported conversations with a "white lady" who came to her in

visions, Catherine appeared before the Parisian magistrates in 1430 as a "hostile witness to Joan" (Warner, *Joan of Arc* 83). In 1431, however, according to the Bourgeois of Paris, Catherine had gone back to the Armagnac side, and in the sermons preached in Paris to justify the burning of Joan, Catherine and Pierrone are both alleged to be heretical followers of Brother Richard. Although Brother Richard's fate is unknown, the Bourgeois of Paris reports that Pierronne was burnt, not for her association with Brother Richard but rather for her loyalty to Joan (Warner, *Joan of Arc* 83).

4. Frank Taylor and John S. Roskell, eds. and trans., *Gesta Henrici Quinti: The Deeds of Henry the Fifth* (Oxford: Clarendon, 1975; London: Oxford University Press, 1975), xxiv.

5. James Hamilton Wylie and William Templeton Waugh, *The Reign of Henry the Fifth*, vol. 3 (Cambridge: Cambridge University Press, 1929), 85. The Lollard John Oldcastle was condemned on September 25, 1413, and he escaped from the Tower of London on October 19, 1413. Although Oldcastle was purported to have led a rebellion of Lollards against Henry V on January 10, 1414, Paul Strohm has recently shown that the construction of the events of that day as the "Oldcastle Rebellion" is part of a Lancastrian propagandist strategy in which Henry V as *electus Dei* opposes the seditious scourge of Lollardy. See chapter 3 of Strohm, *England's Empty Throne*.

6. Wylie and Waugh, *Henry the Fifth*, 87.

7. Margery Kempe, *The Book of Margery Kempe*, ed. Sanford Meech Brown and Hope Emily Allen, Early English Text Society o.s. 212 (London: Oxford University Press, 1940), 129, hereafter *Margery Kempe*. Beverly Boyd points out parallels between Margery Kempe and Joan of Arc in her article, "Wyclif, Joan of Arc, and Margery Kempe," *Mystics Quarterly* 12.3 (1986): 112–18. She also discusses the significance of Lollardy, as well as the involvement of Lollard-hunting clerics, in the cases of both Joan and Margery. She does not, however, discuss Bedford or his involvement with both women.

8. *Margery Kempe*, 132.

9. Nancy F. Partner, "Reading *The Book of Margery Kempe*," *Exemplaria* 3 (1991): 33. On the early establishment of a Lollard community in Leicester thanks to Philip Repingdon, see Anne Hudson, *The Premature Reformation: Wycliffite Texts and Lollard History* (Oxford: Oxford University Press, 1988), 43.

10. RP IV, qtd. in Wylie and Waugh, *Henry the Fifth*, 85.

11. *Margery Kempe*, 134. Interestingly, while Bedford is evidently willing to pay handsomely to obtain Margery, and, later, even more handsomely to acquire Joan of Arc, the archbishop of York is willing to pay to get rid of Margery. After Margery has convinced him she is not a Lollard, he asks, "Wher schal I haue a man þat myth ledyn þis woman fro me?" (ibid., 128). The first volunteer is dismissed as "to ȝong," and the second volunteer, "a good sad man of þe Erchebischopys meny," asks "a nobyl" for rendering the service. The archbishop, though willing to pay, is not willing to "waryn so mech on hir body," and they settle for five shillings (ibid.).

12. Wylie and Waugh, *Henry the Fifth*, 47 n. 7. Given John, duke of Bedford's later involvement with Syon, it seems likely that he had knowledge of the ongoing process

of realizing the foundation, and indeed he may well have participated in it. In 1422, Henry V moved the community from Twickenham to the manor of Isleworth. On February 5, 1426, John, duke of Bedford, then regent, laid the foundation stone of their new chapel there (John Henry Blunt, ed., *The Myroure of Oure Ladye*, Early English Text Society e.s. 19 [London: Kegan Paul, 1873], xvii). He also gave a ring to each of the sisters first professed at Syon (ibid.), as well as "duos pulcros libros officii sororum et vnam legendam" (MS BL Add. 22285 fol. 5v, quoted in A. Jeffries Collins, *The Bridgettine Breviary of Syon*, Henry Bradshaw Society 96 [Worcester: Henry Bradshaw Society, 1969], iv n. 5).

13. *Margery Kempe*, 133.

14. Ibid.

15. Ralph A. Griffiths, *The Reign of King Henry VI: The Exercise of Royal Authority 1422–61* (London: Benn, 1981), 85.

16. Ibid.

17. The grandson of Ralph Neville, earl of Westmorland, was the "Kingmaker" Richard Neville, earl of Warwick, who married Anne, daughter of Richard Beauchamp, earl of Warwick.

18. G. E. Cockayne, *The Complete Peerage* vol. VI (London: St. Catherine Press, 1926), 195; see RP III:426–27.

19. Griffiths, *Henry VI*, 132.

20. John, Lord Greystoke, was himself an important figure in Anglo-Scottish affairs. "On 22 Mar. 1420/1 he was appointed Keeper of Roxborough Castle, for 4 years, at a salary of £1,000 a year in time of peace and £2,000 a year in time of war. He was appointed a commissioner to treat of peace with the Scots, and concerning violations of the truces, &c" (Cockayne, *Complete Peerage* 196).

21. Paul Strohm, *Hochon's Arrow: The Social Imagination of Fourteenth-Century Texts* (Princeton, N.J.: Princeton University Press, 1993), 125. Ruth Nissé Shklar has also noted the connection between Margery Kempe's supposed Lollardy and "domestic treason" in "Cobham's Daughter: *The Book of Margery Kempe* and the Power of Heterodox Thinking," *Modern Language Quarterly* 56:3 (1995): 301. Shklar observes, regarding Margery's involvement with Lady Westmoreland and Lady Greystoke, "Not surprisingly, the final substantive charge brought against Kempe is for domestic rebellion involving the nobility. . . . The suffragan represents Kempe through contemporary chroniclers' propagandistic images of the middle-class Lollards' seduction of the nobility into treason, only recast at a domestic level. Like Oldcastle's putative Lollard teachers, blamed in some accounts for his fall, Kempe becomes the agent responsible for leading this noblewoman away from her class into a feminine revolt" ("Cobham's Daughter" 303).

22. Strohm, *Hochon's Arrow*, 124.

23. *Margery Kempe*, 133.

24. Ibid., 116.

25. Shklar, "Cobham's Daughter," 297.

26. Strohm, *Hochon's Arrow*, 125.

27. Barrett, *Trial*, 100–101.

28. On Joan's refusal of her parents' chosen mate for her, see Warner, *Joan of Arc*, 153.

29. Barrett, *Trial*, 316.

30. Ibid., 333.

31. Ibid.

32. Jules Quicherat, ed., *Procès de condamnation et de réhabilitation de Jeanne d'Arc, dite La Pucelle*, 5 vols., (Paris: Renouard, 1841–1849), I:490.

33. Paul Strohm observes, "Royal and other interests alike are ultimately served by the institution and protection of an accessible and influential model of hierarchy at a level close to the lived experience of most members of the middle strata" (*Hochon's Arrow* 125). In *Families in Former Times*, John-Louis Flandrin argues, "The authority of the father of the family and the authority of God not only legitimized one another: they served to legitimize all other authorities. Kings, lords, patrons and ecclesiastics have all represented themselves as fathers and the representatives of God" (119–20, qtd. in Strohm, *Hochon's Arrow* 125 n. 4).

34. Barrett, *Trial*, 338.

35. Ibid.

36. Ibid.

37. Joan "professed to submit to the Church Triumphant and refused to submit herself to the Church Militant, so declaring her erroneous opinion in respect of the article *Unam Sanctam*, etc., and in all this showing herself at fault. She said it was for God, without an intermediary, to judge her, and she committed herself, her acts and her sayings to Him and His Saints, and not to the judgements of the Church" (Barrett, *Trial* 232). To compound the problem, both Margery and Joan claim to have divine guarantees that they will get to heaven, guarantees that obviate the need for the clergy in the economy of salvation. See, for instance, Barrett, *Trial*, 73, and *Margery Kempe*, 16–17.

38. *Margery Kempe*, 132.

39. W. T. Waugh, "Joan of Arc in English Sources of the Fifteenth Century," *Historical Essays in Honour of James Tait*, ed. J. G. Edwards et al. (Manchester: n.p., 1933), 388.

40. Ibid., 388 n. 6.

41. Valerie R. Hotchkiss indicates, "In the preliminary lists of accusations and admonishments, the charge of transvestism occurs almost thirty times, and two of the final twelve charges against Jeanne concern male dress. Above all, article five condemns her transvestism as blasphemy" (*Clothes Make the Man: Female Cross Dressing in Medieval Europe*, New Middle Ages 1, ed. Bonnie Wheeler [New York: Garland, 1996], 59).

42. Barrett, *Trial*, 83.

43. Ibid., 137.

44. Susan Schibanoff, "True Lies: Transvestism and Idolatry in the Trial of Joan of

Arc," *Fresh Verdicts on Joan of Arc*, ed. Bonnie Wheeler and Charles T. Wood, New Middle Ages 3, ed. Bonnie Wheeler (New York: Garland, 1996), 44–47.

45. Ibid., 47.

46. For a summary of the story of the female pope, frequently called Joan or Johanna, as well as a comparison of different versions of the legend, see Hotchkiss, *Clothes Make the Man*, chapter 5. Significantly, Jan Hus, whose brand of heresy was in Lancastrian eyes so closely linked with Lollardy, "frequently cited the example of the papess to refute claims of apostolic succession" (ibid., 73; see Jan Hus, *Documenta Mag. Joannis Hus*, ed. Francis Palacky [1869; reprint, Osnabrük: Biblio-Verlag, 1966], 61, 178, 229, 291. See also Jan Hus, *Tractatus de Ecclesia*, ed. S. Harrison Thomson [Cambridge: Heffer, 1956], 48, 103, 107, 141, 223). In the Norwich Lollard trials, several defendants make a distinction between "the office of pope and its holders" and similarly deny apostolic succession (Norman P. Tanner, *Heresy Trials in the Diocese of Norwich, 1428–31* Camden 4th ser. 20 [London: Offices of the Royal Historical Society, 1977], 17). John Eldon of Beccles declares, for instance, "the pope is Antecrist, and hath no poar in holy Church as Seint Petir hadde but if he folwe the steppis of Petre in lyvyng" (Tanner, *Heresy Trials* 135), and John Skylan of Bergh says, "ther was never pope aftir the decesse of Peter" (Tanner, *Heresy Trials* 147).

47. *Margery Kempe*, 112.

48. Carolyn Dinshaw notes that Margery Kempe's wearing white clothes "seems to confirm suspicions of heresy" (*Getting Medieval: Sexualities and Communities, Pre- and Post-Modern* [Durham, N.C.: Duke University Press, 1999], 145), and, significantly for the purposes of comparison with Joan, Dinshaw calls Margery's attire "a kind of transvestism" (*Getting Medieval* 148). Dinshaw's reading of Margery as a "queer" figure, as one who challenges categories, also provides a particularly apt point of comparison between Margery and Joan. It is interesting to note that both Margery and Joan serve as touchstones for questions of "queer" identity in contemporary culture; see, for instance, Robert Gluck, *Margery Kempe* (New York: High Risk Books, 1994), and Joan Acocella's article "Burned Again" from *The New Yorker* (November 15, 1999), in which she notes that the "queer studies people" are "on [Joan's] trail" while at the same time the "St. Joan of Arc Anti-Defamation League" will give "a talking to" anyone who thinks that Joan was "a transvestite, a lesbian, a feminist, a Protestant, or a Wiccan" (106).

49. Schibanoff, "True Lies," 47.

50. Jean-Joseph Goux, *Symbolic Economies After Marx and Freud*, trans. Jennifer Curtiss Gage (Ithaca, N.Y.: Cornell University Press, 1990), 3.

51. As Steven Weiskopf observes, the Lancastrians' fear of Joan is in part a "fear that the powerful body of the English monarchy, once represented by Henry V, is being unmanned 'bi litel and lytel'" ("Readers of the Lost Arc: Secrecy, Specularity, and Speculation in the Trial of Joan of Arc," *Fresh Verdicts on Joan of Arc*, 124).

52. Goux, *Symbolic Economies*, 21, his emphasis. Schibanoff astutely observes that in Joan of Arc's trial "what was 'at stake' was not merely God, King, and Nation but the traditional constituent of all three, manhood" ("True Lies" 53).

53. Goux, *Symbolic Economies*, 224.

54. Strohm, *England's Empty Throne*, 141. Joan in male attire also resonates with Lancastrian fears concerning Lollardy and counterfeiting, which, as Strohm has shown, have remarkably close connections in relation to Lancastrian symbolic undertakings. He argues, "Lollards (whose heightened respect for the spiritual encourages respect for matter's stubborn resistance) and counterfeiters (who cynically impose life-giving signs upon inert or dead matter) pose a closely allied, if not identical, threat to the Lancastrian symbolic" (ibid.). Joan the "false lie" counterfeits masculinity; she also (at least from the Anglo-Burgundian perspective) counterfeits her own sanctity and Charles VII's royal legitimacy with her voices and visions. Just as the false groats purportedly produced by William Carsewell in conjunction with John Oldcastle threatened the value of the king's good money (see Strohm, *England's Empty Throne*, chapter 5), so too Joan herself and her report of a crown brought from heaven as a sign to Charles VII threaten to debase the value of the symbolic coin circulated by the Lancastrians in their efforts to gain representational credit.

55. Margery's loquacity, that stereotypically feminine trait that helped get her into trouble, in this case helped get her out as well. Because she is able to tell a "good tale" of which the archbishop approves, he acquiesces to her request that he give her his letter and seal, indicating that she has demonstrated her orthodoxy and assuring all that, as she says, "no-thyng is attyd ageyns me, neiþyr herrowr ne heresy þat may ben preuyd vp-on me" (*Margery Kempe* 134).

56. A. Hamilton Thompson, *Visitations of Religious Houses*, 3 vols., Lincoln Record Society 7, 14, 21 (Lincoln: Lincoln Record Society, 1914–1929), II:xv.

57. Ibid.

58. Margery was quite pleased when those who wanted the privileges objected to the conditional offer made by Alnwick and decided to hold out for full privileges, which they expected to gain through legal proceedings. They "obeyd not ne lyked not þe menys whech wer proferyd hem . . . &, as God wolde, þei wer deceyuyd of her entent, and for þei wold han al þei lost al" (*Margery Kempe* 60). Thus was Margery's revelation that the chapel would not gain the privileges fulfilled. On these events, as well as an earlier attempt made when Margery was a child and involving her father, who also opposed the efforts, see *Margery Kempe*, Appendix III, 372–74.

59. Boyd, "Wyclif, Joan of Arc, and Margery Kempe," 117.

60. I say "seemed" to increase because it is possible that in both 1417 and 1430–31 what actually increased was Lancastrian awareness of Lollardy as a political threat. Indeed, it has been argued that the rebels of 1430–31 were not, religiously speaking, necessarily Lollards at all. Adding to the tension in 1431 there was once again, as in 1417, trouble with Scotland. A truce had been negotiated in March 1424 after James I of Scotland married Joan Beaufort, daughter of the earl of Somerset and niece of Bishop Beaufort, but "the search for peace continued without conclusion" (Griffiths, *Henry VI* 157). The truce was due to expire on May 1, 1431, and violations of its terms, which had occurred since its institution, continued without letup on both sides. The com-

bination of an intensified Franco-Scottish alliance and the possibility of becoming caught up in a war on two fronts made the situation especially tense for the English, since in 1430 France was "absorbing all their energies" (ibid., 159). On January 19, 1431, an agreement was reached on a partial truce on land and a general truce at sea which would last for five years. As Griffiths indicates, though, "It was not an entirely satisfactory outcome and could hardly remove English anxieties about the state of the frontier" (ibid., 160).

61. Ibid., 139.

62. John A. F. Thomson, *The Later Lollards, 1414–1520* (Oxford: Oxford University Press, 1965), 61.

63. Margaret Aston, *Lollards and Reformers: Images and Literacy in Late Medieval Religion* (London: Hambledon, 1984), 34–35. See also Thomson, *Later Lollards*, 59–61.

64. Griffiths, *Henry VI*, 139.

65. Ibid.

66. William Perkins also used as a pseudonym "Jack Sharpe of Wigmoreland." As Margaret Aston observes, "The title—which in fact, if not by intention, commemorates a long-lasting Lollard association with the marches of Wales, and Oldcastle's native county—may possibly be evidence of a wish to be identified with the duke of York and the Mortimer claim to the throne; cf Jack Cade *alias* Mortimer in 1450" (*Lollards and Reformers* 32 n. 122).

67. Griffiths, *Henry VI*, 140.

68. Ibid.

69. Ibid.

70. Cambridge University Library, MS Dd. 14.2 fol. 286v, printed in Aston, *Lollards and Reformers*, 46. Nicholas Bishop, born sometime after 1368, was son and heir of Bartholomew and Isabella Bishop of Oxford. The manuscript is a volume of his collected papers, "primarily a personal cartulary though it also incorporated matters of wider interest, including the brief chronicle of English kings" from which the account of the 1431 Lollard rising is taken (Aston, *Lollards and Reformers* 44).

71. Thompson, *Visitations*, III:405.

72. Thomas Ryngstede subsequently attended many of the heresy trials held between 1428 and 1431, including that of the well-known female heretic Hawisia Moone (see Tanner, *Heresy Trials* 139).

73. Thompson, *Visitations*, III:414.

74. Ibid., III:415. The prioress is then accused of having plotted to be alone with Thomas by sending the other nuns and servants "ad diversa negotia facienda que ipsa assignavit eisdem" (ibid.)

75. Ibid., III:416.

76. Ibid., III:415–16.

77. "Item compertum est quod priorissa non reddit compotum singulis annis, ut tenetur juxta exigentiam injunxionum predictarum" (ibid.).

78. Ibid., III:416.

79. Ibid. In the Norwich heresy trials, beliefs concerning the celibacy of priests and nuns which resonate with those ascribed to the prioress are called into question on ten occasions (Tanner, *Heresy Trials* 11). These defendants are "charged with holding, in one way or another, that it was more meritorious for priests and nuns to marry 'and bring forth fruit of their bodies' than to remain celibate, or that it was lawful for them to do so" (Tanner, *Heresy Trials* 17). For instance, Edmund, an archer from Loddon, confesses, "Also Y have holde, beleved and affermed that chastite of monkes, chanons, freres, nonnes, prestes and of ony other persones is not commendable ne meritorie, but it is more commendable and more plesyng unto God al such persones to be wedded and bringe forth frute of hare bodyes" (Tanner, *Heresy Trials* 166). Shklar discusses the *Twelve Constitutions of the Lollards* and Roger Dymmok's response to them in his *Liber contra duodecim errores et hereses Lollardum* in "Cobham's Daughter," 281–82, noting the prominence of an accusatory rhetoric of sexual misconduct in both texts, as well as the juxtaposition of sexual and economic sins. She writes, "For both sides, promiscuity, whether of the overly well-fed religious orders or the lawless heretics, is a metaphor for and a sign of misrule and the abuse of possessions" ("Cobham's Daughter" 282). Dinshaw too discusses the ways in which "deviant sexual practices seem to have been linked to Lollardy—in Roger Dymmok's refutation of the 1395 *Twelve Conclusions* as well as in William Ramsbury's 1389 heresy trial and in *The Chastising of the Children of God*" (*Getting Medieval* 145).

80. Thompson, *Visitations*, III:416.

81. Ibid., III:417.

82. Barrett, *Trial*, 343. One marvels that the prioress, presumably protected by her enclosed and professed status, and Margery Kempe, presumably protected by her social status, got off so lightly compared to Joan when they balked at acknowledging the Church's authority. Interestingly, Johanna Tate, another Redlingfield nun accused of incontinence who claims she was "provocata ex malo exemplo priorisse" (Thompson, *Visitations* III:416) is given the classic penance for sexually and economically transgressive women; much like Eleanor Cobham, who was punished for threatening the king through sorcery by being compelled to undertake a penitential procession, Johanna is put on display. She is enjoined to "penitentiam subscriptam, videlicet ad incedendum coram solemni processione dicti conventus die dominica proxime sequenti more penitentis, corpore curtello solomodo induto, capite velo destituto et flameola alba induto" (Thompson, *Visitations* III: 417). For the relevance of display in the punishment of Joan of Arc, see Steven Weiskopf, "Readers of the Lost Arc;" on Eleanor Cobham, see Sheila Lindenbaum's unpublished paper "London Women on Display: The Case of Eleanor Cobham." My thanks to Sheila for kindly providing me with a copy of her paper.

83. Barrett, *Trial*, 343.

84. Ibid., 217.

85. Ibid., 216.

86. Ibid., 83, 91, 92.

87. Ibid., 217.

88. Ibid., 159. The Latin reads, "Item dicta Johanna, habita familiaritate dicti Roberti" (Quicherat, *Procès* I:219).

89. Barrett, *Trial*, 160–61.

90. Ibid., 162–63.

91. Ibid., 163.

92. Weiskopf makes a related point about Joan's symbolic capital, comparing it to the value of the coins circulated by the English in France representing Henry VI as "the coming savior of the French kingdom" ("Readers of the Lost Arc" 127). He writes, "Had the enigmatic powers of the *Pucelle* from the tiny village of Domrémy, a recognized savior of the French kingdom in her own right, actually forged a spiritual coin of the realm worth more in symbolic capital than all the real coins that the English had circualted in France?" (ibid.).

93. Barrett, *Trial*, 10–11.

94. Ibid., 7.

95. Ibid., 9.

96. As Schibanoff observes, in an age that "often saw little or no distinction between *res* and sign" an attack on the latter "was tantamount to an assault on the former" ("True Lies" 50).

97. Warner, *Joan of Arc*, 47.

98. Quicherat, *Procès*, II:8 n. 1.

99. Ibid., III:242.

100. Pierre Cauchon's connections with the Lancastrians are well documented. As Warner observes, Cauchon was a member of the duke of Bedford's council from 1423, for which he received "a handsome stipend." Furthermore, "his niece Guillemette, the daughter of his sister Joan, married King Henry VI's French secretary, Jean de Rinel, who later penned the letter granting full amnesty to all who had taken part in the trial of Joan of Arc" (Warner, *Joan of Arc* 47).

101. Barrett, *Trial*, 17.

102. Quicherat, *Procès*, I:13.

103. Ibid., I:14.

104. Ibid., V:178–79. On this tax, see also Warner, *Joan of Arc*, 111.

105. Quicherat, *Procès*, V:136.

106. Ibid., V:162.

107. Ibid., V:192. The notion of Joan's sorcery also lived on well after her death. A letter written by the duke of Bedford three years after Joan's execution reiterates her "fals enchantement and sorcerie" (Waugh, "Joan of Arc in English Sources" 320). The portrait of Joan as sorceress was solidified in Tudor-era chronicles and famously in Shakespeare's *Henry VI Part 1*.

108. The *Chroniques de la noble ville et cité de Metz*, written in 1445, recounts that the chronicler saw Joan alive in Metz in 1436. The *Chroniques* is included in Quicherat, *Procès* vol. 5. On this reappearance, see also Weiskopf, "Readers of the Lost Arc," 129.

109. F. R. Johnston, "English Defenders of St. Bridget," *Studies in St. Birgitta and the Brigittine Order*, vol. 1, ed. James Hogg (Salzburg: Institut für Anglistik und Amerikanistik Universität Salzburg; Lewiston, N.Y.: Mellen, 1993), 271.

110. *Consilium Basiliense, Studien und Quellen zur Geschichts Conzils von Basel*, qtd. in Johnston, "English Defenders," 269–70.

111. Jean Gerson, *De probatione spirituum*, vol. 9 of *Oeuvres complètes*, ed. M. Glorieux, 10 vols. (Paris: Desclée, 1960–1973). On the overlap and interconnection of the roles of female saint, heretic, and witch, see Dyan Elliott, "The Physiology of Rapture and Female Spirituality," *Medieval Theology and the Natural Body*, ed. Peter Biller and Alistair Minnis (Woodbridge: Boydell and Brewer, 1997), 141–73. In her discussion of the inclusion of treatises on discernment in the vitae of female mystics, she observes, "The progressive caution of hagiographers reflects a dangerous collapse in the representation of the familiar polarities of female spirituality. As the famous example of Joan of Arc would suggest and as a number of scholars have recently argued, women as vessels of devotion and vessels of depravity were fast becoming virtually indistinguishable" (ibid., 167). Paul Strohm similarly notes that, as in Joanne of Navarre's case, the female roles of mediatrix and sorceress are "superficially opposite twin[s]" and "[e]ven superficially the two narratives converge in some respects" (*England's Empty Throne* 166). For instance, he points out, "Both mediatrices and sorceresses might . . . be regarded as rule-breakers, operating, if not outside conventional expectation, at least outside the normal rules governing social interactions" (*England's Empty Throne* 166).

112. Gerhild Scholz Williams, "On Finding Words: Witchcraft and the Discourses of Dissidence and Discovery," *The Graph of Sex and the German Text: Gendered Culture in Early Modern Germany, 1500–1700*, ed. Lynne Tatlock, Chloe 19 (Amsterdam: Rodopi, 1994), 46.

113. Barbara Newman discusses the contested boundary between heresy and sanctity in her analysis of the Guglielmites. See *From Virile Woman to WomanChrist: Studies in Medieval Religion and Literature* (Philadelphia: University of Pennsylvania Press, 1995), 182–223.

114. Richard Kieckhefer argues against reading sanctity and sorcery as flip sides of the same coin, saying that "if they mirrored each other, it was in nonsystematic ways" ("The Holy and the Unholy: Sainthood, Witchcraft and Magic," *Journal of Medieval and Renaissance Studies* 24 [1994]: 372).

Index

Barron, Caroline: 209n. 41, 216n. 49
Bartlett, Anne Clark: 18, 191n. 83, 197n. 5,
   217n. 56
Bartlett, Edmund: 60, 208n. 25
Baudricourt, Robert: 178
Baxter, Margery: 217n. 58
Beauchamp, Richard. *See* Warwick, Richard
   Beauchamp, earl of
Beauchamp, Thomas: 111, 238n. 132
Beauchamp, Walter: 227n. 4
Beaufort, Henry (bishop of Winchester): 112,
   254n. 60
Beaufort, Margaret: 225n. 116
Beckett, Neil: 121–22, 230n. 46, 231n. 51,
   232n. 69
Beckwith, Sarah: 212n. 10, 218n. 60,
   218n. 64
Bedford, John of Lancaster, duke of: xi, 112,
   113, 164–72, 173, 181, 249n. 3, 250n. 11,
   250n. 12, 257n. 100, 257n. 107. *See also*
   Kempe, Margery; Joan of Arc; representa-
   tional strategies: Lancastrian
Bell, David: ix, 31, 183n. 11, 191n. 82,
   207n. 11
Bell, Rudolph: 203n. 42, 228n. 14
Benedict, Saint: 34–36, 38, 46, 49, 51, 85,
   200n. 22
Benedictine Order: autonomy of nuns in, 64–
   65; and *Book to a Mother,* 85, 87, 92; chapters of, 16–17, 187n. 16; divine service in,
   200n. 22, 201n. 29; everyday practice in,
   62–69; importance of, x; learning in, 38,
   41–43, 48, 52, 203n. 50; and Margery
   Kempe, 94–95; ritual for benediction of
   abbess in, 69, 196n. 141; role of superior
   in, 9–10, 28–29, 39–42, 100, 194n. 121,
   196n. 141, 203n. 46, 203n. 50. *See also*
   Benedictine Rule; profession: Benedictine;
   visitation: Benedictine; *Ordo consecrationis
   sanctimonialium*
Benedictine Rule: Fox's translation of, 34–35,
   36, 41–43, 48, 49, 50–51, 80, 199n. 18,
   201n. 24, 203n. 49; Latin version of, 34,
   39–44, 200n. 22; prose translation of, 33–
   37, 43–44, 47, 81, 158, 161, 199n. 18,
   200n. 19, 202n. 39, 203n. 46, 203n. 50;
   verse translation of, 28, 29, 33–34, 36–42,
   47, 49, 52, 81, 100, 158, 161, 199n. 18,
   200n. 19, 201n. 33, 202n. 39, 202n. 41.
   See also Benedictine Order; Fox, Richard
   (bishop of Winchester); learning: and Benedictine Rule; St. Mary's Abbey, Winchester

(Nunnaminster); translation: of monastic
   rules for women
Bernard, Saint: 143, 145, 244n. 25
Birgitta of Sweden, Saint: xi, 25, 46, 56, 57–
   58, 106, 188n. 36, 224n. 107, 235n. 114;
   as "English" saint, 114, 120, 182, 231n. 54;
   and Henry V, 118–19, 124, 125, 127, 129,
   135; and Henry VII, 133; and Lancastrians,
   118–19, 124, 125, 135, 214n. 30; *Liber
   celestis*, 12, 127–28, 189n. 53, 218n. 59,
   228n. 22, 234n. 109, 235n. 114; and Margery Kempe, 58, 93, 99, 101–3, 104–6,
   115, 166, 217n. 59, 219n. 67, 223n. 97;
   Officium Sanctae Birgittae, 224n. 107; *Reue-
   lationes extravagantes*, 45, 52, 205n. 69;
   revelations of, 12, 13, 45–46, 93, 99,
   101–3, 104–5, 107, 114, 118, 120, 124,
   127–28, 189n. 53, 199n. 18, 204n. 67,
   205n. 69, 205n. 70, 206n. 77, 217n. 59,
   222n. 90, 223n. 97, 224n. 106, 228n. 22,
   234n. 109; and Yorkists, 79, 125, 127–29,
   135, 214n. 30, 234n. 109, 236n. 122. *See
   also* Brigittine Order; *Myroure of Oure
   Ladye*; representational strategies: Lancastrian; representational strategies: Yorkist;
   Rewyll of Seynt Sauioure
Bishop, Nicholas: 174, 255n. 70. *See also*
   Lollardy: rising of 1431
Blackborough Priory: 67
Black Prince: 232n. 60
Bloom, Harold: 244n. 27
Blount, Thomas: 181. *See also* Joan of Arc;
   sorcery
Blunt, John Henry: 48
Boccaccio, Giovanni: *De claris mulieribus*,
   239n. 1
body, female: corruption of, 81; inferiority of,
   32, 35, 44, 49–50, 81, 204n. 62; and property, 73, 75, 86–87, 220n. 71; spiritual
   value of, 52–54, 138–40; unruliness of,
   37–38, 43, 110, 204n. 59
Bokenham, Osbern: 135–37, 147–62, 179,
   239n. 1, 241n. 6, 245n. 38, 246n. 48,
   246n. 50, 246n. 51, 247n. 55, 247n. 60,
   248n. 61, 248n. 62, 248n. 65, 248n. 66,
   248n. 67, 248n. 70, 249n. 71; *Legendys of
   Hooly Wummen*, xi, 127, 135–37, 147–62,
   195n. 30, 239n. 1, 246n. 46, 246n. 48,
   246n. 50, 247n. 51, 248n. 65, 248n. 67,
   248n. 70. *See also auctoritas*: and Osbern
   Bokenham; lineage: literary; patrons:
   female; representational strategies: literary;

Fox, Richard (*continued*)
  Benedictine Rule: Fox's translation; St.
    Mary's Abbey, Winchester (Nunnaminster)
Franciscan Order: everyday practice in, 55,
  58–62; importance of, x; and Margery
  Kempe, 92–94, 97–99, 100, 220n. 75;
  origins of, 13, 55–56, 199n. 18; and other
  monastic traditions, 13, 21–22, 189n. 37;
  role of abbess in, 9–10. *See also* Agnes of
  Prague, Blessed; Clare, Saint (of Assisi); Isabella, Blessed; Minoresses; poverty: apostolic; profession: Franciscan; *Rewle of Sustres Menouresses Enclosid*; Urbanist Rule;
  visitation: Franciscan

Galopes, Jean: 134
Gascoigne, Thomas: 48
Gaunt, John of: 83, 107, 126, 167, 234n. 100
gender: and claustration, 16–18, 25, 28, 78–
  79, 84–86, 87; and exegesis, 80; and language, 31–33, 36, 37–38, 44, 45–46, 53–
  54, 198n. 10, 199n. 17; and Lollardy, 167–
  68, 171, 176, 212n. 13, 251n. 21; and profession, 7–8, 204n. 60; and religious identity, 5, 7, 14, 16–21, 62, 78–81; and translation, 197n. 2; and visitation, 14–21,
  190n. 65; and writing, 7, 10, 14, 42–43,
  90–91, 106, 142–45, 158–62, 188n. 32,
  224n. 106, 240n. 4, 242n. 15, 244n. 24,
  244n. 25, 248n. 66
George, Saint: 115, 120, 125
Gerson, Jean: 182, 214n. 30, 242n. 17; *De
  probatione spirituum*, 182
Gesta Henrici Quinti: 115–18, 120, 121–22,
  137–38, 165, 166, 229n. 31, 229n. 36,
  229n. 37, 229n. 38, 231n. 57, 231n. 60,
  236n. 130. *See also* Henry V; representational strategies: Lancastrian
Gibson, Gail McMurray: 218n. 59, 220n. 75,
  221n. 76, 222n. 85, 223n. 97, 239n. 2
Gilchrist, Roberta: ix, 5, 63, 65, 186n. 13,
  186n. 15, 197n. 5
Gloucester, Humphrey of Lancaster, duke of:
  111
Gluck, Robert: 253n. 48
Godstow Abbey: 17, 21, 197n. 5
Gokewell Priory: 20, 21
Goux, Jean-Joseph: 75, 171
Gower, John: 158, 159, 160, 248n. 66; *Con-
  fessio Amantis*, 248n. 66
Gracedieu Priory: 21
Grandsen, Antonia: 229n. 38, 237n. 132

Gratian: 187n. 30
Gray, William (bishop of Lincoln): 16, 17, 37
Greatrex, Joan: 42, 201n. 24
Great Schism: 112, 119, 198n. 12
Greystoke, Lady Elizabeth: 166–68, 251n. 21
Greystoke, Lord John: 166–68, 251n. 20
Greystoke, Lord Ralph: 167
Griffiths, Ralph A.: 226n. 4, 255n. 60
Gybbes, Elizabeth: 129

Hadcock, R. Neville: 199n. 12
Hale, Rosemary Drage: 243n. 17, 243n. 19
Haliwell, J. O.: 235n. 115
Hanna, Ralph III: 34
Harding, Wendy: 218n. 64, 224n. 108
Harvey, Barbara: 67, 210n. 57, 210n. 61
Harvey, John H.: 231n. 60
Henry IV (king of England): 58, 122, 126,
  131, 231n. 60, 232n. 69, 234n. 109,
  245n. 35, 249n. 2
Henry V (king of England and France): 107,
  111, 126, 131, 146, 167, 173, 229n. 32,
  231 n. 58, 235n. 112, 250n. 5, 253n. 51;
  and foundation of Syon, 56, 118–24,
  129, 130, 166, 180, 184n. 16, 230n. 46,
  232n. 69, 251n. 12; as king of England,
  115–16, 118–22, 124, 138, 166, 229n. 38,
  231n. 60; as king of France, 113, 114,
  116–18, 119–20, 123–24, 127, 132–33,
  134, 137–38, 166, 229n. 38; and St. Birgitta, 118–19, 124, 125, 127, 129, 135;
  and Virgin Mary, 113, 118, 134, 137,
  239n. 2. *See also* Birgitta of Sweden, Saint:
  and Henry V; Birgitta of Sweden, Saint: and
  Lancastrians; *Gesta Henrici Quinti*; Incarnation: and Lancastrian politics; kingship;
  lineage; representational strategies: Lancastrian; Syon Abbey: foundation; Syon
  Abbey: and Lancastrians; Virgin Mary: as
  political figure
Henry VI (king of England): dual descent,
  128, 230n. 42, 235n. 111, 235n. 112,
  236n. 122, 242n. 13; and Joan of Arc, 179–
  82; minority of, 111–12, 131–32, 163–
  64, 173, 227n. 4; reign of, 114, 125, 126,
  167, 169, 171, 182, 233n. 92, 234n. 96,
  238n. 145, 257n. 92; religions foundations
  of, 129–30. *See also* Incarnation: and Lancastrian politics; lineage; representational
  strategies: Lancastrian; Syon Abbey: and
  Lancastrians; Wars of the Roses; Warwick,
  Richard Beauchamp, earl of

Julian of Norwich: 93–94, 218n. 59, 218n. 61
Justice, Steven: 185n. 3

Kantorowicz, Ernst H.: 228n. 29
Karras, Ruth: 185n. 8, 193n. 103
Katherine, Saint: 240n. 3
Kemp, Theresa: 158
Kempe, Margery: xi, 58, 88, 92–110, 115,
    135, 150, 155, 165–72, 173, 176, 178,
    179, 217n. 59, 218n. 60, 218n. 61,
    218n. 62, 218n. 64, 219n. 65, 219n. 67,
    220n. 69, 220n. 71, 220n, 75, 221n. 76,
    221n. 80, 221n. 81, 221n. 82, 221n. 83,
    222n. 85, 222n. 91, 222n. 94, 223n. 95,
    223n. 96, 223n. 97, 224n. 108, 224n. 109,
    226n. 135, 241n. 8, 246n. 44, 250n. 7,
    250n. 11, 251n. 21, 253n. 48, 254n. 55,
    254n. 58, 256n. 82. See also Bedford, John
    of Lancaster, duke of; Benedictine Order:
    and Margery Kempe; Birgitta of Sweden,
    Saint: and Margery Kempe; Brigittine
    Order: and Margery Kempe; chastity: and
    Margery Kempe; claustration: and Margery
    Kempe; clergy: and Margery Kempe;
    clothing: and Margery Kempe; Franciscan
    Order: and Margery Kempe; Hundred
    Years' War; identity, religious: and Margery
    Kempe; literacy: and Margery Kempe;
    Lollardy: and Margery Kempe; marriage:
    and Margery Kempe; poverty: and Margery
    Kempe; property: and Margery Kempe;
    Syon Abbey: and Margery Kempe
Ketteryche, Joan: 60–62, 63. See also Denney
    Abbey
kingship: Christological, 116–18, 126, 128,
    171–72, 228n. 29, 229n. 32, 230n. 42,
    232n. 60, 234n. 98, 235n. 112; sacral,
    115–16, 117, 126, 128, 138, 170, 171–72,
    228n. 29. See also Incarnation: and Lan-
    castrian politics; Incarnation: and Yorkist
    politics; lineage; representational strategies;
    Virgin Mary: as political figure
King's Langley: vii, viii, xi, 183n. 2. See also
    Dartford Priory; Dominican Order
Kipling, Gordon: 229n. 30, 230n. 40
Knapp, Ethan: 244n. 27, 245n. 29, 245n. 35
Knowles, David: 199n. 12

labor: of male religious, 16–18, 38, 68,
    75, 77, 103, 116, 152, 153, 187n. 28,
    212n. 12; maternal, 53–54, 73–76, 89–91,
    100–105, 138–40, 152–55; of nuns, 17–

18, 38, 68; of women, 73–77, 89–91,
    100–106, 138–40, 152–55. See also
    Eucharist: as male reproductive work;
    Incarnation: and maternity; maternity: as
    female work
Lacan, Jacques: 146, 242n. 16
Langley Priory: 20, 21
Langlond, Thomas: 175–76. See also
    Redlingfield Priory
La Rochelle, Catherine de: 165, 249n. 3. See
    also Joan of Arc
Lateran IV. See Councils, Church: Lateran IV
Latin: as language of authority, 32–33, 34–
    35, 36, 37, 38, 39, 46, 49–50, 54, 155,
    161, 198n. 10, 224n. 109; masculinity
    of, 33, 36, 37–39, 155, 161, 198n. 10,
    247n. 56. See also Benedictine Rule: Latin
    version; literacy: Latin; translation
Lauritis, J. A.: 244n. 23
Lawton, David: 160, 217n. 59, 220n. 75,
    221n. 76, 224n. 108, 240n. 4
learning: and Benedictine Rule, 38, 41–43,
    48, 52, 203n. 50; and Brigittine Order: 48,
    49–52, 108; at Dartford Priory, viii. See also
    books; libraries; literacy; reading; texts
lecherie: 82–86, 215n. 37
Leclercq, Jean: 63, 206n. 85, 216n. 56
Legenda Aurea: 246n. 51
Legend of Good Women (Chaucer): 121,
    239n. 1, 248n. 65, 248n. 66. See also
    Alceste
Legendys of Hooly Wummen (Bokenham): xi,
    127, 135–37, 147–62, 195n. 30, 239n. 1,
    246n. 46, 246n. 48, 246n. 50, 247n. 51,
    248n. 65, 248n. 67, 248n. 70. See also auc-
    toritas: and Osbern Bokenham; lineage: lit-
    erary; patrons: female; representational
    strategies: literary; representational strate-
    gies: Yorkist; texts: female commissions of;
    translation; vernacular
Lerer, Seth: 240n. 4
Leyke, Agnes: 65, 66
Leyke, John: 66
Liber celestis (St. Birgitta of Sweden): 12,
    127–28, 189n. 53, 218n. 59, 228n. 22,
    234n. 109, 235n. 114. See also Birgitta of
    Sweden, Saint: revelations of
Liber contra duodecim errores et hereses Lollar-
    dum (Dymmok): 256n. 79. See also Lollardy
Liber Metricus (Elmham): 138, 242n. 14
libraries: of monks, 17, 31; of nuns, 13, 17–
    18, 27–28, 31, 183n. 11, 191n. 82,

marriage (*continued*)
18, 185n. 8, 186n. 13; and Joan of Arc,
169, 252n. 28; and Margery Kempe, 94–
97, 219n. 65, 219n. 67; and profession,
4–5, 6–9, 12, 18, 25–29, 87, 94–95,
185n. 7, 188n. 30, 195n. 128, 219n. 65;
spiritual, 88. *See also* bride of Christ;
dowry; mysticism: nuptial; profession:
nuptial imagery in
martyrdom: 155–58, 246n. 48
martyrs, virgin: 26–27, 150, 155–57,
246n. 48
Mary Magdalene, Saint: 136, 148–53, 157,
246n. 46, 246n. 48
Mary, Virgin. *See* Virgin Mary
maternity: and abbess, 9–11, 23–24, 28–29,
42, 47–48, 62, 69, 77, 124, 196n. 141; and
abbot, 42; in *Book to a Mother*, 88–92, 100,
101; in Brigittine Order, 23–24, 90, 100–
106, 143; and female authority, 9–11, 28–
29, 42, 62, 69, 74, 77, 205n. 70; as female
work, 73–76, 89–91, 100–105, 138–40,
150, 152–55, 222n. 83; and intercession,
103–5, 224n. 107; and Margery Kempe,
100–103, 104–5, 171, 221n. 80, 221n. 81,
221n. 83, 223n. 97; and profession, 9–
13, 25–26; and salvation, 53–54, 76–77,
101–5, 138–40, 141, 153–55, 207n. 88,
221n. 81, 222n. 83, 224n. 107; spiritual,
89, 100–101; and tears, 103, 104–5,
222n. 83, 222n. 94; and texts, 54, 142–45,
244n. 24. *See also* Benedictine Order: ritual
for the benediction of an abbess in; Benedictine Order: role of superior in; Brigittine
Order: maternity in; Brigittine Order: role
of abbess in; Franciscan Order: role of
abbess in; Incarnation: and maternity; lineage: female; labor: maternal; profession:
maternal imagery in; Virgin Mary: and
maternity
maumetrie: 82–85
McCarthy, Adrian: 83, 215n. 39
McKenna, J. W.: 232n. 77, 235n. 111,
235n. 112, 236n. 122, 242n. 13
McLachlan, Laurentia: 195n. 126
McNamara, Jo Ann Kay: ix, 25, 185n. 11,
186n. 13, 190n. 62, 193n. 115
McSheffrey, Shannon: 212n. 13
Meale, Carol M.: 108
Meditationes Vitae Christi: 98, 134, 239n. 2,
244n. 23
meekness: 12, 34, 36, 40, 41–42, 43, 47, 88,

94, 99–100, 106, 141. *See also* conduct,
female: and meekness; obedience
Melton, William: 98, 221n. 75
Mertes, Karen: 225n. 116
Methley, Richard: 109
Meyer-Lee, Robert J.: 241n. 5
Milly, Margaret: 59
Minoresses: 13, 15, 24, 94, 223n. 100; aristocratic heritage, 58; temporal independence
of, 55–56, 58–62, 65; wealth of, 24. *See
also* Denney Abbey; Franciscan Order; Isa-
bella, Blessed; Isabella Rule; London
Minories; *Rewle of Sustres Menouresses
Enclosid*; Urbanist Rule
miracle of the pregnant abbess: 73–77, 80,
81, 82, 88, 89, 92, 100, 104, 108, 110,
136, 137, 140, 153, 176, 212n. 9,
219n. 64. *See also Alphabet of Tales*
Miracles de nostre dame par personnages:
212n. 9, 239n. 1
Mirror of the Blessed Life of Christ (Love): 90,
98, 109, 216n. 53, 221n. 76
Moleyns, Lord Robert: 107
Moone, Hawisia: 255n. 72. *See also* Lollardy:
heresy trials
Mooney, Linne R. 235n. 111
Morrison, Susan Signe: 198n. 10
Mortimer, Anne: 234n. 100
Mortimer, Edmund: 234n. 100
Mount Grace Charterhouse: 109–10,
221n. 76. *See also* Love, Nicholas
Myroure of Oure Ladye: 18, 42, 45–54, 74,
106, 123–24, 226n. 119. *See also* Birgitta
of Sweden, Saint; Brigittine Order; Syon
Abbey; *Syon Additions for the Sisters*; translations: of monastic rules for women
mysticism: female, 4, 87, 106, 112,
224n. 108, 258n. 11; nuptial, 4, 87,
219n. 65

Neville, Anne Beauchamp: 131, 132,
238n. 143, 251n. 17. *See also* "Pageant of
the Birth, Life, and Death of Richard Beau-
champ, Earl of Warwick"
Neville, George (bishop of Exeter): 236n. 115
Neville, Ralph. *See* Westmorland, Ralph
Neville, earl of
Neville, Richard. *See* Warwick, Richard
Neville, earl of
Newman, Barbara: 39, 189n. 44, 202n. 38,
204n. 60, 205n. 73, 207n. 88, 258n. 113
Newnham Priory: 16

texts: access to, 27–28, 206n. 79; female commissions of, 92, 135–36, 137, 147–49, 150–51, 157–58, 159, 245n. 38; as food, 91–92; production of, 31, 43, 45–46, 62, 92, 105–6, 142–45, 161, 224n. 108, 224n. 109. *See also* books; conduct, female: and reading; libraries; literacy; reading; *ruminatio*; writing

textual economy: 7, 10, 24, 185n. 3

Thomas, Saint (of Canterbury): 236n. 122

Thomas à Kempis: 182

Thompson, A. Hamilton: 19, 21, 64, 192n. 97

Thompson, Sally: 186n. 13, 190n. 61

Thornton Abbey: 19

The Title and Pedigree of Henry VI (Lydgate): 241n. 5

Tractatus de Regimine Principum ad Regem Henricum Sextum: 114

translation: consequences of, 197n. 3, 198n. 10; and gender, 197n. 2; and Incarnation, 54; as interpretation, 200n. 20; of monastic rules for women, 26, 28, 29, 30–54, 194n. 126; of relics, 30, 196n. 1; of Scripture in *Book to a Mother*, 81. *See also* Arundel's Constitutions; Bokenham, Osbern; *Legendys of Hooly Wummen*; Love, Nicholas; vernacular; vernacular theology

Tree of Jesse: 123–24, 140, 232n. 77, 235n. 112. *See also* lineage: female; lineage: male; Virgin Mary

Troy Book (Lydgate): 240n. 3

Tudor-Craig, P.: 237n. 132

Tullius: 145, 160. *See also* lineage: literary

Twelve Constitutions of the Lollards: 256n. 79. *See also* Lollardy

Ullerston, Richard: 198n. 9

Urbanist Rule: 190n. 62. *See also* Franciscan Order; Isabella Rule; Minoresses; *Rewle of Sustres Menouresses Enclosid*

Ursula, Saint: 155–57

Usk, Adam: 121, 242n. 14

Vadstena: 13, 122

Vauchez, André: 113, 190n. 63, 198n. 12, 203n. 42, 205n. 74, 227n. 12, 228n. 13, 228n. 22, 231n. 54

Vere, Elizabeth. *See* Oxford, Elizabeth Vere, countess of

vernacular: dangers of, 43; and the feminine, 31–33, 38, 44, 45–46, 53–54, 158–62, 224n. 109; and the masculine, 158–62, 199n. 17; negative associations of, 31–34, 49–50, 158, 200n. 21, 200n. 22; spiritual value of, 53–54, 161; status of, 30–31, 158–59, 248n. 62. *See also* Arundel's Constitutions; Bokenham, Osbern; Hoccleve, "Remonstrance Against Oldcastle"; translation

vernacular theology: 27–28, 44, 206n. 79. *See also* Arundel's Constitutions; Lollardy; Love, Nicholas; translation

virginity: 5, 117–18, 138, 145, 168, 171, 221n. 83

Virgin Mary: xi, 12, 76, 82, 98, 100, 108, 141, 154–55, 205n. 69, 243n. 17; Annunciation, 89, 90, 102, 117, 118, 141, 143–45, 154, 230n. 40, 230n. 42; *compassio*, 101, 141, 221n. 81, 221n. 83; co-redemption, 12, 23, 47, 53–54, 101–3, 189n. 53, 205n. 73, 243n. 21; as female authority figure, 9–12, 23, 46–47, 69, 73–74, 77, 108, 114–15; Marian trinity, 10, 189n. 44, 194n. 122, 205n. 73; and maternity, 69, 89–91, 101–3, 104–5, 116–18, 123–24, 137–47, 222n. 90, 243n. 17, 243n. 19, 243n. 21, 244n. 24; as model for abbess, 47, 48, 124, 194n. 122; as model for women, 12, 73–77, 141–42, 212n. 9, 216n. 52; as political figure, 113, 114, 116–18, 121, 123–24, 132, 134, 137–38, 230n. 42; as Queen of Heaven, 45–46, 69, 141. *See also* Brigittine Order: maternity in; Brigittine Order: role of abbess in; Incarnation; lineage: female; Tree of Jesse

visitation: 3, 19–21, 14–25, 80, 175–77, 178; Benedictine, 14–21, 24, 67, 68, 69, 190n. 64, 190n. 65; Brigittine, 21–25, 55, 69, 100; financial costs of, 15–16, 22, 190n. 70; Franciscan, 21–25, 55, 69, 100, 223n. 100; and religious identity, 14, 22, 55, 62; symbolic consequences of, 15, 190n. 70. *See also* gender: and visitation; injunctions, episcopal

vowess: 88, 97

vows, monastic. *See* chastity: monasic vows of, obedience; poverty: monastic vows of

Walker, Simon: 115, 238n. 141

Wallace, David: 121

Walsingham, Alan de: 58

Walsingham, Thomas: 83–84, 242n. 13, 242n. 14; *Historia Anglicana*, 83–84,

Acknowledgments

The task of thanking the many people who have helped me bring this book to completion is without a doubt one of the most pleasurable I have undertaken since beginning the project. My first and deepest thanks must go to Paul Strohm and Sheila Lindenbaum—outstanding scholars and teachers, inspiring mentors, and true friends for whose ongoing interest in my work I am profoundly grateful. I also want to express my heartfelt thanks to Larry Clopper and Dyan Elliott, who always made intelligent and perceptive suggestions and whose welcome influence continues to lead me down productive paths.

The communal nature of the monastic life I study resonates with the communal nature of academic life. Without my scholarly "sisters and brothers" I could never have written this book. Special thanks go to the Medieval Reading Circle at Indiana University for years of stimulating discussion and moral support. The students in my courses on medieval women at the University of Michigan and Utah State University asked probing questions which helped me clarify my ideas; I only hope they learned as much from the classes as I did. For astute comments on versions of chapters, I thank Alan Ambrisco, Sarah Beckwith, and Rita Copeland. For wise advice and perceptive insights, I am grateful to Robert L. A. Clark, Theresa Coletti, Sylvia Federico, Michael Hanrahan, Dan Kline, Peggy McCracken, Dorothy McFarland, Eric Metzler, Karen Winstead, and Steve Yandell. For his intelligent suggestions, extraordinary generosity, and great kindness, I owe a special debt of thanks to David Wallace. Nicholas Watson and Sharon Elkins read the entire manuscript for the University of Pennsylvania Press; their discerning comments and keen observations helped me to make this a better book. I also want to express my thanks to the editorial staff of the University of Pennsylvania Press, who made what might have been a difficult process a real joy.

Earlier versions of several chapters have appeared elsewhere, and I extend my thanks for the permission to use this material. Sections of Chapter 2 were published as "Saving the Market: Textual Strategies and Cultural Transformations in Fifteenth-Century Translations of the Benedictine Rule for Women," *Disputatio* 3, ed. Carol Poster and Richard J. Utz (Evanston, Ill.: Northwestern University Press, 1998), 34–50. Some material from Chapter 4 in an earlier form was published as "Pregnancy and Productivity: The Imagery of Female Monasticism Within and Beyond the Cloister Walls," *Journal of Medieval and Early Modern Studies* 28 (1998): 531–52. Excerpts from Chapter 5 appeared as "Kings, Saints, and Nuns: Gender, Religion, and Authority in the Reign of Henry V" in *Viator* 30 (1999): 307–22.

Finally, and most pleasurable of all, I must acknowledge the innumerable debts I owe to friends and family. Sheila and Peter Lindenbaum offered warm hospitality on many occasions, and my colleagues at Utah State University have made a transplanted Southerner feel very welcome in the West. I am thankful for my brother Michael's sense of humor and strong arms on more than one cross-country odyssey. Most beyond recompense, though, are the debts I owe to my parents, Michael and Martha, and to my husband, Bill. Without their unflagging encouragement, unbridled enthusiasm, and unconditional love, this book, and so much more, would never have been possible.